Wilber E. Bradt, Lt. Col.
No. 0182711, Hq. 152nd F. A. Bn.
A. P. O. 43, c/o Postmaster
San Francisco, Calif.

Mr. Hale V P Brodt
204 Broadway
Bangor
Maine

U.S. ARMY POSTAL SERVICE
43 SEP 19 1944 A.P.O.

---

Wilber E. Bradt, Lt. Col.
No. 0182711, Hq. 152nd F. A. Bn.
A. P. O. 43, c/o Postmaster
San Francisco, Calif.

Wilber E Brodt

Miss Valerie E. Brodt
204 Broadway
Bangor
Maine

U.S. ARMY POSTAL SERVICE
SEP 1 1944 A.P.O.

AIR MAIL 6 CENTS UNITED STATES OF AMERICA

---

Wilber E. Bradt, Lt. Col.
No. 0182711, Hq. 152nd F. A. Bn.
A. P. O. 43, c/o Postmaster
San Francisco, Calif.

Wilber E Brodt

Mr. Hale Brodt
Box #75 RFD #1
Dillsboro
Indiana

1944 U.S. A.P.O.

# COMBAT AND NEW LIFE

## WILBER'S WAR

☆ ☆

**WILBER'S WAR TRILOGY**
*Citizen Soldier* (Book 1)
*Combat and New Life* (Book 2)
*Victory and Homecoming* (Book 3)

BOOK 2

# COMBAT AND NEW LIFE

## WILBER'S WAR

An American Family's Journey
through World War II

★ ★

Hale Bradt

*Combat and New Life*
Book 2 of the *Wilber's War* Trilogy:
*An American Family's Journey through World War II*
www.wilberswar.com

Copyright © 2016 by Hale Bradt

Van Dorn Books
P.O. Box 8836, Salem, MA 01971
www.vandornbooks.com

All rights reserved. This book may not be reproduced in part or whole without the express written permission of the publisher. For permission to reproduce any material from the book, kindly contact the publisher at the address above or through info@vandornbooks.com

For information about bulk sales,
please contact the publisher at info@vandornbooks.com

Every effort has been made to trace and credit accurate copyright ownership of the visual material used in this book. Errors or omissions will be corrected in subsequent editions provided notification is made in writing to the publisher at the address above.
Book Editor: Frances B. King, HistoryKeep.com
Book design: Lisa Carta Design, lisacartadesign@gmail.com
Typefaces: Minion, Chaparral Pro
Book and case front-cover images: U.S. Army
Back-cover images: Bradt family
Printed by Friesens, Canada, http://www.friesens.com

*Wilber's War* (the trilogy)
ISBN 978-0-9908544-0-1
Library of Congress Control Number: 2014922173

Limited First Edition

The individual books (if separated from the set)
ISBN (Book 1, Citizen Soldier): 978-0-9908544-1-8
ISBN (Book 2, Combat and New Life): 978-0-9908544-2-5
ISBN (Book 3, Victory and Homecoming): 978-0-9908544-3-2
Library of Congress Control Numbers:
Book 1 (Citizen Soldier): 2014922166
Book 2 (Combat and New Life): 2014922168
Book 3 (Victory and Homecoming): 2014922167

*In memory of Wilber and Norma*
*And for Valerie and Abby*
*—this is their story too*

# CONTENTS

*Preface*     *xiii*
*Maps and Charts*     *xvii*

### PART I   Jungle combat

1   *Lovely little shiny bombs*     *3*
     Rendova, July 1943

2   *The enemy is all around you*     *19*
     Munda action, July 1943

3   *Get your head down! That ain't all!*     *37*
     Sasavele Island, August 1943

4   *It was a depressing and unfortunate affair*     *59*
     Baanga Island action, August 1943

5   *The old 169th just keeps rolling along*     *75*
     Arundel Island action, September 1943

6   *My whispering chorus of observers*     *85*
     The Arundel Story, September 1943

### PART II   Interlude 1983, Japan and Solomon Islands

7   *Kyushu, Japan*     *121*
     Hiroshima and Colonel Kinoshita, March 1983

8   *Guadalcanal: the way in*     *127*
     May 1983

9   *Battle areas, New Georgia*     *135*
     Munda, May 1983

10   *Kolombangara: the way out*     *151*
     May 1983

**PART III  Ondonga palm grove**

| 11 | *Swan doesn't polish those insignia very much*<br>Ondonga, New Georgia,  October 1943 | *159* |
| 12 | *Norma Day*<br>Ondonga, November 1943 | *179* |
| 13 | *Poor Nana*<br>Ondonga, December 1943 | *195* |
| 14 | *He'll have a little trouble with me*<br>Ondonga, December 1943–January 1944 | *209* |
| 15 | *Civilization is catching up with me*<br>Ondonga, January 1944 | *223* |

**PART IV  Western civilization at last!**

| 16 | *Before their souls could be hurt*<br>Guadalcanal, February 1944 | *233* |
| 17 | *Our plan is to get away from soldiers*<br>Tour of New Zealand, March 1944 | *249* |
| 18 | *I'm taking over another battalion*<br>Matakana, New Zealand, April–May, 1944 | *267* |
| 19 | *I've asked for the point of honor*<br>New Zealand,  June–July, 1944 | *285* |

**PART V  Interlude 1984, New Zealand**

| 20 | *Waldo and Wilber*<br>Rhode Island and New Zealand, September–October, 1984 | *311* |
| 21 | *Olive and Margaret*<br>Wellington and Auckland, October 1984 | *319* |

| *Acknowledgments* | *329* |
| *Bibliography* | *333* |
| *Index* | *337* |

# FIGURES

## CHARTS

Chart 1. Bradt, Sparlin, and Bourjaily families . . . . . . . . . . . . . . . . . . . . . xix
Chart 2. Organization of 43rd Infantry Division, 1942–1943 . . . . . . . . xx

## MAPS

Map 1. Command Areas and Wilber's voyages . . . . . . . . . . . . . . . . . . xxiii
Map 2. Cartwheel area and Hale's travels . . . . . . . . . . . . . . . . . xxiv, xxv
Map 3. Dual Allied thrusts . . . . . . . . . . . . . . . . . . . . . . . . . . . . . xxvi, xxvii
Map 4. Solomon Islands . . . . . . . . . . . . . . . . . . . . . . . . . . . . . . . . . . . xxviii
Map 5. Landings on New Georgia group . . . . . . . . . . . . . . . . . . . . . . xxix
Map 6. Bomb pattern, Rendova Harbor . . . . . . . . . . . . . . . . . . . . . . . . xxx
Map 7. Initial drive toward Munda . . . . . . . . . . . . . . . . . . . . . . . . . . . xxxi
Map 8. Final drive to Munda . . . . . . . . . . . . . . . . . . . . . . . . . . . . . . . xxxii
Map 9. Clean-up drives after Munda capture . . . . . . . . . . . . . . . . . . xxxiii
Map 10. Baanga Island, cove and beach . . . . . . . . . . . . . . . . . . . . . . xxxiv
Map 11. Arundel Island . . . . . . . . . . . . . . . . . . . . . . . . . . . . . . . . . . . xxxv
Map 12. Blackett Strait . . . . . . . . . . . . . . . . . . . . . . . . . . . . . . . . . . . xxxvi
Map 13. New Georgia, artillery positions . . . . . . . . . . . . . . . . . . . . . xxxvii
Map 14. New Zealand . . . . . . . . . . . . . . . . . . . . . . . . . . . . . . . . . . . xxxviii

## ILLUSTRATIONS

### PART I  Jungle combat

Rendova Harbor, aerial view . . . . . . . . . . . . . . . . . . . . . . . . . . . . . . . . . 7
LCI-69, Rendova . . . . . . . . . . . . . . . . . . . . . . . . . . . . . . . . . . . . . . . . . . 7
Japanese bomber formations . . . . . . . . . . . . . . . . . . . . . . . . . . . . . . . 10
LCI-24 and LCI-65 listing . . . . . . . . . . . . . . . . . . . . . . . . . . . . . . . . . . 11
Lt. Christopher Tompkins . . . . . . . . . . . . . . . . . . . . . . . . . . . . . . . . . . 12
Landing craft with troops . . . . . . . . . . . . . . . . . . . . . . . . . . . . . . . . . . 15
Troops debarking at Zanana . . . . . . . . . . . . . . . . . . . . . . . . . . . . . . . 15
Linemen with wire reel . . . . . . . . . . . . . . . . . . . . . . . . . . . . . . . . . . . 16
Four native scouts . . . . . . . . . . . . . . . . . . . . . . . . . . . . . . . . . . . . . . . 17
Battery C en route Sasavele . . . . . . . . . . . . . . . . . . . . . . . . . . . . . . . . 18
Telegram, Wilber wounded . . . . . . . . . . . . . . . . . . . . . . . . . . . . . . . . 25
Maj. Devine and men, Laiana . . . . . . . . . . . . . . . . . . . . . . . . . . . . . . 26
Postcard, Hale to Norma . . . . . . . . . . . . . . . . . . . . . . . . . . . . . . . . . . 29
Pillbox, Munda . . . . . . . . . . . . . . . . . . . . . . . . . . . . . . . . . . . . . . . . . 30
Letter, Hale to Norma . . . . . . . . . . . . . . . . . . . . . . . . . . . . . . . . . . . . 35
Telephone loop circuit, sketch . . . . . . . . . . . . . . . . . . . . . . . . . . . . . . 39
Fire direction center . . . . . . . . . . . . . . . . . . . . . . . . . . . . . . . . . . . . . 42
Lt. Donald Mushik, relaxing . . . . . . . . . . . . . . . . . . . . . . . . . . . . . . . 47
Empty shell cases, Sasavele . . . . . . . . . . . . . . . . . . . . . . . . . . . . . . . . 49

## ILLUSTRATIONS Continued

Capt. Downen and captured gun...................................51
Tank in jungle, Munda.............................................52
Graveside service...................................................52
Wounded soldiers in landing craft..............................53
Lt. Louis Christian 1934...........................................54
Maj. Donald Downen 1944........................................55
Clardie and Donald Downen.....................................55
Lt. Norbert Heidelberger..........................................60
Wilber and coastal gun............................................65
Front line July 1943, sketch.....................................67
Landing on Arundel................................................74
Loading ammunition, Bustling Point..........................79
Howitzer firing, Bustling Point..................................79
Wilber, Maj. Bailey, & Capt. Ryan..............................82
Maj. William Naylor 1943 and 1983...........................90
Command post, Bomboe..........................................95
Bomboe village......................................................95
Kolombangara from Arundel....................................96
Col. Sugg and Capt. Van Tusk...................................97
Troops wading to Stepping Stone Is..........................97
Tank and marine crew...........................................101
Col. Douglas Sugg in boat......................................103
Halsey, Griswold, and Lodge in boat........................113

## PART II  Interlude 1983, Japan and Solomon Islands

Seishu Kinoshita, 1942 and 1983.............................123
Naylor and Kinoshita meeting.................................126
Gun on Beach Red, Guadalcanal..............................129
Stacey Wally, age three..........................................129
American memorial...............................................130
Japanese memorial................................................130
Three boys, Guadalcanal........................................131
Salia, age 11........................................................133
Landing craft relic in trees.....................................133
Munda field from cockpit.......................................134
Air terminal, Munda..............................................134
Alfred Basili with recoil spring................................136
Coastal gun and Hale, Baanga, 1983........................137
Beach in cove, Baanga..........................................138
Children waving, Sasavele.....................................139
Three children, Sasavele.......................................139
Hale in Basili's canoe............................................140
Relic vehicle, Sasavele..........................................141

Scenic channel, Arundel . . . . . . . . . . . . . . . . . . . . . . . . . . . . . . . . . . . . 144
Abandoned American tank . . . . . . . . . . . . . . . . . . . . . . . . . . . . . . . 145
Scarecrow with U.S. helmet . . . . . . . . . . . . . . . . . . . . . . . . . . . . . . 150
Ian Warne family . . . . . . . . . . . . . . . . . . . . . . . . . . . . . . . . . . . . . . . . 153

## PART III  Ondonga palm grove

Promotion party . . . . . . . . . . . . . . . . . . . . . . . . . . . . . . . . . . . . . . . . 161
Capt. Charles D'Avanzo and Wilber . . . . . . . . . . . . . . . . . . . . . . . . 162
Wilber portrait with signboard . . . . . . . . . . . . . . . . . . . . . . . . . . . 169
Camp Street, Ondonga . . . . . . . . . . . . . . . . . . . . . . . . . . . . . . . . . 174
Signpost with Rhode Island towns . . . . . . . . . . . . . . . . . . . . . . . 174
Howitzer (155-mm), Bibilo Hill, Munda . . . . . . . . . . . . . . . . . . . 177
Artillery team in battle, sketch . . . . . . . . . . . . . . . . . . . . . . . . . . . 180
Wilber in his tent office . . . . . . . . . . . . . . . . . . . . . . . . . . . . . . . . 181
Munda military cemetery, 1944 . . . . . . . . . . . . . . . . . . . . . . . . . 186
Capt. Russell Davis . . . . . . . . . . . . . . . . . . . . . . . . . . . . . . . . . . . . 190
Trucks ready for inspection . . . . . . . . . . . . . . . . . . . . . . . . . . . . . 196
SCAT cartoon flying instructions . . . . . . . . . . . . . . . . . . . . . 206-207
169th FA passing in review . . . . . . . . . . . . . . . . . . . . . . . . . . . . . 211
Band concert . . . . . . . . . . . . . . . . . . . . . . . . . . . . . . . . . . . . . . . . 212
Officers of 169th FA and chapel . . . . . . . . . . . . . . . . . . . . . . . . . 212
Wilber and Lt. Mushik . . . . . . . . . . . . . . . . . . . . . . . . . . . . . . . . . 213
Path, Ondonga . . . . . . . . . . . . . . . . . . . . . . . . . . . . . . . . . . . . . . . 216
Capt. McAuliffe and Lt. Mushik . . . . . . . . . . . . . . . . . . . . . . . . . 226

## PART IV  Western civilization at last

Rain flooded tent, Guadalcanal . . . . . . . . . . . . . . . . . . . . . . . . . 236
USAT Holbrook loading troops . . . . . . . . . . . . . . . . . . . . . . . . . . 247
Mt. Egmont aka Mt. Taranaki . . . . . . . . . . . . . . . . . . . . . . . . . . . 256
Mt. Ngauruhoe in eruption . . . . . . . . . . . . . . . . . . . . . . . . . . . . 257
Drop Scene, Whanganui River . . . . . . . . . . . . . . . . . . . . . . . . . . 258
New Zealand trees, sketches . . . . . . . . . . . . . . . . . . . . . . . . . . . 260
United Services Hotel, Christchurch . . . . . . . . . . . . . . . . . . . . . 261
Franz Josef Glacier . . . . . . . . . . . . . . . . . . . . . . . . . . . . . . . . . . . . 263
Waiho Chapel and glacier . . . . . . . . . . . . . . . . . . . . . . . . . . . . . 263
Wilber with three hikers . . . . . . . . . . . . . . . . . . . . . . . . . . . . . . . 264
Stationery printed by Hale . . . . . . . . . . . . . . . . . . . . . . . . . . . . . 273
152nd FA staff . . . . . . . . . . . . . . . . . . . . . . . . . . . . . . . . . . . . . . . . 292
Minnie & Sidney Smith 1942 . . . . . . . . . . . . . . . . . . . . . . . . . . . 302
Sam & Olive Croker . . . . . . . . . . . . . . . . . . . . . . . . . . . . . . . . . . . 303
Jones girls . . . . . . . . . . . . . . . . . . . . . . . . . . . . . . . . . . . . . . . . . . . 304
Olive Madsen with corsage . . . . . . . . . . . . . . . . . . . . . . . . . . . . 306

**ILLUSTRATIONS** Continued

### PART V  Interlude 1984, New Zealand

Waldo Fish and Hale .......................................... 313
Dawn Jones Penney ........................................... 314
Minnie & Sidney Smith ....................................... 315
Olive Madsen 1944 ............................................ 320
Olive Madsen and Hale 1984 ................................. 321
Wilber and Capt. Davis, Wellington .......................... 322
Inscription by Wilber in book ................................ 324

# *Preface*

This is the second of the three-volume story of the Bradt family in World War II. It carries my father, Wilber Bradt, through several important phases of his military service in the South Pacific Theater: intense combat over three months in the Solomon Islands; a decompression phase of defensive duty; and finally rehabilitation and retraining in New Zealand, with its opportunity for social engagement with the people there. Many aspects of his earlier combat experience resurface in Wilber's mind and appear in his letters during the latter phases. On the home front, our family became fragmented against the backdrop of an America in the midst of a world war.

Wilber was a skillful and (fortunately) compulsive letter writer, and this story is told in large part through his letters, which I located in Indiana, Virginia, Maryland, Florida, and elsewhere in the early 1980s. There are some 700 of these letters (about 400,000 words), constituting a unique contemporaneous view of the Pacific war. This trilogy contains about 37% of their content, or about 150,000 words. The work also includes letters by relatives and associates that shed light on the characters and activities of Wilber and his wife Norma.

The journeys I took to uncover the story are an important part of this account: I sought out Wilber's letters, associated photographs, and documents; interviewed his family and colleagues (plus one Japanese opponent) during the 1980s; and visited Pacific battle and rehabilitation sites in 1983–84. As the son of Wilber and Norma, I offer my personal responses to his letters and to all of these events, which are another important part of this story.

Choosing which letters and which parts of Wilber's letters to retain was difficult because they contain so much interesting and germane material. Whole letters are omitted without indication, and a deletion within a letter is indicated with an ellipsis. Wilber often wrote of the same events to multiple recipients, albeit with different spins, and he wrote of mundane items, like requests for personal supplies (radio batteries, razor blades, foods), the status of the mortgage, and about other family members. I retain samplings of such writing but delete most of it.

# COMBAT AND NEW LIFE

The remaining content of the letters has undergone some light editing for minor corrections and formatting, all without indication. For the most part, however, the inconsistencies of Wilber's impromptu writings are left untouched. Brief clarifying comments by me are presented within [square brackets]. Infrequent abbreviated references also in brackets provide a sense of my sources, which are more fully described in the bibliography.

The remarkable overall clarity and drama of Wilber's writing made heavy editing unnecessary.

## SYNTHESIS OF BOOK 1

The first volume (Book 1: *Citizen Soldier*) of this trilogy began with the untimely death of my father, a much decorated army officer, six weeks after his return home from the Pacific Theater at the end of World War II. The book then stepped back and introduced its central character, Wilber E. Bradt (1900–1945), and his wife, Norma Sparlin Bradt (1905–1986), he an Indiana farm boy and later a college chemistry professor and she a Washington State musician and writer. The story followed them through their very different upbringings, their marriage, and the births of their two children: Hale (myself, this book's narrator) and my sister Valerie (Chart 1; charts and maps follow this preface). In 1936, our family moved from Washington State to Orono, Maine, where Wilber became head of the University of Maine Department of Chemistry and Chemical Engineering.

Wilber had been in national guard units since shortly after World War I and was a member of the Maine National Guard when it was ordered to active service in February 1941. He was a captain of artillery. His unit, the 43rd Infantry Division, went through training in Florida and Mississippi and deployed overseas in October 1942 to New Caledonia via New Zealand (Map 1). Several months later, it advanced by convoy to the just-captured Guadalcanal Island in the Solomon Islands and suffered a torpedo plane attack en route. From there, it transshipped to the Russell Islands, which became the American front line in the Solomons.

In the Russell Islands, Wilber's battalion suffered Japanese bombing attacks and witnessed overhead air battles. Wilber, now an army major, rose to the command of his unit, the 169th Field Artillery Battalion, a Rhode Island outfit and one of the four artillery battalions of the 43rd Infantry Division. His immediate boss, commander of the division artillery, was Brig. Gen. Harold R. Barker (Chart 2), a demanding, effective, profane national guardsman from Rhode Island. Wilber's new command merited the rank of lieutenant colonel, so a promotion was expected.

*Preface*

As Wilber entered active military service in February 1941, Norma and their two children, Valerie (age 8) and I (age 10), moved to New York City where Norma could pursue her musical and writing interests. The plan was for her to develop some independence in the event that Wilber was lost at war. In early 1942, while in New York, the family was befriended by a 49-year-old Lebanese-born journalist, Monte Bourjaily, who had held high positions in the 1930s but was by then twice divorced and between jobs with few resources. Wilber had met him on one of his military leaves and thought well of him. In January 1943, three and a half months after Wilber had gone overseas, Norma became pregnant by Monte and chose to carry the pregnancy to term while hoping to keep it a secret from everyone, including and especially her husband. To maintain this secrecy, she sent Valerie and me to summer camps in July and then arranged for us to attend boarding schools immediately afterward.

x·o·ø·o·x

The 43rd Division, after its reorganization for greater mobility in January 1942 (Chart 2), consisted of three infantry regiments, four field artillery (FA) battalions, and other supporting units. The four artillery battalions—one of which Wilber commanded in 1943—were organized as the 43rd Division Artillery, commanded by General Barker. Each of the three artillery battalions was assigned to support one of the division's three infantry regiments. The fourth artillery battalion, carrying larger howitzers, was used for general support as needed. Each of the infantry regiments, with its artillery battalion and other supportive units, could operate quite independently and was known as a regimental combat team (RCT).

The 43rd Division had been commanded by Maj. Gen. John H. Hester since the end of the Louisiana maneuvers in September 1941. He would lead the division (and also the entire New Georgia Occupation Force) into the Munda combat but would be relieved of these commands in the midst of that action. The next higher level of command during most of the Solomons campaign was the XIV Corps, commanded by Maj. Gen. Oscar W. Griswold.

---

Our story resumes in the midst of World War II in July 1943. At that time, the Axis powers (Germany, Italy and Japan) controlled most of Europe and the entire western Pacific, areas they had conquered in 1939–42. The Allies (America, England, China, and Russia) had just begun to claw their way back, but there was a long way to go. The Germans and Italians had been driven from Africa, and the invasion of Sicily was set for July 10. In the Soviet Union, the Germans had been driven back from the gates of Moscow and had suffered a major defeat at Stalingrad. On July 5, the Germans initiated a major battle for Kursk. In the South Pacific, the Americans had secured the island of Guadalcanal and the Russell Islands, and Wilber's unit, the 43rd Infantry Division, was about to make the next move to New Georgia, under the command of the navy's Admiral William Halsey. In parallel with this advance, Gen. MacArthur was preparing to move up the New Guinea northeast coast to the Huon peninsula (Map 2). The war was flaring up on all fronts.

# MAPS & CHARTS

★ ★

*Maps and Charts*

## BRADT

Abram Bradt (b. 1805) — Margaret Van Antwerp

Isaac Henry (b. 1840)
- m1 — Ann E. Bastow
- m2 — Julia Bugbee Bradt Seelinger*

*Isaac died when Julia was 21 and Hale 15 mos.; she married Phillip Seelinger 4 years later.

- Mary Ann
- Will
- Charles

Fletcher "Hale" — Elizabeth Peak

- **Wilber** E. (b. 1900) — **Norma** Sparlin
  - "Hale" Van Dorn (b. 1930)
  - Valerie Evelyn (b. 1932)
- Mary — Willys Higgins
- Paul — Josephine Irey
- Rex — "Gerry" Enos
- Ruth — Jack Wilson

## SPARLIN

Andrew (b. 1805)
- m1 — Elizabeth Spurgeon | 10 children
- m2 — Mary Myers

Stonewall J. (b. 1866) and 10 others
- m1 — Ethel Richmond
  - **Norma** (b. 1905)
  - Leota
  - Jesse
  - Beatrice "Beto"
  - Milton
  - Evelyn — Clarence Ayer
- m2 — Lucille Milton
  - Stonewall E "Stoney"
  - Gerald
  - Vida

## BOURJAILY

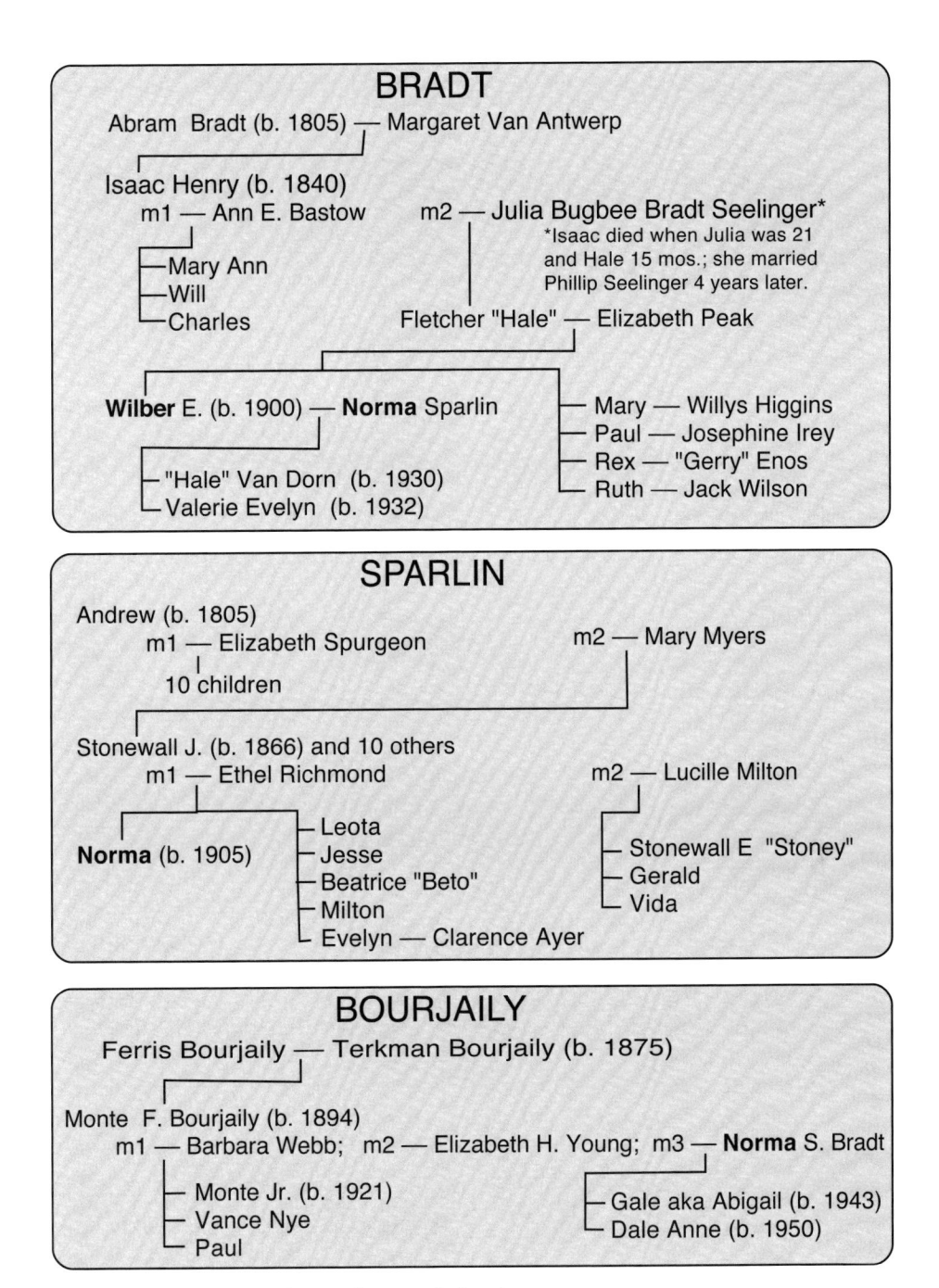

Ferris Bourjaily — Terkman Bourjaily (b. 1875)

Monte F. Bourjaily (b. 1894)
- m1 — Barbara Webb;  m2 — Elizabeth H. Young;  m3 — **Norma** S. Bradt
  - Monte Jr. (b. 1921)
  - Vance Nye
  - Paul
  - Gale aka Abigail (b. 1943)
  - Dale Anne (b. 1950)

*Chart 1. The Bradt, Sparlin, and Bourjaily families.*

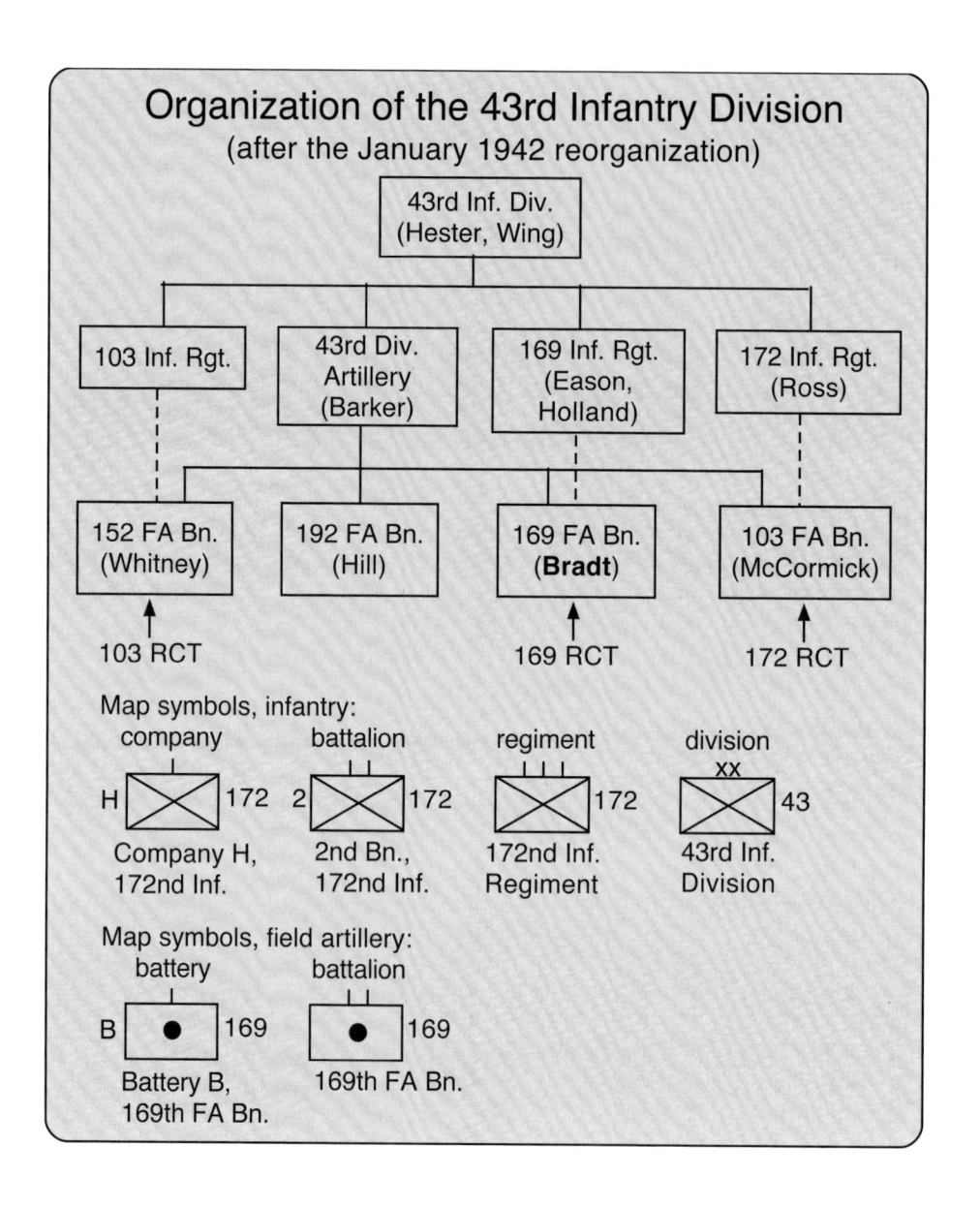

# Organization of the 43rd Infantry Division
## (after the January 1942 reorganization)

- 43rd Inf. Div. (Hester, Wing)
  - 103 Inf. Rgt.
  - 43rd Div. Artillery (Barker)
    - 152 FA Bn. (Whitney)
    - 192 FA Bn. (Hill)
    - 169 FA Bn. (**Bradt**)
    - 103 FA Bn. (McCormick)
  - 169 Inf. Rgt. (Eason, Holland)
  - 172 Inf. Rgt. (Ross)

152 FA Bn. ← 103 RCT
169 FA Bn. ← 169 RCT
103 FA Bn. ← 172 RCT

Map symbols, infantry:

| company | battalion | regiment | division |
|---|---|---|---|
| H ⊠ 172 | 2 ⊠ 172 | ⊠ 172 | ⊠ 43 (xx) |
| Company H, 172nd Inf. | 2nd Bn., 172nd Inf. | 172nd Inf. Regiment | 43rd Inf. Division |

Map symbols, field artillery:

| battery | battalion |
|---|---|
| B ● 169 | ● 169 |
| Battery B, 169th FA Bn. | 169th FA Bn. |

*Chart 2. Organization and commanders of the 43rd Infantry Division, 1942–1943.*

1. The commanding officers (C.O.) shown are those in command during the Solomon Islands actions who were mentioned in Wilber's letters.

2. The division (Div.) had numerous other supporting elements.

3. The three "light" field artillery (FA) battalions (103rd, 152nd, and 169th) had 105-mm (4-inch) howitzers, which had a range of about five miles. The "medium" battalion (192nd FA) had 155-mm (6-inch) howitzers, which had a greater range.

4. A field artillery battalion consisted of about 500 men and 12 howitzers divided into three batteries (A, B, C) of four howitzers each and a headquarters battery.

5. An infantry regiment (Inf. Rgt.) consisted of three infantry battalions, 1st Bn., 2nd Bn., and 3rd Bn., each with about 500 men in four companies, designated A, B, C, and D in the 1st Bn., E–H in the 2nd Bn., and I, K, L, M in the 3rd Bn.

6. The four artillery battalions were under the command of General Barker, but could be assigned to regimental combat teams (RCT), which could operate independently of one another. The three light artillery battalions were normally assigned to the infantry regiments shown (dashed lines), but assignments could vary. The medium artillery battalion was reserved for general support where needed.

7. The National Guard origins of these units were:
Connecticut: 169 Inf. and 192 FA.
Maine: 152 FA and 103 Inf.
Rhode Island: 103 FA and 169 FA.
Vermont: 172 Inf.

8. Army officer ranks in ascending order in 1943 were: 2nd lieutenant (Lt.), 1st Lt., captain (Capt.), major (Maj.), lieutenant colonel (Lt. Col.), colonel, brigadier general (one-star insignia), major general (two stars), lieutenant general (three stars), and general (four stars). A five-star rank, General of the Army, was reactivated in late 1944.

*Maps and Charts*

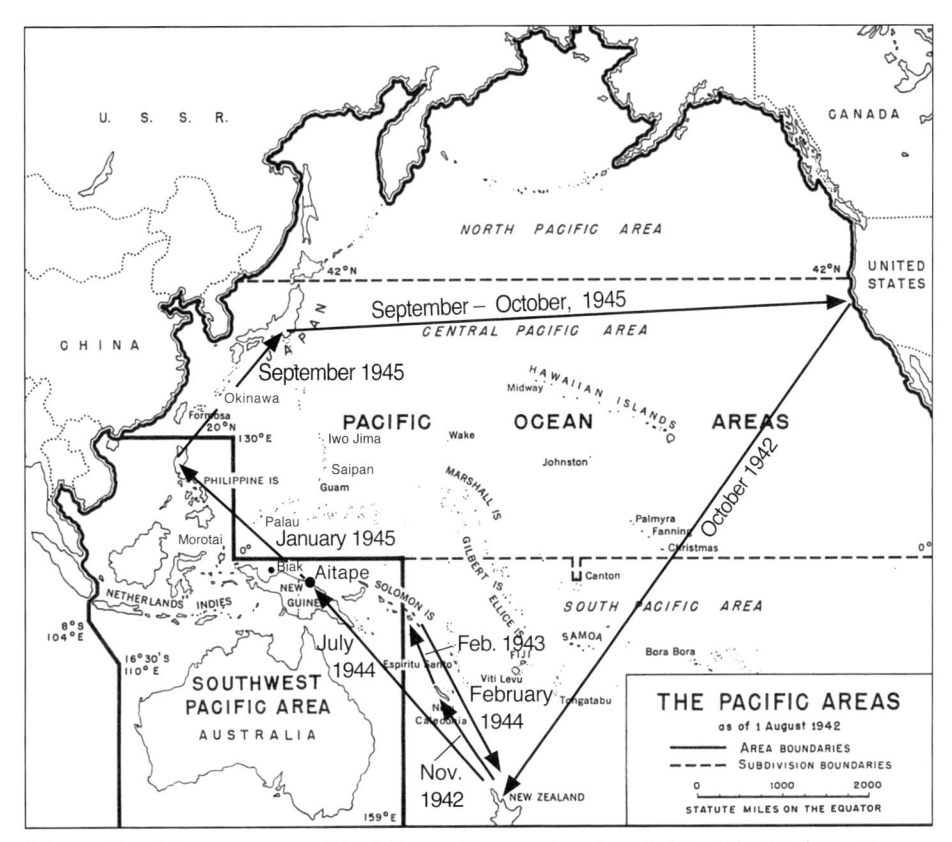

*Map 1. The eight sea voyages (black lines with arrowheads and dates) the 43rd Division made in the Pacific Ocean during its three years overseas. Three additional (overnight) voyages were made within the Solomon Islands. Also delineated are the four military command areas of the Pacific Theater. The North, Central, and South Pacific Areas were the domain of the U.S. Navy (Admiral Chester Nimitz), and the Southwest Pacific Area, the domain of the U.S. Army (General Douglas MacArthur).* [UNDERLYING MAP: R. JOHNSTONE, IN MILLER, *CARTWHEEL*, MAP 2, P. 3]

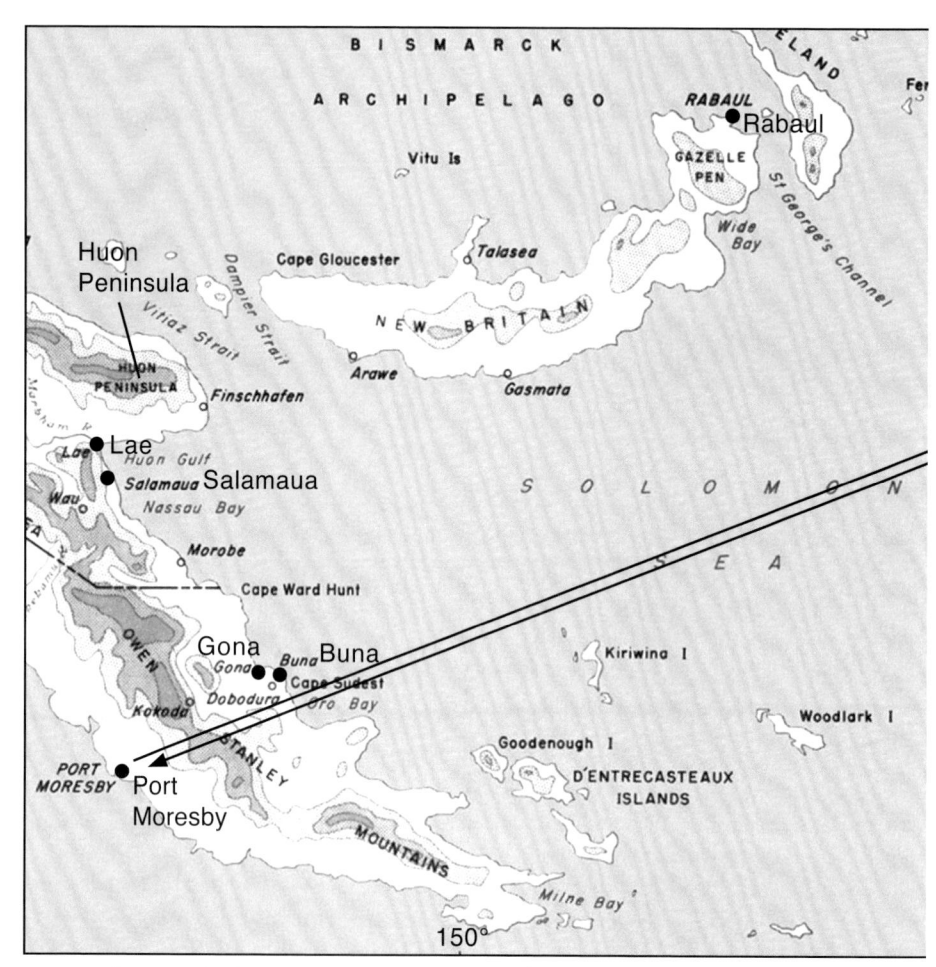

*Map 2. The Cartwheel area and my travels: New Guinea (lower left, left panel), Bismarck Archipelago (top of left panel), and Solomon Islands (right panel). The dark lines, some with arrowheads, represent my flights in May 1983 to, through, and out of the Solomon Islands, beginning and ending in Port Moresby (lower left, left panel). The longest three segments were in high altitude jets. The others were in low-flying small propeller planes.*

The Japanese had been driven from Guadalcanal (lower right, right panel) and the Gona-Buna area on New Guinea in January–February, 1943. When the 43rd Division began *its attack on Munda airfield, Solomon Islands, in July 1943, the Japanese had retreated to the Lae-Salamaua area of New Guinea. Simultaneous drives up the Solomons (under navy command) and up the New Guinea coast (under army command) were intended to isolate and eventually neutralize the major Japanese naval base at Rabaul (upper right, left panel). The advances in the two theaters were coordinated to allow the use of common naval and air resources. This strategy was given the name "Cartwheel."* [UNDERLYING MAP: MILLER, *CARTWHEEL*, MAP 3, P. 23]

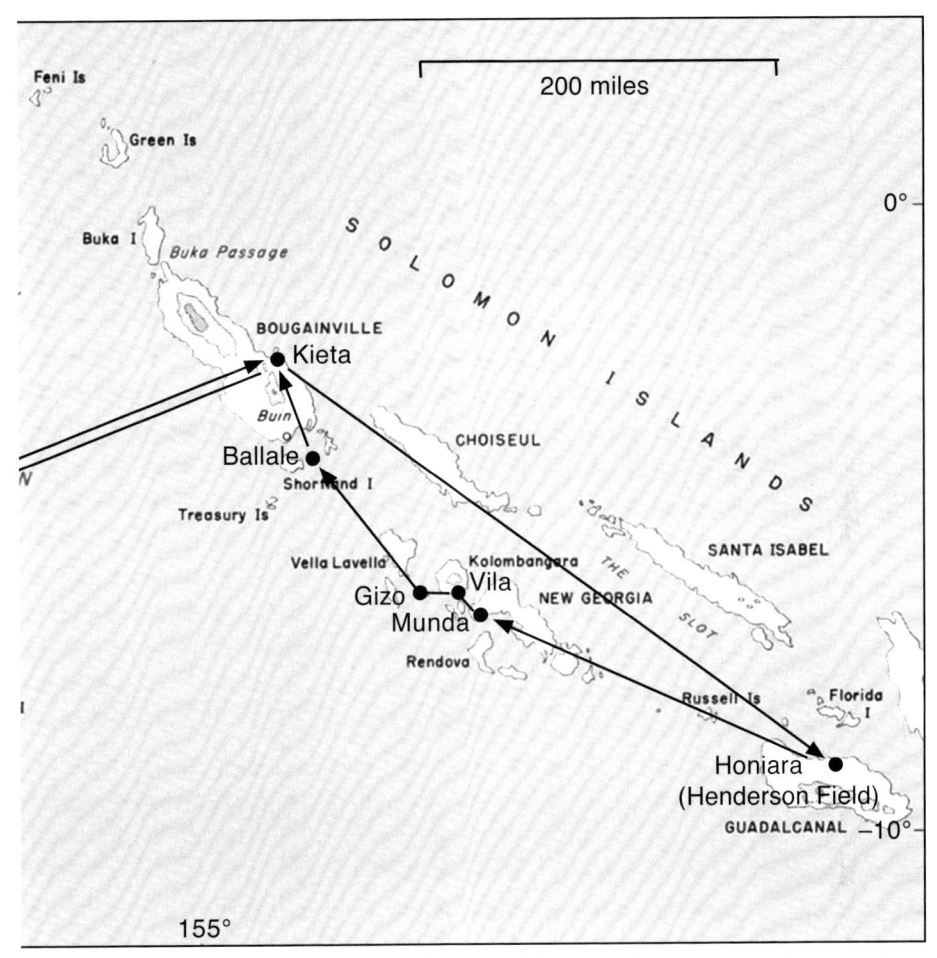

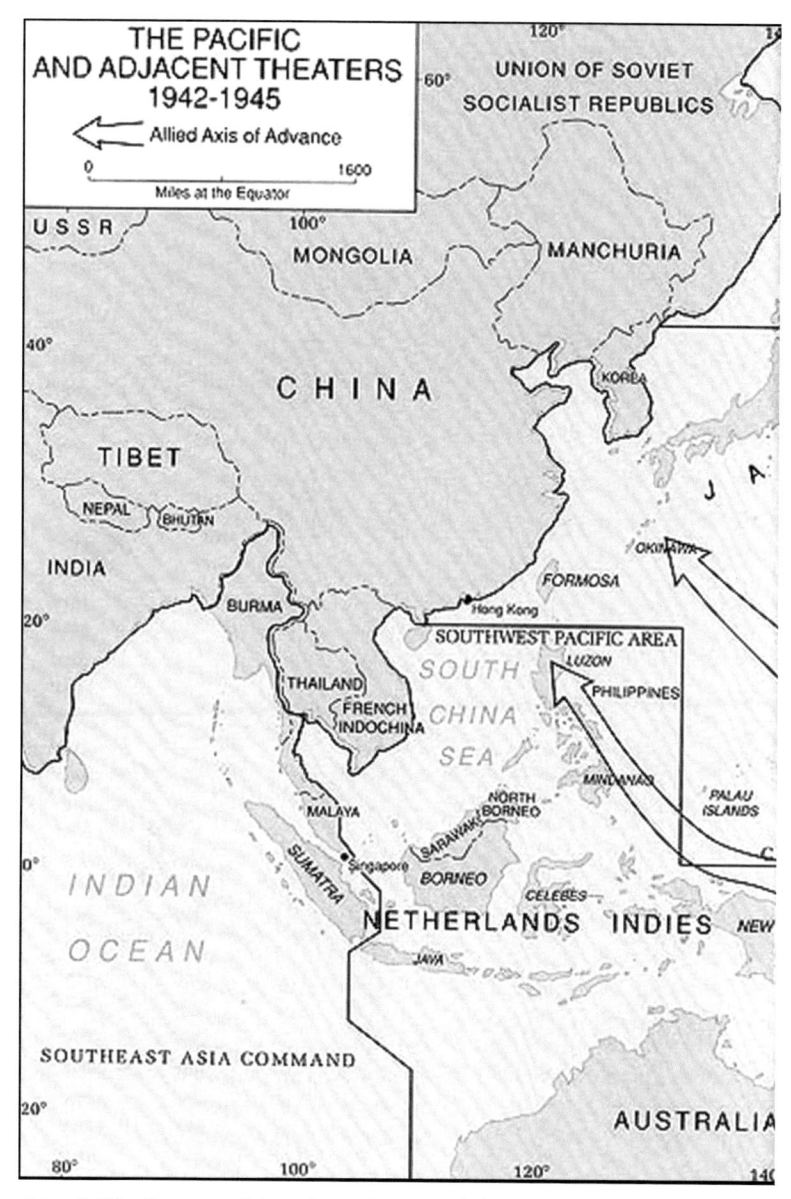

*Map 3. The Command Area boundaries and dual Allied thrusts in the Pacific. The U.S. Navy, under Admirals Nimitz and Halsey, controlled the Central and South Pacific Areas, while the army under General MacArthur directed operations in the Southwest Pacific Area. In the early months of the war, the navy directed the fighting in the eastern Solomons*

*Maps and Charts*

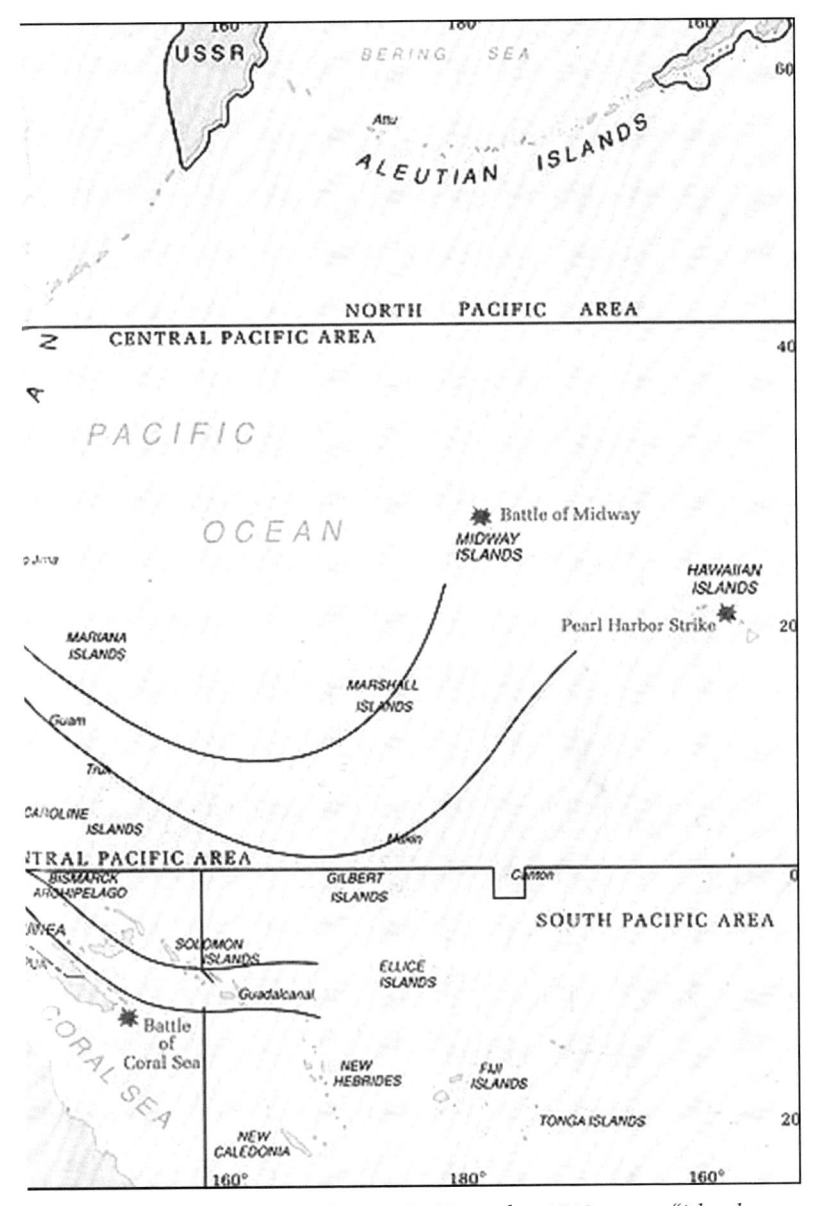

*and MacArthur that in New Guinea. In November 1943, a new "island hopping" thrust was opened in the Central Pacific under Nimitz. MacArthur directed the southern thrust up the New Guinea coast toward the Philippines. The two thrusts shared fleet and air resources.* [MAP: CONCISE HISTORY OF WWII, U.S. ARMY CENTER FOR MILITARY HISTORY]

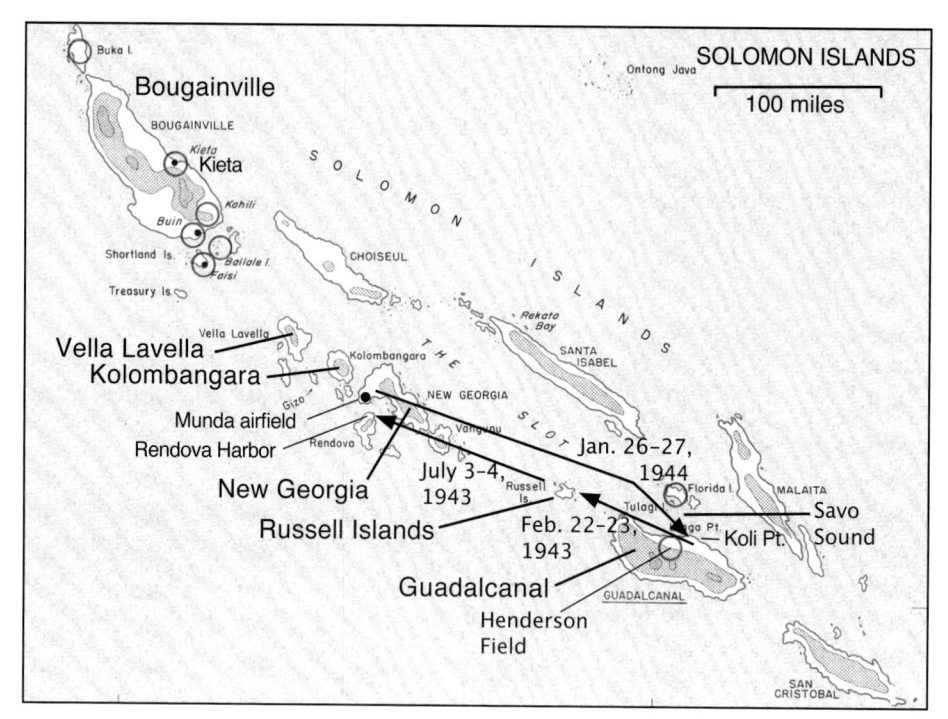

*Map 4. Solomon Islands including Guadalcanal, the Russell Islands, and the New Georgia group. The circles indicate Japanese bases prior to the marine landings on Guadalcanal in August 1942. The major Japanese stronghold at Rabaul was on New Britain Island, 200 miles farther to the northwest. Another Japanese airfield was built on New Georgia at Munda during the Guadalcanal fighting. The three moves of the 43rd Division during its 11 months in the Solomons are shown.*

*During the battles over Guadalcanal, Japanese ships would approach Guadalcanal from the northwest through "the Slot," while American ships would approach from the southeast. Both were trying to reinforce and supply their troops on Guadalcanal. Many ships were sunk in Savo Sound ("Ironbottom Sound"), which lies between Florida Island and Guadalcanal.* [UNDERLYING MAP: MILLER, *GUADALCANAL*, MAP III, CROPPED]

*Maps and Charts*

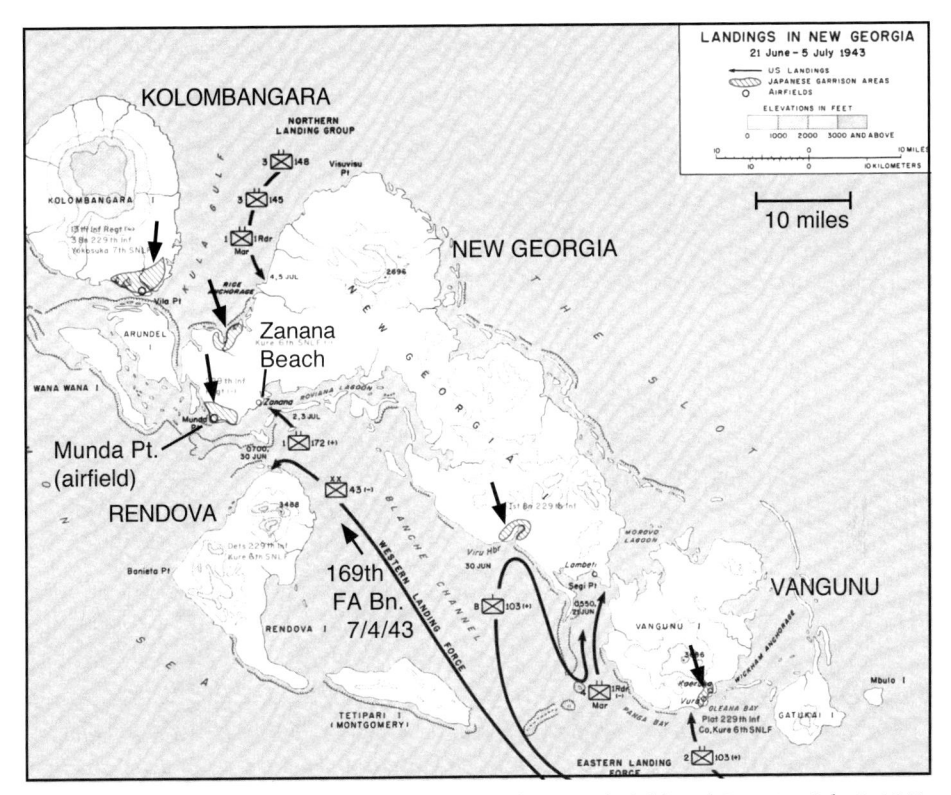

*Map 5. Allied landings in the New Georgia Island Group (solid lines) June 21–July 5, 1943. The outlined hatched areas (arrows) indicate Japanese strongpoints. The long tracks show the approach of the American Western, Eastern, and Northern Landing Forces. Wilber was wounded on the north end of Rendova Island on July 4. The attack on Munda airfield was mounted to the east of Munda at Zanana Beach. See Chart 2 for meanings of unit symbols.* [UNDERLYING MAP: MILLER, *CARTWHEEL*, MAP 11, P. 69, CROPPED]

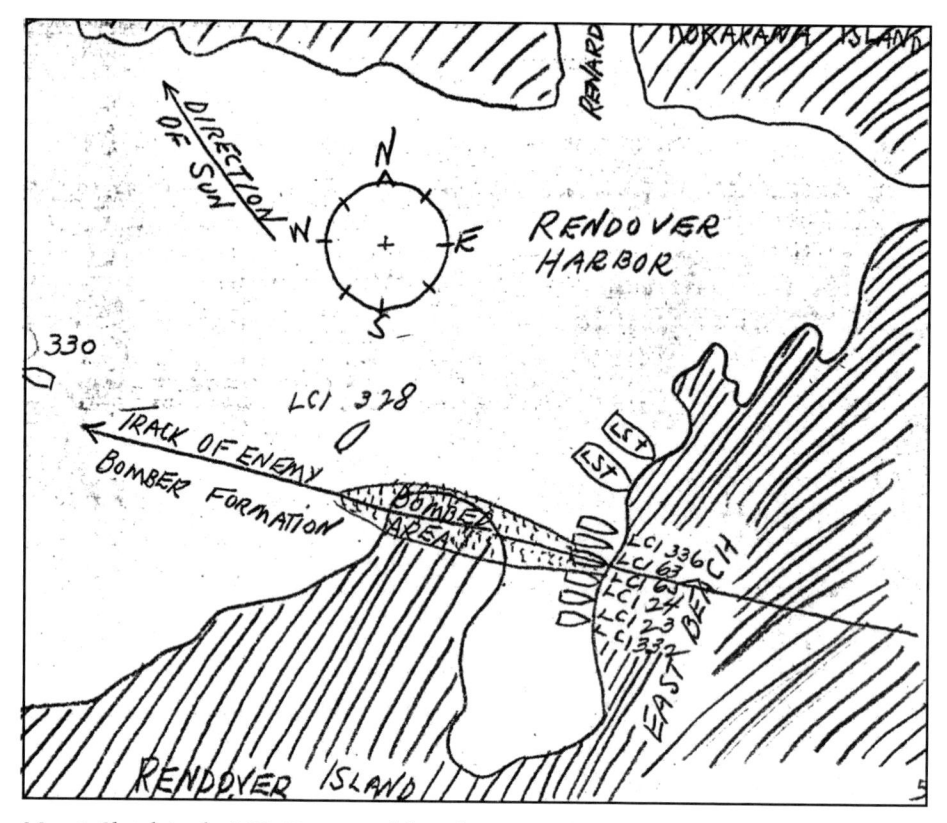

*Map 6. Sketch in the LCI-65 report of the July 4, 1943, bombing strike in Rendova (misspelled "Rendover" in map) Harbor. The dotted bomb pattern starts between LCI-24 and LCI-65, the third and fourth LCIs from the top.* [ACTION REPORT, LCI-65]

*Maps and Charts*

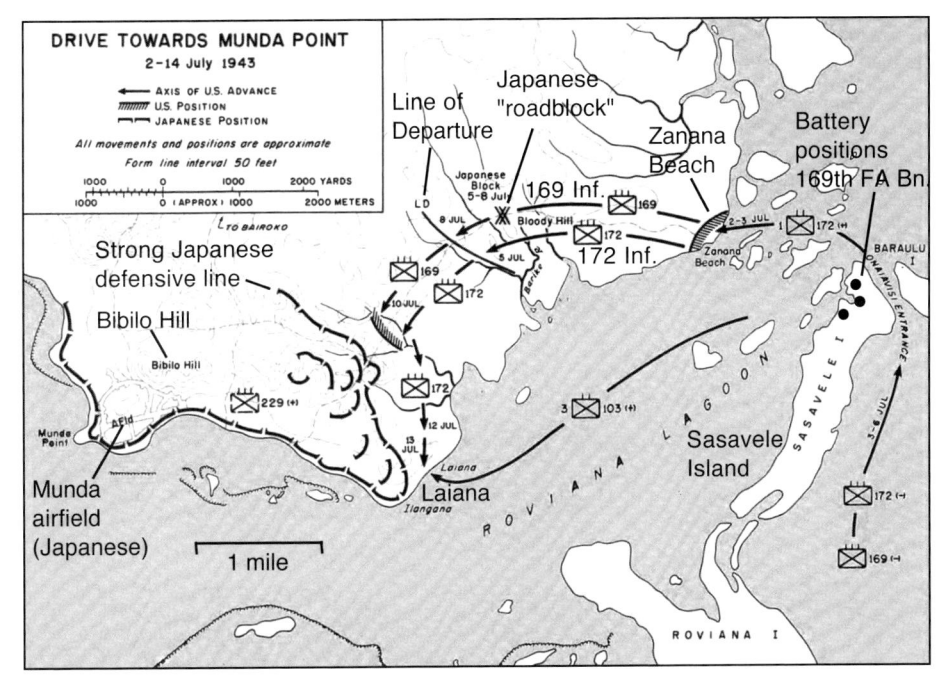

*Map 7. The American landings on Zanana Beach (upper right) and the initial drive toward Munda airfield by the 169th and 172nd Infantry Regiments beginning July 2–3, 1943. The Line of Departure ("LD") is shown. The advance stalled at the most advanced positions shown on about July 10, after which the 172nd Infantry drove south to Laiana beach to shorten supply lines. The howitzers of the 169th Field Artillery Battalion were emplaced on the north end of Sasavele Island (far right); from there the battalion could support the entire advance toward Munda airfield, six miles distant at the far left.*
[UNDERLYING MAP: F. TEMPLE IN MILLER, *CARTWHEEL*, MAP 9, P. 107. LOCATIONS OF 169TH FA BATTERIES: DIXWELL GOFF, WHO SURVEYED THE POSITIONS (PVT. COMM.); SEE ALSO BARKER, MAP P. 50.]

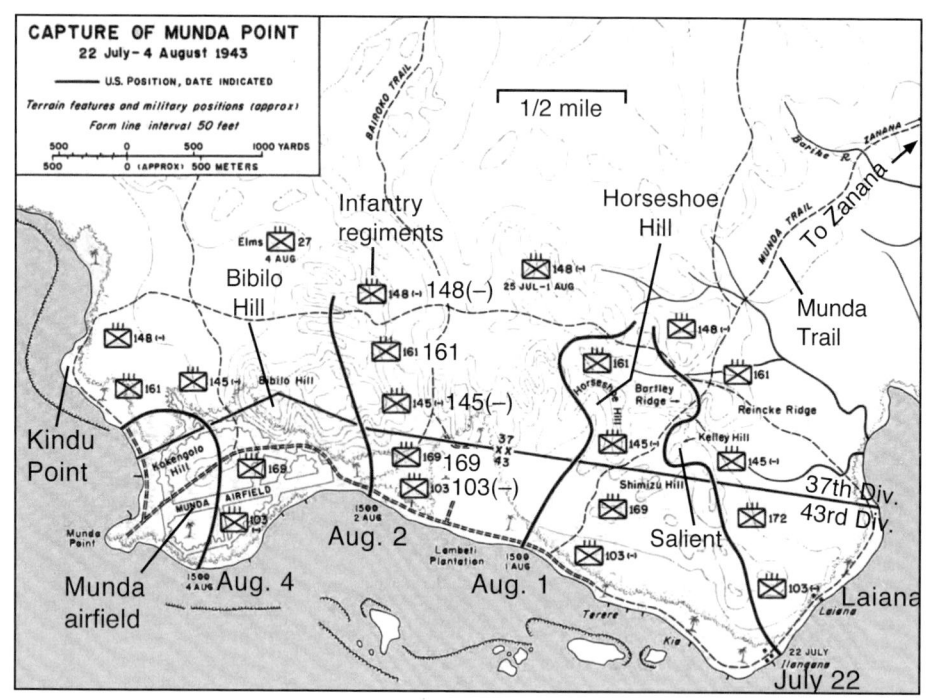

*Map 8. Final westward drive on Munda airfield (lower left), which began July 25. The American front lines on four different dates are shown (dark lines originating on the southern coast). The horizontal dark line was the boundary between the two infantry divisions, the 43rd below and the 37th above. The July 22 front line was more or less in place from July 10 to 25 while the 43rd Division was regrouping and the 37th Division was being brought in, but the fighting never ceased. The salient (protrusion) in that line is described in Wilber's letter of August 24, 1943.* [UNDERLYING MAP: F. TEMPLE IN MILLER, *CARTWHEEL*, MAP 10, P. 145.]

*Maps and Charts*

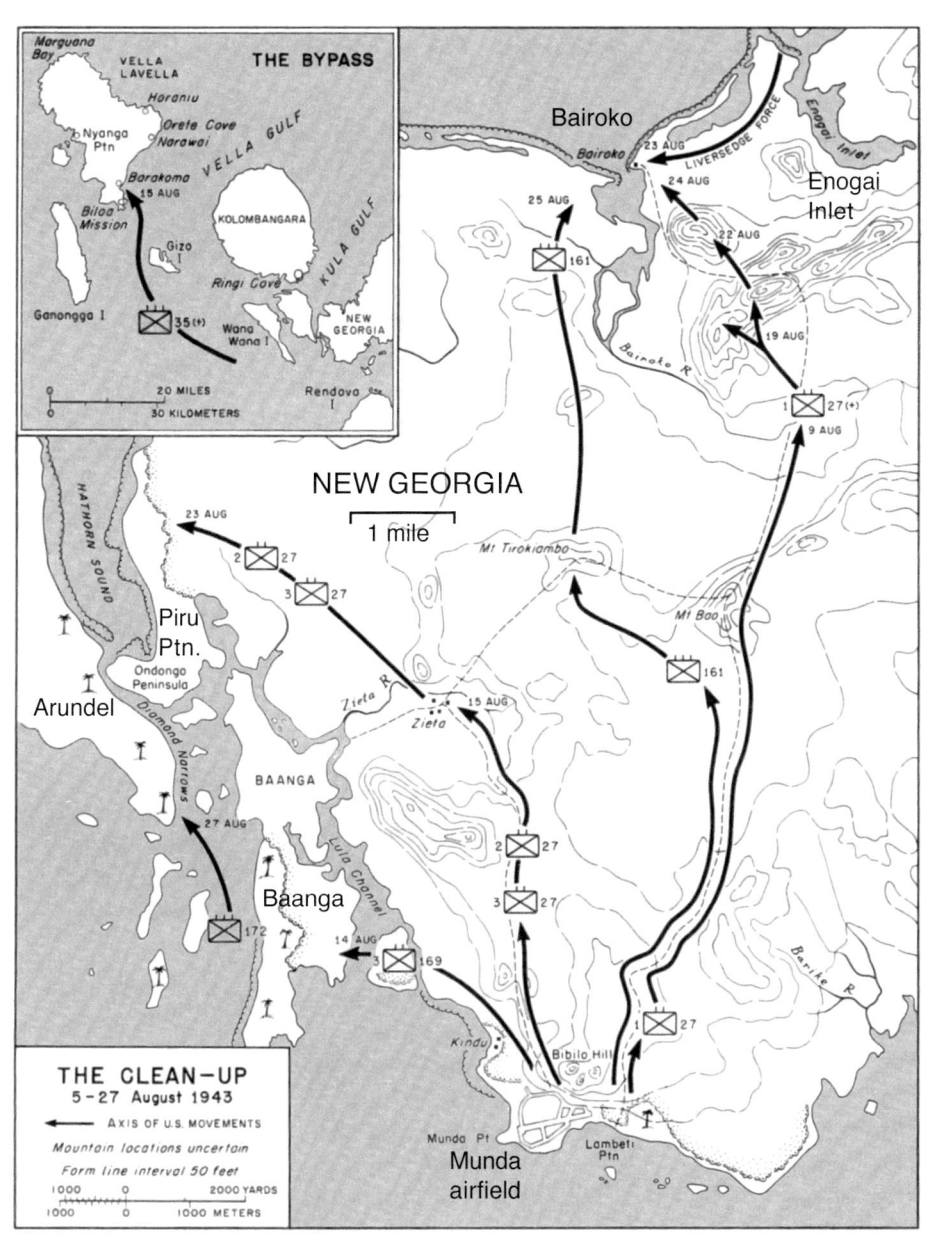

*Map 9. Clean-up after the capture of Munda airfield on August 5, 1943. The advances onto Arundel Island by the 172nd Infantry (leftmost dark line), onto Baanga Island by the 169th Infantry (lower left), to Piru Plantation (center left), and to Bairoko in the north are shown. The August 15 landings on Vella Lavella (inset) bypassed the Japanese stronghold of Kolombangara.* [MAP: D. HOLMES, JR. IN MILLER, *CARTWHEEL*, MAP 11, P. 166]

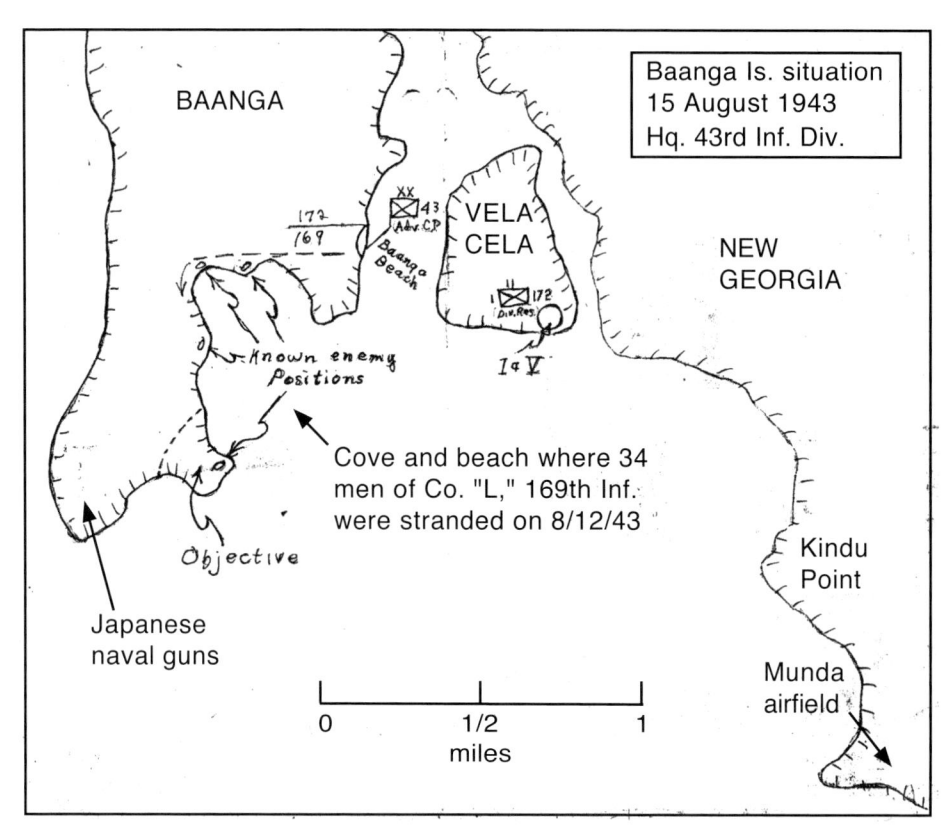

*Map. 10. Cove and beach on Baanga Island where Company L (169th Infantry) troops were ambushed and 34 men stranded on August 12, 1943. On August 14, a depleted company of 42 men, probably also of Company L, attempted unsuccessfully to reach them from Vela Cela Island and Baanga Beach northeast of the cove. Lieutenant Heidelberger, one of Wilber's officers, was with the latter group and was fatally wounded. The next day the 169th Infantry (and later, the 172nd Infantry) mounted a concerted effort from Baanga Beach to overcome the Japanese resistance and rescue the stranded men. The advanced command post (Adv CP) of the 43rd Division was on Baanga Beach indicating that the then-division commander, General Barker, was close at hand. Wilber was probably at or near Kindu Point when, in the early dawn of August 17, he heard and saw the flashes of the Japanese coastal guns on Baanga and proceeded to silence them with a massive artillery barrage.* [UNDERLYING MAP: ACCOMPANIED FIELD ORDER #16, 43RD DIVISION, 8/15/43]

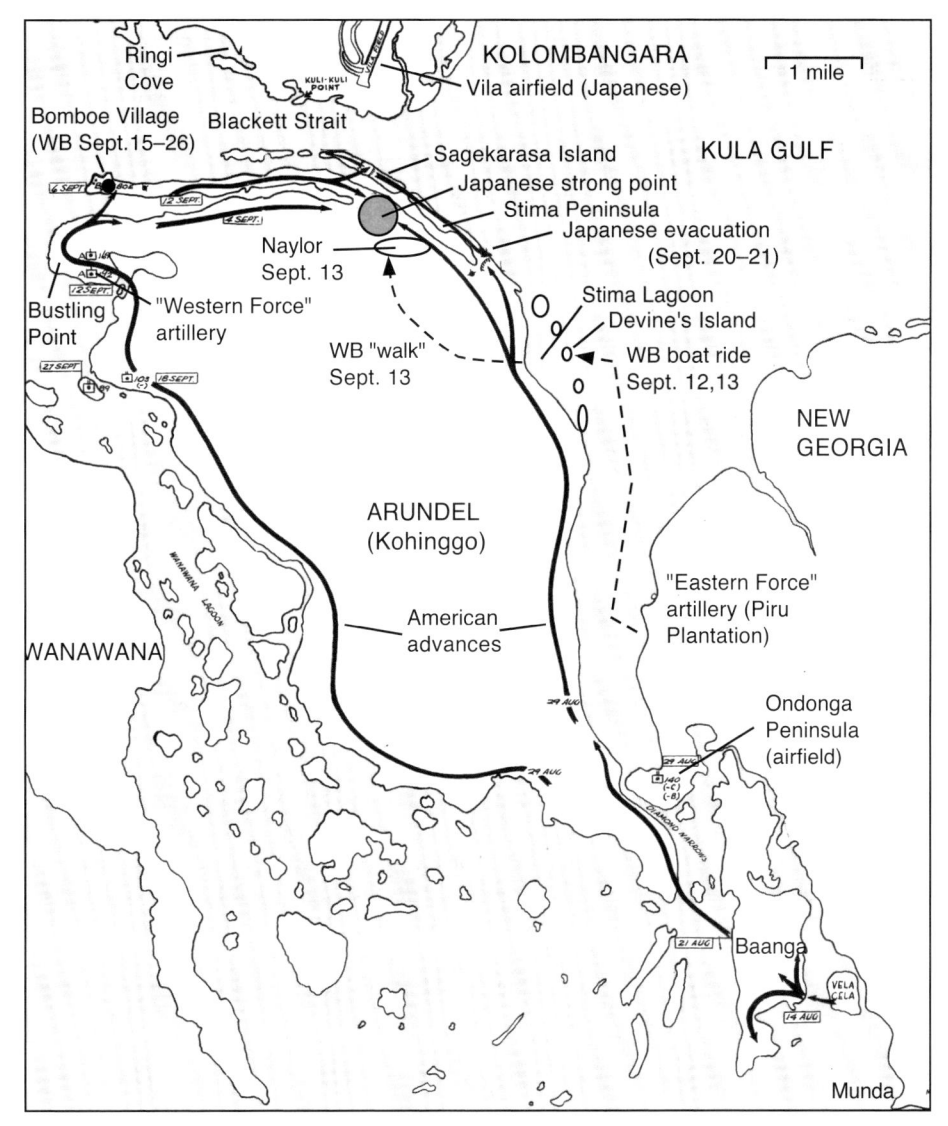

*Map 11. Arundel Island showing places and actions mentioned in Wilber's account. The initial infantry landings took place at the southern end of Arundel, August 29, 1943. When the infantry encountered Japanese on the north end, Wilber became involved. The position of Devine's Island is approximate. The long dark arrows show the advances of American units. The Japanese evacuated Arundel for Kolombangara on the night of September 20–21. In 1983, I circumnavigated Arundel in the clockwise direction in Arthur Basili's canoe.* [UNDERLYING MAP: BARKER, P. 96]

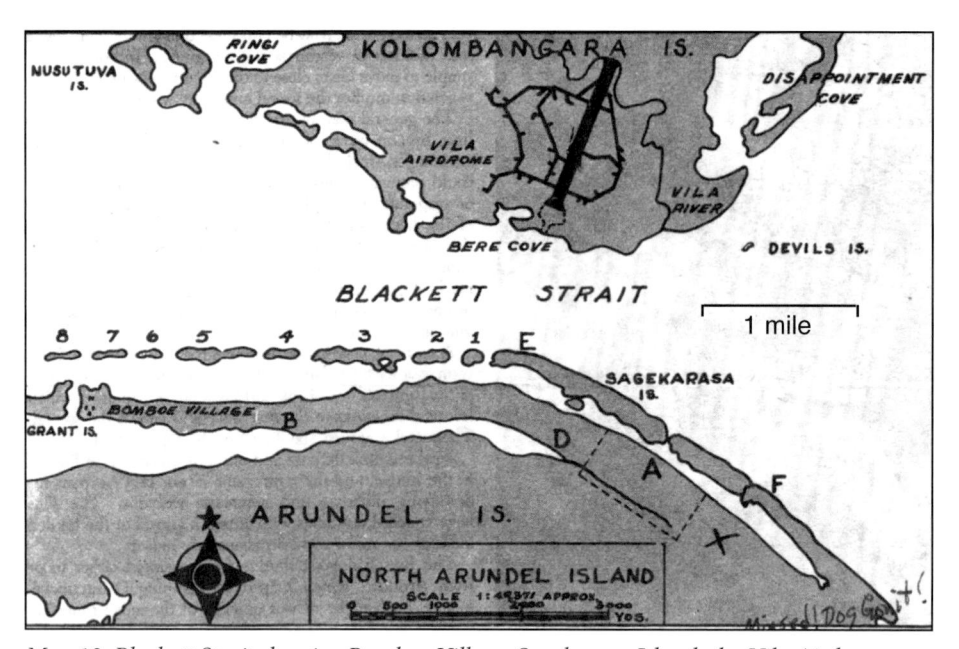

*Map 12. Blackett Strait showing Bomboe Village, Sagekarasa Island, the Vila Airdrome (Japanese) on Kolombangara, and Devil's Island to the right. Wilber wrote about this map: "I crossed Arundel on foot [from lower right] with a patrol of 20 sick men to reach our Infantry trapped at X [his mark]." The Japanese were strongly entrenched at A and on both ends of Sagekarasa Island, especially the west end (E). For most of the subsequent action, Wilber was at Bomboe village (far left) directing artillery located at Bustling Point, southwest of Bomboe. He boated several times along the long lagoon (just below B) between Bomboe and the battle area D where the tank attacks took place. One of his forward observers was on Island No. 1. The small Stepping Stone Island (unlabeled here) is just above the letter D. The notation in the lower right, "Missed! Dog Gon it!", was Wilber's reference to the text of the associated article about the artillery missing the Japanese float plane.* [MAP: FROM "TANKS AND TACTICS ON ARUNDEL ISLAND," INFANTRY JOURNAL, SEPT. 1944, PP. 18–20; ANONYMOUS AUTHOR]

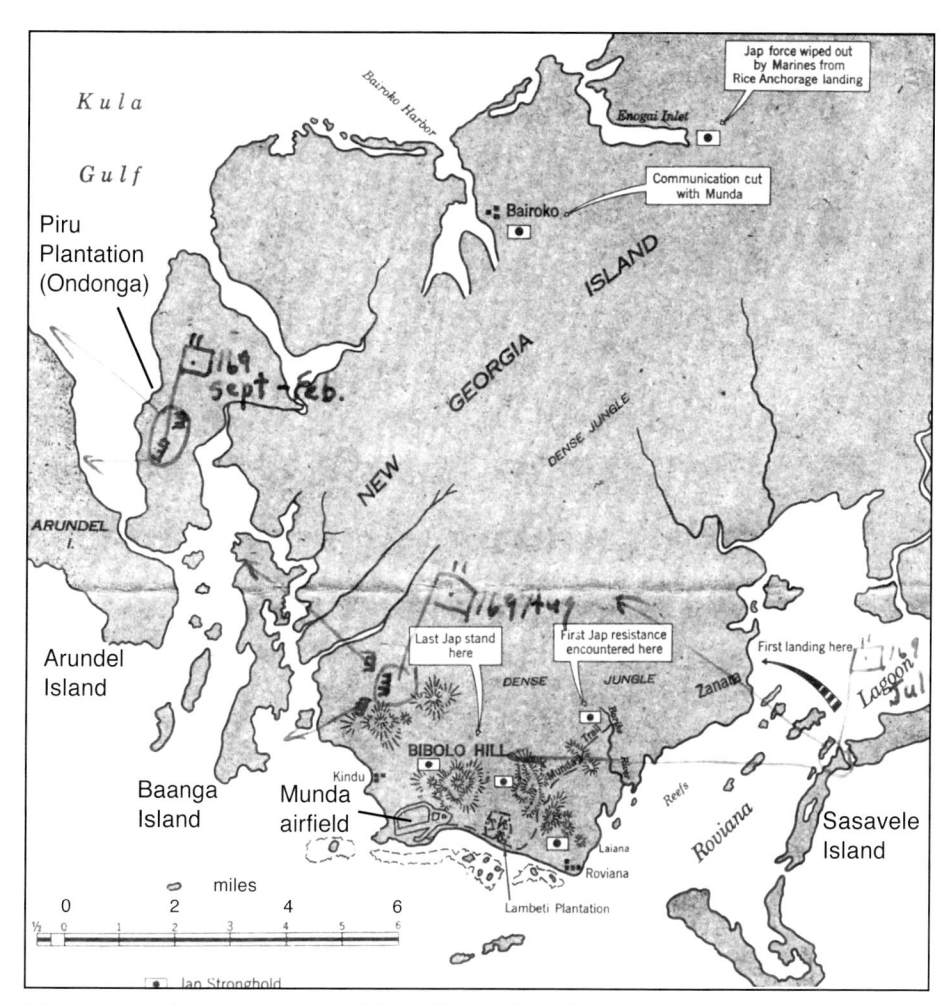

*Map 13. Munda region annotated by Wilber to show the three locations of the 169th FA Bn. during the three phases of combat in the Solomon Islands: on the north end of Sasavele Island during July 1943; north of Bibilo Hill during August; and on Piru Plantation, Ondonga, from September 1943 to February 1944. For most of the latter period, Battery A of the 169th FA was with the Provisional Battalion on northwest Arundel. Wilber showed the fields of fire with long arrows.* [UNDERLYING MAP: FROM DUPUY, R. ERNEST, "BIBOLO [SIC] HILL—AND BEYOND," *INFANTRY JOURNAL*, JANUARY 1944, P. 21-26]

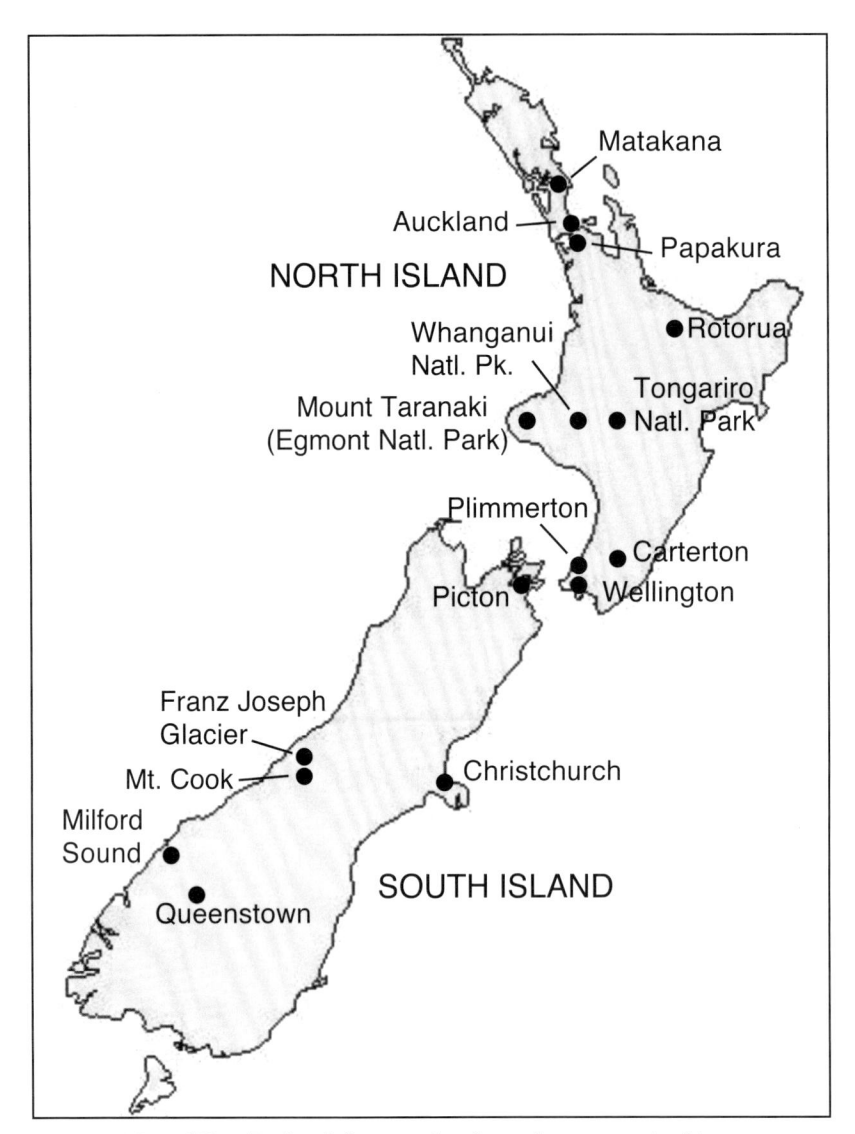

*Map 14. Map of New Zealand showing the places that appear in this story. Wilber's units were stationed at Papakura and Matakana and trained near Rotorua. On leave in March 1944, he and Davis visited the three indicated national parks on North Island and also Plimmerton and Wellington. On South Island, he visited Christchurch, Mt. Cook, and Franz Joseph Glacier, and possibly also Queenstown, Milford Sound, and Picton. Miss Madsen's home was in Carterton when I visited her in 1984.* [MAP OUTLINE: GEOGRAPHY.ABOUT.COM/LIBRARY]

# PART I

# JUNGLE COMBAT

NEW GEORGIA ISLAND GROUP, SOLOMON ISLANDS
JULY—SEPTEMBER 1943

★ ★

## 1

## *"Lovely little shiny bombs"*

### Rendova
### July 1943

The capture of Guadalcanal in the eastern Solomons had required six months of bitter fighting on land and sea (Map 4). The Japanese evacuated it in February 1943. That same month, the 43rd Division, Wilber's unit, advanced to the Russell Islands. In June 1943, the division was ready to move farther forward to capture the recently built Japanese airfield at Munda Point on New Georgia Island, 120 miles to the northwest (Map 5).

The drive up the Solomons took place in the South Pacific Area, the domain of the U.S. Navy (Map 3), under the command of Adm. William "Bull" Halsey. The fighting in New Guinea was in the South*west* Pacific Area, the domain of the army and Gen. Douglas MacArthur. In a complex command arrangement, Halsey had two bosses, MacArthur for strategy and Adm. Chester Nimitz, commander-in-chief of the Pacific Fleet, for logistics. MacArthur was based in Australia and Nimitz in Hawaii.

x·o·ø·o·x

In New York City at the beginning of July, Norma, now more than five months pregnant, had gone to great lengths to keep her pregnancy secret. She had just sent me off to summer camp and Valerie to relatives and later summer camp, so we would not know about it. We mailed letters to her at the Hotel Altamont in Baltimore. Her actual living arrangements remain a mystery to me to this day, and they may have changed over time. The Altamont was probably a fictional residence and mail drop point when, in fact, she was living in the town house that Monte Bourjaily, the baby's father, had rented in the upscale Georgetown neighborhood of Washington, D.C., at 2919 Q Street NW. He and his mother Terkman shared the residence.

By this time, Monte had obtained a high position in the wartime government with the Board of Economic Warfare, and had established himself again as a man of importance. Combining their households would have been a natural move, especially since Monte was apparently willing to take responsibility for the pregnancy. Norma and Terkman would maintain the home and provide support for each other while Monte would bring home the paycheck. Norma may have used some of her military allotment to help with the rent on the Q Street house.

Why did Norma need a fictional residence in Baltimore? She could not live openly in Washington, D.C., because Wilber's brother Paul and his wife lived there and would expect to see Norma on occasion, and Wilber himself would expect such meetings. Also, Wilber surely knew that Monte had moved to Washington, and a Washington address for Norma as well might have been a worry for him.

Baltimore, only 50 miles away, probably seemed like the perfect place for a fictional residence. But perfect it wasn't. Managing her correspondence with Wilber would prove to be awkward. Also, how did Monte explain Norma's presence in his home to his neighbors and social acquaintances? Did she have to wait until night to leave the row house, or retreat to the upper floor when visitors came? Either scenario—that she lived alone in Baltimore or that she lived in Washington at Monte's home—is sad to contemplate. Many years later, around age 80, she told me that she had not been able to share her plight with even her closest sister. Making the burden even heavier, she said this had been the only time in 40-plus years that she had been without her beloved piano.

I cannot help but wonder how Monte dealt with all this. Would he have preferred that Norma abort their out-of-wedlock fetus that was already complicating his life? Could he have felt put upon by Norma's insistence on carrying the pregnancy to term? Was his support of her grounded in a sense of duty and obligation, or was he simply enamored of her and pleased at the prospect of their having a child together? There may well have been an element of pride at fathering this baby, but given the circumstances and the societal expectations of the day, he must have had serious worries about the consequences of their actions. Did they have a long-range plan? Perhaps. We can surmise it only from their subsequent actions.

As a youngster, I was totally unaware of the reason for the family separation and went about having a healthy and productive summer in 1943 at Grace Boys Camp in Bear Mountain State Park, Southfields, New York. At age 12, I became a confident swimmer, canoeist, and hiker. Valerie, after an extended visit with her Uncle Paul (Wilber's brother) and Aunt Jo in Washington, D.C., attended Camp White for the Sheltering Arms, Bantam, Connecticut. She was 11.

x · o · ø · o · x

In the South Pacific, the thrust toward Munda airfield by the 43rd Division would begin with the capture of the lightly defended Rendova Island a few miles south of the targeted airfield. Rendova would serve as a staging area, and artillery emplaced there could fire upon Munda. The first elements of the 43rd Division occupied Rendova on June 30 with minimal resistance. Two days later, on July 2, they were completely surprised by a Japanese bombing raid that resulted in more than 200 dead and wounded [Barker, p. 49].

The day after the air attack, July 3, Wilber was still on Pavuvu Island in the Russell Islands awaiting the sea-going vessels, landing craft, and destroyers that would carry him and his men the 120 miles to Rendova. He wrote to Norma, and she forwarded the letter to me at Grace Boys Camp.

**[PAVUVU, RUSSELL ISLANDS] JULY 3, 1943**
*[Note from Norma to me at the top of this letter:] Dear Hale: This tells the story of the trip to New Georgia and the preparation for the fighting. These letters are very personal. I wish you could care for them, read to Valerie sometime and return as we must save them. Mother*

Dearest Norma — If you listened to the radio last night, you know business is picking up in this theatre. There will be no chance to mail this until later so this letter is just to say I'm thinking now of you and the children. It's a good day. We worked hard all day yesterday until late and now are at it again.

Just now I'm sitting on a coral rock under the ever present palm tree. A column of army ants is going by me six inches from my elbow. Only a few scouts have trespassed so far. This is my last hour on this beach [on Pavuvu] and I'll be looking for another palm [on Rendova] for the next letter.

COMBAT AND NEW LIFE     PART I: JUNGLE COMBAT

The other day when a lot of our planes were overhead, [Corporal James H.] Swan [Wilber's orderly and driver] said "We are sure fighting with the right army." The Air Force is certainly a good morale builder. The boys on the ground feel that they have to hold up their end so they work all the harder.

> An orderly is a soldier assigned to a senior officer as a personal assistant to support him in his official duties. The officer would pay the orderly from his own funds for strictly personal assistance. Swan served as Wilber's driver as well. A senior officer would rarely if ever drive his own car.
>
> Wilber embarked on the 158-foot Landing Craft Infantry 65 (LCI-65), which, after an overnight voyage, dropped anchor in Rendova Harbor at 8:45 a.m. It then waited for other LCIs in its flotilla to unload and clear the small beach [log of LCI-65]. During the wait, Wilber continued his letter.

**JULY 4 [ABOUT 11:45 A.M.]**

Can you imagine I would ever celebrate the Fourth [of July] on a boat. We are waiting to unload now and have been waiting for three hours. This is a lovely little harbor with little cocoanut plantations on parts of the shore. Back inland, the mountains tower into the clouds. Nearby our artillery is firing on the enemy installations across from us. We have not yet been committed and the men are thrilled to hear their sister unit [192nd Field Artillery Battalion located on the adjacent "offshore" Kokorana Island] firing in battle. There are a lot of questions such as "Are they really firing at the Japs?" They can hardly believe that they finally have reached that phase. This is of course all old to you by the time you receive it for the radio has been announcing things in great detail.

There is also a lot of individual praise for our Airmen who stay overhead so faithfully and keep the air clear for us. The ships that brought us up are the same type used for landing in Africa and they surely pitch and toss a lot. It was quite rough, and I enjoyed the trip a lot except for the fact it was pretty tough for all the men with normal stomachs. It's a job to stay in bed tho. I banked myself with a pillow against the wall and let her roll. I slept most of the way, in fact from seven P.M. to five the next morning.

I have told you war is mostly waiting, mud, and work. Our work is ammunition. The estimated amount of ammunition we fire in one day's combat is sixty tons. So you can guess at the amount of work our men have been doing lately. They have loaded and unloaded this ammo so often that all they want now is a chance to shove it in the breech of a howitzer and kiss it goodbye.

Darlings, I wish we might have had this Fourth together. It would have been fun to shoot firecrackers with you, but it is definitely a more definite way to celebrate

CHAPTER 1   *Lovely little shiny bombs*

*Aerial view of Rendova Harbor where the 43rd Division landed in preparation for the assault on nearby Munda airfield. The protected harbor, just inside Renard Entrance (right foreground), is where the LCI-65 was anchored waiting for a place at the beach. The landing beach where the LCI-65 and 24 were damaged on July 4, 1943, by a Japanese bomb is on the left side of the small inlet just left of the center of the photo. The offshore Barabuni Island, today Mbarambuni, to which the 169th Field Artillery Battalion was sent after the bombing, is just off the photo to the left of the long foreground Kokorana Island. Long-range 155-mm howitzers of the 43rd Division, some emplaced on the right end of Kokorana, were firing on Munda airfield when Wilber's unit arrived on July 4.*
[PHOTO: NATIONAL ARCHIVES 80-G-42070; SEE ALSO BARKER, MAP, P. 50]

*Landing Craft Infantry, LCI-69, en route from Rendova Harbor to the offshore islet, Kokorana, July 13, 1943. This was the type of ship on which Wilber voyaged to Rendova nine days earlier.* [PHOTO: U.S ARMY SIGNAL CORPS, SC 184497]

the Fourth if you have real ammunition. Anyway I hope you are having a good time and I love you all a lot.

I remember too that it was a July 4 in 1927 when I took Nana out on a picnic above the Snake R. canyon. We walked a path together over the river and the flowers were lovely and the air was fresh and cool. Later it rained and we sat under a blanket and talked. On the way home Norma sat on my lap [probably on a crowded bus], and I wished we might never get home. It was one of the perfect days of my life. We are moving now [toward the beach] so I must stop again. — WEB

> LCI-65 beached on Rendova at 12:20 p.m. on July 4 and disembarked its troops and supplies. Unfortunately, Rendova had become saturated with men, vehicles, and supplies. Vehicles to move goods from the beaches became mired in the deep soft mud and new troops could not be accommodated. Wilber was ordered to re-embark his troops and equipment and to establish them on a small offshore islet called Barabuni that lay at the entrance to Rendova Harbor. In a letter he wrote over the next two days, he described what transpired next.

x · o · ø · o · x

### JULY 5, 1943 [PROBABLY EARLY A.M. ON BARABUNI ISLAND]
Hello again Family of mine — Times are still a bit rushing and I'll try to just give you a report of my continual well being. Yesterday I landed two of my batteries on a beach [on Rendova Island] and called Hq. [Headquarters] reporting my arrival. We received orders to move immediately to another island to land all batteries. I was told to hold my former ship if possible. You can picture me dashing out into the ocean waving my arms and yelling "Bring that ship back to shore." Valerie would love this war because that is just what I did. This so called ship is about 125 [actually 158] feet long and will quarter about half of my men. Anyway he stopped and I waded out to one ship [LCI-24], walked the length of it and jumped across to the one I hoped was mine [LCI-65].

The skipper, a young navy lieutenant from Richmond, Va., named [Lt. Christopher] Tompkins was a bit upset and said he would have to get an OK from the Commodore. I gave a few generals as my authority so he started to signal to the commodore about my problems. The answer was "wait" so we did and soon found out why.

Just then from sixteen to twenty four Jap bombers Mitch 97s came over us. They had a formation like this [sketch] and were beautiful silver birds. I could see

CHAPTER 1   *Lovely little shiny bombs*

when they dropped their bombs way up high and noticed how the sun glinted on them as they fell. They looked like little drops of mercury. At first, as I stood on the deck, I thought about a slit trench for me, but they had forgotten to dig any in the deck. Next I considered jumping in the water but decided that was a bad place to be too. All this time (one second) those lovely little shiny bombs were sliding down a steep curve toward the ground. I was quite concerned that they appeared to be headed for our infantry nearby and was wishing them all luck possible. However an instant later I decided they would land on my troops. I was scared to death then at the thought of all those men; of [Maj. René L.] DeBlois' baby he has never seen, of the girl [Lt. Wm. A.] Farrell couldn't get leave to marry, of [Capt. Edward J.] Keegan the Reliable, of Green the Texas lawyer, of Swan, and others. I don't know how long those bombs took to fall but I did a lot of thinking while they did. About that time it suddenly dawned on me that I was in the wrong place so far as the bombs were concerned.

So your old man decided to get off the hatch cover he had been sitting on and very efficiently lay down on the deck against a steel bulkhead. The next thing I knew the hatch cover went bye bye and I found I was OK. The first bomb had landed on the other side of my battery [Wilber's troops on the beach], the second one along side my L.C.I. less than eight feet from me, and the others dropped in the harbor. By this time the bombers looked like this [sketch], and I was told all were shot down before they cleared the harbor. After it was all over I asked the Skipper what about getting on about our business. He said "Hell! We're sunk." I looked down the hatch and saw it was all torn to pieces inside and half full of water. The [other] ship [that] I had climbed on too was also full of holes and down. It seems I hold a record for this outfit, that of having a ship sunk under me in ten feet of water.

Seriously tho, Norma and Hale and Valerie, I thank each of you for the prayers that saved me from harm. It would only have been Divine protection for I was within less than ten feet of a five hundred pound bomb and only received one minor cut on my forehead. Less than four feet below me a hole six feet across was blown thru the steel side of the ship. My map case which I was holding has a hole thru it where a piece of steel about the size of a pea went thru it [and] thru my maps but failed to go thru the Firing Tables and tore around it and went on its way. I certainly feel that I was well protected by all of your prayers and those of your friends. I personally thought of Mrs. Estes [of Bangor, Maine, a Roman Catholic] in that connection as soon as I found I was OK.

> The 500-pound bomb landed at 2:11 p.m. in the water between the two LCIs, the one Wilber was on, LCI-65, and the one he had crossed, LCI-24, and blew a large hole in the side of each. A photograph shows the two ships

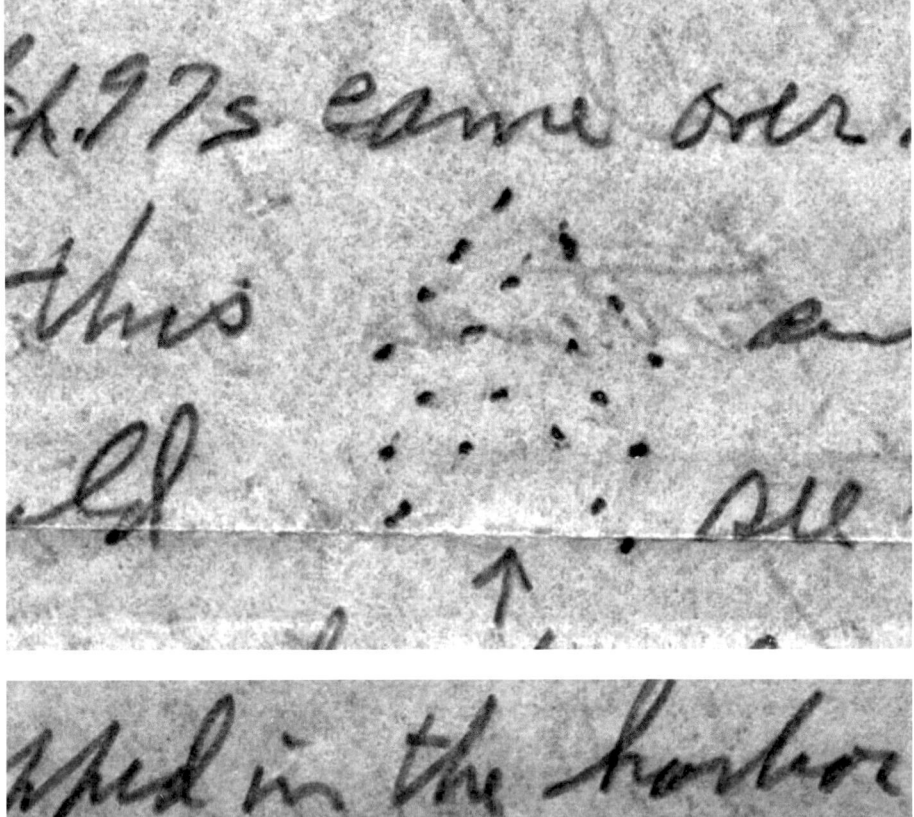

*Wilber's sketches of Japanese bombers before (above) and after (below) the bombing of July 4, 1943. All but about four of the planes were shot down.*

just off the beach listing toward each other. Wilber was hit by a small piece of shrapnel that lodged in his right eyebrow. A sailor on his ship was killed by shrapnel entering his forehead, and two on the adjacent LCI-24 were killed.

I was the only casualty in my battalion, and it has worked out well because I came wading out of the ocean with a bloody head and later a bandage that made me look like Capt. Kidd and went ahead about my business. Mainly I needed to keep going because of the tendency to be shaky. It has paid good dividends tho

CHAPTER 1    *Lovely little shiny bombs*

*LCI-24 (left) and LCI-65 after the bombing attack, July 4, 1943, Rendova Island. A 500-pound Japanese bomb had landed and exploded between the two landing craft, penetrating the hulls of each and leading to significant flooding and listing. Three sailors were killed. Wilber was on the forward deck of LCI-65 only about eight feet from where the bomb landed.* [PHOTO: U.S. NAVY, U.S. NATIONAL ARCHIVES 80-G-52772]

because the men have steadied a lot. One of the finest compliments I ever received was when one corporal rather shamefacedly said the men wanted me to know that after I was as "calm" as I had been, they would not worry any more about anything. He was a bit confused, but I was very flattered. They have no idea how scared I really was.

We got three other smaller boats that evening, and, when I gave the order to load and move out, the men really hove to. They didn't think much of that place and its Fourth of July fireworks. It's a great life. When we were in those cockle-shells and moving out to sea without a pilot to find an island none of us had seen and after being bombed, they sang "Roll Out the Barrell [sic]", "The F.A. Song" and the others. We landed that evening about dark [on Barabuni Island] and settled down to an all night job of unloading guns, trucks, and ammunition.

Much later, after the Solomons combat, Wilber wrote Norma more about his injury.

# COMBAT AND NEW LIFE   PART I: JUNGLE COMBAT

**OCT. 22, 1943**

… I was lying on that hatch cover, shoulder and arm and head across it and slipped myself off just at the last minute. I don't stand around during a bombing or shelling. I got off it because I thought the edge would cause broken bones in case I was blasted against it. The blast did break the bands inside my helmet liner, and the blow over one eye was likely caused by my head being struck by the inside of the helmet. That over the other eye was a cut by a piece of steel. You can see from my photo that the damage was negligible.

In 1982, I visited the Navy History Division, then at the Washington, D.C., Navy Yard. There I easily obtained the log of the LCI-65 and that of its flotilla. It contained an action report for July 4, complete with a sketch of the ship deployments at the time of the attack (Map 6). With much more difficulty, because of poor cataloging, I found a photo of the two damaged ships in the National Archives. They are each listing toward the sides that were flooded through the hull ruptures created by the bomb blast between them.

My contact with the skipper of the LCI-65, Christopher Tompkins, then 74, was memorable and gratifying. Wilber's letter had given Tomkins's

*Lieutenant Christopher R. Tompkins (1909–1985), in 1942 and in 1981. Tompkins was the skipper of LCI-65 when it was bombed on July 4, 1943. The 1981 photo was taken at a national decathalon where he placed second in several events in his age group (70–75). He died shortly after his 76th birthday in August 1985.* [PHOTOS: C.R. TOMPKINS]

hometown as Richmond, VA. After calling information in Virginia, I had him on the phone within minutes. It was August 20, 1983. He told me the whole story of that attack and remembered that Wilber had left a signed statement to the effect that the LCI-65 gunners had downed one of the Japanese bombers. The bombing, he said, was the most dramatic of his war experiences. I sent him copies of the photos of the ships I had found. In 1983, at age 74, Tomkins was competing successfully in decathlons and complaining about how hard it was to beat the younger competitors, ages 70 and 71, in his age group. Regretfully, I never met him in person. He died shortly after his 76th birthday in August 1985.

(Serendipitously, many years later, a young man named Tomkins walked into my office at MIT inquiring about graduate studies in physics. He turned out to be the grandson of Tompkins's brother. I was able to reach into my bookshelf and show him photos, maps, and the story of his late great-uncle's biggest moment in the war.)

Wilber's story had nearly ended on that July fourth. One inch in his head's location made all the difference. It was incredible that he continued on, not missing a beat in carrying out his duties despite a painful head wound. The shrapnel in his eyebrow would bother him for the rest of his life. He simply turned his attention to the assault on Munda.

x·o·ø·o·x

A direct frontal attack on the Japanese Munda airfield was ruled out as too risky. The Japanese had protected that approach to Munda with two five-inch (120-mm) coastal defense guns (called "naval guns" by Wilber) that may have been captured from the British at Singapore and moved to the Solomons. Instead, landings on New Georgia Island would take place at Zanana Beach, five miles east of the airfield (Map 7). The infantry would drive westward through the jungle to the airfield. Artillery would be situated on small offshore islands from which the guns could support the infantry all along its drive to Munda.

Wilber's job was to get his howitzers moved the six miles from Barabuni Island (Rendova) to the small island of Sasavele (just off New Georgia Island), and positioned for firing. His officers had been laying out positions and communication wire during the previous several days. Already on July 5, his howitzers were being moved to Sasavele, one or two at a time in small boats (Landing Craft Tanks, or LCTs) as Wilber described in this continuation of his letter of July 5:

### JULY 6 [ACTUALLY LATE JULY 5]

We are still heaving ammunition but today [July 5] [was] a big day. Today I took onto Jap shores [at Sasavele Island] my first howitzer. Her name was Betsy Ann and I walked into the jungle and shed a few tears. This is the last time I make these boys heave this ammunition except into the breech of their guns. Do you realize that my men have carried on and off boats by hand three hundred tons or a total of 600,000 pounds of ammunition in the last three days. Most of it was while wading in water often knee deep. I hear often men cursing the army [a shell] like this "G-D you. I hope you kill thirty Japs the next time I move you."

[General] Barker shows up once in a while with [Capt. James R.] Ruhlin, and I gather we are doing all right. It is late evening and I have two guns in position ready to fire and eight others on my island ready to move in. We also have two and a half days supply of ammunition on the island. It takes an hour for a boat to travel from this island [Barabuni] to the position area island [Sasavele], so it is slow work. There has been no more bombing in my neighborhood. My head is improving normally. It was quite painful last night but is improving now to the stage of an ordinary headache. It looks now like a wet night but a safe one for us. Good night Darlings All. I love you and am thinking of you. — XXXOOØ Wilber

> Wilber usually closed his letters with kisses (X) and hugs (O) and sometimes Ø, the significance of which I do not know.

x · o · ø · o · x

> On July 2, the first infantry troops of the 43rd Division had gone ashore at Zanana Beach, which hardly deserved to be called a landing beach because it could accommodate only a few boats at one time. The channel to it was narrow and shallow and confusing; an attempt to land during the previous evening had been a failure. By July 6, with the help of native scouts, the two infantry regiments, 169th and 172nd, were ashore and assembled and the division command post set up. Fortunately, there was not yet any Japanese opposition.
>
> Wilber managed to get another note off the next day. It is doubtful that any of these letters were mailed right away because of censorship. He held them for later mailing.

### [BARABUNI ISLAND] JULY 6, 1943

Dear Family of Mine — This is another day of work. My last howitzer is on the boat sailing for my position area, with another day's ammo. The boat I'm leaving here on will carry another and my anti aircraft guns. By the way one of "B"s [for

CHAPTER 1  *Lovely little shiny bombs*

*Boats loaded with men of the 43rd Division head for New Georgia, July, 1943, probably toward Zanana Beach on July 6 or 7.* [PHOTO: U.S. ARMY SIGNAL CORPS, SC 181786]

*Signal Corps wire crews of the 43rd Division (43rd Signal Company) landing on a New Georgia beach to establish a message center and communication system, July 6, 1943. Note the soldier to the left (arms raised) guiding in another craft. This, given the date, is surely at the tiny Zanana Beach, five miles behind Munda airfield, where the 43rd Division made its landings over several days.* [PHOTO: U.S. ARMY SIGNAL CORPS, SC 185878]

*Soldiers laying out telephone wire in the jungle of New Georgia, July 6, 1943, after the first landings at Zanana Beach.* [PHOTO: U.S. ARMY SIGNAL CORPS, SC 183168]

B Battery] gunners shot down a Jap bomber on the Fourth of July raid. Your little notebook [given him by Norma] is carrying a note to publish him in orders. The little notebook has had a hard time lately. It has been under salt water many times and is a bit damp yet. I'm writing all these details of our work, boat trips, getting into place so you can get a better picture of the preparation for battle. This is the part not in the movies or newsreels [news movies], but it is what counts in saving men's lives during battle.

> Wilber's "little notebook" was apparently lost, to my regret. The American army approach to a battle was to methodically plan, organize, and execute all preparations in advance of an attack. The goal was to minimize casualties while accomplishing the mission. Rushing impulsively into battle with swords raised was not the army way.

Barker just came by while I was airing my feet. He always asks about my head and I tell him it's fine. Maybe he thinks it's cracked. He always was a bit puzzled by me anyway. [Capt. Dixwell] Goff, [Lt. Robert W.] Patenge + [Lt. Earl M.] Payne

CHAPTER 1    *Lovely little shiny bombs*

*Native scouts for the 3rd Battalion, 145th Infantry Regiment, August 3, 1943. From left, Chief (of Munda) Talasasa, Baku, Makini, and Bidi. I met Bidi on my visit to Munda in 1983.* [PHOTO: U.S. ARMY SIGNAL CORPS, SC 364393]

were my advance detail for this action. It is due to their early work that we are so far ahead of other battalions in our preparations. Payne had laid all our [communication] wire within our area before we arrived. Goff had found and selected positions for all our installations and Patenge had cut roads thru the jungle for all batteries. All this was done before we brought our troops in at all. They worked close behind the Infantry and of course were in some danger all the time. The general says everything seems "to be going fine." I told him we would know soon. Today DeBlois is working on the position island [Sasavele] while I am hanging onto my boats. They are hard to keep [because others want them]. DeBlois is a real help especially since we are short five officers including one major. He does the work of two or three and is in my opinion the finest gunnery officer in the division. I recommended him for the Legion of Merit last month because of his outstanding work.

They are bombing the Jap [Munda] Air field now. I can see our planes and the Jap AA [anti-aircraft] fire and hear the bombs land. It's harder to keep men working

17

*Lt. Francis McAuliffe (facing camera) on way to Battery Position. This boat, probably a Landing Craft Tank (LCT), carried the men and equipment of Battery C (McAuliffe's unit), 169th Field Artillery from Barabuni Island off Rendova to Sasavele Island off Munda in New Georgia, a one-hour trip. The battery moved in two segments on July 5 and 6, 1943. [169 FA Bn. Journal]. Wilber wrote about organizing these boat trips as his battalion was being positioned for the attack on Munda.* [PHOTO: CAPTAIN LAWRENCE S. PALMER, DDS, DC, COURTESY OF HIS SON DAVID PALMER]

while we bomb them than [it is] while they [the Japanese] are over us. My position area [Sasavele] will let me fire on the field [Munda], but that is a secondary mission for us, our primary one being to fire in support of the advance of our Inf. regiment [the 169th]. I must stop now

Dear Ones. I hope you are all OK and taking care of each other. Remember no whining and no quarrels. — XXXOOØ Wilber

Wilber's first real battle was about to start.

# 2

## *"The enemy is all around you"*
### Munda action
### July 1943

Wilber's 169th Field Artillery Battalion was initially in direct support of the 169th Infantry Regiment of the 43rd Division. (It is important to distinguish the two 169ths; they were independent units within the division.) A fire direction center (FDC) for Wilber's artillery was established on Sasavele Island in a protected pit in the ground with telephone and radio connections to the front lines and to the three nearby batteries, each with its four howitzers. Each of the three infantry battalions of the 169th Infantry Regiment on (mainland) New Georgia had artillery officers from Wilber's unit with them: a liaison officer and a forward observer. The observers were on the front lines with the foot soldiers. They would spot where artillery shells landed and communicate with the FDC by telephone or radio to make adjustments. Telephone wires had to run through the water and coral separating Sasavele Island and New Georgia. The coral and the Japanese were quick to damage the lines, so maintaining communications was a continuing task.

The 105-mm artillery howitzers could hurl shells five or more miles. The 33-pound shells contained five pounds of explosives that were usually fused to explode upon contact. The observers would spot and report the locations of the explosions relative to the target position, (e.g. "50 yards left", or "100 yards over"), to the FDC. There, soldiers known as "computers" would calculate the gun-pointing corrections in azimuth (left-right) and elevation (up-down), which were then passed by sound powered phone to the gun crews. The poor visibility in the jungle complicated the task of the observers. They would sometimes have to resort to using the sounds of the blasts or the smoke from special "smoke" shells to locate the explosions.

Wilber's operations officer (S-3) and executive officer (second in command), Maj. René DeBlois, ran the FDC, while Wilber was nearly always at the front with the infantry during the month-long drive on Munda airfield. It was Wilber's job to ensure that the infantry got effective artillery support. At the front, he could stay in touch with the infantry commander, assess the tactical situation first-hand, and ensure that his forward observers had what they needed. Liaison officers were assigned to do much of this, but he apparently felt that his presence was more valuable at the front than back on Sasavele with his howitzers. I suspect he was also drawn to the drama of being near the action; recall that he had been an infantryman in the Washington State National Guard.

Wilber's letters were sparse during the heavy fighting, but he wrote about it during breaks in the action and at later times. He was at the front with the infantry almost continuously from July 8 to 25.

x · o · ø · o · x

On July 7, the 169th Field Artillery began its support of the 169th Infantry as it moved from the trailhead at Zanana Beach toward the line of departure (explained in Wilber's letter below) two miles to the west (Map 7). Wilber spent the day with the infantry, and returned to his battalion on Sasavele in the evening. The next morning, July 8 at 7:30 a.m., he again left for the mainland (New Georgia), this time with a party of three officers and 20 enlisted men he would deliver to the infantry as liaison and observer parties. He went to a 10 a.m. meeting at the division command post regarding coordinating artillery fires in the attack scheduled for the next day, July 9 [169 FA Journal]. It was probably there, perhaps while waiting for the meeting to start, that he found time to write to us. He would not write again for six days.

Wilber was too preoccupied at this point to deal with the dispersion of his family. He would send this letter to Norma when censorship allowed and trust her to share it with Valerie and me.

### [NEW GEORGIA "MAINLAND"] JULY 8, 1943
Darling Wife + Beloved Children — The last day and today have been busy preparation days for us. Yesterday we completed getting the last howitzers in position

to fire and registered one battery. That is customary and all that is needed to give us accuracy. I am now in what was four days ago Jap territory. Do you remember in the old correspondence courses about the Line of Departure? It is supposed to be the line on which troops form [in preparation] for an attack. All yesterday and today we have been fighting [the Japs] to get in our L.D. Funny that never came up in the problems [in military courses]. Our infantry is OK. I have had three [infantry] officers + some men with them [working with me], and my men are also doing a good job.

The Japs slip a bomber thru now + then but none very near to me. This is still not the attack proper, just the preliminaries.

I saw a naval battle the other night. Of course I don't know what happened but there was [sic] a lot of fireworks on the horizon. I hope our navy liked the results and have a lot of confidence in it.

Right now I am sitting between high, high roots of a mahogany tree. Barker has been here several times to talk with me. He said he wished he had as much confidence in the other battalions as in us. You have no idea what a man DeBlois is. He is doing a wonderful job. I am on one island [New Georgia] and he on another [Sasavele] but I know he does his + my work there....

My head is still improving and I see no reason to be concerned about it. Bill McCormick is alongside now. — Love Wilber

> The Japanese were sending reinforcements to Munda from their bases further north. The naval battle that Wilber saw was most probably the Battle of Kula Gulf in which three groups of Japanese destroyers came south with troops intended to reinforce Munda. They were intercepted by a task force of three American cruisers and four destroyers. In a running battle of some five hours in the early hours of July 6, one American cruiser, the Helena, was lost as were two Japanese destroyers. Sixteen hundred Japanese troops and supplies were successfully landed on nearby Kolombangara Island at Vila. This action took place 20 miles north of Wilber's position. [Morison, v. VI]
>
> Wilber often referred to units by the name of the commanding officer. Part of Bill McCormick's 103rd Field Artillery Battalion was also on Sasavele Island with the balance on adjacent Baraula Island. They were supporting the 172nd Infantry Regiment in the drive on Munda, which was on the left flank of the 169th Infantry (Map 7). The 172nd Infantry and 103rd Field Artillery had been on the SS Coolidge when it sank with all equipment the previous October (1942) and had been in the New Hebrides and on Guadalcanal since then. Having their sister battalion, the 103rd Field Artillery, finally alongside after all those months was highly significant news.

## COMBAT AND NEW LIFE   PART I: JUNGLE COMBAT

x·o·ø·o·x

The two regiments reached the line of departure, launched their attack, and in the next two days advanced southwestward another mile. There they encountered strong Japanese defenses that stalled the advance on about July 10, but intense fighting continued as the Americans attempted to take well-defended Japanese positions in the rolling hills. It was another two miles to the airfield at Munda. During this standoff, the American 172nd Infantry drove southward to Laiana Beach on July 12 and 13. This shortened the distance to the front lines for supplies and reinforcements. Air parachute drops could be reduced.

Within those few days, American inexperience in jungle warfare led to severe demoralization in some units. Normal jungle noises were mistaken for Japanese nighttime harassment. Soldiers panicked at real and imagined threats. They wounded and possibly killed their own comrades with undisciplined knifing, shooting, and grenade throwing. Men abandoned their posts in large numbers, including officers and non-commissioned officers [Fushak, pp. 46–52].

Neuropsychiatric casualties, otherwise known as "combat fatigue" or "war neurosis," equivalent to today's post traumatic stress disorder (PTSD), occurred in far greater numbers than in other combat situations, and it was the 169th Infantry that was the most affected. At a reunion of the 43rd Division Association in August 2011, a 90-year old former enlisted man of the 169th Infantry told me, "The Japanese grenades were raining down from the trees." They might well have been American grenades bouncing off trees! What mattered, though, was his perception of that time; the trauma was real and lasting.

After a visit to New Georgia on July 11, General Griswold recommended to Maj. Gen. Millard Harmon, commanding general South Pacific Area, that additional troops were needed, stating—perhaps with some hyperbole—that the 43rd "was about to fold up" [Miller, *Cartwheel*, p. 124]. In fact, while the total number of 43rd Division psychological casualties in the Solomons was large (about 15%), the bulk of the division was unaffected and soldiered on creditably [Fushak, p. 2].

In response to the situation, heads fell. The commanding officer of the 169th Infantry, Col. John D. Eason, a good friend of Wilber's, was relieved of his command on July 11 along with other officers. Eason was replaced by Col. Temple G. Holland, a regular army officer.

CHAPTER 2   *The enemy is all around you*

x·o·ø·o·x

Back in America, I was not aware of the extreme conditions my father was just then facing. My letters from Grace Boys Camp showed some normalcy in our lives. They also reflected the attention Norma was directing our way. She was ever the conscientious, responsible mother.

**July 11, [1943], Southfields, N.Y. G.B.C.**
*Dear Mother — I am enclosing your post card with the answers on it.... I am also enclosing a leaflet describing how to get here on visitors' [day] if Valerie comes or anybody else. Will you leave money for next month in camp or leave it at the Church [Grace Church in NYC] if I come here [back to camp] next month. I have been writing Daddy regularly....*

*The answers to your questions on the letter dated Friday are: About working hard I didn't have to work hard, and I did the 300 approx. yd. swim in 7 minutes 12 seconds. I take all three pills the same time. I sleep well and am not cold.*

*I have to write to Daddy now so. — Your loving son, HB*

*Please send me envelopes non-sticking except when wetted and if we have it, "Mutiny on the Bounty" by Charles Nordhoff + James N. Hall.*

x·o·ø·o·x

On July 13, Wilber returned to Sasavele for a brief respite, so brief that by his own account [letter 7/25/14] he did not shave or bathe. He was on Sasavele for a full day and a half, the nights of July 13 and 14 and all day on the 14th [169th FA Journal]. The combat was desperate and there was much to do. While there, on July 14, Wilber learned that one of his forward observers, 1st Lt. Earl M. Payne, had been killed by Japanese machine-gun fire. He was the officer who so competently set up the battalion communications in advance of the unit's arrival on Sasavele. That same day, Wilber wrote his first letter since July 8. It was a piece of subterfuge as it told nothing of his present activities. Norma sent it to me; she was keeping her children aware of their father's activities.

**[SASAVELE ISLAND] JULY 14, 1943**
*[Note from Norma to me at camp:] Please send on to Valerie. "Camp White for the Sheltering Arms," Bantam, Conn.*
Dear Hale, Valerie and Nana — You probably have missed some of my letters for

mail connections here are not yet very good. However this will probably get thru pretty promptly now. I am well and feeling good. The last two weeks have been pretty strenuous but we are doing our work as well as usual.

Just now I'm in my chair in a two-officer tent that DeBlois and I share. The tent is in the jungle on a small island and the essential comforts of life are available. I have not tried to get the news with my radio for lack of time. I probably won't do it in the jungle anyway.

Dearest I've lost my Vit. C. [Vitamin C] pills, my Gillette razor, my polished metal hand mirror. If you can replace them I will appreciate it a lot. In the meantime I still have a small glass mirror and can borrow another razor. The Vit. C. helps a lot to keep me going. I think a lot of perspiration depletes the level in the system.

I wonder what you are doing. I hope the weather isn't too hot in N.Y. and that you are happy together. I want my children to be as courteous and considerate to each other and to Nana as they can. It would be too discouraging to come home to a quarrelsome, unloving, selfish family. This war will I hope be over some day and we can be together again. Be sure I love you and that it is only a very important job that keeps me away.

If any reports come thru that I have been wounded, don't believe them unless the word comes from another officer of this Bn. It is too easy to have rumors start here that may cause confusion at home. I am in perfect health, tired, and absolutely "in the pink." Let that stop all rumors to this date. — I love all of you. XXXOO Wilber

> This letter was to be mailed immediately and hence could not mention the ongoing combat or the earlier preparations for it. Wilber had been wounded twice, on July 4 and, as he recounted below, again on July 9 or 10. He was probably still holding the July 5 letter that described his first wounding. He was concerned that a formal notice (such as a telegram) from the War Department to us about his woundings would not make clear how "superficial" the wounds were. We did receive a telegram on August 19, almost seven weeks after his first wound, informing us that, on July 19th(!), Wilber had been "slightly wounded." Also, he seemed unaware, or had forgotten, that his family was no longer together. Norma, at the same time, was crafting her own letters, which were another bit of subterfuge. Unfortunately, they did not come down to us; Wilber likely buried or otherwise destroyed them.

x · o · ø · o · x

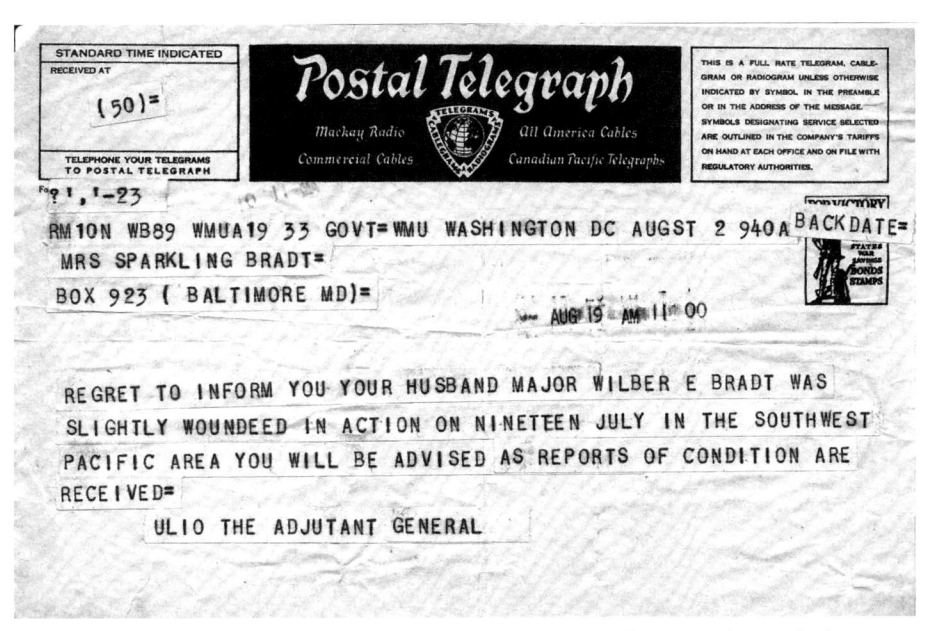

*Telegram notifying Norma of Wilber's wounding in the Munda action, but with the wrong date. Wilber was wounded twice, first on July 4 by a Japanese bomb, and again on July 9 or 10 by a sniper's bullet.*

On the night of July 17–18, the division command post near Zanana, far from the front lines, was attacked by the flanking Japanese. Not expecting this, the Americans mounted only a makeshift defense; artillery was called in at some risk because it was not registered (calibrated) for that area. It saved the day, and the Japanese were driven off. But, at another place and time, a party taking wounded soldiers to the rear was ambushed, and several of the wounded were killed. Both events illustrated the chaotic and fluid nature of the combat.

The high command made more changes to revive the stalled drive toward Munda. General Griswold, whom Wilber admired greatly, was brought in as XIV Corps commander on July 16 to oversee the New Georgia Occupation Force, thus relieving the 43rd Division commander, General Hester, of this extra responsibility. Also, two regiments (148th and 145th) of the 37th Division were brought in from Guadalcanal to assist the 43rd Division along with the 161st Infantry Regiment of the 25th Division.

The battle-weary 169th Infantry was relieved of combat duties on July 20 and returned to Rendova Island, piecemeal, for rehabilitation and replacement of men and equipment, and Colonel Holland reverted to his former command of the 145th Regiment, which was now in the battle line

(Map 8). The 169th Infantry would be back in the fight on New Georgia less than a week later. [Ops. Report, 169th Inf. Rgt.; Miller, *Cartwheel*, pp. 137, 144, 147, 149].

The 161st Infantry, also in the line, was Wilber's national guard unit from Washington State. The friends he had known in the 1930s and had met on Guadalcanal the previous February were with the 161st. A major attack toward Munda by all these units was planned for July 25, and his friends would be only a few hundred yards from him in the front lines. It was not to be a happy reunion.

Through all this turmoil, Wilber's unit, the 169th Field Artillery, stayed the course on Sasavele Island and continuously supported infantry units in the line, the 148th, the 145th, and for a short period, the 161st, as well as

*First hot meal in 21 days for Maj. James Devine (right), C.O. of 3rd Battalion, 172 Infantry Regiment, and Lt. Chris Christopules, at a kitchen at Laiana behind the lines during a lull in the fighting, July 21, 1943. One company at a time would come back to eat, bathe, and clean up. The 172nd Infantry had been in active combat since the June 30 landings on Rendova. The beards reflect that time interval but appear to have been recently trimmed.* [PHOTO: U.S. ARMY SIGNAL CORPS, SC 186150]

the 169th. During the preparations for the July 25 attack, units were given brief opportunities to wash, shave, and eat a hot meal.

x · o · ø · o · x

Wilber wrote his next extant letter, this one to me, after a gap of nine days. In it, he describes his second wounding. He was still in the front lines on New Georgia. Preparations for the July 25 attack two days later were nearing completion.

**[IN THE FRONT LINES, MUNDA] JULY 23, 1943**
Dear Son — I thought you might like to get a letter written on a battlefield during a battle. Just now things have quieted down right here. However there are some Jap snipers in the trees around me. The men shoot one out every so often. Some fall; some are tied up so they stay. I have a very satisfactory slit trench with poles and dirt over it. I am in it now.

I told you I was wounded by a bomb on the Fourth of July but that it didn't amount to much. On the tenth [July 9 in Wilber's notebook], I was scratched in the ribs by a Jap bullet. Again it was nothing and is all healed now. I have the bullet for a souvenir. It came in thru my jacket, hit me in the side, and [amazingly!] dropped in my pocket.

> I myself had this bullet for some time. It was bent and so had struck some hard object before striking Wilber.

July 24 — [Corps commander General] Griswold was in the next foxhole to mine the other day. I was reintroduced to him as commanding the "finest g—d— artillery in the world," by the infantry commander, Colonel Holland. I appreciated that and said the Lord had been leading me by the hand. He [Griswold] said "I am well aware that you are adding a lot of high technical ability and skill to that. I'm glad you are here Bradt."

The Bn. is doing a great job and I hope we continue to do it. Things are going well with me. I know your and Valerie's and Norma's prayers are protecting me. Don't let Norma worry about me. I am taking care not to be foolish, and beyond that I am trusting God to do with me what needs to be.

I love you Norma, Hale and Valerie but must stop now. "Times is busy." This letter cannot be mailed until after this job is done. Please read it to N + V. — Your father, Wilber

> It appears that Wilber really did trust in God. He was also proud that Griswold knew who he was. His pride in his unit was justified. During the

Munda action, the 169th Field Artillery hurtled 28,975 rounds of high explosives toward the front lines [letter 8/5/43 and Barker p. 62], each with great precision. A minor pointing error or a slip in procedure on any one of those rounds could have killed and wounded American soldiers, and this went on day after day and night after night. Wilber recounted [letter 11/25/43] that it was only near the end of the Arundel campaign, after nearly 48,000 rounds total, that a round falling short had injured (or perhaps killed) an American soldier. The gunners, together with the telephone linemen, surveyors, forward observers, and others who constantly supported them, were all true heroes.

x · o · ø · o · x

The concerns that occupied me at Grace Camp were minor by comparison, but of course were important to me.

**GRACE BOYS CAMP, JULY 24, 1943**
*Dear Mom — Tonight 20 boys (12 years or over) are going to a dance. I am planning to go. I will tell you later whether I went or not and what happened. I have the powder for my athlete's foot (Mennen's talcum powder)....*
*There are some deases? [sic] going around here. They are a fever nothing else. German measles and pink eye and ear aches [are] generally over....*
*Please tell me what I am to do after I arrive on [the] bus. I expect to meet Monte there. — Your loving son, Hale*

As the first month of camp ended, I was a bit concerned about whether or not I would be met in New York since we no longer had a home there to which I could go. Apparently Monte stood ready to meet Valerie and me, as needed, during Norma's pregnancy. In fact, later that same day, I heard from Norma that plans had changed. I would be staying at camp for another month.

x · o · ø · o · x

**SOUTHSFIELDS, N.Y., JULY 24, 1943 [POSTCARD]**
*Dear Mother — I got your two letters. I am staying next month. Thanks for the letters. — L O V E, Hale*

CHAPTER 2    *The enemy is all around you*

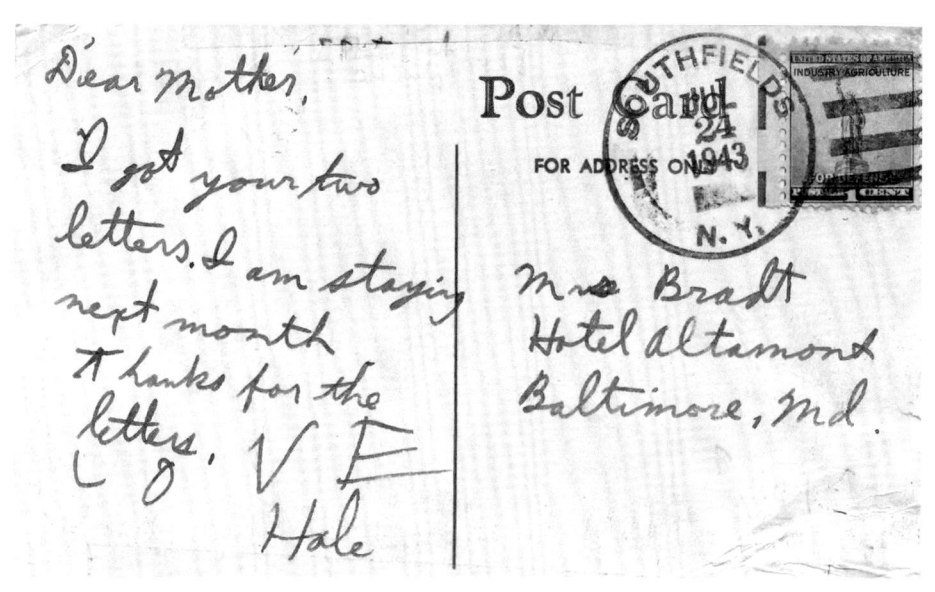

*Postcard from me at Grace Camp to Norma. The postage was one cent. Norma's location at the time was uncertain, and Valerie and I had no place we could call home.*

x · o · ø · o · x

The next day, July 25, the attack on the Munda defenses with the reorganized forces began (Map 8). It was slow, difficult going; the Japanese use of pillboxes with overlapping fields of fire, along with the lack of visibility in the jungle, hindered reconnaissance and artillery observations. It would not be until August 5 that Munda would be securely in American hands. Remarkably, Wilber found time to write on the attack day about the politics and uses of artillery in jungle warfare.

### [NEW GEORGIA] JULY 25, '43
Dearest Norma and children — This is another letter that cannot be mailed until after this action is ended. This is a hot day and is the big push we hope is final. I have been at the front since the sixth [actually July 7] except for one day [July 14] when I returned to the Bn. Goff is here with me and has been most of that time. This morning was a lot like the movie type of battles. Early this morning the FA began to fire a "preparation" fire. We lay in our hole and listened to the shells whistle over our heads. There were so many that it was a continuous hum. Then the Navy came by and added its share a little farther out from us and the air sent over

*Japanese pillbox made from coconut foliage, logs, and coral, on Munda, New Georgia, September 1943. Several such pillboxes, located to protect one another with machine guns, created a very strong defensive position.* [PHOTO: U.S. ARMY SIGNAL CORPS, SC 380618]

Liberators with block-busters [large bombs]. Dix said he bet the Japs thought an attack might be coming up. Of course, after that the ground troops go to work. We, because we were a way ahead of the rest of the line, have not yet moved and won't until the rest of the line reaches us. I am in no great personal danger because I am at the Regimental C.P. [command post of the 145th Infantry].

Don [Capt. Donald C. Downen] and Cris [Lt. Louis K. Christian] and [Clare] Langley and the other Pullman [Washington] boys are just now only 400 yards away from me. Their regiment is next to the one I am supporting but they don't suspect I'm here. Maybe I can send a message later. You see I am alongside my boys in fact as well as in spirit. They just came into the action a day or so ago, so should be quite fresh.

The Bn. is still doing a good job and it makes me both proud and humble to be its CO. Barker seems very happy about our being so effective. Now we are functioning in another division by special request of the regimental commander [Holland] in that division because of the fine work he watched us do for our own regiment [the 169th Infantry]. When they [the 169th Inf.] were relieved [and Holland returned to command of the 145th Inf.], he asked and fought to get us. He is Col. Temple Holland, Reg[ular] Army, and we work well together. I have been introduced to three generals and half dozen Cols as the "Finest G—D— artillery in the world." He told me he never had much use for artillery before, but that he wanted me to know we had saved the day for him several times.

Once, the Japs came at us thru a narrow valley and Goff went out to the edge of our troops and adjusted our fire so close in to us that fragments were falling over us. He then walked the Bn. fire up that valley and swept it clear of Japs, trees and machine guns and we slept safely another night. Another day Dick [Capt. Richard N.] Rainey brought down fire on a ridge the Japs held. We had lost men trying to take it. Dick went up front to the foot of the ridge and telephoned orders back bringing the Bn. fire down in front of him. Then he shifted the Bn. fire up and down and across that ridge until it was clear. We took the ridge without the loss of a single man. [Capt. Edward W.] Wild did the same thing with a barrage [of artillery], then followed it in with the infantry and shot ten Jap machine gunners with a borrowed pistol.

> Wild was later awarded the Distinguished Service Cross for his actions during this drive on Munda [letter 11/27/43].

[Lt. Norbert J.] Heidelberger nightly adjusted a night protective barrage we called "Charlie One" along a ridge that was only 250 yards away from us from which the Japs continually fired on us with rifles, machine guns and mortars. We would get all our men down in their holes and he would bring it in close and sweep them out. Then we would fire there every hour all night to keep them out.

It hasn't been all officers [who have been heroic] either. Telephone linemen have laid and repaired wire under sniper fire and until they could hardly stand. Survey groups have surveyed thru the jungle while being shot at by Japs. Cannoneers [men who load and fire the howitzers] have fired all day and thru the night every night for nearly three weeks, stopping now and then to shoot a Jap in their own area. A driver from Service battery was chased by two Japs. He said " I ran like hell". Then a third Jap headed him off and so he dropped when they shot at him. He decided it was easier to go thru one than two so he shot the one thru the chest. Then he went up and "shot him thru the head and in the stomach to be sure he was dead," and went on after his car. You know Service Battery men are supply men, not combat troops, so I phoned DeBlois [and told him] "Service Battery is no longer a virgin." Not original but it fitted.

So you see why I am proud and humble about my Bn. DeBlois back at the Bn. and his Fire Direction Center go on forever and has [sic] saved my and scores of other lives both day + night by putting fire exactly where we asked for it. This is the stuff the 169th is made of....

You have no idea how dirty I am. No bath for over three weeks, sleeping in a hole and living in a hole; no bed rolls here. No shave for three weeks. I carry clean sox in my pockets + change every couple of days. I'm glad I'm not fighting in the north country. Warm nights simplify clothing loads. The golf spikes are life savers. I am sure footed when others slip and that is worth a lot here. Thank you again. The Rose Bud type [of spikes] come out when shoes are wet all the time.

I like your plans for the children. My pay as a Lt. Col. will be about $80.00 more a month so you should be all set. By the way I probably am a Lt. Col. now (no, not on Aug 4 – WB) for the papers have been in nearly a month. If anything happens to me you draw pay for six months after my death. It should be as at a Lt. Col. [level]. However don't get concerned, I expect to draw my own pay much longer than that. I did not draw it on July 1 because I could not mail it to you then. (Nor in Aug either – WB).... I must stop now and get my part of the war rolling again. I have been waiting for some of our tanks to clear out of my zone of fire. I love you all. — XXXOOØ Wilber

> It might seem surprising that Wilber wrote when the letter could not be mailed; he held it until at least August 4. His writing was a way to commune privately with his wife and children, but he seems to also have been motivated by a desire to record what was happening for future readers. It was also a way of preserving the record of his own life, in case he was killed. He knew that unmailed letters in his possession at his death would be forwarded to his family.

x · o · ø · o · x

> In the midst of this second drive toward Munda, on July 28, one of Wilber's forward observers, 2nd Lt. Arthur F. Malone of Jamaica Plain, Massachusetts, died in the line of duty. Wilber was at the front at the time and was most likely close by when this occurred. Malone was awarded the Silver Star posthumously. The citation, probably written by Wilber, was for actions two days before his death. It reads in part,

*... When a party of infantrymen was subjected to intense enemy mortar and artillery fire near his forward observation post, Lieutenant Malone observed two men fall to the ground, one was dead and the other severely wounded. Leaving the protection of his foxhole, he courageously crawled to the wounded man and brought him back safely to cover where he administered first aid.... (General Order #457, Hq. United States Army Forces in the South Pacific Area, 31 March 1944)*

> Malone is remembered by name in a memorial on the campus of Northeastern University in Boston, Massachusetts.

CHAPTER 2   *The enemy is all around you*

The following day, General Hester was relieved of command of the 43rd Division by order of General Harmon who felt that Hester had exhausted himself [*Cartwheel*, p. 149]. The slow progress of the division, compared to expectations, was surely also a factor. He was succeeded temporarily by Maj. Gen. John R. Hodge. And on this date, July 29, Wilber found time to write his father and me from a front-line foxhole. He made life in the jungle come alive.

**JULY 29, 1943**
Dear Father — I am writing this in a foxhole at a regimental C.P. [145th Infantry] on the front. This month has been a pretty active one for me.…

Actually the jungle is far different from that taught in school. We seldom can see [the enemy] from the ground. Anyone in a tree is shot as a sniper. The enemy is all around you and often in your own area. I have stayed awake several nights and watched Japs near my slit trench. Their object seems to be to draw fire so they can wipe out our automatic weapons. We sat with pistols and bayonets and knives through their antics and used the silent methods preferably.

> Silent methods? Wilber never mentioned any of his men using a knife or bayonet. He was probably referring to the "silent" withholding of pistol fire.

We adjust our fire (F.A.) by listening to the sound and carefully walking the bursts back to our observer. When the fragments begin to fall in front of him he moves it a little farther away and we go into fire for effect. We have had to make some hard decisions and try some very difficult targets such as firing in front of, in rear of, and on both sides of ourselves, or such as firing in a narrow lane through our own troops.…

One good thing about the war in the tropics is that one is not cold. There are no bedrolls at the front here. One Inf. Col. [infantry colonel] had two men carrying a very heavy one. I suggested to the Col. that it be hauled in one of my observer's cars. We did to the next thicket and dumped it. I was very sorry! — Wilber

x · o · ø · o · x

And he could find humor in a foxhole.

**JULY 29, 1943**
Dear Hale — … I hope you are having a good time and getting a real coat of tan. Norma says you are really growing up to a man's size.

The other day I saw a green snake about three feet long. It climbed up some vines into a tree. It is the first time I ever saw a tree-climbing snake but this one was obviously a tree dweller.

Also a few nights ago I was sleeping in my hole and a big land crab with a body about as big as the palm of my hand crawled across my chest. I knocked him off on to Capt. Goff's feet and he gave it a kick clear out of the hole. It was very dark and we couldn't see a thing but we heard it land and then some soldier in that direction made some very nasty cracks about whoever had thrown a crab on him. Goff and I lay there and nearly burst to keep from laughing out loud.

Another night it rained and we slept in two inches of very muddy water. Whenever one of us turned over there was a lot of splashing, and whenever one turned we all did because there were four of us in a hole dug for two. It's a good thing it's warm here for we are often soaked.

I must stop now. Never forget that I still am thinking of you every day and that I love you very dearly. — Your father, Wilber

> Wilber by now had my camp address and was writing me there. I often credit this story (of the muddy foxhole) with my joining the U.S. Navy Reserve, rather than the army or marines, in 1951 during the Korean conflict. Wilber had told me in 1945 never to join the marines because "they waste their men's lives." This statement (setting aside the question of its validity) and the army's foxholes with two inches of water made my choice an easy one! (Was I following a noble Bradt tradition of voluntary military service? I found the relative safety and clean, dry sleeping arrangements of the navy quite attractive, especially when confronted with the draft, which most likely would have thrust me into the mountains of Korea. It wasn't at all noble, but military service was in my heritage.)

x·o·ø·o·x

In great contrast to jungle fighting, Grace Camp's end-of-the-month festivities were approaching, and I was hoping to swim the length of the lake.

**July 29, [1943]**
*Dear Mother — The day before yesterday most of the camp went to Island Pond. It is a place on another lake about ten miles from Grace. It was a good hike and we passed a [sic] iron mine.*

*Yesterday was HOBO DAY. We could do anything you wanted to do. I went swimming more often and our cabin ate out as the rest of the camp did; breakfast in* our fireplace and dinner in an island. This morning we had the Pentathlon in which I could have done better. This afternoon I am going to try to swim the length of the lake 1 1/2 miles. — *Your loving son, Hale*

I recall that I struggled along for about a half mile and then quit.

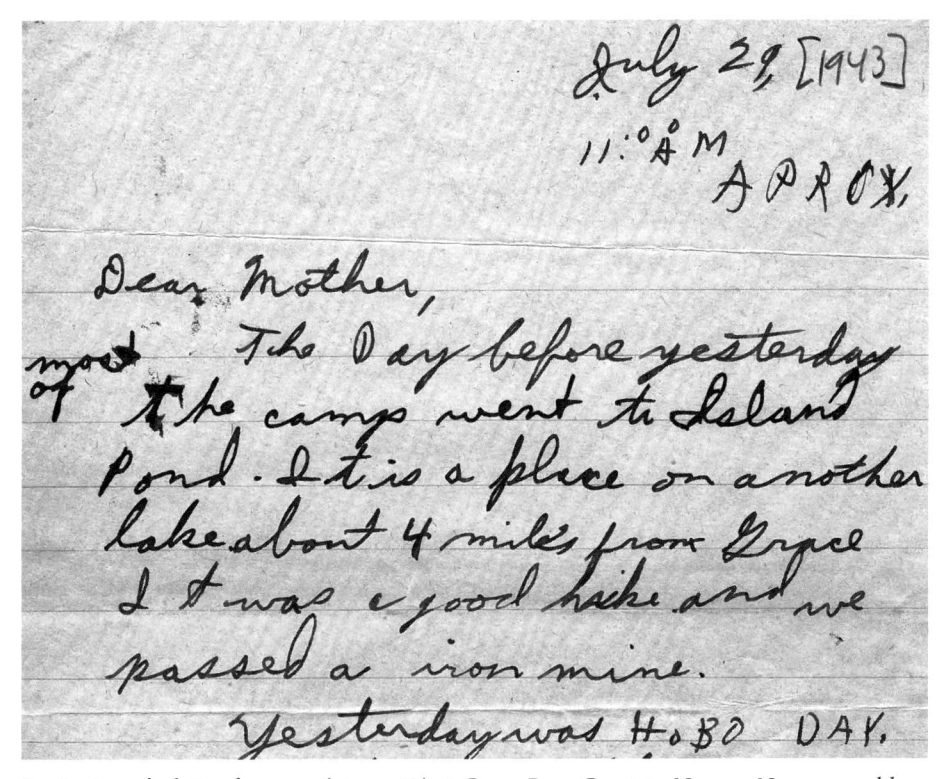

> Dear Mother,
> 
> The Day before yesterday most of the camp went to Island Pond. It is a place on another lake about 4 miles from Grace. It was a good hike and we passed a iron mine. Yesterday was H₀ 80 DAY.

*Beginning of a letter from me (at age 12) at Grace Boys Camp to Norma. Norma would send our letters on to Wilber, and he would send them on to his parents; hence some of ours survived as inserts to his. Wilber was in the midst of the final drive on Munda airfield when I wrote this. Ordinary civilian life at home continued on with little connection to the experiences of the fighting soldiers.*

## 3

## *"Get your head down! That ain't all!"*

### Sasavele Island
### AUGUST 1943

Wilber was ordered to the rear by General Barker on July 30. It is probable that his 23 days of nearly continuous service at the front was beginning to wear on him, and Barker sensed that. He arrived at 9:20 a.m back to the relative comfort of Sasavele Island where his battalion was located [169th FA Journal]. While there, he had time to reflect on what he had just been through. He first wrote a letter that could be mailed; it told nothing about the combat. The letters home had been rare, and he was anxious to get another off to us.

**JULY 30, 1943**
Hello Darlings — I know you must be worried because I have sent so few letters. This is just to tell you I am all right and still love you. Things have been a bit rushing this month and you have been neglected. Please remember I have faith in the protection of your prayers and am counting on you for that protection.

The boys in the outfit are doing a great job and I am proud and very humble about being their commander. Someday I can tell you about it but have no time now. It is raining now, and the jungle is full of the drip, drip from the trees. It reminds me of rain at Bar Harbor [Maine] and you.

… Your plans for the schools and summer sound fine. I hope you are all well. Must stop now. Generals don't wait. — I love each of you. Wilber

x·o·ø·o·x

The next day, he wrote a "real" letter to Norma. Recollections of his previous three weeks began to flow. His artillery on Sasavele was still firing in support of the advance toward Munda.

**[SASAVELE] JULY 31, 1943**
[Note on top of page:] Aug. 1: The pictures just came. They are fine and you all look just wonderful to me. WB
Hello Flower of my Heart — I am answering your letter of July 9. It is such [a] sweet letter. I came back to the battalion position [on Sasavele Island] yesterday after three weeks [on New Georgia]. It is very quiet here compared to my forward command post. The howitzers pound away every little while and you sit comfortably above ground knowing the shells will land five miles away.

[When I was] forward, I would order fire, hear them wham thru the phone, next hear Ray [DeBlois] say "On the way", wait a few more seconds and the rumble of my guns would reach me across the jungle, and, almost immediately after, the shells will go "whish, whish whish-whispering and whirring" overhead. I take off my helmet and notice their direction and the time they seem exactly overhead, then a few seconds later the sound of the bursting shells comes back to my ears as a series of heavy explosions. I count seconds during that last wait and then calculate how far beyond me the shells landed and authorize the necessary shifts. Sometimes the bursting shells can be seen, but often in the jungle we are limited entirely to sound methods.

It is so quiet here. Birds are singing in the trees, lizards go by looking for ants, and an occasional monkey chatters in the nearby trees. At night the jungle noises change and seem to increase. Most of the signals and noise-making terrorisms that the marines credited to the Japs are really perfectly normal jungle noises. I have had reason to be very thankful for the days I spent in the jungle during these past months. When the jungle noises are normal at night, I know no Japs are moving near me. When they change and strange ones start, I know things are cooking.

A couple of weeks ago I heard the Jap whistle that I thought had usually been used by them as a signal to assemble. You know my ability to imitate birds [with] whistles. I gave the signal to disperse (as I thought it was meant). We kept it up for fifteen or twenty minutes using the same tone but a different combination of long + shorts. By the time I stopped there were several different Japs blowing their lungs out with different signals. I had a hunch their plans were a bit confused, for the whistlers gradually receded to a more distant area where they probably tried to decide who had his signals mixed. By the time they came back, my artillery fire was adjusted and the night was handled the American way.

Some funny things happen. The other day I was talking with Ray and we were firing. Our phones were connected by a double circuit like this [sketch] so if one

*Wilber's sketch of the telephone wire hookup between Ray DeBlois and himself (WB). If one section of the wire was cut, the other could carry the signal. Both voices could also be heard at each side of the cut because the line was continuous through WB and Ray.*

was cut the other might still be good. It happened circuit B was cut and we were talking over A. An innocent and conscientious lineman came along and found "B" broken, connected his phone on one end and said "What line is this?" DeBlois + I said as one voice "This is an artillery line. Get off." The lineman said "I'm out here to fix this line." Again we each said "Get off this line. We have a fire mission going on." Fire missions are classed as urgent. The lineman tried once more. "But this line is broken and …" Ray said with great finality "This line is OK. Get off Bud." The poor lineman said desperately "How in the H— can it be OK when I am holding one end in one hand and the other end in my other hand?" and to himself very amazed "How come I hear both of them too?" He gave up in disgust. I didn't figure out what had happened until later that night and Dixwell [Goff] + I lay in our slit trench and laughed for ten minutes at the bewilderment of that poor lineman.

When I came back here yesterday, I had a three weeks beard and looked like the prospectors that used to come out of the Idaho Mts. It was a real job to get them off with a safety razor. I thought something of having my picture taken, but one look in the mirror convinced me the perpetuation of such evidence would be dangerous.

What a shame he didn't get that photo.

… I know you will never leave me for a career. I just want you to know how necessary to me you are. Life with you and life away from you is complete as long as your love and sympathy and understanding are with me. If I lost that, all this effort + trouble would be wasted so far as I am concerned. You know I think you are beautiful, but I doubt if I can ever see you as you really physically are because the glory and beauty of your love has dazzled me. I have joy in your loveliness but I live in your sweetness and love. Dear Norma I am your very much-married husband. I am waiting until I can again sit in your presence, hear the music of your voice, and feel the touch of your hand. You are my lovely adorable and charming wife. I never address a letter to "Mrs. Wilber E." without a thrill.

Keep up your courage, My Darling. These are hard days, but the sun will shine again and your faith and mine will carry us back to the sunshine. I love you and lay my cheek on your lovely breasts. How I will love to really do that. I must stop now Dearest. Give the children a kiss for me. — XXXOOØ Wilber

>Wilber had put Norma on a pedestal. His words suggest that he needed her totally: "I know you will never leave me for a career" and "If I lost that [your love], all this effort … would be wasted."

x · o · ø · o · x

>Wilber revealed more about his quarters on Sasavele and noted that Barker was very serious about Wilber not returning to the front. But the battle for Munda was not yet over.

**[SASAVELE] AUG. 1, 1943**
Hello There Darling — It's a new month and the sun is shining and it is Sunday and I am just back from a Roman Catholic Mass. It's quiet and peaceful and I love you. My tent is under and between about six large trees. A very muddy road goes by on one side and on the other is our Fire Direction Center where all calls for fire are processed and delivered to the guns. – It's an hour later, has rained, and blue sky.

Aug 2, 1943 — It's another day and raining. I'm still back at the Bn. position area and am under orders from Barker to stay here until he releases me. So I am getting quite a rest because this end is DeBlois' job, and I don't interfere.… I love you Sweet Rose of Mine. Don't worry about me. The Lord has already demonstrated that he is saving me for some later work. I hope that means my family. — 4:00 P.M., XXXOOØ Wilber

>Why was Barker so adamant that Wilber not return to the front? He may have sensed that Wilber was nearing the end of his tether under the constant pressure, night and day, for those 23 days. Wilber could well have become fixated, even to the point of obsession, on the needs of his forward artillery officers and the details of artillery support and might have come to believe himself indispensable, even to the point of neglecting his own well-being. He did go without sleep for "six days and nights" during the drive for Munda [letter 10/4/43]. Or, Barker may have seen the symptoms of combat fatigue setting in; all soldiers in continuous combat will eventu-

ally succumb to it [Fushak, pp. 89, 116]. His letters showed no sign of any imbalance at this point, though it might have been there. Never again, in any other letters, did we hear of Barker reining Wilber in; Wilber may have learned to better pace himself in later combat situations.

That night, ten hours after Wilber signed this letter, Jack Kennedy's PT boat, PT-109, was rammed by a Japanese destroyer and sunk a few miles north of Gizo Island, 65 miles northwest of Wilber. The subsequent rescue of Kennedy, later our 35th U.S. President, and his crew became the stuff of legend. The unsuccessful mission of the PT boats had been to intercept Japanese naval forces bringing reinforcements into Vila on Kolombangara. The 43rd Division had faced and would again later the Japanese troops from Kolombangara.

x·o·ø·o·x

Wilber wrote again late that evening from an unusual location.

**[FDC DUGOUT, SASAVELE] AUG. 2, '43, 9:30 P.M.**
Dear Wife of Mine — This is tomorrow's letter. I'm in the F.D.C. [fire direction center] dugout listening to rain outside and news from our front line. This dugout is about six feet deep and is dug into the solid coral rock. Overhead are logs covered with sand bags filled with dirt and covered by a tent. It really is quite a snug place. Before we left Frisco we bought light bulbs that would work from car batteries. Now we have electric lights in here so [artillery] fires can be plotted and calculated at night. All this is carefully covered so no light shows and a pair of guards is on duty outside to add to the care about light leaks and to take care of emergencies. So you can see how much I value DeBlois and his contributions. He sits at the nerve center of the Bn. and is a pretty critical guy. It's good to be under a roof during a rain and not in a slit trench in the jungle. However I feel a bit guilty about my present comfort because so many are out in the rain tonight. Of course it is warm, but it makes such good mud that one doesn't appreciate sleeping in it.

We are fortunate to have an Army Signal Corps photograph of the FDC of the 169th Field Artillery Battalion, the very place Wilber described. It is preserved in Barker's book, p. 106; it is not to be found in the National Archives.

Barker called me this evening to assure himself I'm not up front again. He is right about it. My job there is done now, but I think he suspects I was just up there for fun. Anyway I have received some nice comments for some reason not quite clear to me. For example [Major] Pat Kenny [executive officer of 152nd FA

*Fire Direction Center of the 169th Field Artillery Battalion in a pit on Sasavele Island. Major René DeBlois, the S-3 sitting at left center, is on the phone receiving reports from his forward observers. The assistant S-3, Capt. Russell Davis, is standing just behind him. The human "computers" for Batteries C, B, and A, are the three soldiers sitting in the rear. The "chief computer," Sergeant Easton, is behind them. They communicated with their batteries via the sound powered phones hanging around their necks. In the foreground, a journal clerk records the action on a typewriter.* [PHOTO: U.S. ARMY SIGNAL CORPS, IN BARKER, P. 106]

Bn.], the snooty major who taught English at Brown, called me yesterday to say he was "proud to know me." I was a bit embarrassed and said he should not believe everything he heard. Whitney said Col. Eason [recently relieved C.O. of the 169th Inf.] had said some very fine things too. I didn't ask what.

However the remark that Griswold [C.O. XIV Corps] made really pleased me. I had been introduced to him by Col. Holland as the "Finest G—d— artillery in the world." … That was a thrill all the more because it happened in a foxhole not 400 yards from the Jap lines. I told Ray [DeBlois] over the phone that night and he said "You sure find it in funny places but I didn't expect to find it in the jungle." Being dumb I asked, "what?" and he said "Baloney." The Dope.

We have had a quiet day and things go well with us here. I've been getting a hold of administration details again that have been allowed to ride. Among other things, I found [that] my promotion papers are still lying on a desk. Col. Files [Exec. Officer of Division Artillery] is stirring them up again and hopes to get

Maj. Gen. Hodge to sign them soon. It seems Happy Jack [Hester], didn't get to it while he was Div. Commander. I haven't met our new C.G. [Commanding General, Hodge] yet, but he is supposed to have done a good job in Guadalcanal.

I've met a Col Baxter too and gave him some artillery help in an emergency so he too is a booster for our Bn.... So, when his [Baxter's] regiment [148th Infantry] went into the line [against the Japanese] he asked for us. We were already supporting Holland, and they had quite an argument about who got us. The [37th] Div. commander got disgusted and said "For __ Sake! Haven't we any artillery in this division [37th] as good as this 169th." They both said "No." and we have spent the past two or three weeks in a strange Div. as honored members. I hope to terminate the relationship in good standing soon. However we took care of both of them for a week. Those were busy days. — Good Night Dear. I love you. Wilber.

> Wilber's battalion did support those two regiments when the 169th Infantry was not in the line, and his unit received commendations from the commanders of both regiments after Munda was captured.

x · o · ø · o · x

> After four intense weeks of fighting, Munda airfield was pretty well in hand by August 4, but it was officially captured on August 5. The relief was palpable, but more combat on nearby Baanga Island was in the offing. Wilber was still on Sasavele when he wrote this.

**AUG. 4, 1943, 5:00 P.M.**
It's My Darling, I'm thinking of now — This is a lovely time of day and I am sitting between two big trees in my jungle C.P. Our part of the campaign is about over. There are still little mopping up jobs for the infantry but the battle has been won. July 4 to Aug 4 seems short now, but they were busy days. I spent twenty-three of those days at the front supervising and planning joint efforts of infantry and artillery in the advance. It was fascinating, strenuous, and sometimes exciting. Because of my having stayed in spite of two excuses [two wounds] for getting back, I am in a very enviable position in the Bn. The men have decided that I may be a strict + hard boiled Major, but they have also decided I can be relied on in a pinch. I hope the reorganization period when I begin again to talk about sanitation and neatness isn't too much of a shock to them.

> Wilber was still a major with a lieutenant colonel's job.

Incidentally our health has been fine thru the past month. The acclimatization of the men and their training has helped a lot while officers were busy with more active matters. During the past month the Bn. has come to the stage where we don't need to tell the men they are in a good Bn. All that is needed now is to tell them the things we have done. As soon as the story is complete and all our men are back from the front, I intend to call them together and list those actions + accomplishments of which we are proud.…

Today I mailed you my delayed letters, those that could not be mailed until the job was done and the censorship restrictions changed. That was done today so you will know I thought about you even in the busiest days. I thought of all of you so often. You seemed a long way from me some of the days, but at night I could feel your presence and knew you were wishing me well. You probably worried too much because of the radio news. Remember the news always selects the "horror" items. It is never as bad as they picture. Most of the times I felt perfectly secure. Occasionally I thought I was seeing my last sun but not often, and the idea was usually eliminated by some artillery fire.

> How reassuring that he only occasionally thought he was seeing his last sun!

You would be surprised how often, after fighting a losing battle to keep communications functioning all day, and seeing things get more + more critical, that by some miracle, here would come a telephone wire or a radio would start to function. Radios do not work well in the jungle so we were always trying to find a cleared space where they would function. The sight of a lineman coming in to report the necessary repairs were made was often a welcome sight.

This is the quiet night of all quiet nights. No firing tonight. 9:30 P.M. – I am in the FDC pit where we have light and [I] have been reading "One World" [by Wendell Wilkie, presidential candidate in 1940].… Barker just called a little while ago and said he was taking steps to have us returned to our division. That probably means the official end of this campaign for us.… — XXXOOØ  Wilber

> One of Wilber's battery commanders, Howard Brown, at the 43rd Division's 65th reunion in 2011, told me a story that pertains to "here would come a telephone wire." At one point at the front, Wilber was struggling with a defective phone line. He had to yell to be heard and could barely hear the other party, probably DeBlois on Sasavele. While this was going on, a lineman came in with a new line and a connection that was loud and clear. He or another soldier tried to hand Wilber a phone connected to that line. Wilber, not tolerating any interruption in his struggles to communicate, impatiently

CHAPTER 3  *Get your head down! That ain't all!*

waved him off several times, not realizing the other phone would end his frustration. He eventually did get the point and accepted the other phone. Brown told me this with a chuckle. The C.O. was not always right!

x·o·ø·o·x

On the day Munda was captured, Wilber found time to write separate letters to Norma, me, and Valerie, each with a different tone.

**AUG. 5, 1943 9:00 A.M.**
Lover Mine — Today we are being officially released from our battle assignments. That is really the end of the fight for us until the next major move for the division. It hardly seems possible that it is over for us. Last night we did not fire. Neither did the other artillery in this vicinity. The silence was so unusual that I could not sleep well. It is odd how clear the silence seems at night.…

One river [the Barike] that we crossed three times within a mile was clear and cold and swift, so you see we were well up toward the mountains. At one crossing I was in a hurry so did not walk the engineers' foot bridge but instead jumped in + waded across. It was about waist deep and seemed as cold as ice. However I haven't seen ice lately. Anyway a whole column of soldiers followed me thru and things were speeded a little. – A letter dated July 17 came just now from Hale. He had just been on a two-mile hike [at Grace Boys Camp]. I wonder if you realize how much I like to get letters from my children. Hale writes very interesting letters.…

> I visited the Solomons in 1983 and found the Barike River to be a small stream, perhaps six feet wide and one or two feet deep. Upstream a bit from the road it widened to a small pool. On the hot afternoon we passed by there, we walked up to the pool and I had a refreshing dip.

The Japs tried to bomb us yesterday and my boys shot down two "Zeros" [Japanese fighter planes].… All in all they are pretty pleased with themselves.

I love you Sweet and know these two letters are the ones you have been waiting for and am glad you can forget the worries of the past month. You have been sweet and courageous. I wish I could have kept those letters I buried up front for there is much you mentioned that I have not answered. They were sure welcome. The U.S. mail does go thru even during battle. Good bye now. — XXX OOØ Wilber 4:30 P.M.

> I fantasized, as I was being driven around those hills east of Munda airfield in 1983, that I would stumble upon Norma's lost letters 40 years after they were buried. I didn't, but I did see other artifacts there that had been collected by the native residents, such as a rusted old helmet and a dog tag

(the metal identification tags worn around every solder's neck). There were two tags in each set so that one could be removed and recorded by a body identification team if the worst happened.

x · o · ∅ · o · x

Norma's life that summer remains unknown to us. She could have been in New York, Baltimore, or Washington, D.C. She had gone under cover, but still wrote frequently. Unfortunately—in fact, tragically—her voice remains buried somewhere deep in the dirt of New Georgia Island in the Solomons and elsewhere in the Pacific, from New Zealand to Japan. Nevertheless, we do obtain occasional glimpses of her through her notes on letters sent to Valerie and me and most of all as reflected in Wilber's letters back to her. He wrote how "sweet and courageous" she was; her letters must have been calming and reassuring to Wilber. The apartment was now vacated, and the children were settled into their summer activities. She had determined her course through the pregnancy and was now embarked on it. Her ship had left the dock.

**AUG. 5, 1943**
Dear Son Hale — Your very interesting letter written to me on July 17 is here. Your two earlier letters had been delivered to me in a slit trench of the front lines during a battle. I read them, then tore them up so the Japs could not read them. After that I buried them so they would not find them. When this one came it was the last day of the battle, and I was sitting peacefully back at my command post resting after everything had stopped. It seems very quiet not to hear machine guns and mortars and howitzers and cannons off and on during the night and day.

You would like one of my officers, named [Lt. Donald] Mushik. He is a lst. Lt. He worked for about two weeks conducting our fires from a hill that the Japs could both see and shoot to. Day after day while he was talking over the telephone I would suddenly hear a loud crash on the phone, then he would say "Gemeny!" and there would be silence for a while, then he would be back saying "200 left. l00 over" which means the last volley we fired was 200 yards left and l00 yards beyond where we wanted the next one to fall. I would guess he was shot at fifty times a day, sometimes by rifles, sometimes by mortars and occasionally by a high velocity dual-purpose gun. He was wounded in the arm and didn't tell me. I was told tho and sent him back to the rear to have it dressed and to get a rest. Two days later I sent for him again and he went back on his hill. Since then he has stayed with the infantry with some of my other officers during their last advance, which cleared out the Japs. I am going to recommend him for a decoration.

Wilber did, and Mushik was awarded the Distinguished Service Cross, an award for valor exceeded only by the Congressional Medal of Honor. Such an award for one of its members engendered great pride throughout the entire battalion. Wilber thought very highly of Mushik and mentioned him again in later letters. He was from Mandan, North Dakota. In the early 1980s, I called him and had a pleasant chat. He remembered Wilber, but without many specifics. More recently (ca. 2012), I shared these letters and photographs with Mushik's sister, daughter, and nephew.

Another of my officers named Bert [Heidelberger] was on another hill for several days. The Japs held a hill that overlooked us and they kept firing mortars and machine guns at us. Just at that time, we couldn't spare troops to capture this hill so Bert would clean them out with our artillery fire. The Japs were so close to us that whenever Bert did this we had all our troops lie down in their holes. He would bring the shells down right beside us. We would hear the crash of trees being cut down, rock and dirt and fragments of steel would whiz by over our heads, Japs would scream and run and all their firing would stop. We called that particular mission "Charlie One" because it was #1 for "C" battery.

*Lt. Donald Mushik relaxing, probably at Ondonga, October 1943. Mushik was awarded the Distinguished Service Cross for his forward observing during the drive on Munda. Three of his fellow observers were killed.* [PHOTO: CAPTAIN LAWRENCE S. PALMER, DDS, DC, COURTESY OF HIS SON, DAVID PALMER.]

Charlie One saved a lot of American lives almost every day for a week. A couple of times we left the "C" battery guns laid on [aimed at] "Charlie One" all night. In the middle of the night when the Japs were all in there again and getting pretty brave, I called Maj. DeBlois on the phone and said "Fire Charlie One, Three and

Three." He said "Coming right up." In less than two minutes 24 shells weighing 50 pounds each blasted into that ridge and those Japs never made an attack again. "Three and Three" meant three volleys [twice] with quick fuse that explodes the shell above the ground and three volleys with delay fuse that lets the shell dig in about three feet before it explodes. We used to say "Three to knock them into their holes and three to dig them out again." — Wilber – I love you.

> The phrase "three and three" meant that each of the four howitzers of Battery C would be fired three times as rapidly as it could be reloaded (six to ten seconds). After a delay, this would be repeated. The "quick fuse" was most likely a timed fuse, set to explode at a fixed time after firing. (The proximity fuse, which used radio waves to detect the approaching ground, was, it appears from my limited inquiries, not available for army artillery until 1944 because of fears that unexploded shells would make the technology available to the enemy.)
> Sadly, Heidelberger later became the third observer of the 169th Field Artillery to be lost to enemy fire.

x·o·ø·o·x

> In the letter to Valerie, Wilber revealed more about the fire direction center of the 169th FA Bn. On my 1983 visit to Sasavele Island, I was shown its probable location, in a garden. The older natives had moved there after the war and remembered it as a large pit, about chest deep, with sandbags.

**AUG. 5, 1943, 8:00 P.M.**
Hello There! Cute and Darling [Valerie] — How is the Young American Travel Girl? I imagine you must have had a pretty busy time in Washington. What did you think of the statue of Lincoln? I thought he was really still sending a message to me when I saw it. How do you like Paul [Wilber's brother] and his wife? I've thought of him often during the past month and been glad he wasn't here.

By the way, right now, I'm down in our Fire Direction Center dugout. We have electric lights here. On the walls are maps and photographs and charts on tables, all used to put the fire of the Bn. on the right spot in the front lines. I used to sit up in the front and decide where to shoot and pick out the spot on the ground and map. Then I'd phone or radio to Maj. DeBlois where, when and how much. He would do some calculating, his [human] computers would do some figuring and issue orders to their batteries. Next Maj. DeBlois would say quietly "Fire" and on the phone to me he would say, "On the way, Bill." In about half a minute I would hear the noise

CHAPTER 3     *Get your head down! That ain't all!*

*Stacks of empty 105-mm howitzer shell cases on Sasavele Island, August 3, 1943, just as Munda was being captured. Wilber's battalion (169th Field Artillery) fired 28,975 shells from this island during the Munda campaign in support of five different infantry regiments. It is likely that these are the shell cases that held those projectiles before they were loaded into the 169th's howitzers.* [PHOTO: U.S. ARMY SIGNAL CORPS, SC 256474]

of the guns come booming across the jungle for five miles. An instant later my shells would whisper Whish! Whish! Hurry! Hurry! Whish! Hurry! over my head and I would say into the phone "They passed here going the right way all right." DeBlois would say "Get your head down. That ain't all" and here would come some more. One day he sent out over 2,500 shells in one day and altogether we sent out 28,975 during the whole (Munda) battle. Since each one weighed 50 pounds you can calculate how much they weighed in pounds and tons. Anyway, after we heard them over our heads we would almost at once hear the blast and roar and crash of the shells exploding in our next door neighbor's front yard. Sometimes we put them in his back yard, sometimes in his side yard, and even in his lap.

The Japs don't like our artillery fire. One day there were a lot of them on a hill where our boys couldn't get at them. Capt. Rainey decided he would help the Japs get closer to us. So he dropped our shells well behind them at first, then closer to us and kept moving them closer and closer to us. Pretty soon a lot of them were running to get away from the bursting shells. They should have stayed in their holes to be safest. However, they got excited and ran toward our soldiers just as if they were attacking us except they had thrown away their guns. As soon as they were close enough our infantry went to work on them, and pretty soon "no more Japs" were there.

There are supposed to be barking lizards here. I hear the barking at night, and I see the lizards in the daytime but I have never been able to catch one in the act. However the soldiers have all decided they do bark. It sounds just like a little dog, but I haven't seen any dogs. The fireflies are quite thick in the jungle and seem very bright at night. A lot of rotting wood glows green light at night with phosphorescence. The soldiers use it sometimes to mark paths at night. We don't quite agree with all the news commentators that the Air Corps and Marines earn all the credit. Don't forget the Army was here too.

I love you Dear. Please write to me when you can. — Your Daddy, Wilber XXXOOO

> The "no more Japs" was pretty callous stuff to be writing to 12-year-old Valerie. It was not characteristic of Wilber, who would catch an indoor fly with his hand and then release it outdoors unharmed. In combat, human life, at least the enemy's, had become cheap in Wilber's eyes. He seemed to share his less palatable, dehumanized thoughts with his young daughter, passing them off almost as a joke. This was not the only time we see this in his letters to her [letter 3/25/45, Book 3]. He suppressed this aspect in his letters to Norma and me. In the letter above to me, combat was treated as a technical exercise without personalizing the targets on the other side. His daughter provided Wilber with a needed outlet; he could voice (confess?) the depersonlization inherent to the military without reproach. This window into his psyche was slammed shut with the abrupt transition to "barking lizards" and "phosphorescence." The "barking lizard" reference might have been the barking gecko, plentiful in the cooler climes of southern Australia.

x · o · ø · o · x

### [SASAVELE] AUG. 7, 1943

Dearest Wife — It's 4:35 P.M. and raining. Ray [DeBlois] + I have just moved into our dugout tent. It is dug into the ground about three feet with a dirt and log wall up on the outside. The tent sits over the hole and furnishes some protection from the rain. The total space would accommodate three cots without leaving any floor space. Our two cots leave a narrow floor space where we can walk, have a small table and take turns having a chair. Over our cots we have stretched our shelter-halves [small half-tents] to shed such rain as comes thru the tent roof. All in all we are pretty cozy and have the advantage that if the Jap air raids us we don't have to get up at night to go to some hole. Our cots are dug down low so we are well below deck.

CHAPTER 3    *Get your head down! That ain't all!*

Yesterday Ray + I went back to the main island [New Georgia] to show him the effect of our fires on some of the more "historical" areas.... A nice young corporal, now 1st Lt. [Kenneth P.] French, that you may remember and Cris fought their last fight. I know how you will feel about Cris and we felt the same way. Don [Downen] and [Lt. Robert W.] McCalder felt it pretty strongly. McCalder had lived with Cris for quite a while. Don said it was a good way to go tho, and we were glad on that score.

> McCalder was later killed at Balete Pass in Luzon, in the Philippines, on April 29, 1945.

Don looks tired (this was his first day after the job was finished) but well. He wears a mustache and seems highly regarded by his men and fellow officers. It is just like having a brother here to see him. I felt that he was glad I came up even tho I could only stay a few minutes. I hope to be able to have him down to my Hq. before any more moves develop.

We drove back thru the airport [Munda] that was the objective of this action. It seemed funny to be able to drive safely thru an area, which we had considered an objective for so long. The artillery is quite the service now. We are, of course only temporarily, now given a lot of credit by the infantry. Soon they will be convinced they won [the battle], but now they feel pretty generous.

... I wrote Dan Downen [Don's father] about Don and what a great job he is doing and that I had happened on purpose to put some of my fires where they would "soften" his zone for him. I love you Nana. Don't forget that Aug 28 [Wilber's and Norma's wedding date] was the greatest day of my life. If I could just be with you I'd tell you. WB. — Wilber XXXOOØ

*Capt. Donald Downen with a Japanese gun his company captured near Munda, August 1943. Downen was a close friend of Wilber's from Washington State. Wilber mentioned him often in his letters. I corresponded with and then met him in the early 1980s.* [LIBRARY OF CONGRESS PHOTO COLLECTION; LOT 4281; FILED UNDER "ARUNDEL."]

COMBAT AND NEW LIFE   PART I: JUNGLE COMBAT

*Marine tank on patrol in deep mud in the jungle of New Georgia, July 29, 1943.* [PHOTO: U.S. ARMY SIGNAL CORPS, SC 395877]

*Graveside service at a Munda cemetery, August 11, 1943. Lt. Col. F. Kirker, 37th Division chaplain, conducted the service. Note the numerous grave markers in the background.* [PHOTO: U.S. ARMY SIGNAL CORPS, SC 186018]

CHAPTER 3   *Get your head down! That ain't all!*

*Wounded, probably from Munda, being evacuated from Rendova to a PBY Catalina seaplane for flight to a hospital, July 1943.* [PHOTO: CHARLES D'AVANZO]

The tragedy and horror of battle are chillingly on exhibit here. Donald Downen wrote me letters in 1981 about how Christian (Cris) and French had died. Christian was wounded by an American mortar shell that fell short. He died of blood loss at the aid station with Don at his side on July 27. Lieutenant French was crushed by a withdrawing American tank that backed over and crushed him and three enlisted men on July 28. Christian and French were both posthumously awarded the Distinguished Service Cross—Christian for eliminating a concealed Japanese machine gun and French for assisting a tank attack two days before his death. Recall that Lieutenant Malone, Wilber's forward observer, was also was killed on July 28.

Wilber's letters, and official and unofficial histories of the battle and of the 161st Infantry Regiment, glossed over these sad facts. They tell of the tank incident wherein a squad leader and three of his men were crushed, but do not identify the men. I have little reason to doubt Downen's written testimony that Lieutenant French was that squad leader. Downen had been in the same national guard unit as both Christian and French since prewar days; he was from their home town of Pullman, Washington, and he was in the front lines with them when they died. Understandably, our culture discourages discussion of amicide, the wartime killing of one's friends; but this only further serves to disguise the reality of war.

*Prewar (1934) photo of Lt. Louis K. Christian as an enlisted man in Company E of the 161st Infantry Regiment of the Washington State National Guard. He was a personal friend of Wilber and Norma in Pullman, Washington. He was awarded the Distinguished Service Cross posthumously.* [PHOTO: WASHINGTON NATIONAL GUARD]

CHAPTER 3   *Get your head down! That ain't all!*

Did Wilber suppress the reality of what was happening to his friends and forward observers, or was it simply that he did not discuss it in his letters? (Perhaps it was censorable material.) Stoicism was required of his position and it was also his nature. But he did bring up the losses of these men several times in later letters; he had a deep affection for his observers and his old Company E comrades of the 161st Infantry. It was a deadly game they played, and the psychological costs for the survivors were not small.

I visited Don Downen at his home in Pullman, Washington, in 1986. He was full of memories of Wilber and their meetings in the Solomons.

*Major Donald C. Downen, after the Munda action, probably 1944. He was from Pullman, Washington, and a close friend of Wilber's.*
[PHOTO: DONALD DOWNEN]

*Clardie and Donald Downen, Pullman, Washington, 1985. She died in 1988 at age 76 and he in 2001 at 86.*
[PHOTO: HALE BRADT]

55

He was most interested in the Wilber-Norma story. They had been his close friends and neighbors in Pullman 50 years earlier. Don died in 2001.

x · o · ∅ · o · x

On August 10, General Hodge, C.O. of the 43rd Division, returned to his Americal Division and later became a corps commander. Gen. Harold R. Barker, Wilber's superior, became acting commanding general of the 43rd Infantry Division [Barker, p. 83]. It was unusual for an artillery commander and especially a national guardsman to be given command of an infantry division. Barker's aggressive and fearless pursuit of excellent performance must have appealed to Griswold and Harmon. And it was apparently just what the 43rd Division needed; the capture of Munda had not been accomplished with the alacrity the generals had expected.

x · o · ∅ · o · x

**AUG. 11, 1943**
Dear Norma — … Yesterday Goff + I went over to the C.P. [command post] of our infantry [169th Regiment, probably near Munda] and received a royal welcome from their officers. It was really fine to be able to talk casually to them and standing right out in the open. Roads are of course terrible, and it is amazing to see what some drivers can get their vehicles thru.

> The 169th Infantry was the unit that Wilber's artillery had supported through much of the Munda campaign and that had been pulled from the front lines for a short while. This was a welcome reunion.

The average soldier is busy now trying to get himself on salvage and clean-up details. It is such a good chance to get souvenirs. The price on Jap sabers was $250.00 the other day. Some men have queer ideas of what they want. I saw one proudly carrying a bench, which was made out of rough poles like the rustic camp chairs in state parks. It was crudely made and carried no suggestion of Jap origin. He had probably been morbid during the past month about lying in slit trenches and having no "setting" equipment. Others collect large shells, heavy pieces of planes, trucks and Jap trunks and boxes. Others go in for Jap shoes, hats, buttons and lapels off uniforms. I saw one carrying home a Jap fly trap. He may have been a practical minded type for the flies are pretty thick.

I've been a poor souvenir hunter because of other duties and a lack of interest in going thru some dead Jap's personal effects. The compass interested me because we had shot up the equipment of which it was a part. I'll send it along when the arrangements can be made for shipping it. It will be an addition to the children's exhibit anyway.

Barker was very embarrassed the other day when he felt he had to commend his Bn. C.O.s. He hemmed + hawed and said he was no good at saying that sort of thing and ended by saying "Anyway you know as well as I do you did a good job." So that was that. I take it "we done OK."

> Barker was much more at ease and effective when profanely castigating his officers for their shortcomings and failures.

Wild wrote me a funny letter from the hospital. I had cautioned him on taking too many chances while on the front lines. He wrote: "I was sitting in a hole when I was hit and taking all due caution as you instructed. It was a tree burst from that dual-purpose gun right overhead. There was another hill between it [and] me, so I couldn't adjust [artillery fire] on it, either by sight or sound."

If he was in a hole, I'm sure it was an accident, for the only reason he was not wounded sooner was that he moved so often + so fast. The infantry considered him a wonder and I'm pretty proud of him myself.

… Some of the most worthwhile training we did was to have men used to the jungle, especially at night. It's a noisy place and one needs to know what noises are normal. We have the land crabs that travel over leaves and pieces of wood with a crusty rattle and scratchy noises. The lizards are very interested in climbing over tent tops and thru the brush. The tree frogs and similar animals squeak, and trill and chatter. …

We eat twice a day; at 8:30 A.M. and 4:30 P.M. Today for supper I had mashed potatoes, tomatoes, Vienna sausage, mixed spinach + green beans, crackers and peanut butter and finally canned fruit cocktail. You see we are doing pretty well just now. The fact that a big ration dump just moved in probably helps a lot. However the standard morning meal is pancakes. Occasionally I force the kitchens to vary their breakfasts and a loud squawk comes from the men. It reminds me of the Maine potato eater [who] used to refuse your salads.… Good bye Dear Family — XXXOOØ Wilber E. Bradt

x · o · ø · o · x

> So ended the Munda action. And as it did, Valerie and I were dealing with the daily issues of camp life. But we remained well aware of our father who was far, far away in another world.

**Grace Boys Camp, Aug. 17, 1943**
*Dear Mother — This letter will be short because I had to help with canteen and will not have much time.*

*I went on a little hike this morning with a counselor and three other boys. It was my first hike this month. We walked about two miles. It was an easy hike, as that is all I should do so soon [perhaps after being ill].*

*I sent Valerie Daddy's letters and told her to send them to you.*

*I think Daddy would like some "Blondie" funny books for X-mas. You know how he liked Blondie or maybe Popeye. If I have any better ideas I will let you know. — Your loving son, Hale*

The capture of Munda airfield was not the end of combat in the New Georgia group for the 43rd Division. A sudden crisis in the form of a Japanese ambush was now thrust upon the division.

---

During the drive to Munda airfield, Allied forces were active in the Mediterranean and in the Soviet Union. The German offensive for Kursk, begun on July 5, was stopped and reversed by Russian counterattacks on July 12 and August 3, which then drove westward some 150 miles to the Dnieper River. On July 10, U.S. and British troops landed in force on four beachheads of southeast Sicily. Two weeks later, on July 25 with fighting raging in Sicily and Kursk, the Italian upper classes arrested Mussolini and began secret negotiations with the Allies, hoping to forestall a German occupation and defense of Italy.

By mid-August 1943, Sicily was completely neutralized. Negotiations between Italy and the Allies continued as Allied forces prepared to invade Italy proper. In the Solomon Islands, on August 15, Allied troops landed on Vella Lavella, northwest of New Georgia and Kolombangara, thus bypassing the Japanese forces on Kolombangara (Map 9 inset).

---

# 4

## *"It was a depressing and unfortunate affair"*
### Baanga Island action
#### AUGUST 1943

Wilber became involved in the capture of Baanga Island, a scant three miles west of Munda airfield, which was now in American hands (Map 9). Reconnaissance on August 11 had located enemy troops on Baanga who could threaten the airfield. Company L of the 169th Infantry attempted to land on a beach in a cove on Baanga on August 12 (Map 10). It encountered machine gun fire from several locations and withdrew, leaving 34 men stranded on the beach. Wilber's letter six days later told what happened next.

**[NORTH OF BIBILO HILL, MUNDA] AUG. 18, 1943**
*[Note by Norma:] Dear Valerie, please send to Hale at St. Bernard's School, Gladstone New Jersey – Mom. Hale: Daddy tells how he acted as a Brigadier General – took Gen. Barker's place for a while. This was the capture of Baanga Island. I couldn't find it on a map.*

Dearly Beloved — I'm in business [combat] again. One of our cleanup jobs [Baanga Island] is in process. The battalion was not in that area but Barker and I were. He is acting Division commander now, so he temporarily tossed the [division] artillery into my hands …

Luckily I had had a hunch [that artillery might be needed] and already had some communication and observer personnel [Heidelberger et al.] with me. We had artillery fire from two borrowed batteries within two hours and eventually worked in another battalion and started to cut some grass [with artillery] for the "doughboys." Now the powers "that be" have allowed me to get my battalion on the job so we are moving in today.

Ordinarily I couldn't mail this until after the entire operation but the censorship regulations have been relaxed. You notice the radio now announces the names of divisions in various operations.

I only have time now to say how much I love all of you. Please take care of yourselves. — XXXOOØ Wilber — Aug 19 [I am] Still OK.

> Wilber had anticipated the need for artillery and had left Sasavele at 8:30 a.m. on August 13 (a Friday!) with Heidelberger and ten enlisted men [169 FA Bn. Journal].
>
> On August 14, in an attempt to reach the stranded men, a "depleted" company of 42 men (probably from the same Company L) landed north of the cove and drove west and possibly south (Map 10). Wilber sent Heidelberger and several men with them to provide artillery support. The company encountered resistance and returned to battalion lines the next day leaving six wounded behind. According to Wilber's eloquent oral account after he had arrived home in 1945 (as recalled by me and hence possibly not entirely accurate), the infantrymen had panicked and abandoned their wounded.

*Lt. Norbert J. Heidelberger, a forward observer of the 169th Field Artillery Battalion killed in action on Baanga Island, August 15, 1943. Wilber felt his loss deeply. He wrote Heidelberger's mother upon his death and several times later including on the next two anniversaries.* [PHOTO: CARA K. HEIDELBERGER.]

CHAPTER 4   *It was a depressing and unfortunate affair*

Among the wounded left behind were the artillery observer, Lieutenant Heidelberger, and three of his party. Heidelberger and Cpl. Norbert F. McElroy did not survive. Heidelberger was reported missing for some time after his body was found because of difficulties in identifying it. He was not officially declared killed until November.

Artillery observers were hindered in their movements by their heavy radio equipment. In this case, artillery could not be used because the jungle impaired radio communication and telephone lines had been cut by the Japanese. The "Report of Operations of the 169th Field Artillery (August 12–September 10)," signed and probably written by Wilber, commented self-critically on this sad experience:

*This practice, however, was found unsatisfactory in that one observer was lost in action and his party of three men severely wounded while accompanying a company of only 42 men. It is not felt advisable to send artillery observers into un-reconnoitered areas with less than a full company, unless, of course, the need is very urgent and communication to the rear can be maintained.*

Other attempts to dislodge the Japanese by the 169th Infantry on Baanga also failed. On August 16, elements of the 172nd Infantry were brought in, and they arrived singing as they marched toward the front. It was a heartwarming and encouraging sound, as Wilber recollected in 1945. "We knew it was going to be OK," he said then. Finally, on August 21 the stranded soldiers were reached, a full nine days after being isolated. Four survived, 20 were dead, and the ten others had managed to swim away from the beach. Several American regiments had been in the vicinity, and it still took nine days to accomplish the rescue.

During this action, Wilber commanded all of the divisional artillery (August 11 to 21) while Barker was division commander. On August 17 and 18, Wilber's own unit (169th Field Artillery) was brought up to the vicinity of Munda airfield (north of Bibilo Hill, Maps 8 and 13) so it could also fire on Baanga Island. The low point for Wilber was the loss of Heidelberger and McElroy, and a high point was his personal involvement in the elimination of two Japanese coastal defense guns with borrowed artillery on August 17 (see below).

The Japanese finally evacuated Baanga by boat on August 21 and 22. Wilber later (October 22) commented to Norma: "I never wrote up the battle of Baanga for you. It was a depressing and unfortunate affair in several ways."

COMBAT AND NEW LIFE   PART I: JUNGLE COMBAT

Wilber's oral account of the Baanga story told to us in 1945 was prompted by the visit of his brother Paul and his wife Josephine a few days after Wilber's return home from overseas. It was a monologue that must have gone on for a couple of hours. The story clearly had resonated strongly with him and affected him deeply. At age 14, I was fascinated and continue to have strong, clear impressions of it to this day. How sad he never wrote it down or that we did not record his telling of it. Nevertheless, his letter above and those written later give us glimpses of it.

x·o·ø·o·x

In New York, the end of my second month of camp was approaching, and I took exception to the arrangements for getting me to St. Bernard's School in New Jersey. I made clear, however, that I would obey orders. I was the little soldier.

**Saturday, Aug. 21, 1943**
*Dear Mother — I received your letters telling me to come home [to NYC] next Friday. If it could be arranged I would like to come home on Monday instead of Friday because I would miss a lot of things the last two days [of camp]. Of course I would rather see Monte and Valerie if it can't be arranged. I can take a train or bus home if necessary on Friday. I love you! — Hale*

x·o·ø·o·x

**[About August 22, 1943]**
*Dear Mother — When I go home Friday or Monday, whichever you say, I don't know where to send my baggage by express or if it is necessary. I think it could be arranged to take it back on the train or bus. I can hardly wait to see Valerie and Monte, but I wish I could see you.*
*I love you a whole lot, — Your loving son, Hale*

Norma was now almost seven months pregnant and, to hide the fact, she could not come to meet me (or Valerie). I seemed oddly acquiescent about this; I had probably been fed a convincing enough story for a 12-year-old. We would be delivered directly to our boarding schools in New Jersey by Monte. Was Monte still living in New York or was he commuting up from Washington for this purpose? In either case, he was paying his dues.

CHAPTER 4    *It was a depressing and unfortunate affair*

x·o·ø·o·x

The command of the 43rd Division changed yet again on August 21. General Barker returned to his command of the divisional artillery, and Wilber reverted to his command of the 169th Field Artillery Battalion. Command of the division was assumed by Brig. Gen. Leonard F. Wing, the assistant division commander, who, as a consequence, would soon be promoted to major general. Wing remained commander of the division through the rest of the war, and it came to be known as the "Winged Victory Division." Wing was a national guardsman from Vermont and had served in all ranks therein from private to general.

Wilber, in my memory of his oral account, felt that the poor execution of the Baanga action was a significant, if not determining, factor in Barker's relief of divisional command. It was not necessarily due to Barker's own shortcomings, but as commander he carried the responsibility. Contributing factors could well have been Wing's greater seniority (if so) and the fact that artillery officers were rarely appointed to infantry positions. Interestingly, Wilber himself would make that same transition in 1945.

x·o·ø·o·x

After the Japanese evacuation of Baanga, Wilber recalled more aspects of the Baanga and Munda actions for his father.

**AUG. 22, 1943**
Dear Father — Happy Birthday to you from me [the elder Hale is 72]. It's a pretty good day for me too for I have completed my second battle. The second was not so long as that for Munda, but in some ways it was less convenient for me....

The latter action was particularly interesting to me because Barker was acting as Division commander and I was the only other artillery commander present when things started. Barker told me I should take care of all artillery arrangements with the comment that he wanted to have the best brains on the job. I looked around and didn't see any other artillery brains so decided he meant the only brain. Anyway I went to work and had some artillery in the war as soon as the infantry was ready. I guess the high spot in the Baanga I. action for me as an individual was the fact that I located, adjusted my artillery fire on, and knocked out the two biggest Jap guns yet found in this area. They fired a little too early in the morning and I saw their flashes. Four minutes later I had four guns firing on them; six minutes later eight and in less than ten minutes twenty were dropping shells on them. In another ten minutes they were all thru, and two days later, I walked over to see them. We had just put shell holes all around them and had ruined all the less massive parts. They were approximately 4.7 [inches diameter] and were a naval gun with a fifteen-foot tube. Since they were firing on Munda field [now American], everyone from the corps commander and air commander were shouting for action.

All these Jap guns fire as one or two guns. They have not yet ever massed the fire of all their guns on one target as we do. Because of this they are always called Pistol Pete. Whenever P.P. starts firing it is always news, and everyone wants us to knock him out immediately. Of course the job is to find him.

> Wilber expanded on this event in a letter to me several weeks later (November 7): "It was about five in the morning and we [Davis and I] woke up saying 'That firing doesn't sound like ours.' We jumped out of our foxhole and ran down to the beach [at or near Kindu Point] and saw the flashes from these guns. He had started too early and it was dark enough to let his flashes show. I grabbed the phone and said in it '907-Ten volleys.' Then to another battalion, '905 is 200 right 500 short. Fire at will.' Four minutes later the Jap guns were thru for this war."
>
> Those coastal defense guns on the southern tip of Baanga were still there when I visited in 1983. The pedestals were standing, but the tubes were on the ground because the brass parts had been removed. Wilber sent me the gun sight, a telescope about two inches in diameter and three feet long, which the Japanese had buried nearby in the sand.
>
> As I recall his oral story in 1945, he had just sent the gun sight back with an orderly, when an infantry colonel came up saying he was interested in having the gun sight. Wilber told him it was not on the gun and that the Japanese had probably buried it somewhere nearby and then left the colonel there kicking up the sand looking for it. He felt no guilt about this deceit, because the infantry had had absolutely no part in the silencing of those guns; it was all his artillery.
>
> His letter to his father continued:

I am allowed now to tell you more of the Munda battle.… It was necessary for me to stay at the front all the time because of the situation. It was on this [Munda] trail that I was wounded the second time. Snipers are very much over-rated. If one keeps moving, one is pretty safe. I have had a good many twigs clipped within six feet of me but did not feel in too much danger if I was on the move. If you stop on the trail to rest, it is wise to get in the undergrowth so a sniper cannot so easily locate you. The one that scratched me caught me at a phone.

CHAPTER 4   *It was a depressing and unfortunate affair*

*Wilber with a coastal-defense Japanese five-inch (120-mm naval) gun his artillery put out of action August 17, 1943. This was one of the two guns emplaced by the Japanese on Baanga Island to defend the approaches to Munda airfield.* [PHOTO: U.S. ARMY SIGNAL CORPS, 161-43-9009, 8/19/43]

Of course you have read the wild horror tales told by the marines of Guadalcanal. I had all the same experiences and found the facts much less vivid.… Sometimes they [the Japanese] show a childish tendency to perform antics. One night one dropped a fish line and hook between the logs over the foxhole where one of my Lts. was sleeping (?). He could have dropped a grenade and the Lt. was ready to shoot if he made any sudden moves. He however didn't want to shoot because only outside perimeters were supposed to fire and I had instructed my officers to stick to artillery as much as possible. Anyway my Lt. pulled on the string; the Jap pulled; they repeated this several times until my Lt. cut the string and kept the hook. Mr. Jap left with a few very disgusted jabbers.

It's a weird war and a lot different from the European type either past or present. The fact that so few prisoners are taken (I have only seen two) is because of a fight to the finish attitude on both sides. No one wants to be a prisoner. One U.S. officer sat over a foxhole l5 minutes talking to an English-speaking Jap armed with a bayonet, trying to get him to come out and surrender. The Jap understood he would be well used, that if he refused he must be killed. He never came out.

I forgot to mention that I saw the first U.S. planes land on Munda Field and was a bit thrilled.

I hope this debunks and explains a bit of the flashy news stories and gives you an idea of what I'm doing now. — Wilber

What was the reality? The "flashy news stories" and "wild horror tales told by the Marines"? Or the antics of a Japanese with a fishhook or one just curious (letter of August 24 below)? Perhaps there was truth in all of it. It was indeed a "weird war."

x·o·ø·o·x

### Tuesday [August 24 1943?]
*Dear Mother — I got Monte's letter and I am going back [to New York City] on Friday and I will mail my baggage to [St Bernard's] school.*

*If you have found a film [for my camera] and it will get here in time please send it.*

*I had a temperature Sunday but it went down so I got up this morning. I am all well and will go in the water as instructed by the nurse with my head above water. — Your loving son, Hale Bradt*

I did leave camp on Friday, which meant that I missed the end-of-camp activities and festivities. As a result I did not have the opportunity to try again to swim the length of the lake (1.5 miles). I was rather relieved about that.

x·o·ø·o·x

Wilber wrote Norma with more reflections on the Munda combat that complemented those he had sent to his father two days earlier.

### AUG. 24, 1943
Dearest Wife of Mine — Several letters came from you today. It was wonderful to hear from you and to have time to sit + think of what you say.… For a time the front line looked like this [sketch showing front lines with American salient].

You see, we were on a finger, which left the Japs on three sides. So each night we would fire artillery fire at [locations] a, b, and c [on three sides of the salient]. DeBlois + I would set up a schedule and if the Japs got active in the night I would call up + say "Fire Charlie" or "Fire Able" or "Fire Baker" or "Fire battalion." Ray would say "coming up" and in a minute or two "On the way," and the shells would

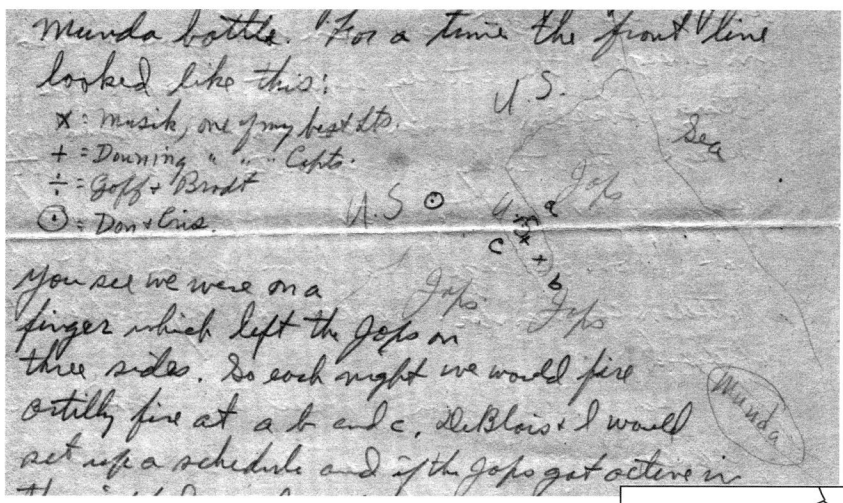

*Pencil sketch and my traced drawing of the U.S. front lines, the salient in them, and Munda airfield, from Wilber's letter of August 24, 1943. The sketches show the salient into Japanese-held territory (Map 6) and the locations of Mushik the forward observer (x), Capt. Edgar S. Downing, the liaison officer (+), Wilber and Goff (÷), and his friends "Don and Cris" of the 161st Infantry (circled dot). The a, b, and c indicate target areas for the American artillery.*

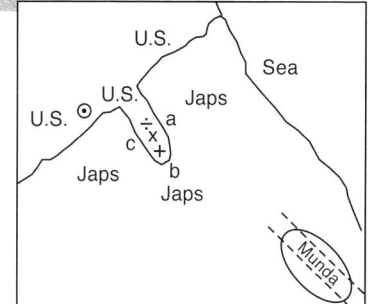

whisper over and crash into the trees. So you see we were "boxed." You have no idea how [much] the average infantryman likes that. He can sleep when we have his protective fires going. The Japs don't like it + it always stops their night harassing.…

Don't believe all the horror stories that come out of here. It is a fight to the finish war and different from the European type and one is often within ten yards of Japs, but so is he ten yards from you which should worry him. In some ways they are shrewd; in others they react as a ten year old boy would if he found he could run in and out of the enemy camp without being caught. Much of the nightmare stories are based on these antics and a failure to realize what they are.

For example at night I have had single Jap soldiers creep up to my slit trench + peep in. I would be covering him with a pistol + he could drop a grenade on me, but no, he would only be curious + go on. I leave the individual combat to the infantry if I can, and try to stick to my business of artillery. That too is my instruction to my officers. However Wild did borrow a pistol + shoot up a machine gun crew for which I should court martial him but will probably recommend a citation.…

It isn't all fun or screwy. There are tragedies and mistakes and there is mud and work and sleepless nights and cracked nerves but the best, or rather worst, stories come from the news boys or those who imagine more than they see. Don't worry about me. It doesn't effect [sic] me as it does some. I'm usually the busiest when the going is the toughest. The hardest part for me is to send my friends + men + officers where I know they may die. Anyway it's a better way to go than the Fascist way that you described.…

The other day Barker + I went over the Baanga area, which was recently captured. You would have been interested in the type of things the Japs had left. Tissue paper was common. Pastel shades of cloth, thousands of little jars + bottles of pastes, salves + pills, cards and notebooks, and dishes and hand grenades. One meal was still in the plates on a table. They aren't very clean. In fact they must have been filthy in their quarters. We found one British truck [from Singapore probably]. I've seen others. Their graves are marked (when marked) by a single vertical post with writing on it. There are several in our present position area.

I'm enclosing a few papers I found. Note the touching child's crayon work and the family aspect. I send it so the children will see these are people too with homes and children. They [should] realize they are wrong because they have the wrong government policies, not because they are Japs.

> Wilber had retained some ability to see the humanity in his enemy, though his use of the derogatory "Japs" suggests otherwise. In 1945, I must have asked him about shooting people, because I recall him telling me that shooting Japanese in the jungle was like "shooting rats in a dump."

Your letters are lovely messages, Dear. I know you are my mate and I love you dearly. Don't worry. Times is OK and I'll be along some day to tell you how I do love you + the children. — XXXOOØ Wilber

> Should we believe the stories of Japanese "running in and out of the enemy camp" like ten-year olds, dropping fishhooks, or peering into American foxholes out of curiosity? They certainly run counter to our knowledge of warfare as described in books, the cinema, and the news media. However, there is no sign here that Wilber was frightened or imagining events or that he was dreaming of them. They were dispassionate observations by a mature objective observer. Warfare at night in the jungle between soldiers from radically different cultures was so far removed from the normal experiences of either that almost anything was possible. It was, as he said, a "weird war" and "screwy." Consider the pranks of high school kids! I choose to accept his testimony at face value.
>
> He does not deny, however, the other reality, that "there are tragedies and mistakes and there is mud and work and sleepless nights and cracked nerves."

*CHAPTER 4*   *It was a depressing and unfortunate affair*

x·o·ø·o·x

Turning to his present location, Wilber described his New Georgia camp, north of Bibilo Hill, Munda.

### AUG. 28, 1943

Sweet Heart Mine — After a few busy days, I'm back at letter-writing again. We have been in an ideal artillery situation lately. A good bivouac area, sunshine, breezes, no Japs near, and a fine outfit to toss ammunition a few miles up the way where there are Japs. It's a deluxe setup for us. The area is improving steadily as a place to live. The enemy was shelling it when we moved in so the boys can now say they occupied a position under enemy fire, but it really was pretty casual.

This was a busy battlefield a few weeks ago so the men had a mess to clean up and a chance to see how the Japs had lived and fought. Flies were very bad but we are getting them under control now.…

I have the children's winter addresses now. Hope CBS can't get along without you. I take it you now are on the "little job as pianist." Hope you like it + Good Luck. Happy anniversary, Lover Mine. Maybe our next will be together. — Love. XXXOOØ Wilber

Here is our first hint of what Norma was telling Wilber, namely that she had tried for and failed to get a job at CBS and was now working as a pianist. But where and in what kinds of venues and establishments? It was surely a complete fiction.

x·o·ø·o·x

### AUG. 31, 1943

Dear Nana — Here are some pictures [of the Japanese naval guns on Baanga Island] that might interest you.…

… I'll write to Box 923, Baltimore Md. from now on. What about [the address for] my identification tags? Should I go back to the U. of Maine address? Or to 204 Broadway? I seem to be a man without a home address just now. I'm a bit confused about your residence. Do you live at the Altamont? You say it's too far to go after rehearsals. Where do you stay? Don't get yourself too much adrift, so you can get lost by some accident and not be missed.…

The mess kits are beginning to rattle [it was time to eat] so I'll stop. I love you Dearest. Please send my love to the children. When does their school start? I have a kiss here for you. — XXXOOØ Wilber

COMBAT AND NEW LIFE  PART I: JUNGLE COMBAT

Wilber had begun to feel at sea with no home address and without knowing what Norma was doing or where she was. It seemed she was working on her own with no one close by to keep track of her. This weighed heavily on him during this short break in the combat.

x · o · ø · o · x

Valerie and I finished our summer camps in late August. Monte Bourjaily met us and took us directly to our boarding schools in New Jersey: me to St. Bernard's in Gladstone and Valerie to St. John Baptist in nearby Mendham. The latter was run by an order of Episcopal nuns, and the former had a strong Episcopalian tradition. I arrived at St. Bernard's a week or so before the school opened and was immediately recruited to help with farm tasks. St. Bernard's kept costs low by using the students as farm workers and dormitory cleaners. The students were a rougher bunch than I had been used to at Grace Church School, so I rapidly learned more about self-reliance and self-defense there. During the school year I was thrust into many new areas: football (reluctantly), caring for cows and horses, scouting, and print shop work.

**[St. Bernard's School] Tuesday [September 7(?), 1943]**
*Dear Mother — I am in the Old Schoolhouse [dormitory] for a week or so right now. I am having a good time here herding cows, washing them, helping spread lime on a field (12 tons), etc. We get up at 5:45 approx. Everything went as planned in New York except I came home with Jess at about 8:00.*

*I got a letter from Daddy which I am sending you [with] four letters from you and a postcard from Valerie at Camp White. I did not bring my trunks up to my room because I will go to the New School [dormitory] soon. — Your loving son, Hale*

x · o · ø · o · x

**[Monday, September 13, 1943]**
*Dear Mother — I just moved to the "New School" and regular classes start tomorrow. I just sent Daddy's letters to Valerie. They were very interesting and exciting. I almost took Latin I, but Mr. Nichols said it couldn't be arranged. He said if I did well this year, I could be sure of having it next year. (If I am here.) I am going to take up printing if I can which I will take during manual work [period].*

*I got the candy, which is very good and thanks a lot. I am eating a piece now. Goodbye now. I am going to write Monte now. — Your loving son, Hale*

I was preparing to write Monte, and not Daddy! Was I equating Monte with Wilber in my life and letter writing? Likely not. This was probably a letter Norma had reminded me to send, thanking Monte for meeting me in New York. At St. Bernard's, we were required to wear suit jackets at dinner. I was wearing hand-me-down suit jackets that Monte had given me. The overly large 1930s adult double-breasted business jackets were hardly the style for a 12-year-old.

Saint Bernard's School was not as academically challenging as Grace Church School where I had, for example, studied Latin the previous two years. After one month at St. Bernard's, I was moved up from 7th to 8th grade, where I also did well. Each class had about 10 or 12 students. The challenges for me were the non-class activities and interactions with my fellow students. I grew up a whole lot that year.

x·o·ø·o·x

Valerie arrived at her boarding school, St. John Baptist in Mendham, New Jersey, for her first full year away from home at age 11. The school was run by nuns of the order of St. John Baptist, who dressed at the time in the full regalia my generation associates with Catholic nuns. The isolated hilltop rectangular school building and the nuns who ran it could make a forbidding impression. Here Valerie told of her first arrival at the school for the sixth grade in September 1943. She wrote this essay seven years later (in 1950) for a contest sponsored by *The Living Church*, a magazine of the Episcopal Church. (She had returned to St. John Baptist for high school.) It won The Living Church Award that year and was published in the magazine. It contains the flowery syntax and upbeat tone of a high school senior trying to win a prize, but it did paint a graphic picture of her arrival and life there. She entitled it "My Reason."

### St. John Baptist School, Mendham, N.J. (1950)

*It was strange and alien; this bare rectangular stone building, standing erect with dignified pride at the summit of a wind swept hill. How odd it seemed, to carry my bags through the door, from a life securely bounded by activity. The bare, brown and white linoleum squares under my feet spun and twisted, multiplying to lengthen this endless cavern of a hall. Overwhelming loneliness swelled inside me to blur those maddening geometric squares, and to roar painfully in my ears. Suddenly, a door slammed, then another, and bright laughter bounced down the stairs a step ahead of its owners. Some of the inhabitants of this strange, separate world had come to meet the new girl.*

*Just then, the little brown study hall clock began to chime, and its joy gaily penetrated the wax-like cloud of my sadness. Outside a dog barked, and was faintly yet laughingly answered. Then, when I began to listen carefully, the jumbled strains of "Chopsticks" bobbed down the hall, making each brown and white square dance with uncontrolled rhythm. Unable to prevent this contagious happiness from enveloping the strangeness of a new existence, I felt one happy tear shine in each eye, and it told me through emotion, that in this atmosphere, I would be happy, and loved.*

*Moods were not accepted among us; we untangled problems ourselves, and laughed away the tantrums as if kicking and screaming were the silliest things in the world. In my associations with other young people, I gradually began to understand what was expected of me, and how to go about it. Sunshine always came through the clouds of remorse following an argument, and two girls became faster friends as a result.*

*How gay we were! Saturdays we walked into town, stocked up on food, and for the rest of the week, spent an hour "after lights-out" sitting on the window sills in the moonlight munching large green dill pickles, or crackers and cheese. Sometimes a streak of daring seized us, and we gave the seniors a merry chase through the halls. A reprimand always followed these escapades, yet I fancied I saw a twinkle in the Sister Superior's eye when she chided us for disturbing the peace. [©The Living Church, April 23, 1950, pp. 21–22]*

Much later, in 2009, Valerie further recalled her early days at the school:

*It was during World War II, when most of our parents were serving somewhere far away—my father was in the Pacific. Strangely, one of our favorite games out among the pine trees was inspired by an English student. We pretended to be a bomber crew with missions, names, and ranks. The English student signed that yearbook, "Skipper Savory." Another signed as "Sgt. McNeal." In our war, the good guys always won.*

Wilber was far from the worlds of his children. The Baanga operation was barely completed when his attention was drawn to the next island, Arundel, less than a mile west and north of Baanga. These islands were all part of the New Georgia Island group. Arundel was separated in one place from (mainland) New Georgia by a narrow channel of width only about 100 yards. Wilber's combat experiences in Arundel turned out to be unlike any he had encountered before.

---

Italy surrendered unconditionally to the Allies on September 3, 1943, the same day Allied troops came ashore in Calabria, in the boot of Italy. On

September 9, British and American troops landed farther north at Salerno, on the west coast south of Naples. The German response was to occupy Italy, take Italian soldiers prisoner, brutally put down any resistance, and most important, to resist the Allied landings. The Salerno beachhead was in danger of being overcome by the Germans in the first week, but Allied air and naval support carried the day. It would not be until October 1 that the Allies would enter Naples and begin the slow drive up the Italian peninsula toward Rome against strong German defensive positions.

*Unopposed landings on southern Arundel by 2nd Battalion, 172nd Infantry, on August 29, 1943.* [PHOTO: U.S. ARMY SIGNAL CORPS, SC 186126]

# 5

## *"The old 169th just keeps rolling along"*
### Arundel Island action
#### SEPTEMBER 1943

Arundel Island (now called Kohinggo Island) was probably named by Maine sailors after the town by that name in Maine. It is about ten miles long and five miles wide (Map 11). Arundel provided an approach to the nearby volcanic island of Kolombangara to the north, a Japanese stronghold, and the location of yet another Japanese airfield at Vila. The airfield was just across Blackett Strait from Arundel.

Since about August 29, the 172nd Infantry had been driving northward up both the east and west coasts (Map 11), intending to drive the Japanese from the island. Wilber's artillery, the 169th, initially supported this effort from its position near Munda airfield.

As the advance moved northward beyond the range of the 169th's howitzers, the battalion was moved northward in two sections to keep within artillery range of the action. On September 10, Battery A was emplaced on Bustling Point on the west side of Arundel; it would be part of a newly formed and named Provisional Battalion with the mission of providing interdiction fires on Kolombangara and support for American troops on Arundel. On September 11 and 12, Batteries B and C moved to Piru Plantation on Ondonga Island, which was really part of mainland New Georgia but isolated by a swamp. The latter move was made under combat conditions. The Bustling Point artillery was called the Western Force and the Ondonga artillery the Eastern Force. When firing on Japanese on Arundel, each force was firing toward the other, a highly unusual situation. [History Rpt of 169th FA Bn.; see also Barker, p. 100.]

Wilber first wrote of the Arundel action in letters to Valerie and me.

### SEPT. 7, 1943

Dear Daughter of Mine — There isn't much time today for me to write but at least I'll start a letter.… The Catholic medal [I enclose] may be of interest to you because I found it at the front. The Japs were very close (about fifty yards) and we had had a fire fight with quite a bit of business. I found this where there had been quite a few casualties and carried it myself all thru the rest of the Munda and Baanga actions.

Breakfast is coming, and then I'll have to go up to the Arundel I. front. That is the island we stand on when we want to spit on Kolombangara. It is also the same island that the Japs stand on when they want to spit at us. They spat a few times last night, and I want to be all ready if it develops into a real contest. Down here the fellow that spits the "fustest and furdest" gets along the easiest.… I love you. — Wilber, the ole man XXXXXOOOOO

x·o·ø·o·x

Wilber took note of my being on my own at a new school [St. Bernard's] for the first time and offered some fatherly advice. I am not sure I took it to heart. I probably thought I would not be making the mistakes he considered an inevitable part of life.

### SEPT. 9, 1943

Dear Son — You are probably starting another year of school next week. I want you to enjoy it and to make it a worthwhile session. It is going to be your first year on your own and you will be making decisions for yourself. I know you will make some wise and some not so wise decisions. However, I do want you to know that in either case I'll be on your side. We'll take care of the mistakes together. It will be a great year, I'm sure, and I want you to tell me about it when you can. I'm making an allotment of $5.00 a month to both you and Valerie. That will maybe take care of the extras so you won't have to ask Nana for any special funds. You can consider it as coming from my pay as a Lt. Col.

… Yesterday I went up to the island of Arundel.… I talked with a native and asked him if he saw any Japs. He said "me see Japs" "Jap, he good fella too." He told us where there was a spring of good water and probably had told the Japs too. I hope they don't try to use it the same time we do or someone may be hurt.

I must stop now and write to Norma. Good Luck, Old Top! I just heard Italy had surrendered [on September 3]! Someone must have scared them. — I love you, Wilber

Those monthly green government $5.00 checks (about $60 today) were very much welcomed by Valerie and me. In later letters, he asked us to record what we did with the money and to send him monthly reports. That turned out to be a futile request. However, it might have been why, during my college years, I kept a small notebook where I listed absolutely every penny I spent, always with an underlying fear that I would waste money and then find myself with none.

x · o · ø · o · x

Wilber wrote Norma the same day.

**SEPT. 9, 1943**
Hello There Dearest — Yesterday I was on Arundel Island. Probably some old Kennebunkport [Maine] sailor landed there years ago and named it. I'm back to the [our] area today but will go again [to Arundel] tomorrow....

Cronin gave a service to some natives on Roviana I. The church had no floor because the Japs had used the lumber. The natives sang all our hymns with the portable organ using their native tongue. Later one prayed in English. Afterward Cronin held a service for the soldiers of [Lt. Col. George M.] Hill's battalion [192nd FA] and they [the natives] attended. Then the Chief made a speech saying it was the first service they had had for two years and how much they appreciated what Cronin and the Americans had done by giving them this service. He ended by saying "We can do nothing to show our thanks. We have no planes, no ships, no tanks, no cannon. We can't fight, but we will help all we can. We will bring in the pilots that fall and the sailors that are wrecked and the soldiers that are wounded."

Since that service, there has been a steady stream of canoes bringing in U.S. pilots, sailors, + soldiers that have been missing. Recently it was a pilot with both legs fractured. He was down in a mangrove swamp and had no chance to live except that the natives brought him out. Another time they brought a cocoanut shell in which was written "Need immediate assistance. Men badly burned. Natives will guide you" Signed — Lt USN. The natives guided a rescue party out and saved nine lives. The practical Christianity of these so-called inferior people shines like a light while the two "civilized?" nations concentrate on death + destruction.

I'm sorry the moon just went behind a cloud and I can't see. This is probably pretty terrible [writing].... — I wish I were with you now. (Major W. Bradt) Love WB

Re X-mas I'm all set. WB

## COMBAT AND NEW LIFE    PART I: JUNGLE COMBAT

Writing by moonlight? His penmanship was larger and thus easily readable. They were in blackout conditions (no lights allowed) because they were in range of Japanese aircraft and artillery.

The rescued navy lieutenant was surely John F. Kennedy, whose patrol boat (PT-109) was sunk near Arundel on August 2. One never reads of Kennedy's rescue as possibly stemming from a Christian service offered by an army chaplain. In 1983, I spent a touching hour with two of Kennedy's rescuers in Bomboe Village; see the following Interlude.

x · o · ø · o · x

In early September, troops of the 172nd Infantry had reached northern Arundel and were encountering Japanese pockets of resistance. In response, the Japanese sent reinforcements into northern Arundel from Kolombangara Island. By September 10, small units of American and Japanese troops were in contact in the dense jungle of northern Arundel, but with no well defined lines. It was a confusing situation for both sides. American artillery, placed on either side of Arundel—the Western and Eastern Forces—relied on good forward observations so as not to injure friendly troops. It was the job of the artillery to get observers to these infantry units, not an easy task in the jungle terrain.

On September 13, Wilber accompanied a patrol to bring artillery support to an isolated American infantry unit and ended up at the command post of a completely different regiment (the 27th Infantry) at Bomboe Village in northwest Arundel (Maps 11 and 12). It consisted of a few huts on a ridge overlooking the volcanic Kolombangara Island three miles distant. From there Wilber directed the Western Force artillery on Bustling Point about one mile to the southwest, while DeBlois directed the Eastern Force at Piru Plantation.

After Wilber's arrival at Bomboe Village, the Japanese on Kolombangara sent troops to Arundel for a few days and then evacuated them for a day or two. Wilber's artillery was used to impede both actions, to support the infantry fighting on Arundel, and to bombard Kolombangara. It was a week full of high drama. One week after his last letter, he was in the midst of this action at Bomboe Village and gave Norma only hints of what was going on because of limited time and censorship. But greater detail was soon to come.

CHAPTER 5    *The old 169th just keeps rolling along*

*Ammunition being loaded onto a truck at Bustling Point, Arundel Island, September 24, 1943. These shells were for the 155-mm howitzers of the 192nd Field Artillery Battalion. Getting the shells to the guns was the hardest part of the job. The never-ending hard work was done by the enlisted artillerymen so much admired by Wilber.* [PHOTO: US ARMY SIGNAL CORPS, SC 259147]

*Howitzer (155-mm) of 192nd Field Artillery Battalion under camouflage netting at Bustling Point, Arundel Island, September 24, 1943. The gun is being loaded after firing a shell onto Japanese-held Kolombangara Island. The artillery at Bustling Point was the Western Force that Wilber was directing from Bomboe Village, September 15–22. The Japanese had completed their evacuation of Arundel on the night of September 21–22.* [PHOTO: U.S. ARMY SIGNAL CORPS, SC 182104]

COMBAT AND NEW LIFE     PART I: JUNGLE COMBAT

**SEPT. 16, 1943**

Darling Norma — Here I am on another island [Arundel] again. This is at least a scenic spot. From my bunk (yes I have one), I can see a great tall volcanic mountain [Kolombangara]. I'm glad to report it is an extinct one and beautiful. The white clouds hang around the top of the cone which is a little over a mile high. The sides are covered by the deep green of the jungle and the base by Japs. So I'm not doing any climbing over there.

Maw, I been shootin' some more Japs again. The old 169th [Field Artillery] just keeps rolling along. Now I'm with a regular [not national guard] army infantry regiment [27th]. I just happened to come out of the jungle on their side of this island; the troops I had been supporting were on the other side. There [on this side], this Colonel [Douglas Sugg, C.O. of the 27th Infantry Regiment] was, so I introduced myself and was practically "hired on the spot." Gen[erals] Wing + Barker heard I was here + sent word up that anything I said was OK was good with them. So we sowed a few seeds of wrath in the suburbs of the Jap areas and still are. However in this action I'm operating from a nice quiet comfortable rear C.P. with hot meals and a bed.

> The "169th just keeps rolling along" is adapted from the line, "And those caissons go rolling along," from the Field Artillery song popularized by John Phillip Sousa in 1918. Caissons were carts carrying ammunition chests that accompanied the cannon.

While I was on this recent trek [hike through the jungle], the rumor was out that I was trapped so if you hear any such story don't be concerned. As Mark Twain said "The report … is very much exaggerated." Your spikes were invaluable again and I thanked you for them several times. It's often the little things that make the difference between continued good health and the possibility of trouble. Being sure footed is a real help....

I feel fine and don't want you worrying about my wounds or health. This is better for me physically than teaching in a U. [University]

By the way Gen. Griswold [corps commander] again today told me I was doing a "fine piece of work here." Boy, Am I modest! However I do want you to know that the C.G. XIV Corps has so stated twice now. No raise in pay tho. I'm now an official associate "Wolfhound," as are all the personnel of this regiment [27th] because they were in Siberia in the last war.

Answering your letter of 12 Aug:

1. The 1st wound was, the second was not painful. Neither very bad. I wasn't brave. In fact I was scared like nobody's business. 2. I was not wounded a third time. Right now I have calluses on my bay-window [belly] from hugging the ground so hard the other day during an attack while I was coming thru the jungle. 3. The paper

CHAPTER 5   *The old 169th just keeps rolling along*

should have said the 25th, 37th, and 43rd Divisions were in the Munda battle. 4. My eyebrow [where wounded] has a hump in it covered entirely by the hair. I can feel it, but can't see it. Tough? I love you Sweet. Good night for now. Keep 'em turned up at the corners for me. — Wilber

Answering [your letter of] July 7. I got the film and pictures too. WB

x · o · ø · o · x

### Saturday [September 18?, 1943]
*Dear Mother — I am sending you the letters you sent me from Daddy. I do not know my weight and height. I do not have any vitamins.... I received the apple candy at camp. Thanks for the chocolate bar. I got the new clothes. I have only tried the hat....*

*I am going to go see Valerie Sunday afternoon (tomorrow). I am sorry about Cris [Washington State friend who was killed]. — Your loving son, Hale*

Norma was supplying needed items to all three of us—Wilber, Valerie, and me. She was the loyal distant provider. I didn't appear to be too distraught about Cris's death. I probably did remember him then, though I do not now.

I did get to see Valerie, and was pleased that I could give her some attention. I saw her only a few times that year. Her school, six miles distant, seemed far away. I could have arranged rides, I suppose, but people with autos were way above my place in the social pecking order, and gas rationing discouraged automobile use. Unfortunately, I did not appreciate how a brother's visits would have been valued by a "fatherless" younger sister.

x · o · ø · o · x

Wilber, still in Bomboe Village, wrote again to Norma.

### [BOMBOE VILLAGE] SEPT. 20, 1943
Hello Dearest — ... This is a lovely spot [Bomboe Village] but quite close to enemy artillery.... Oh yes, I'm now an artillery Lt. Col. and am very busy being congratulated. Gen. Wing said it had been a long time earned which I thought was one of the nicest compliments I had ever heard....

This present job is nearing completion and the 169th [Field Artillery] can say it has helped its fifth infantry regiment in battle. They were the 169th, 27th, 145th, 148th, and 172nd.

*Wilber (left), Maj. William N. Bailey, and Capt. Hugh E. Ryan on the occasion of Wilber's and Bailey's promotions (Wilber to lieutenant colonel and Bailey to major), on Arundel Island near the end of the action there, probably on September 20, 1943, when Wilber wrote of the promotion. This was the first time Wilber had worn the lieutenant colonel's leaves. Bailey was one of Wilber's officers in the 169th Field Artillery and temporarily commander of the Provisional Battalion on Bustling Point. Ryan (of the 192nd Field Artillery) was most likely also temporarily assigned to the Provisional Battalion.* [PHOTO: BRADT FAMILY]

I love you dearly, My Own. Don't be too lonely because I'm still with you. — XXXØØØ Wilber

Finally, the long deserved promotion had come through. He celebrated his first time wearing the silver oak leaves of his new rank by having his photo taken with two other officers.

Wilber's list of the regiments he supported did not include the 161st Infantry, his old Washington State unit, probably because the support was minimal and may not have been an official assignment. It was mentioned, though, in the commendation he received from Colonel Files after the Solomon actions and Wilber had mentioned firing in their support [letter 8/7/43].

Wilber guessed that Norma was lonely, which was surely the case, even if she was with Monte and his mother, Terkman. She was cut off from personal contact with everyone in her nuclear family, and could not share her situation with them or even with her own siblings. Nor did she have a close woman confidante she could turn to, except possibly Terkman; her closest friends in Maine and Washington certainly would have been equally constrained by societal norms and would not have taken the news of Norma's pregnancy lightly. Although Wilber was unaware of her true situation, he wanted to support her, but he could not spend much time dwelling on it; he was heavily occupied with artillery business.

On Arundel, during the night of September 20 and 21, the Japanese completed their evacuation, but with a large loss of life due to American fire. The battle was over. Kolombangara was the next target, but it would be bypassed. This completed the Solomon Island campaign for the 43rd Division. Wilber remained at Bomboe Village until September 26 when he returned to his battalion at Ondonga. There, his troops would have several months of decompression, rehabilitation, and training. This gave Wilber time to recollect and reflect on the just-completed three months of combat.

x · o · ø · o · x

On his last two days on Arundel, Wilber wrote to Valerie.

**SEPT. 25, 1943**
Hello there Tumblebug [Valerie] — This is a special letter to tell you I am now officially a lieutenant colonel of field artillery as well as the commanding officer of the 169th FA Bn. It has been a long time since I wrote you the secret that I was to be promoted. Since then I have been in three battles.… During the Arundel battle I received a radio message that I was a Lt. Col. so I jumped right into my foxhole to make it legal. So now you can call me "Colonel." I wish I could hear you do it for a Christmas present.

Our latest battle is over now and the radio has announced that Sagekarasa and Arundel Islands are now cleared of Japs. That is right except for a lot of dead ones. Sagekarasa I[sland] is also cleared of a lot of trees that I cut down around the Jap's ears.…

This is Sept. 26. My letters are always interrupted by something. Yesterday a letter written to you & Hale came back because I had used the N.Y. address. It is pretty old but I'll put it in with this one. It had gone to N.Y., then to Baltimore then to me.

Today I'm going back to my battalion and rest (?) for a while. The Battle of Arundel I. is over and I will go back to the rear until the next one starts. My job during battle is up front but we keep the guns back a good ways and hide them so the Japs cannot find them. Now that everything is quiet again I'll move them into a good place and let them settle down for a little sleep.… Good bye and good luck Precious. — I love you, XXXOOO, Wilber

# 6

## *"My whispering chorus of observers"*
### The Arundel Story
### September 1943

Exactly one month after combat ended on Arundel, Wilber sat down to tell the story of his Arundel adventures in four long letters written on three successive October days. He wrote them on Ondonga Island where his unit was recuperating and on defensive duty. It is, to my mind, a most remarkable account and the single most coherent extended story among all his letters. It features: a patrol he joined himself out of fear that he would lose yet another forward observer; firefights on that patrol; an infantry and tank attack; unorthodox artillery usage; and a jungle encounter with Admiral William Halsey and Massachusetts Senator Henry Cabot Lodge.

I present his account here stripped of unrelated material in the openings and closings of the four letters. That material will be presented later at its chronological place because it portrays the ambiance of Ondonga, not Arundel. Here is the first part of Wilber's Arundel Story, with headings I have added.

### [ONDONGA] OCTOBER 20, 1943 [A.M.]
Do not broadcast [i.e. do not publish]

Dearest Wife — It is nearly a month since the end of the Arundel Action so I can now describe some of the happenings in it for you.…

### [Background and Preparations]
Our part of the Arundel Action came quite unexpectedly. Another battalion of artillery [140th] from another division was rather casually supporting the infantry

regiment [172nd] that McCormick [C.O. of 103rd FA Bn.] usually supports. In other words, the Vermonters. They had gone thru most of Arundel and found very few Japs. This other division [25th] got orders to move out [to Arundel] just as Japs showed up all around the [172nd] infantry, and of course that took the artillery Bn.

My Battery A [169th FA Bn.] had just moved [September 10] up on the west side of Arundel [Bustling Point] to fire on the Japs on Kolombangara. The rest of my Bn. still sat peacefully near Munda, and this definitely wasn't my war. Six hours later I was looking for positions to fire on the Arundel Japs. We found the artillery [140th FA Bn.] busily firing, so busy in fact they didn't dare stop to let us move in. We had to go into their positions [September 11 and 12 on Piru Plantation] because there were no others. So we pulled one of their pieces out, moved one of mine in and registered it while they kept their others firing. Then we started our #1 pieces firing with their #3 and #4 of each battery and replaced their #2. We eventually replaced them "by piece" without interrupting the fire for the infantry even for one minute. The same thing was done with firing charts, phones, switchboards, etc. So we were in, and they were relieved [at 1:40 p.m., September 12; 169 FA Journal] and no one bothered. (This wasn't taught at [Fort] Sill [Field Artillery School]. It's horrible to do these things!)

> Relieving another battalion while firing was a tour de force. Each battalion had three batteries, each with four howitzers ("pieces"). The three #1 pieces of the 140th were replaced more or less simultaneously by the three #1 pieces of the 169th; then the three #2 pieces were replaced, and so on. Wilber's task, then, as battalion commander was to get forward observers and liaison officers to units that would need artillery support.

However, when it came to replacing their liaison parties and forward observer parties, the Japs and the navy were to be considered. There were three infantry units to be covered which I will call Item, Devine and Naylor, the last two being battalion commanders [3rd and 1st Battalions of the 172nd Infantry, respectively; Item refers to Company "I" of the 3rd Bn.] The most urgent was Item who was very much alone and pretty weak, so he needed artillery pretty badly. My predecessors had pulled out, and I had no boat to get in to Arundel. Anyway by about four P.M., I got a boat and took Lt. [Joseph W.] Mayne and three men to go to Item [as a forward observing party].

We went by this boat across Kula Gulf to a little island about the size of our lot at home, called "Devine's I," then by raft across a lagoon [Stima] to Arundel I. We landed on Carrigan's beach. Carrigan is also a Bn. CO [of 172nd Inf.], and it was his beach as long as he held it. By the time we were ashore and [had] met our infantry patrol to guide us to Item, it was 5:00 P.M. The patrol wasn't coming back, so I decided not to take Mayne to Item but to send him. When I said "Well, so long, and Good luck. Keep your head down." He looked awfully lonesome but plugged on up the trail, which was beginning to look pretty dim and full of shadows. I was worried until I returned to the FA Bn. C.P. [at Piru] because it was his first time up front, and I had wanted to be there then. However, when I got back he was already on the job and yelling for fire, so I knew he had really arrived.

On this same trip, I had taken Mushik and [Lt. Michael J.] Butler as far as Devine's I. and left them with Devine because it was too late to get them in to Naylor who was deep in the jungle near the other side. On this same day, [Col. David] Ross who was the regimental commander [172nd Infantry] had gone in to Naylor with one hundred seventy men, and that should have put everything under control.

> Mushik and Butler were additional forward observers. It was impressive that Ross, the infantry regimental commander, a full bird colonel, would go on such a mission with so few men. It may have set the stage for Wilber's subsequent actions.

The next morning [September 13], I had seen that DeBlois [managing the artillery at Ondonga] was all set and went over to start Butler and party in [to join] Naylor [as a forward observer]. Since I expected to walk in and return the same day, I only wore my shoulder holster [with .45 Colt pistol] and carried on my pants belt one canteen and left my pistol belt and aid kit and extra magazines and issue pistol at home. When I got to Devine, he told me Ross [Ross's unit] had been cut in two and that about a third of his men had returned to Item, but no one knew if Ross had gone through or was in serious trouble. Since firing had not been continuous it was assumed he had reached Naylor. Of course, all telephone wires were out [cut by the Japanese]. The Japs still occupied the trail. You have read of their "road blocks." This was one. He (Devine) was sending a small patrol around the block to lay a new wire to Naylor. It was to be 21 men. They were all men who had been or still were sick. Two officers were along. I looked at Butler with his big grin and all at once he looked just like Heidelberger to me. I remembered it was Sept. 13 just exactly a month since I had sent Heidelberger into Baanga. It wasn't so cheering for he had been the third officer I had sent in not to come out.

Consequently, I said to Butler, "You act as liaison to Devine, and give me your sulfanilamide and First Aid Packet." He did, and I picked up a grenade and away we went across the lagoon. Devine had protested a bit because of the danger, but I felt I couldn't face just then the idea of a fourth officer being killed on my orders. He said it would be individual fighting and every man for himself if we hit the Japs. Anyway I went, and he apparently tried to clear himself of the responsibility by phoning the news back to Division that he advised against it, for it turned out to be considered quite something back there.

This scene was amazing: a field artillery battalion commander voluntarily heading into a perilous situation with an infantry patrol because of his fear that one of his junior officers would be lost. This was not his job and would have been considered foolhardy and reckless. These were the same circumstances in which Heidelberger had been lost: an artillery observing party accompanying an understrength infantry company. This was an even smaller group, a patrol of 21 "sick" or recently sick men. I have no idea why the sick were chosen. Devine must have felt that all other available troops were critically needed elsewhere. The 172nd Journal states simply that "0755: Haffner and a party of 15 EM [enlisted men] left for Naylor's Bn. with a 284 [field radio] and [telephone] wire...."

The discrepancy in numbers might suggest that Wilber had a party of artillery with him, for example a radioman, but he later explicitly states that he did not. If so, he intended to work as a solitary forward observer at his destination. Why would Wilber have taken this impulsive and, some would say, ill-advised action? Surely the loss of Butler would have been more than he wanted to face. Perhaps there was also at play a taste for risk and adventure.

### [Walk into Arundel, September 13]

The trip to Naylor was a most interesting experience. It was probably not over three miles air line but it took from 9:00 A.M. to 6:00 P.M. The officers were Capt. Haffner in command and Capt. Shreve who was rejoining his company. They are two of our most competent [infantry] officers, so you see I was in expert hands. We also had with us a Coast Guard boy who had been running the boat I had been using. He had been a bit of a nuisance by frequently asking if he couldn't take me clear to Kolombangara every time I stepped in his boat. [Kolombangara Island was held by the Japanese!] He had apparently asked once too often if he could go on patrol. Anyway, after we were well in the jungle I saw him stumbling along in the file carrying a borrowed rifle and very pleased with himself and obviously worried by the fact that no one would even believe he had really gone in the jungle with the infantry.

> Wilber introduced a bit of comedy about the coast guardsman into this tense situation and continued to play on it as the patrol proceeded. Regrettably, he never gave us the sailor's name.

We carried telephone wire [on a large spool] and laid it as we went, also a radio, for Naylor's seemed to be out. This, and the fact the men were not well and the need to go quietly, is why we went so slowly. I stayed near the radio in the file because that was my way to get DeBlois to put fire where I needed it. If we got cornered, I expected to get artillery fire on all sides and let the Japs figure the next move. That meant I had to know where I was all the time. There was no trail, guessing distance was mainly guess, and all I could do was take compass directions to the sound of my guns. Altho that varied a bit, I at least could tell something of my location.

We traveled in a single file, sometimes five, sometimes three, paces apart. The distance was controlled from the lead and was passed back by hand signals and whispers.

Sometimes the jungle is just a forest of huge trees, sometimes it is heavy bush, sometimes long grass-like plants [that] are barbed, and vines are common. Often coral is so rough, one must watch each step or risk a broken ankle and a bad fall; at other places the ground is easy walking, or on the contrary swampy and soggy. We went thru all these types during that day. We traveled west and in so doing crossed three different recent Jap trails going N–S [north–south]. Consequently we knew there could be Japs in any part of the Jungle near there. The trails indicated quite large groups. All in all, we were quite all right. One thought continually about three things: First, where do I set this foot next and how to do it most quietly; second, is there on either side of me now a long enough open space for a Jap to find a lane of fire for a machine gun, and, if so, is there one in that place; and third, if a Jap machine gun opens up on us where do I jump for a hole and cover.

It all boiled down to that. If you walked quietly and securely you could fight or withdraw. If you saw the possible gun positions the Japs could use, you at least didn't loiter there. And if you did know where to jump at the first shot you could face the next on even terms. The nervous strain of such a trip must be terrific for a nervous type or the imaginative type of individual. At the end of the day I was exhausted as if I had walked twenty miles because of this strain.

After we had gone along for about four hours, we tried to cut back to the trail thinking we were west of the block. It was a bit embarrassing to walk right into a Jap camp. We did and we were. We don't know yet how many there were, but we saw five and heard a lot of chopping farther in. The ones we saw were evidently sentries, but our being quiet paid well. Haffner wanted badly to shoot the five but his orders were definite "To avoid combat and get to Naylor," so we pussyfooted back a ways and I mean pussyfooted. Compared to us a cat would have sounded like a horse walking on a tin roof.

The Coastguardsman's legs looked a bit limber by this time but he came right along with his freckled face looking mighty serious too. Anyway we were off again until our wire was nearly gone, and we cut back to the trail a second time, very cautiously, too. We saw no Japs but they had been there. Those Japs had been pretty conscientious about the way they cut our wire. There had been about six U.S. telephone wires along that trail. We followed that trail west for more than a mile and all wires were cut as often as every twenty yards. So we telephoned to Devine [that] we

COMBAT AND NEW LIFE    PART I: JUNGLE COMBAT

*Major (later General) William H. Naylor (left), C.O. 1st Battalion, 172nd Infantry, at the end of the Arundel campaign, September 28, 1943, and at the August 1983 meeting of the 43rd Infantry Division Association. Wilber's small party joined Naylor's "depleted battalion" during its walk into Arundel.* [PHOTOS: WILLIAM NAYLOR AND HALE BRADT]

were going on and left our wire end tied to a tree as a monument of good old U.S. underestimation [They had come to the end of their roll of wire.].

**[With Naylor's battalion (1st Battalion, 172nd Infantry), September 13–14]**
That evening just before dark we reached Naylor, and I think he appreciated my being there. At least two of his men dug a hole for Haffner and me. Naylor said Ross had not shown up, so that deepened the mystery, and Naylor and I decided not to use artillery on that account except in an emergency. He [Naylor] had been attacked seven times the preceding day and was low on ammunition and rations but had a local water supply. However he expected a quiet night because the Japs had left booby traps around him. It was a quiet night. We radioed our arrival back to Devine and went to bed in our hole. No noise, no rain, and it was a pretty good night.

The next morning [September 14], Devine radioed that Ross had returned to Carrigan beach with his group and that we were pretty much on our own. Ross was to have brought more ammo and supplies, so it didn't look so good. Next we were told to join the 27th Inf. [Regiment], which had landed on the west shore of Arundel at Bomboe Village. That was all right except they had a strong group of Japs in front of them and between them and us. Also getting two fighting units together in the jungle without shooting each other up isn't done by the "Yoo Hoo!" method. So it was arranged by radio for us to fire an automatic rifle for ten rounds each fifteen minutes so [Col.] Sugg's patrol (27th) could find us. It worked too, except all the Japs around found us too, which was OK if we liked it.

> Colonel Douglass Sugg was C.O. of the 27th Infantry Regiment. He had set up his command post at Bomboe Village on the northwest tip of Arundel, just north of Bustling Point where the Western Force artillery was emplaced.

The next thing that happened this day of surprises and guesses was for a friendly patrol to walk in [from the east, possibly from Devine] saying there were no Japs on the trail. They had come straight thru and seen none. We were a bit nonplussed, but then it could be true. So Naylor sent three wounded back with Haffner who was supposed to return [back to Devine] with his 21 and the C.G. [coast guard] man. They started out on the back trail, and Shreve and I stayed with Naylor. The coastguardsman had a look in his face of wanting to feel a boat under his feet again.

About two that afternoon a Lt. and about a dozen men came thru from Sugg. They had found a trail through a swamp around the Japs and laid a telephone wire so we could talk to Sugg about how and when to join him. Before anything could be done about moving, a scout reported a heavy Jap group coming down the old trail. Everyone checked up on rifle and ammunition and fox-holes. I shared mine with this Lt. from Sugg.

> The patrol from Sugg reported finding "a very depleted composite [American] Battalion of about 250 men suffering from fatigue and shortage of rations." [Operations report, 27th Rgt., p. 60.]

The Japs opened up on us a short time later with the heaviest small arms fire I ever underwent. They were on our front and one flank. It was really something to watch and hear. It would have been very comforting to use artillery but of course Haffner was out there somewhere, so that was only a last resort. So I lay there and tried to see the situation as clearly as possible just in case I should suddenly find myself in command. That is one of the hazards of being a Field Officer. The boy who dug my hole really dug it for the Thin Man. I bulged badly and some Jap has his eye on my general location. Every time I'd look up he would begin to spatter me with twigs and dirt. He wasn't a good shot, but I didn't know I could count on it, so I bobbed now and then. The attack started with heavy Jap fire and then was increased by ours, matched by ours, and finally smothered by ours. Do you remember the old correspondence courses about fire superiority? We took it away from them and they were thru for the time being. All was quiet. Naylor was passing inquiries around about ammunition and the answers were all bad.

Just then, from our free flank, in came Haffner. He had gone down the trail, met some Japs, had a fight, come back up the trail found Japs on that side of him, had another fight with Japs on two sides, pulled out into the jungle, and just gotten back to us in time to find us in another fight. The coastguardsman was still along. His legs looked like cooked macaroni, they were so limber, and he carried that rifle as if he had suddenly found it was his best friend. He looked now as if he never expected to see the sea again.

The Japs didn't wait long to get going again. This time they opened up with a few good college yells, which were variously interpreted as "Banzai" but didn't sound like it to me. It sounded a bit like "Yea! Yea!" and I halfway expected it to end in "Yale" or "Purdue" or "Wash. State". However they didn't know all the words, and away we went thru the routine again. By this time, I knew where all our troops were – Devine, Ross, Haffner, Item, [and] Sugg; and I could use the artillery. However the radio was torn down and [ready for the] move to Sugg. It was good tho to know I could, for I knew I would get a chance soon. The Japs added a few acts to their show this time such as more machine guns and some of our own mortar shells they had "collected" somewhere. One burst in a tree over me again reminding me of the deficiencies of my fox hole. It didn't do any damage and pretty soon we had the Japs silenced again.

Now we moved to join Sugg. A rear guard kept fire on the Japs to hold them down, and Naylor's men started out. I watched this group and that leave, until I began to wonder if I was the rear guard; but [I] finally decided to stay with the radio [when its carrier left]. I was no good away from it anyway. This time it was the same thing as to quiet and order, but the Jap mortar shells kept coming near and kept one from worrying too much about little things.

It was on this move that we went thru a swamp that surpassed all my ideas of swamps. It was deep, slimy, stinking, sticky, sucking mud under about six inches of very nasty water. There were vines and rotten logs to climb over and really every step was over crotch deep. Several times I doubted if I could pull a leg out of the depth to which it had sunk. It would have been a bad place to have the Japs open up on me. However, they didn't, probably because our rear guard kept them busy where they were. Neither did their mortar shells cause any casualties because of no good observation, altho I walked thru several shell holes. About 4:00 P.M. we reached Sugg or rather one of his battalions [2nd Bn., C.O. Lt. Col. B. F. Evans].

> Wilber had now reached an infantry battalion of a regiment (27th) belonging to a different division (25th). With Evans, the infantry battalion commander, were two 43rd Division artillery officers, Lieutenant Wild and 1st Lt. Ewart M. Blain; both were well known to Wilber. They were temporarily assigned to the Provisional Battalion on Bustling Point and were acting as liaison or forward-observer officers to Evans's battalion. Wild had returned to duty after treatment for the wound he had received in the Munda action.

**[With Evans's battalion (2nd Bn., 27th Inf.), September 14–15]**
I found Wild and Blain with him [Evans], and we started to do business. I knew where the Japs were and where all our troops were so it was a set up. No sooner had we started [firing artillery] than Ross, Wing and Barker all ordered us to cease fire! I radioed that I was doing it and asked for authority to resume fire. So Wing and Barker radioed back that all fires approved by Bradt were OK. They were too. So we slept quietly another night. When I showed up, Lt. Wild said, "Who is with you?" I said "No one!" He said "Haven't you any party?" I said, "Nope, have you a place for me to sleep?" He did and I did under a bush.

The next morning (Sept. 15) Haffner went back by boat. The coastguardsman looked pretty cheerful about that and very well pleased with himself as a veteran. I told Haffner to write a note signed officially that he had been on that patrol and in three fire fights and had conducted himself well. He told me later he had done it and that Ross too had added to it. No doubt that coastguardsman is most unpopular in his unit. The same morning I started back by water to the 169th FA Bn., but Sugg kidnapped me. That is the next chapter, and in the meantime I love you Sweet girl of mine. — Your Husb. Wilber

COMBAT AND NEW LIFE    PART I: JUNGLE COMBAT

x · o · ⌀ · o · x

Later in the evening, writing under a gasoline lantern, Wilber picked up the story in a second letter.

**OCT. 20, 1943**
**[En route Bomboe Village]**

Yes Dearest I'm back again — … Now back again to the lives and loves of WEB in the Arundel action. On the morning [Sept. 15] after Naylor had succeeded in joining one of Sugg's Bns, I busied myself about getting back to my own Bn. I was on the west side on Arundel while DeBlois and the battalion except [Battery] "A" were across six miles of jungle and two or three miles of the Kula Gulf [to the east]. Btry "A" was under [Capt. Richard N.] Rainey and was detached from my Bn. and placed under a provisional one commanded by [Major William N.] Bailey [who also was detached from Wilber's Battalion]. I had no authority over Bailey [who reported directly to General Barker] and Rainey, but did have quite a bit of influence especially in Barker's absence. So I started west to get to the west shore and then to catch a boat around the south end of Arundel up thru Diamond Narrows to Ondonga I. where DeBlois was. That was over fifteen miles and looked like a day's job.

About eight A.M., I left Naylor who had been assigned only passive jobs until his men had a couple of days rest and started walking back [westward] along the telephone lines. This is the easy way to get back and forth between friendly units. It was about a half hour walk along a ridge, then a half hour ride in a long narrow lagoon in a boat much like we used to rent at Spirit Lake. The water varied from twelve inches to six feet deep. Sometimes the soldier running it had to lift the outboard motor nearly out of the water to clear the coral. At the next stop, I shifted to a bigger personnel boat of the smallest type used for landing operations [LCVP?] and went still further along the deeper end of the lagoon to Bomboe Village where Sugg had his regimental Command Post (C.P.).

I do wonder about the wisdom of walking alone between units.

This long lagoon (Map 12) was a lovely place. The water was clear and full of fish and interesting coral. The edges were mangrove swamp. A mangrove is a tree of about six to twenty legs. During the next days, I made numerous trips up and down this lagoon and grew to know its beauty spots. The sun shone in early morning along its length and gave it color and brightness and an impression of security far beyond the reality. Occasionally a trail would go into the jungle from the lagoon, and we knew they had been Jap routes a week or so before.

CHAPTER 6   *My whispering chorus of observers*

*"Lion" Command Post (large tent barely visible behind the house) of the 27th Infantry Regiment at picturesque Bomboe Village, Arundel Island, September 13, 1943. Wilber arrived there on September 15 and remained until September 26. "Lion" (sign on tree) was a code name for the regiment, which was known publicly as the "Wolfhounds" after its service in Siberia during World War I.* [PHOTO: U.S. ARMY SIGNAL CORPS, SC 263807]

*Soldiers resting and reading newspapers under native-built homes in Bomboe Village, Arundel Island, September 13, 1943. I visited Bomboe in May 1983 and conversed with villagers in the shade under one of these homes. The command post of the 27th Infantry Regiment is behind the house to the left.* [PHOTO: U.S. ARMY SIGNAL CORPS, SC 263535]

*The mile-high inactive volcano, Kolombangara, reaching into the clouds, viewed from Arundel Island across Blackett Strait, 1983.* [PHOTO: IAN WARNE]

### [Bomboe Village (Command Post of 27th Infantry), September 15–26]

I arrived at Bomboe Village about ten o'clock [the morning of September 15] and went up to report to Sugg on what I knew of the forces opposing him. His C.P. was in a beautiful spot on the end of the ridge that made Bomboe peninsula and formed the lagoon I had just traveled. The climb up from the landing was a stairway of rock, lined with red-leaved shrubs and green-leaved shrubs bearing red and yellow flowers. The Village proper consisted of a half dozen abandoned native type houses and a lovely garden of bananas, lime trees, papaya trees, vegetables and fruits I did not know and many shrubs and trees obviously planted for beauty or novelty. This ridge ended here and one could look south at the jungle of Arundel, west into Wana Wana Lagoon at scores of islets and the most beautiful sunsets reflected from the sky to the water. To the north across Blackett Strait was the mile high inactive volcano Kolombangara and on the side near us, Vila Airfield. Kolombangara was so near it seemed to lean over us and to be watching our every move. The shores were so close one could see without glasses if the Japs we saw were wearing headgear or not, if the headgear was big enough.

It, Bomboe, was truly a lovely spot and must have been something particularly special before the war. I was told a missionary had lived there for years and developed

CHAPTER 6    *My whispering chorus of observers*

*Colonel Douglas Sugg (right), C.O. 27th Infantry Regiment, explaining to Captain Van Tusk where and how he wanted a mortar barrage laid down, September 13, 1943.* [PHOTO: U.S. ARMY SIGNAL CORPS, SC 395879]

*Infantrymen of the 27th Infantry Regiment wading to Stepping Stone Island from which they could access the center of Sagekarasa Island where the Japanese were entrenched at both ends. Arundel, September 13, 1943.* [PHOTO: U.S. ARMY SIGNAL CORPS, SC 186142]

it. However as a C.P., it was a bit public so far as the Japs were concerned and they did shell it now and then according to the reports I received on the way thru.

Col. Sugg turned out to be most cordial [and] was very interested in what I could tell him about the situation in front of his regiment. It developed that he had another battalion [3rd] then on one of the fringing islands [Sagekarasa Island] still closer to Kolombangara. This Bn. was commanded by one [Maj. Charles W.] Davis who had earned the Congressional Medal of Honor and was at the moment holding the middle of this island with Japs holding each end. It was quite long but narrow and he had entered thru a swampy connecting island which we called Stepping Stone Island. The long one was Sagekarasa I.

When I inquired of Sugg about boats, he said "Oh, but you're staying here, Major." I allowed as how I'd like to, but that my war was on the other side. His answer was that he had no artillery advisor and he wanted me and needed me. So I said OK I'd check with Barker when he came up to see Bailey. I moved into Sugg's tent with his S-3 and Exec. [Lt. Col. George E. Bush], brushed some of the mud off my denims, borrowed his razor and installed a phone, also borrowed. That afternoon Bailey told me Barker was coming up to see me, and he showed up at Bomboe a little later. He was a bit surprised to find me moved in, but Sugg put up a pretty strong case for my staying. Barker asked me what I thought, so I told him DeBlois could handle the "Eastern Force" all right, so I was glad to help out. So I was put in direct support of Sugg and a regular army regiment with less [F.A.] equipment and personnel than I had ever used in combat. Barker did go in his boat and get some of my officers and their parties and bring them around to me. He also brought Swan, and Swan brought my roll, clean clothes, toilet articles, and I was all OK the next day (Sept. 16, I think).

**[Dodging Japanese shells]**
That day was pretty well wasted by the time I was definitely told I could stay and had done a little of the preliminary cleaning up of Bradt. Sugg's tent was laid out with his bunk on one side, Bush's on the other and all the center was a double fox hole. His S-3 and I were under a fly at the end of his tent. I was told that in case the Japs shelled us during the night, I should get in the Colonel's hole too. I accepted the offer and went to bed on a real cot under blankets, no mosquito bar, but no mosquitos. It is a pretty general custom for the Jap artillery to fire with one gun and to fire about three to five shells very rapidly with very small or no shifts. Consequently if one shell comes by, one expects the other two quite suddenly.

I had these little customs in the back of my mind as I went to bed as well as an idea that the beauty of Bomboe was a poor reason for not being behind the ridge instead of on top of it. In the dark of the night, I woke with a loud, very close and very fast "Whish" ringing in my ears. It also seemed to me that it had practically gone under my bunk, which made it seem quite logical for me to be sailing thru the air. I recall thinking how glad I was to have remembered just where that foxhole was. Sure enough, just as I landed in the bottom of the hole, the next shell went over, well over the bunk too. After that I was a bit embarrassed to find Col. Sugg and Lt. Col. Bush and the S-3 following me into the hole. I had had the farthest to go, but had arrived first by a good lead. The next day there was quite a bit of kidding about my efficiency and also the fact that all one end of the bank [of dirt] was knocked down where I had ended my trip by a slide that would have done any baseball player credit. In fact the story was so good, most of the generals that strayed by were regaled with it to everyone's fun.

> More humor in the trenches! Wilber told me after his return home that the soldiers who failed to take the little precautions were more likely to be killed. For example, when taking a compass bearing, one needed to keep the mirror covered except for a brief instant, lest the enemy see the sun's reflection from it. Other examples he noted were wearing a helmet, not walking on an exposed ridge, and moving rapidly to a foxhole. Wilber had a very healthy interest in staying alive.

The days are a bit blurred that I spent with Sugg so I'll deal more with events than days. The first day or so were used in preparation for a main push and the getting up of supplies. We did some firing of a routine type and I placed officers and parties with all three of Sugg's Bn.s. Two officers BeBlois sent over were pretty new. One so new that forty-eight hours after he reached the 169th, he was in combat under fire with Mushik. Of course Mushik is my standby and the only officer in the Bn. with more front line service than myself, so this new officer, [Lt. W. H.] Van Camp, was in good hands. The other [Mike Butler?] I put on an island we call "No. 1" because it was next to [west of] Sagekarasa and only fifty yards from the Japs (Map 12). There were other observers on other islands, some also close to the Japs. Each observer whether infantry or artillery had a phone and could report to the C.P. anything he saw. About this time the moon began to be very bright so we could see. Jap planes would fly over at night looking for our batteries and troops. One of the regular visitors was a float plane. It would set down in Blackett Strait and once taxied near our C.P. for a takeoff. We nearly ruined ourselves that day getting an antitank gun where we could fire out at it, if the pilot did it again. He didn't.

### [Artillery against boats and planes]
In the evening I would have all the observer phones and my phone to the Bailey Fire Direction Center [at Bustling Point] connected into a big party line. Just about dark

the reports would start, usually in whispers so the Japs wouldn't hear them speak. Because the Davis Bn. [on Sagekarasa Island] had woken up one morning to find two Jap machine guns everywhere there had been [only] one the evening before, we decided the big artillery job was to prevent or make expensive Jap reinforcement of their Sagekarasa forces. That became my chief occupation, and it was all night work. As I said, at dark the whispered reports would come in. "Major, I see a light on Devil's Island" or "Major, A boat is coming out of Bere Cove." or "Major, three barges are going east past Vila Point" or "Major! Six barges just left Devil's Island coming this way!" or "Major! A plane is coming!" or "Major the Japs are doing some talking on Sagekarasa" and so it went from dark until two or three in the morning.

These messages came fast. Sugg had a monitor on the party line who kept a time record of all reports and an abstract of action taken. It would show entries every one or two minutes for periods of four continuous hours. Sugg showed it to most of the visiting generals, and since I was furnishing the action, every other entry mentioned what I did and the artillery fire. We fired at boats when they came out of coves, when they passed points, when they tried to hide in Vila River, when they went to Devil's Island, and then gave them our barrages when they tried to land on Sagekarasa. I'll never forget my whispering chorus of observers. They would get excited and tell me to "Hurry! Hurry!" and I'd say "It'll leave when we get shifted." and "Don't forget the cannoneers do the work, we just see the results" or some other comment.

The effect of our fire in actually sinking the barges was not too encouraging. As the news would say, I had four downed and several "probable." Near misses were common and they played hob [caused mischief] with the Jap morale. Those barges would run all up and down the coast of Kolombangara with us dropping shells around them every time they stopped or passed a point on which we had adjusted. One night we completely broke up three organized efforts to get boats across to Sagekarasa. The Japs on Devils Island would signal with lights to those in Sagekarasa so we stopped that too. When barges would get close, the Japs in Sagekarasa would get excited and talk and jabber, so we would stop that too.

Once an observer said there was a light on Devil's Island, so I said to Bailey "Put out the light on Devil's Island." Pretty soon four shells landed on D.I. and the light was out. Sugg had never seen artillery used to put out lights before. When I used it to keep the Japs from talking too, he proclaimed that we were the most aggressive artillery support he had ever seen, and he liked it too, and he told all the generals that too. Another time the float plane went into Bere Cove and we started firing on it. We were using a 6-inch [155 mm] battery at the time and it was too slow, but we scared that pilot so bad or crippled his plane for he never did come back to either Blackett Strait or anywhere else around Arundel. That too caused a lot of publicity except the instructors at Sill would probably have court martialed me if they ever heard of it. Barker said, "It used to be the tanks, then boats, now planes. What's next for artillery?"

**[Tank attack, September 17]**
By such means we stopped the Jap reinforcements, and after two nights had Blackett Strait under control. In the mean time, we moved in some tanks manned by marines. There are two types of marines that I like to consider as good soldiers. Those in tank companies and the so-called Defense battalions with the big coast defense guns. Those two types are really OK. A Capt. Carlson commanded these tanks, and he and his men were really on the job. In the first place, it was tough getting the tanks into Arundel anywhere near the front. A Chinese officer, Capt. Chak, built the roads and piers and did that in a very short time. Then Carlson came in, and we went up front to see where his tanks could jump off. Next he sneaked them in quietly, if you can imagine a tank going in quietly, so the Japs would be surprised.

It's a real job to keep control of tanks in the jungle because of the brush, which keeps them from seeing each other. However it was done and well. I enjoyed watching

*Marine tank crew, September 1943, on Arundel Island. The marines supported the 27th Infantry in Arundel with tank attacks on September 17, 18, and 19. Wilber observed and described the first attack.* [PHOTO: U.S. ARMY SIGNAL CORPS]

a Regular Army regiment prepare for a battle because they were so business-like about things. They didn't make mistakes amateurs would make. Neither did they hurry. They just worked at things until they were sure they were set, then started the real fight. There were three such fights and of course every so often the Japs had to be slapped back because they still had the idea they were on the offensive and we on the defensive. I'll tell you of the actual battles later. My night activities lasted about five [six?] nights [Sept 15–20] of which the first two the Japs tried to get reinforcements in to Sage[karasa] and Arundel and the last two they were trying to get out. I, being a conservative about such things, opposed both efforts.

It's ten o'clock now Lover and I must get to bed. I love you, My wife. — XXXOOO Wilber

x·o·ø·o·x

The next evening, after a day of personal labor in setting up his tent at a new location, Wilber continued the story in a third letter. Japanese troops were still on the mainland of northern Arundel on September 16, as well as on the offshore island of Sagekarasa. To remove the Japanese, the 27th Infantry (2nd Battalion) attacked eastward early on September 17.

## OCT. 21, 1943
### [Tank attack, September 17, continued]
Darling of My Dreams — … The night before the first attack by Sugg's regiment was a busy one for me. I was up all night controlling and directing fire against boats, etc. It was my second such night, and Col. Sugg was worried about me and had planned for me to sleep during the day. When he started up to the front lines [the morning of the attack] I climbed into the boat too. After all, so far I had been living in the lap of luxury so far as combat was concerned. My C.P. was a comfortable bunk under canvas, which had not been true in Munda or Baanga. I sat or lay on my bunk and listened and talked over the phone. It was so interesting, I couldn't have slept anyway. So I went back up the lagoon [by boat] with Sugg that A.M. It was lovely and quiet and peaceful, and the sun and water were fresh and clean and cheerful. We thought (and correctly) the Japs didn't know we had tanks nor that we expected to attack that morning.

When we reached the trail I had come down, the engineer officer had built a road thru the jungle. It was my second trip back to the front, and this time it was well marked with the wide tracks of the tanks. The plan of attack included artillery fire on the Japs' position for a half hour; then the tanks and infantry were to go over the top; only here it isn't over the top. We go in. At the same minute, my fires were

CHAPTER 6     *My whispering chorus of observers*

*Colonel Douglas Sugg (2nd from left) in a boat on a lagoon near Bomboe on September 13, 1943. Wilber rode with Sugg on this boat several times, though not this day.* [PHOTO: U.S. ARMY SIGNAL CORPS, SC 395878]

to lift to a point six hundred yards behind the Japs and continue to fire. We, that way, gave the tanks room to play in and blocked the Japs chance to retreat down the trail. All the plans were made, and our fire adjusted the day before, so now it was all on schedule, and we would soon know about the plans of mice and men.

One could infer from this that Wilber's visit to the front was strictly out of curiosity, and possibly ill advised, especially since he mentioned no specific contribution he made. However it had always been his practice to stay near the action and the infantry commander, in this case Colonel Sugg, so he could rapidly adapt his artillery to a changing situation.

As we left the "put-put" boat and walked up the road thru the jungle, my shells began to whisper over our heads and we could hear them crash into the trees up ahead of us. The road wound around the trees and gulches and rocky ridges so that we missed the Bn. C.P. and reached the front lines quite unexpectedly just as the attack jumped off. My shells were landing about three hundred yards in front of our lines; then without warning except that I knew it was time, the bursts moved much farther away from us. The whispering and wishing overhead went on just the same, except all at once a real bedlam broke loose.

The six tanks moved out with their machine guns and canister firing. All the machine guns in our lines started mowing down the bushes ahead of them and Tommy guns, auto rifles and M 1 rifles started searching for Japs. Our men ignore the tanks and fire at and around where they are, because the marines inside the tanks are safe, and fire close to them protects the tanks from any Jap trying to slip or throw mines under them.

Of course, the Japs also opened up with everything they had too, and there was some pretty heavy fire going both ways for a few minutes. We were pinned down for this period on the edge of the road but in no particular danger. Since a lot of fire was coming against us from one flank, Sugg decided to bring up some extras. So we ran back to his supply dump where he grabbed all men with rifles and started them forward. Just then, word came back that everything was under control, so we went back up front. He didn't mention his lack of confidence to his Bn. C.O. either. I didn't tell.

> A commander should have the self-restraint not to second-guess his subordinate commanders, while at the same time knowing when it was important to intervene. The choice was often not a clear one.

The Japs had broken and taken to cover. As soon as their fire stopped, our men moved in and the Japs left. They don't face tanks, especially surprise tanks. Neither do they all prefer to die to retreat [prefer dying to retreating]. This was the 13th Jap Inf., the so-called "Flower of South Japan," supposedly one of their two best regiments, but they didn't even pretend to fight it out. However they did withdraw well and saved most of their machine guns and weapons.

> There were also tank attacks on the two following days, September 18 and 19. On the 18th, the two American tanks participating were disabled by Japanese antitank gunfire [Estes, p. 52]. (One of those tanks was still, in 1983, sitting where it stopped in the jungle.) The Japanese, "encouraged by this success, counterattacked and were thrown back with heavy losses" [Ops. of the 27th Inf. Rgt. p. 62]. The Japanese battalion commander facing the Americans was Col. Seishu Kinoshita, whom I interviewed in March 1983, shortly before I visited Arundel, as I recount in the following Interlude.

### [General Griswold visits]

We went into the captured area and discussed the situation with the Bn. C.O. Our troops were getting set for either a counterattack or a second attack depending on what they found. Platoon leaders were patrolling to see where the Japs were, and information was coming in to the Bn. C.O. from all directions. The tanks were back for ammunition.

As we sat there discussing the situation, [General] Griswold came up with some of his staff. He wanted to go thru the Jap area to see how it had been organized and to get a Jap light machine gun for Admiral Halsey. So we went around on a tour of the battlefield [with Griswold] while it was still smoking. It was interesting, but of course we really were pretty conscious that we were a guard for G. and kept our eye on him. I found his machine gun and it was sent back for him. Later we went thru the Jap officers' quarters and C.P. and most of the area.

One of G's staff whom I asked to hold my pistol was shocked to find that I had left the safety off and mentioned it. When I snapped it off again when I took it back, he asked why. My answer was that if there were Japs behind "those bushes" (20 yards away), I didn't want to feel silly. He looked a bit serious then and very much so when, a few minutes later, some were found behind some bushes less than fifty yards away. To make a good story, I should say that he hasn't been back since, but he has and [has been] better alerted too. Later we went back to a foxhole while those Japs were being cleared out of another area and talked and ate some rations. G chased one of his staff away and included me in the group (4) [of four persons]. It was a nice thing to do and definitely not necessary or even to be expected. It was a few days later at a dinner for Lodge and Halsey that Barker said G. had said of me that he always seemed to find Bradt where things were the busiest. Barker was quite pleased.

All these things take time, and in the Jungle things pretty well stop moving by three P.M. because of the need to be all organized by dark, and so we started back to the village. G. was pretty well pleased about the day's work and was very anxious about the final count on Jap dead. It was pretty satisfying too. He said he felt particularly good because the Jap regimental commander had become almost a personal adversary and this should set Colonel Tomonari back a bit. Tomonari was killed by a shell the next day [September 18].

> Yes, it was all in a "day's work" to best your "personal adversary." Colonel Satoshi Tomonari was the revered commander of the highly regarded Japanese 13th Infantry Regiment, known as, Wilber wrote, the "Flower of South Japan."

## [Sagekarasa Island]

For the next day [September 18] we had decided to clear the west end of Sagekarasa I. The east end had been cleared by this time [by 2:00 P.M. of September 18] without much trouble, but the west end was strongly held by the Japs. I told you our

[3rd] Bn. C.O. [Davis] there had woken up one morning to find two machine guns looking at him wherever there had been one. We had no chance to get tanks into this scrap because of a swamp where we approached the I[sland].

However we planned to use a lot of mortar and artillery fire before and during the attack. After another night like my earlier ones – lots of business whispers – I went down with Butler [probably on Island #1] to adjust the artillery fire. It was Mike's first time with real soldiers in the way. He struggled thru it OK tho, in spite of my presence. It was really difficult because our troops were attacking toward his guns, and he seemed to be firing at his own lines.

That doesn't really make a difference except mentally. His real trouble was the narrowness of the island and the fact that it was crooked. He had a heck of a time hitting it. Shells would fall on his side in the water and he would shift, and "Old Man Dispersion" would step in and put it in the water on the other side. However he got a series of concentrations adjusted along the length of the Jap held position. Just to keep the Japs from being able to predict us, this attack started at noon [at 3:45 P.M. according to the 3rd Battalion operations report]. We blasted the Japs, the mortars did the same, and the infantry moved just one hundred yards and stopped. The Japs were really dug in deep, and there were a lot left yet. We dropped back.

So I spent another whispering night blasting the reinforcements Togo [the Japanese] was trying to get over to Sagekarasa. We still fired on them whenever they showed a light or talked. That must have made them wonder how we knew when they were talking. They apparently never guessed our OP [observing post] was only thirty or forty yards away [on Island #1] nor realized how sound carried across water. Anyway we maintained quiet in the Jap ranks and sunk a few more barges too. The next morning [September 19] early we cut a few more trees over their heads and caved in some more dug outs, and the infantry went to work again [at 0830]. They fought all day and we fired intermittently all day in front of our lines and at night had only reached the same one hundred yard line with a little margin here and there. However as Davis said, "We haven't gone anywhere, but the Japs are a lot weaker tonight than last night." He also said he had tried every method in the Field Manuals, [the] Infantry Journal, [the] Mailing List, and a few besides, and he was open to suggestions.

> To unfavorably specify the Japanese, Wilber usually used (Shigenori) "Togo" (Japanese foreign minister in 1941) rather than that commonly found in the press: (General Hideki) "Tojo" (Japanese prime minister through most of the war).

### [Japanese evacuating]

That night [September 19] I had trouble keeping the proper discipline among the Japs. They were excitable, kept signaling to Kolombangara and moving around toward the shore. However we worked at it all night. It was this evening too that Togo dropped supplies on Vila [Kolombangara] from the air. We decided he was having his problems. During the night too, now, the moon was beginning to fail us. The early part of the night was dark. The Japs were about out of barges but they apparently towed and drifted over small boats without motors because the OPs saw and heard some. They were too small for artillery targets so we didn't fire at single ones.

The next morning [9:00 A.M., September 20] we hammered again on the door [of the west end of Sagekarasa Island] and it practically fell in. They were weaker all right. Ammunition was practically gone and so were a good many Japs. A lot more were left tho and very dead, and more floated in from the sea where the artillery fire had sunk their boats as they evacuated. Now we know why they had been so nervous in the night. [They had begun to leave the island.]

I had forgotten to mention that one boat had come in to a part of the shore held by us, and that was a mistake on their part. It only had three Japs in it. When it came close to shore they called "Togo! Togo!" That was likely their password. Tonight it was the wrong word, for a U.S. 37 [mm gun] was right there as well as other weapons. Our men didn't bother the artillery about this boat. They did that job then and there. Those Japs screamed and screamed from the first shot until they were dead. I have never heard one of our soldiers let himself go except to say "I'm hit" or some similar word but I've heard the Jap completely lose control of himself because of fear of either death or wounds. A lot of the reports of the fanatic Japs are just Marine fiction played up by the publicity artists.

It's 10:30 P.M. and I must stop. I hope this is interesting to you. Tomorrow or soon I'll wind this up. There "ain't" much more. — XXXOOO Wilber

x · o · ø · o · x

Wilber wrapped up the Arundel story in this fourth and final letter.

### OCTOBER 22, 1943
### [Tactical situation, September 19]

It's evening again Darling … — Continuing and winding up the Arundel story. By Sept. 19 the Japs were trying to get out of Arundel. The Sagekarasa route was closed to them but they could go out on a long peninsula which based [had its base] on the east side of Arundel and extended NW toward Kolombangara. Col.

Ross, now Gen Ross, commanded the 172d Inf. then and was holding that side of Arundel with two of his very badly exhausted battalions and a battalion from both the 169th and 103d Inf. These troops were not all in action at once, but relief was in progress and all were in at one time or the other. DeBlois was supporting this group from Ondonga while I was using my Btry A and two borrowed batteries on the other [west] side in support of the [Sugg's] 27th Inf. and Naylor's battalion from the 172 Inf. This force was driving the Japs against Ross, and Ross never knew when the Japs were attacking him to destroy him or when they were just trying to get away from Sugg. It didn't matter anyway for a fight always resulted. Sugg sent one battalion [3rd] from Sagekarasa to the tip of the peninsula to drive down it to meet Ross who was trying to come up it.

Sugg's other two battalions [1st and 2nd] and Naylor's battalion were driving [west to east] across Arundel proper and pushing those Japs against Ross' rear. All this must have been very confusing to the Japs, for part of our force was trying to make them go where they wanted to be [toward the base of the peninsula] while the rest of our force was blocking them. At all events they didn't like it.

Since the Japs were between our "Eastern and Western" forces, all communication was by radio. I would radio DeBlois where he could and could not fire. We set up a boundary each evening so each "Force" would not fire on the other. Remember, we were firing toward each other. Ross had a reputation of being difficult so far as artillery was concerned. We had supported him in Baanga without any difficulties developing – and found that about all that was needed was not only a willingness but an anxiety to fire. DeBlois kept him happy all right. While I was firing to put out lights, maintain silence, and to sink planes and boats, he was specializing in protective barrages. I asked him later just whom he had been supporting. He said he never bothered to ask, but whenever a patrol moved, he put a rolling barrage in front of it on the way out and followed it by protective fire on the way back. I do know that two battalion commanders were nearly extreme [ecstatic] about how his fires had saved the day for them.

**[Halsey, Lodge, Griswold visit to Bomboe command post]**
Such was the general picture. On my side I was still putting in sleepless nights and chasing around the various fronts in the day. One such attack was almost something. We were all set to attack at one P.M. [with tanks again on Arundel proper, toward the east on September 19]. I had been ready to fire a preparation for the attack when [Senator Henry Cabot] Lodge, [Admiral] Halsey and a lot of brass [including corps commander Griswold] came in on the Bomboe Village C.P. I was low on ammunition and was tempted to proposition Halsey about [getting] a few

more boats but thought better of it. Sugg served some limeade from our own garden trees and thoughtfully spiked it with some rum presented to him by Griswold a few days before as a memento of our first victory in Arundel. I was pretty much background [because of my low rank] and was under the impression Lodge was a newspaper correspondent so we had a very good chat.

Griswold came over and said "Bradt it wouldn't hurt to have quite a little firing while we're here, if you have any targets that would justify the ammunition." I said "General, I'm awfully low in ammunition but I've plenty of targets so I'll do what I can." What I did was spread my preparation out.

Normally we fire preparations for a stated time and pretty rapidly by volleys. Mushik called and said the Bn. CO wanted about fifteen volleys at one o'clock. I said "I'll give you salvos." Mushik said "Yes, it will probably be alright to fire one salvo then the volleys" I said "OK fifteen salvos" (one gun at a time). Mushik thinking his commander was having a relapse said "We'll want volleys." I [then] said to the FDC [fire direction center on Bustling Point] "Is that clear now Sam [Capt. Samuel F. Pierson]? Fifteen salvos for Mushik." Sam says "Which one of you guys is right? What goes on? Is it salvos or volleys?" So I said "That's fine Sam, Fifteen salvos." Mushik says "Well I guess I don't know what goes on, but I don't think my Infantry commander is going to like this." So I say "fifteen salvos starting at one o'clock."

> Miriam Webster: "Salvo: a series of shots by an artillery battery [four howitzers] with each gun firing one round in turn after a prescribed interval." "Volley: one round per gun in a battery fired as soon as a gun is ready without regard to order."

A little later, I went to another phone and told Mushik and Sam Pierson "There is so much brass here, Griswold [a three-star general] looks like a corporal. We fire salvos." So that was all clear. Such rigors in this war. And the shells whispered over while the celebrated guests discussed. We also started a fire or two on Kolombangara on the side and blew up a Jap ammunition dump at the same time. I announced each item of interest to G., and they were casually introduced in the conversation. When they left, G. looked over and nodded, quite pleased; I was really low on ammo for the next couple of hours.

Don't you dare quote [publish] this.

### [Final attacks and Japanese evacuation]
On the day before this [Sept. 18], the Japs committed the social error of attacking just before we did [actually it was after the tank attack; see above], so this attack [at 1 P.M., September 19] was to kick them back out of our position area and to

push them [eastward] back to Ross. After the preparation was over, the tanks and the infantry went thru and started the Japs east. It was their last stand on Arundel proper, and Mushik [the artillery observer] just kept going.

That night [September 20–21] Ross had lots of business. Japs were attacking him on all sides. I received a radio [message] asking if DeBlois could fire on my side of the line [that] we had set up for a boundary. I said "No, not safe." Next a radio from [the 43rd] Division asking Bailey to fire his medium battery on the peninsula. Again I said "no" because of the probable shots falling on our troops. Radio messages didn't clarify things much. Finally Marland at division radioed me: "Navy targets [boats] on peninsula." [The Japanese were evacuating.]

That made sense, so DeBlois and I both went to work and really worked up and down our respective ends of the peninsula. I fired each five minutes until one A.M. and he did about the same. Where the Japs evacuated, there was one pile of twenty-five dead Japs, and officers told me later that anywhere they would walk two hundred yards, there were at least five dead Japs. Of course we didn't know this yet. It was my last busy night.

> September 20–21 was the final night of the Japanese evacuation.

When the Japs evacuated, all their Artillery opened up on us [to protect the evacuation]. But we outguessed them. We did not fire back at them except with one battery. With the other two, we just kept shooting at boats as if it was a nice quiet night. Some Fun.

> Fun? An article in the Infantry Journal [September 1944, p. 20] about those days in Arundel stated, "During the two nights that the Japanese were evacuating Arundel, they departed from their usual method of isolated artillery rounds and actually covered the north shore of Arundel with heavy fires. This was the only time in our experience in the Solomons that anything approaching massed artillery fires has been used by the Japs." Next to the words "massed artillery fires" in his copy, which I still have, Wilber had penned, "Not fun."

The final attack down the peninsula was set for the next morning [September 21]. I had stopped all of the DeBlois' fires, fired a preparation, then stopped my own. Col. Sugg and I went to see it jump off. There was delay, and he and I were up front checking, and some Lt. said "you shouldn't be here." I said "I know but look at that Col. of yours! I promised myself no Inf. Col. would get any farther forward than I would go!" So he thought, "What a screwball!" and let it go. The Japs weren't there anyway, and the war on Arundel was over, except for a few [Japs] to be cleared up that day on the march thru to Ross. The next night, Sept. 22 [Sept 21–22], I slept all night.

CHAPTER 6   *My whispering chorus of observers*

Wilber related his getting "farther forward" comment as a joke, but there was undoubtedly some truth in it. He was not totally free of machismo.

The next day [September 22] we knew the job was done. Captured documents and statements from two prisoners showed that the Jap 13th Inf. and two rapid fire companies and two machine gun companies and some engineers had opposed us in Arundel. Of these, two battalions and the spare parts had come over from Kolombangara during the early days. The prisoners thought the reinforcements amounted to 900 men, and the total force was about twelve hundred. One prisoner said only three barges were used to evacuate. Maybe I had eliminated too many. He thought 420 had gotten away, but we knew between fifty and a hundred he thought escaped were dead on the peninsula. Also a mass of wreckage near Devil's Island floated by our OP a day later and turned out to be fragments of boats and a great many dead Japs. The prisoner said the Jap regimental commander [Tomonari] was killed by a shell burst on his first day on Arundel. The Bn. C.O. who took command was killed the next day and the Bn. C.O. who replaced him was killed some time later. The third successor left Arundel alive.

> The American artillery did kill the regimental commander and two battalion commanders, but one of the latter did not succeed to regimental command. Tomonari was succeeded by the C.O. of the 3rd Battalion, Uichi Takabayashi, who was killed. The second successor as regimental commander was the 1st Bn. C.O. Seishu Kinoshita, who survived the war. Takabayashi's successor as C.O. of the 3rd Bn. was Capt. Kazen Moria. He was the second battalion commander killed by American artillery [Conversation with Kinoshita].
>
> During our meeting in 1983, Colonel Kinoshita told me he had been standing in the water helping to shove off the boats, which had become grounded when taking on their loads of men. All of this was transpiring in the dark under heavy American mortar and artillery fire.

Goff ran the forward C.P. [on Devine's Island] for DeBlois while I was it [the forward C.P.] on the West. He [Goff] did a fine job. Rainey's wife says their children have lost their Daddy [to the war], and [that] their mother is going soon because one [child] is playing the piano, and another the coronet. The little one wants to take up drums.

I think I saw Col. Tomonari's grave. The Japs had built it up with coral and flowers into an unusually imposing mound. No name post was placed on it.

So ends the battle of Arundel as seen by your Old Man. I was given a commendation for my work with Sugg and will enclose it for you to file and show the children.... I love you. — XXXOOO Wilber

COMBAT AND NEW LIFE     PART I: JUNGLE COMBAT

x·o·ø·o·x

This concluded Wilber's extended account of the Arundel action. In an earlier letter (October 7), Wilber gave an expanded account of his encounter with Senator Lodge:

However, a little later, this news correspondent [actually Senator Lodge] came around to me and asked what I was doing. He seemed quite interested so I went into things a little more in detail than usual. After he left one of the Colonels came over and said "What did Senator Lodge say?" I was a bit surprised for it hadn't seemed the logical place for even Republican Senators. After all, I had been practically shot out of my bunk by Pistol Pete only two nights before.

In the 1980s, I examined the archived papers of Henry Cabot Lodge, the former senator from Massachusetts and later ambassador to Vietnam. There was a reference to his visit to the command post but no further enlightening details. I telephoned him to see if he remembered chatting with an artillery officer. About all he could remember, he said at age 80, was a long boat ride. In the national archives, I found a photo of Halsey, Griswold, and Lodge on a small well-decorated boat—probably Halsey's Admiral's "barge"—taken in the New Georgia region most likely en route to Bomboe Village that very day.

The backtalk from Wilber's subordinates about salvos and volleys was a reflection, I suspect, of their national guard origins. His more senior officers were in their late 20s or early 30s and were not afraid to express their differing opinions to a senior officer when there was an appropriate opportunity. Wilber's battery commander, Howard Brown, in 2011, when presented with this view, immediately challenged it: the 43rd Division in World War II was every bit as professional as any regular army unit, he emphatically told me.

Wilber did not take offense at the inference that he might be in error. He thought it all rather humorous. In an earlier, almost contemporaneous letter [letter 9/20/43], he reflected on this event: "I get quite a kick out of the C.G. XIV Corps [Griswold] trying to impress COMSOPAC [Halsey, Commander South Pacific Area] just as I had seen Captains try to impress Colonels. And I suppose COMSOPAC [Halsey] wanted to impress the Senator. What a system!"

The loss of the highly regarded Colonel Tomonari was a grave and dispiriting blow to the Japanese. The names of senior Japanese officers were well known to the Americans and vice versa. Wilber's little note-

CHAPTER 6    *My whispering chorus of observers*

*From left, Adm. William Halsey, Jr. (area commander), Gen. Oscar Griswold (corps commander), and U.S. Senator (Massachusetts) Henry Cabot Lodge on a visit to forward areas of New Georgia Island group, September 1943. This was most likely taken the very day, September 19, of their visit to the 27th Infantry command post that Wilber described so humorously. Note the fancy overhead fringe on their well-appointed "admiral's barge" and the protective craft following them.* [PHOTO: U.S. ARMY SIGNAL CORPS, SC 186140]

book listed the names of Tomonari and all three battalion commanders. It indicated that Kinoshita had been killed. In fact, he and other survivors of the Japanese 13th Infantry Regiment sat out the rest of the war in isolation in the mountains of Bougainville. They suffered greatly from lack of food and supplies; they grew their own crops and stole food from the Australians. Kinoshita was proud of the fact that he and his troops never surrendered. They were taken into custody by the Australians after Japan capitulated in 1945.

x·o·ø·o·x

COMBAT AND NEW LIFE    PART I: JUNGLE COMBAT

Combat for the 43rd Division in the Solomon Islands was finally over. Wilber summarized his service in the New Georgia group by marking a map from the *Infantry Journal* with the three principal locations of the 169th Field Artillery Battalion during the three months of fighting (Map 13). For his service in the Solomons, Wilber was awarded the Purple Heart with cluster in recognition of his two wounds and also the Legion of Merit, a high-ranking medal for exceptional service. The citation reads:

*For exceptionally meritorious conduct in the performance of outstanding services on the way to and in the South Pacific Area, from 24 Feb. 1941 to 21 Sept. 1943. In New Georgia, Solomon Islands, he supervised the direction of fire on 14 July 1943, which helped the infantry to seize strategic Horseshoe Hill. On the following day his battalion's fire forced the retreat of Japanese troops who threatened annihilation of an infantry command post. From 20 to 30 July, his battalion ably supported two infantry regiments and, on one occasion during this period, Colonel Bradt directed all artillery battalions of a division in massed fire which virtually wiped out an enemy command post. His supervision of fire in support of infantry operations on both Baanga and Arundel Islands was outstanding. The continuous superior achievement of Colonel Bradt contributed much to the success of the New Georgia campaign. (G.O. #545, USAFISPA, 30 Dec. 1943)*

His and his unit's performance were further recognized by a personal letter of congratulation from Colonel Files, the executive officer of the 43rd Division Artillery. After noting that Wilber's battalion supported six different infantry regiments (169th, 172nd, 145th, 148th, 27th, and 161st) during the campaign, when one was the norm, Files continued:

*… At times more than one regiment was supported simultaneously. The liaison and observation facilities supplied were at all times not only adequate but outstanding, taxing your reduced personnel almost beyond the limit of endurance. The misfortune whereby several of your officers and men were rendered casualties in the front lines attests to the aggressiveness of this service. You have been almost continuously on duty from the beginning of the battle to [the] present date.*

*From your howitzers have been fired nearly double the number of rounds of ammunition expended by any other artillery battalion of the 43rd Division Artillery. Every change of position has been characterized by the speed and efficiency with which you were able to open fire from the new position. The universal praise by all supported infantry organizations over the assistance you have rendered could hardly be surpassed. The efficiency of your fire direction center should serve as a model for all artillery battalions.…*

Wilber also received a personal commendation from Colonel Sugg, the commander of the 27th Infantry Regiment for his work with that unit on Arundel. Wilber's battalion received unit commendations from the commanders of the 148th and 145th Infantry regiments of the 37th Division.

The military tends to do a lot of self-congratulating after an exercise or action, so it might be reasonable to do some discounting here. Nevertheless, it is pretty clear that Wilber's battalion performed well above the average in several measurable ways. The 169th Field Artillery Battalion saw more combat, fired more rounds, and suffered more casualties than any of the other three field artillery battalions in the division.

Wilber stayed close to the infantry commanders and the action. He was thus able to anticipate their needs, and was quick to volunteer his unit to perform a needed task. The unit's availability was enhanced by its rapid and efficient moves to new positions. Such moves were technically complex; surveys and the installation of communications lines were required before firing could begin.

At the end of a phase of combat, a commander would traditionally recognize individuals in his battalion for exceptional deeds; he would write recommendations for medals that were sufficiently convincing to garner approval from higher commands. Wilber excelled at this; his writing and the greater action his battalion had seen led to his men receiving 39 medals for the Solomon actions while the other three battalions received 15, 7, and 5 respectively [Barker, pp. 235–247]. These numbers exclude Purple Hearts, which were given for a wound or a death.

The number of awarded Purple Hearts was not dependent on writing ability. Rather, the awards attested to the involvement of the unit in combat. Such awards could actually be indicators of individual bravery or carelessness, as well as command aggressiveness, recklessness, or incompetence. There were 15 Purple Hearts awarded to those in Wilber's battalion and four, one, and none, respectively, to those in the other three battalions. As noted, Wilber's own Purple Heart with cluster recognized his two woundings. Four others in Wilber's unit—three officers and one enlisted man—who had been killed in action were awarded the Purple Heart posthumously.

These numbers of casualties indicate that Wilber was indeed an aggressive commander, as Colonel Files noted. Was he overly so? He always claimed to weigh the risks against the benefits in his own personal choices, and I am sure he did this for his men as well. Wilber took the loss of his men to heart and blamed himself especially for the loss of Heidelberger. The ultimate benefit was, of course, the saving of infantrymen's lives, and his artillery did that in abundance.

x · o · ∅ · o · x

Despite the difficulties and setbacks the 43rd Division encountered in the Munda campaign, its objectives were attained to the benefit of the Allies. The jungle environment and well-trained Japanese soldiers were formidable foes, but they were overcome. From these experiences, new strategies resulted and were adopted: placing artillery units on off-lying islands to provide cleared fields of fire (without trees obstructing the trajectories) and better security from raids; using sound ranging to locate artillery bursts; and using artillery bursts themselves to locate infantry units ("everyone watch for the smoke shell"). Other innovations included using flamethrowers to reduce enemy pillboxes; deploying marine tanks in the jungle; and making artillery observations from airplanes. The duration of this campaign—three months—was substantially longer than anticipated, but it led the planners to adopt an effective island-hopping strategy to speed the Allied advance. Japanese positions would be bypassed by means of landings beyond them; the enemy position, cut off from supply sources, would eventually be abandoned.

The 43rd Division of some 12,000 men suffered 5,960 casualties. Of these, 581 were killed and 2,059 were wounded. According to Barker [p. 112], war neuroses claimed 1,552—according to Fushak, p. 2, it was 1,950—malaria 1,171, and "other" causes 597. Many of these soldiers were returned to duty after a short convalescence or never left the field at all. Wilber, for example, took no time off as a result of his two wounds.

The number of war neuroses (akin to today's PTSD) in the Munda campaign was unusually high compared to those in other units under comparable circumstances. Many of the cases developed in the first days when the infantry were first exposed to the nighttime jungle sights and sounds, and the 169th Infantry bore the brunt of them. The causes of these problems were varied and systemic, according to a 1999 study of the 43rd Division's experiences by a student at the U.S. Command and General Staff College [Fushak, 1999]: inadequate jungle training; turnover in personnel (officers and enlisted) during training in the States, which hindered the development of unit cohesion; extensive non-combat duties such as developing infrastructure at the camps and being assigned to cargo handling parties in New Caledonia, which detracted from training time; publicity portrayals of "the

CHAPTER 6    *My whispering chorus of observers*

Japs" as inhuman, superb jungle fighters, rather than city and farm boys equally new to the jungle and generally imbued with a deep unquestioning loyalty to their cause, which could impair their judgment; and finally, the failure to anticipate neuropsychiatric casualties and the improper handling of them. According to Fushak, major lessons of the past, from the very beginning of military history, about the value of unit cohesion and (from World War I) about neuropsychiatric casualties were simply forgotten or neglected. Fortunately, the experience of the 43rd Division led immediately to improved training and better care of these casualties.

The study painted a grim picture indeed, but as the author pointed out, of the 12,000 men in the division, more than 10,000 were not listed as psychiatric casualties; they went on with their duties. Wilber was with the 169th Infantry Regiment during those early days, and his letters showed no sign of the discouragement and setbacks that the regiment must have felt. (In contrast, he did allude to such problems in the Baanga action.) I gather from this that despite the problems, all was not despair and gloom. He and most of his infantry colleagues swallowed the setbacks and continued to move ahead as best as they could. The 43rd Division earned its spurs at Munda and performed creditably throughout the rest of the war, apparently without excessive neuropsychiatric casualties.

x · o · ∅ · o · x

As the New Georgia campaign ended for the 43rd Division in late September, Valerie and I were adjusting to our New Jersey boarding schools; it was our first extended time away from home. Meanwhile, Norma had been in places unknown for those three months, though most probably she was in Washington, D.C., with Monte and his mother. At the end of the Arundel action, she was only a few weeks shy of her due date.

---

During the three summer months of combat in the western Solomons, naval action continued as the Japanese attempted to reinforce Munda, Arundel, and Kolombangara and later as they evacuated troops. In the USSR, by September 30, the Russians had secured five bridgeheads across the Dnieper River. The summer campaign was a disaster for the Germans, and as winter approached the conditions would again favor the Russians. In Italy, the Germans began the defensive campaign that would take advantage of the mountainous terrain of Italy.

The tempo of the bombing of German cities was increasing. The bombing of Hamburg by the British late in July 1943 led to a "firestorm" that killed 23,000 of its inhabitants. Industrial areas were the prime targets, but the bombing of civilian areas as a means of impacting morale was becoming common in the campaign against Germany. This practice had been initiated in Europe by the German raids on London in 1940, and was notably unsuccessful. American bombers of the Eighth Air Force in England were joining the British in the bombing campaign. German resistance to these raids with anti-aircraft fire and fighter planes was fierce. A raid by 229 B-17 bombers on a ball-bearing factory in central Germany on August 17 led to the loss of 36 of those planes.

# PART II

# INTERLUDE 1983

JAPAN AND SOLOMON ISLANDS
MARCH AND MAY, 1983

★ ★

# 7

# *Kyushu, Japan*

## Hiroshima and Colonel Kinoshita
### March 1983

In 1983 and 1984, I visited sites in the western Pacific where my father Wilber had been. I describe these visits in three "Interludes" drawn largely from the journal I kept during those trips. This is the first of them.

In the winter and spring of 1983, I spent a sabbatical leave at Japan's Institute of Space and Astronautical Science. During March of that year, I took a five-day trip to Kyushu, the southernmost of the main Japanese islands; there, I visited the Kagoshima Space Center (now Uchinoura Space Center) where my Japanese colleagues were collecting and analyzing data from a Japanese x-ray astronomy satellite ("Tenma"). On the way there I visited Hiroshima, the site of the first use of the atomic bomb, and also visited Col. Seishu Kinoshita, a surviving senior Japanese battalion commander of the Munda and Arundel campaigns in the Solomons.

In May of that year, I met my colleague, Dr. Ronald Remillard, in Australia for a scheduled period of astronomical observations to be carried out at Australia's Siding Spring Observatory. (From there we could observe parts of the southern sky not visible to northern observers.) En route to Australia, I stopped in Luzon, the main island of the Philippines, for one week to search out the sites and people Wilber had written about. On the return trip, I took another week to visit the places he had been in the Solomons. The trip, including the astronomical observing in Australia, took the entire month of May. The following year, 1984, while en route again to Australia, I visited New Zealand and found the people who had treated Wilber so hospitably on his second visit there, after the Solomons combat. My travels in 1983 and 1984 were a condensed form of Wilber's own three-year Pacific odyssey.

I was driven to visit these sites by my intense curiosity about my parents' story. By then, I knew it well and wanted very much to see its settings with my own eyes. My attraction to these sites was stronger than I can explain here. I was surely searching for my father, and in certain ways, I did find him, particularly in the village of Bomboe on Arundel in the Solomons, the town of Pakil in the Philippines, and in the small town of Carterton, Wairarapa, New Zealand.

I choose to tell the stories through my eyes of 1983–84 by quoting extensively from my (edited) journals. In this interlude, I describe my visit to Hiroshima and my meeting with Colonel Kinoshita and then my visit to the New Georgia group of islands in the Solomon Islands. My visit to New Zealand is presented later in this book and my trip to the Philippines in Book 3.

x·o·ø·o·x

### Hiroshima, March 20, 1983

Visiting Hiroshima was, for me, a very emotional experience. The use of the atomic bomb by the U.S. was a major step for mankind—in a dangerous direction according to my thinking and that of many of my physicist colleagues, some of whom had participated in the bomb's development. On the other hand, its use together with Russia's entry into the war against Japan brought about the end of the war without a costly invasion of the Japanese home islands and very likely the loss then of my father's life.

I spent several hours touring the Peace Memorial Park at Hiroshima and its exhibits, and was deeply moved and saddened by them. The Japanese exhibits made real the agony of that day, but downplayed Japan's role in bringing about the Hiroshima bombing by its own history of atrocities in its conquests, by its indirect participation in Hitler's crimes, and by prolonging the war long after defeat was inevitable. I was, frankly, put off by the one-sided presentation. Yes, it was a horrible, terrible event, and I did and do grieve for the 80,000 innocents who died that day. But the forces that brought about the bombing were large, complex, and not solely American.

For some reason I could not explain, I felt compelled to find the center of the blast, the point under the parachuting bomb when it exploded. I somehow needed to get as close to the explosion as I possibly could. Inquiries led me to a nearby shopping district where there was a relatively inconspicuous

*Major Seishu Kinoshita as commanding officer of the 1st Battalion, 13th Regiment, China, 1942, and when I visited him in 1983. In the latter he is with his wife and daughter-in-law, Kurume, Kyushu, Japan.* [PHOTOS: SEISHU KINOSHITA AND HALE BRADT]

marker. I communed with that awful August 7, 1945, event in the midst of unconcerned passing pedestrians, and then I too carried on.

## COLONEL SEISHU KINOSHITA, MARCH 21, 1983

I learned of Colonel Kinoshita from a historian, Hishashi Takahashi, at Japan's Center of Military History. He told me a senior officer of the 13th Regiment still survived on Kyushu and arranged for me to visit him. My journal of that visit, with some edits, picks up the story.

*Now, 11 a.m. on the 21st of March 1983, I am in the lobby of the plush Zen Nikky Hotel in Hakata, Kyushu, drinking coffee and having cookies. My room will*

## COMBAT AND NEW LIFE    PART 11: INTERLUDE 1983

*be ready soon. I'll dump my bag there and walk the three minutes to the train station for the 40-min. ride to Kurume. There I will meet Col. Seishu Kinoshita, the surviving senior officer of the 13th Japanese Regiment that fought opposite Wilber on Arundel Island as well as on the approaches to Munda airfield. I am armed with maps, photos, etc. to give or show him. His name is mentioned in General Barker's book (p. 47) as C.O. of the 1st Bn. and in my Dad's notes as a battalion commander in the 13th Regiment. Wilber erroneously believed his artillery had killed Kinoshita.*

Two days later, at Uchinoura Space Center, I wrote up my visit with Kinoshita. It was based on notes I took during our meeting.

*I took the 12 noon train to Kurume and there was met by Kinoshitasan, a spry old man, straight-backed, articulate and friendly. He was 72 years old, so he would have been only 32 during the Arundel battles. We took a cab to his home, conversing with my very limited Japanese on the way. I showed him Barker's book with the map of the Arundel area (Sagekarasa and Stima peninsula) and also the listing of his name. He told the cab driver with great enthusiasm why I was there.*

*He lived in a nice 3 to 5 room home with a pretty vegetable and flower garden outside; gardening is his hobby. I was served tea and sweets on "this special holiday upon which we honor dear friends and relatives." I met his wife, son, and daughter in law. I set up my tape recorder on the table as did his son. An English teacher served as translator (a military man) so Kinoshitasan could tell his story quite freely in Japanese.*

*He excitedly pulled out his maps of the battle places in the Solomons. All of his official maps had been confiscated by the Australians, so these maps were created from memory on large poster sheets of paper and were sometimes vague or in error. He spread them out on the floor and got on his knees and excitedly told his stories. He was the battalion commander who fought immediately opposite the 27th U.S. Infantry Wilber was with at Bomboe Village. He also participated in the defense of Munda airfield.*

*A few of the more interesting facts I gleaned from him are:*

*(1) The nighttime attack on the poorly-defended U.S. 43rd Division Command Post at Zanana (east of Munda) was carried out by the entire Japanese 13th Infantry Regiment (2 Battalions), not just a small element of Japanese troops. With a little more persistence they could have done great damage to the Americans by destroying the C.P. and then moving west into the American rear. However, the Japanese were woefully ignorant of the overall situation – or even the geography –and many of the Japanese soldiers were new to combat and badly frightened by American artillery and planes.*

*(2) After the first American attack with tanks on Arundel (Sept. 17, 1943), heroic efforts were made to bring forward an anti-tank gun from Kolombangara and then from Sagekarasa Island to the Arundel "mainland" where the tanks had attacked. This was the only available anti-tank gun of the regiment, and there were only ten shells for it. He described how, on the 18th, the first shell destroyed an American tank, how they damaged perhaps two more [actually one], and how much that cheered the Japanese soldiers. (He did not mention the following attack by his troops with great loss of life.) Later the gun was destroyed. In the next and final tank attack, without the antitank gun, he thought "his days were numbered."*

*(3) The Japanese evacuation from Arundel to Kolombangara was very difficult: The boats would become grounded in the shallow water when loaded and would have to be pushed off by people in the water. Kinoshita was in the water up to his chest. He was now the regimental commander. Both the revered Col. Satoshi Tomonari and his successor, the 3rd Bn. commander Major Uichi Takabayashi, had been killed by artillery fire. The artillery was not bad at the evacuation, but generally it was devastating. Getting the men to the evacuation points was very difficult. "They were panicked, but I cheered up everyone," said K. I believe it; he is so chipper, even now.*

*(4) Kinoshita did not fight on Baanga (before Arundel).*

*(5) After arriving safely in Kolombangara, he left in overloaded small boats for Bougainville with the survivors of his regiment. There the regiment remained more or less intact in the mountains until the war ended. There was no hope of resupply or reinforcements; the surrounding seas were controlled by the Americans. Those were bitter times with much starvation; they grew and stole food from the Australian troops and others. This isolation contrasted vividly with the mobility of the U.S. 43rd Division which went to New Zealand for rehabilitation and training and then went on to fight in New Guinea and the Philippines.*

*(6) Kinoshita joined the Defense Force after the war and instructed many officers now in important positions in the Defense Force. He is obviously pleased about this and took pride in the fact that "my men loved me. Many asked about me after the war." He was extremely grateful that I came to visit. He was pleased we can be friends now. He liked my carrying out my "filial duty."*

*We then went to a traditional Japanese restaurant for supper (the three of us: K, the interpreter and me). We had a delightful meal of tempura complete with sake. Then they saw me to my train and waved goodbye as the train pulled away. Just before – as he said his final warm goodbye – I gave Kinoshita an around-the-shoulder hug which he enjoyed, and the interpreter (Adachi Tsusumu) took a photo.*

Shortly after returning to the U.S., I described this visit in a talk at the August 1983 reunion of the 43rd Division Association. The former 1st Battalion commander of the 172nd Infantry, William Naylor, who had fought directly opposite Kinoshita's battalion at Arundel, was present. In April 1984, he visited Japan, and the two commanders had a private meeting at the Defense Ministry in Tokyo. Both are deceased now.

Was it really filial duty that led me to visit Wilber's adversary? Did I need to atone for Wilber's artillery killing of his revered regimental commander and fellow battalion commander? Or did I instead feel the need to fill out the story by getting Colonel Kinoshita's view of those times and hearing about his later life, a life Wilber never had? All were probably at work in my head.

*General William Naylor (left) and Col. Seishu Kinoshita examining a map in 1984 as they discuss their wartime experiences on Arundel Island. Each was an infantry battalion commander, and the two units were in direct conflict. Naylor arranged the meeting after hearing about Kinoshita in a talk I gave to the 43rd Division Association in August 1983. They met at the National Defense College in Tokyo on April 16, 1984. Their meeting was recorded but not advertised. Both are now deceased.* [PHOTO: WILLIAM NAYLOR]

# 8

## *Guadalcanal: the way in*

### MAY 1983

Two months after visiting Colonel Kinoshita, I was en route from the astronomical observatory in Australia to Japan and had allowed one short week for a stopover in the Solomon Islands. To get to Munda airfield on New Georgia Island, I traveled through New Guinea and the world-famous island of Guadalcanal (Map 2). This chapter of my story began in the isolated—far from city lights—Siding Spring Astronomical Observatory in New South Wales, Australia, 500 miles northwest of Sydney. I wrote this in my journal several days later, after I had reached Munda.

**LEAVING AUSTRALIA, MAY 20 FRIDAY**
*I left Siding Spring Observatory after 1 1/3 nights of time on the AAT (Anglo-Australia Telescope). The rest of the three nights we had been assigned were cloudy. I copped out and slept the entire last cloudy night. Did I ever need the sleep. We, my colleague Ron Remillard and I, flew in the ANU (Australia National University) charter plane to Dubbo, 150 miles distant, for our plane connection to Sydney. We strolled around the town, and I bought a knapsack and mosquito repellent, thinking of the Solomons. A few hours later, we flew to Sydney, after a hassle because the observatory staff had, due to a misunderstanding, cancelled our reservations!*

*Sydney: I had a lovely dinner with Ken and Jill McCracken in a high revolving restaurant with a view of Sydney harbor: We had a nice chat, recalling our days together at MIT many years before.*

## COMBAT AND NEW LIFE     PART 11: INTERLUDE 1983

### May 21 Saturday
*I was up very early for the flight to Port Moresby, Papua New Guinea on Air Niugini. It was sort of scary going to New Guinea, cannibals and all! I met two Australian CPAs (Barry Weir and John Brown) on the plane who told me that Hotel X where I had reservations is sort of sleazy. I thus took a taxi with them and checked into their hotel, the "Islander" – nice tropical setting with pool. We rented a car and drove around town and saw the Australian military cemetery, lots of colorful flowers. I had supper with them after a swim and enjoyed our discussions. Then, to bed.*

### May 22 Sunday: Guadalcanal
*Again an early flight, to Guadalcanal my entry point into the Solomons. The Islander was terribly expensive ($100 per night! – in 1983), but it did give me the idea that this part of the world is the Caribbean of the South Pacific – relaxed, topical, and pleasant. Some of my anxieties about the Solomons began to fade away.*

*I flew into Honiara, Guadalcanal, via Kieta on Bougainville Island, the most northwestern of the Solomon Islands [but formally in the nation of Papua New Guinea]. The flight down the Solomons to Guadalcanal took me right over my destination (Munda) at 30,000 feet altitude. The weather was cloudy so I saw nothing of the ground until we reached Guadalcanal.*

*Honiara's airfield is the famous "Henderson Field" about which the fame of Guadalcanal revolves. The U.S. Marines landed and captured it in August 1942 and defended it heroically from Japanese attempts to retake it. Now it is a little relaxed airport with no bank for changing money, a source of some problem to me as Honiara's bank was closed on Sunday, and I had no Solomon dollars. I decided to rent an Avis car at the airport, taking a lesson from my companions in Port Moresby.*

*This was my only day (afternoon and evening only) on Guadalcanal so I made use of the daylight hours by driving around some of the battle areas. I met friendly Solomon Islanders some of whom, especially children, had blondish hair which I now know is most likely natural. Everyone I went by wanted to chat and did so. I felt safe, secure, and relaxed. Driving a right-hand-drive car on the left side of the road even went OK. There was only one main road along the coast with very little traffic. I relived a lot of history in my four-hour self-guided tour.*

### Beach Red about 1 p.m.
*First I drove a few miles to "Beach Red" where the Marines had first landed. There I saw a large mounted about 3-inch gun on the beach pointing out to sea; it was terribly corroded but was unmistakably a gun; It could have been American or Japanese. I talked to a woman and child on the beach; her husband works for the nearby timber company. They lived in a modest home on the beach, owned I*

CHAPTER 8    *Guadalcanal: the way in*

*Heavily rusted gun on Beach Red, Guadalcanal, May 1983. It may be a Japanese 75-mm antiaircraft gun with the mount deeply embedded in the sand.* [PHOTO: HALE BRADT]

*Stacey Wally, age three, at home on Beach Red, Guadalcanal, May 22, 1983.*
[PHOTO: HALE BRADT]

think by the timber company. I took photos of them on their porch and got a great grin from the boy. I asked for their name and address [and sent them photos later. I received a nice note back.]

COMBAT AND NEW LIFE    PART 11: INTERLUDE 1983

*The memorial for U.S. Marines at Edson's Ridge, Guadalcanal, with Jason Alaikone.*
[PHOTO: HALE BRADT]

*The Japanese memorial on Edson's Ridge, Guadalcanal, with Jason Alaikone. The lower white marker is an indicator of recent visitors.* [PHOTO: HALE BRADT]

CHAPTER 8   *Guadalcanal: the way in*

**BLOODY RIDGE ABOUT 2:30 P.M.**

*I then drove to Lunga Bridge and met Cris of Avis driving by; he had rented me my car at the airport. He directed me to a little dirt road leading to "Bloody Ridge," aka Edson's Ridge after the marine commander, where there were Japanese and American memorials. This is where the Marines desperately defended Henderson Field from aggressive Japanese attacks only a mile from the airfield. As the road became narrower and narrower with tall grass obscuring it, I stopped and asked a little old man who was working in a field for directions. When I told him my Dad had been there with the Americans, he lit up, and offered to take me himself. His name was Jason Alaikone, and he had been a scout for the Americans, he said. He climbed in the car with machete and all. (Hmm … Solomon Island headhunter stories still circulated.) The road in some places had grass as high as the car's hood and was very steep in one place. We found the U.S. memorial OK, then drove on to the Japanese memorial. Both memorials were very simple. The grass around the U.S. memorial had been recently cut. The memorial itself was a white four-sided pyramid about ten feet high with a base about ten feet square set on a square base of rocks about three feet high.*

*The Japanese memorial had high, uncut grass around it. It was a simple post about 8 inches square in cross section and about ten feet tall with painted inscriptions on it. A nearby small stake, painted white with inscriptions, indicated recent visitors.… On the way back to the main road, I dropped Jason off at his home and photographed his three grandsons.*

The three grandsons (Raramo 13, David 9, and Willken 3) of Jason Alaikone who took me to the memorials on Edson's Ridge, Guadalcanal, May 1983.
[PHOTO: HALE BRADT]

The successful defense of Henderson Field on this unpretentious hill was a turning point for the Americans; they could begin to take the offensive against the Japanese on Guadalcanal.

**Beach across from Henderson Field about 4 p.m.**
*I had heard that there were war relics on or near the beach just opposite Henderson Field. The airfield is on the opposite side of the main road from the beach, about a mile from the beach. I drove east 1/2 mile or so on the main road, turned left off the road to try to get to the beach. I encountered a gate through which I could walk. I met a boy who was walking home to Lunga (a few miles) with a partial gallon can of paint he had been given. He promptly adopted me and walked along with me; I carried his paint can part of the time. His name was Salia, age 11. It was a long walk to the beach through the coconut groves. He guided me to relics of airplane parts, two different landing craft rusting in the jungle not far (30 m) from the beach, and wrecked metal wharves.*

*After this, I drove west the few miles into Honiara, dropping Salia off on the way. The entire walk down to the beach and back was out of his way, but he had cheerfully followed me along without being asked. Since I still had no Solomon Isladns money, I gave him a Papua New Guinea coin ($1 maybe). He didn't seem to expect it and seemed a bit baffled when I offered it to him. I do think he followed me all that way because he thought I was just an interesting character who paid attention to him, not because I might part with money.*

*The Hotel Honiara was simple and clean. I had supper and then walked about one mile into town to the fancy Hotel Mendana. On the walk, I chatted with another native "Charlie" who was walking my way. He was very talkative and interested in talking with an American. Keep in mind that these islands were British so that most people knew English. However, now that the SI have become independent (1978), English is becoming less used by the younger children. Before I had left the Hotel Honiara, I had asked if it was OK to walk into town – it was after dark – and was told it was OK. I didn't feel unsafe even though I had been told in Port Moresby to take care in Honiara. I just walked along in the warm night air and talked to "Charlie"; it was all very pleasant.*

*At the Mendana, I had ginger ale as I looked out over the dark waters of "Ironbottom Sound" and mused on the destructive naval battles that had taken place there. Then I got a taxi, had the driver show me the downtown monument to the American dead, which was literally next door to the hotel. Then back to my hotel, to bed and up early (again) for the plane to Munda.*

This was the end of my touring Guadalcanal. I had allowed exactly one week, Saturday to Saturday, for my Solomons visit. Flights were infrequent

CHAPTER 8    *Guadalcanal: the way in*

*Rusted landing craft among trees near the beach opposite Henderson Field. This appears to be the aft end of a 50-foot-long Landing Craft Medium (LCM); its upright pilot house was about five feet tall and would hold only one man, the coxswain. This is one of the relics that Salia showed me, May 1983.* [PHOTO: HALE BRADT]

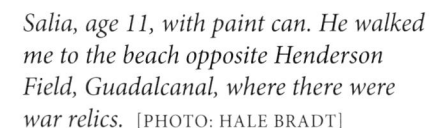

*Salia, age 11, with paint can. He walked me to the beach opposite Henderson Field, Guadalcanal, where there were war relics.* [PHOTO: HALE BRADT]

and, since it took up to two days to get into and then a full day to get out of Munda on New Georgia Island, time was precious.

### MONDAY, MAY 23

My Solaire flight to Munda was a real eye opener. We were at low altitude and it was a beautiful clear day. I was in the copilot's seat with absolutely no qualifications for it. We flew over the Russell Islands, and I could see the characteristic outline of Pavuvu Island there that I knew so well from the maps.

COMBAT AND NEW LIFE    PART 11: INTERLUDE 1983

I was able to see exactly where the 169th Field Artillery had been stationed for four months in 1943. Then Rendova Island came into view, the 43rd Division's jump-off point for the Munda landings. The harbor where Wilber wrote his pre-landing letter on July 4 and was wounded by a bomb was easily identifiable. This was no map; this was the real thing. I was transfixed.

*My view of Munda airfield on New Georgia Island from the copilot's seat as we approached the field.* [PHOTO: HALE BRADT]

As we made the approach for our landing at Munda airfield, I could not believe I was coming to the hard-won objective of the 43rd Division's month of combat in July and August of 1943. By this time, Munda had become almost mythical to me. But we were there, and here I was, standing on New Georgia Island.

In Munda, I was now walking, figuratively and literally, in Wilber's footsteps.

*The terminal at Munda airport, May 1983. It was an expanded Quonset Hut. The Munda Rest House was nearby, possibly that low building to the rear left of the terminal.* [PHOTO: HALE BRADT]

# 9

## *Battle areas, New Georgia*

### Munda
### May 1983

The following is based on rough notes I made in my journal at Munda on May 24. I fleshed them out into the following prose in 1984, when my memory of these days was still quite fresh.

**Monday, May 23 (cont.)**

*Immediately after my arrival at Munda, I met Alfred Basili to whom I had been referred in previous correspondence, saw his canoe and was delighted to see that it had an outboard motor. It was a long canoe (30 feet) so went very fast. Alfred told me a bit about how he had been a scout with the 43rd Division. My correspondents had told me that canoe was the only way to get around the Western Solomons. Thus I had spent some time looking at maps, measuring mileages, and wondering how far I could paddle in a day!*

*Now here I was at the Munda Rest House, a simple set of motel-like rooms facing the beautiful water and only about 15 yards from it. It was just like being in the Caribbean. A small dock near my end of the motel was one of the local docks, with boats occasionally coming into it and young boys swimming off it. The Rest House was a mere 60 yards from the Airport Quonset main building. The whole Munda community looked like it had only about 20 native houses, but probably there were more out of sight. At the other end of the airfield, there was a Christian Mission that I visited later. There were only two or three flights (all small planes) into Munda a day, all Solaire. The Rest House had about six rooms and a restaurant. It was run by Agnus Kera. As I recall she was Caucasian (mostly), but she had lived in the SI all her life. The Rest House is used by transient pilots, government* inspectors, and others. It is to be my home for three nights while I explore Munda, Baanga, and Arundel.

There was a tourist guest (young man) from Australia there with his son: Claude Colomere and Julien, age 4. He had read about Munda as a beautiful place and came for a vacation completely unaware of its war history. Claude was very interested in the carvings of the natives and did professional photography. [I have learned that both he and his son contracted malaria despite taking preventive pills, probably from camping out in Guadalcanal. Their first symptoms appeared after they had returned home. I am not sure how they feel about the Solomons now.]

I asked Basili if the big naval guns were still on Baanga; he replied that one of them was but that it had been damaged. When he wanted to know where I wanted to go first, I immediately said Baanga, which I knew was nearby. That was where Wilber's artillery had disabled two Japanese naval guns and where one of Wilber's forward observers, Heidelberger, was killed.

### BAANGA ISLAND

We got into his canoe and buzzed over to Baanga in about 15 minutes. It was a beautiful sunlit day, maybe 85 degrees or so. We beached the boat on a beach and walked into the jungle – THE jungle! Well it wasn't spooky, creepy, full of mosquitos, or dense with vegetation. It was pretty with dappled sunshine coming through the tall trees. Of course, I did not try to sleep there overnight in a hole in the rain [as Wilber had]; that would have been quite a different experience. We then came out on a beach again: sand, coral, water two or three inches deep sometimes. My running shoes were the perfect thing for this. I just jogged along with them in and out of the water. I wore a long sleeved shirt and long khaki pants as protection against mosquitos, which never appeared.

After about a 20-minute walk, we came to one of the guns. What a moment! I have a picture of Dad alongside one of them just after its capture, and for many years I had its telescopic gunsight. This was one of the same two guns, not any old gun! The long fifteen-foot barrel was on the ground and the main stand was still solidly upright anchored into the ground. The gun had been disassembled by persons seeking the brass bearings. The guns were positioned to fire toward

*Alfred Basili with recoil spring of coastal gun, Baanga Island, May 1983.* [PHOTO: HALE BRADT]

CHAPTER 9    *Battle areas, New Georgia*

*Left: Coastal gun mount of one of the two Japanese 120-mm coastal guns on Baanga Island, and me, May 1983. Right: Fifteen-foot-long barrel (tube) of the same gun. The two guns were put out of action by Wilber's artillery on August 17, 1943.* [PHOTOS: HALE BRADT]

*the southerly approaches to Munda airfield. No wonder the Americans chose to come into Munda through the eastern back door so to speak, even though it did involve five miles of jungle fighting.*

*I asked Alfred if he was sure there wasn't another gun because I knew there had been two. He said, no he was sure there was only one; he had lived in the area all his life and was very sure. Whereupon, I went exploring down the beach, and sure enough found the other one, dismantled the same way. Parts of the guns were still lying about, specifically the recoil springs and their cylindrical containers. Alfred played with one of the springs; it still was very springy. Then several boys came along; they were students at the secondary school on Baanga. We then visited and got a photo of the beach where the men of L Company, 169th Inf. Rgt., were stranded for 9 days.*

*Alfred and the boys had large machetes, which they used to get through the thicker parts of the jungle. They all went about in bare feet through the trees and over the sharp coral. Alfred's feet were large, thick soled and apparently impervious to all kinds of sharp objects.*

COMBAT AND NEW LIFE    PART 11: INTERLUDE 1983

*Beach in the Baanga Island cove where 34 men of Company L, 169th Infantry, were stranded on August 12, 1943.* [PHOTO: HALE BRADT]

*We never tried to explore the swampy region where the attack north of the cove ran into trouble. I never really found out how bad the jungle can be. At the time, I was feeling quite adventurous, but deliberately walking into swamps didn't seem necessary.*

### Sasavele Island

*We returned to the canoe and then to Munda where I had a nice cool beer. Then back into the canoe to go eastward to nearby (about five miles) Sasavele Island where the guns of the 169th FA Bn. had been emplaced during the drive to take Munda. Sasavele is a small island (two miles long) just off New Georgia and within artillery range of Munda airfield (Map 7). The fire direction center (FDC) of the Battalion was on Sasavele, dug into a big pit. Maj. DeBlois and his telephone men and human "computers" controlled the artillery from there day and night for a full month.*

*The visit to Sasavele was a delight; we were followed around by some two-dozen school children. School was out. I was like the Pied Piper. They would all stand and seriously listen to me explain how important their island had been. (It seemed that they understood some of my English.) Then when I would start to take a picture of them, they would all start jumping up and down waving their hands, smiling, and calling out, all very excited. There were many curly blond heads of hair among them.*

CHAPTER 9    *Battle areas, New Georgia*

*Top: Children waving at my camera, Sasavele Island, New Georgia, May 1983. The smoky light streak, center, is a consequence of my camera's brief saltwater bath. Bottom: Three children with three expressions on Sasavele Island. The blond hair is reportedly due to a gene variant found in Melanesians [Kenny, et al.,* Science 336, 554 (2012)]. [PHOTO: HALE BRADT]

*Basili and me in his canoe after several days at Munda; I was completely relaxed by then. The 30-foot canoe with outboard motor really moved along.* [PHOTO: CLAUDE COLOMER]

The village is on the same (northeast) end of the island as the 169th FA Bn. was, but it was established after the war.

At the village there was an old vehicle dump with some six or eight abandoned U.S. army vehicles, still complete with rubber tires. They could well have been 169th FA Bn. vehicles. Along the adjacent narrow channel (only about 100 yards wide), there were the remains of old metal docks. On the way to Sasavele, we had seen similar docks or barge like boats at Laiana beach. We also saw Zanana Beach, so small as to hardly qualify as a "beach"; it was maybe ten yards of sand wide and only three yards deep. Bringing the troops in there in small boats from Rendova must have been a slow, cumbersome operation.

At Sasavele, there was a bit of a problem because we were walking around the village without permission from the chief. Alfred was rather shamefaced about this

CHAPTER 9   Battle areas, New Georgia

*Rusted remains of American WWII army vehicle, Sasavele, Island, May 1983.* [PHOTO: HALE BRADT]

*and hurried off to make amends. I visited the chief's large open (single room) hut and chatted with him and his son and the schoolteacher. Chiefs tend to be quite old and do not get about too well. Also there is a high sensitivity to property rights in the Solomons. There was so much room – jungle areas were easily cleared – that it seemed silly, but it was very serious to those involved.*

*When I asked Alfred about a big rectangular hole, the fire direction center of the 169the FA Bn., he surmised that it might have been where a big pile of stones were.*

On our second visit several days later, we were told by an old man that the stones were a ceremonial place where the headhunters (who were active until early in the 20th century) deposited the skulls they would obtain from expeditions to the eastern Solomons. It definitely was not the FDC. He also showed us a garden where there had been a large pit with sandbags when they first arrived. That was most probably the FDC, the nerve center of the 169th FA Bn. as it fired some 29,000 artillery shells in support of the infantry advance on Munda airfield.

*We then took the canoe back to Munda in time for supper. I covered myself well with mosquito repellant because dusk is mosquito time. We were well removed from the jungle, and I experienced no problem with them.*

*By the way, I was paying Alfred $30 a day plus his gas which was quite expensive – say $40 for two or three days running around. I think these are SD dollars – which*

*I believe are about equal to U.S. dollars. The Rest House was $27/day and included supper. [Again, remember this was 1983.]*

*Then, I went to bed. What a day this was: I woke up on Guadalcanal, flew to Munda, toured Baanga Island to the west, then toured Sasavele to the east, all before supper.*

The next evening, at the Munda Rest House, I wrote of that day.

### Circumnavigation of Arundel Island, Tuesday, May 24,

*Today was some day, only my second here at Munda. Alfred and I circumnavigated the island of Arundel, a distance of 50 miles or so (Map 11). We took a lunch and bought lots of gas before we left at the Mission at Munda. It was there that I accidentally dumped the contents of my knapsack into about eight inches of seawater. My camera was in the water for about ten seconds, and I probably lost the films of Sasavele and the Marine tank we would see later – too bad.*

*I still did not have any Solomon dollars. I had been promising Agnus and Alfred that soon I would have some. But how? There was no Bank at Munda; the closest was back at Guadalcanal, 200 miles to the east. Eventually I entrusted signed traveler's checks (several hundred dollars) to the airline representative, and the proper amount came back from Munda a couple of days later. No receipts were requested or asked for; "it's OK, don't worry" was more or less the attitude. And it was.*

*Right off Munda airfield, slightly submerged in the sea water, is a U.S. fighter plane, the top of which is only about three feet down. I was told it was accidentally shot down by Americans during target practice, and the pilot parachuted safely. It is very impressive; it lies upright on the bottom, almost entirely visible, except for one wing under the sand. A little stick tied to the rudder marks the spot.*

*We took Alfred's canoe up Wanawana Lagoon on the west side of Arundel. There are lots and lots of tiny islands and coral rising up to the surface. It would be very easy to become stranded. Thank goodness I had Alfred and his 15 horsepower motor; his long 30 ft canoe draws very little water and really moves. It was a beautiful ride past green jungled islands, over green and white water sometimes only six inches deep!*

### Bustling Point

*Bustling Point is on the west side of Arundel Island about a mile southwest of Bomboe Village. This was where the "Provisional Battalion" of artillery was located while Wilber was at Bomboe Village directing its fires. Well, the gun positions are still there. Dirt and coral built up in a circle about the gun pit. Albert W. Merck, one of Wilber's officers, had been here a few months ago and showed them to Alfred!*

I called Merck upon my return [home to the U.S.] and had a nice chat with him. Even later (2009), I visited him at his retirement home in the Boston area. He was lively and full of recollections of the war years. He was a chemist and a direct descendant of the original founder of Merck & Co., Inc.; he served on the company's board of directors into the 1980s. Merck was scheduled to give a talk about his trip to the 43rd Division Association at its August 1983 meeting. I brought my 35-mm carousel of slides, just in case I could add something. Well, he canceled at the last minute, and I had the pleasure of bringing the 43rd Division's three-year Pacific saga to life again for the veterans and for their families. They were a large, energetic, and responsive group at that time. (Merck died in August 2014 at age 93.)

## Bomboe Village

*We then carried on in the canoe to Bomboe Village (pronounced Boboi) where I saw about two dozen houses and could identify the low "ridge" where Sugg's tent [the Command Post] probably was. There were lots of trees there. We even found a depression which might have been Sugg's foxhole which Wilber jumped into when the Japanese shell came by, but maybe not. There were probably lots of tents and foxholes around.*

This was the very site where Wilber had sat in Colonel Sugg's tent night after night controlling the artillery at Bustling Point as it supported infantry attacks and fired on boats and a seaplane with the help of his "whispering chorus of observers." I could picture the ghosts of Admiral Halsey, Senator Lodge, and General Griswold sitting and conversing in that tent drinking spiked limeade.

*We talked to the villagers for awhile including two who helped rescue Jack Kennedy (later U.S. President) after his PT boat was run down by a Japanese destroyer in nearby Blackett Strait. They were the village chief, Igolo Koete and Moses Sesa. We also met Peter Evan, Peter August Enoch, and Timothy Koete (son of the chief).*

I later found Igolo's and Moses's names in a detailed description of the Kennedy rescue [Donovan, p. 206]. They were in the party of scouts that the Coastwatcher Evans sent to the survivors after Kennedy's first message was received. They were not among those who later visited the U.S. amid much fanfare while JFK was president.

*We were asked to sit in the shade under one of their raised houses. Lots of villagers stood around and watched as we talked. They brought out a photo of President Kennedy with a dedication to Koete. It was a standard framed presidential photo with the presidential signature. The glass cover was badly cracked. The chief also went off to get a small glass vial that was supposed to contain a gift from the Kennedys. I thought it might contain a PT109 lapel pin. However, it had only a pin with a kangaroo design. I courteously said how nice it was, but then it turned out that they also expected to find a PT109 pin there. It seemed that someone had stolen it. Koete, an old man with a cane, was rather dismayed and disappointed. I told him I would try to get others sent.*

I later ordered some PT-109 pins from the Kennedy Museum in Boston and sent them to my English friends on the neighboring island, Kolombangara. I never heard whether they arrived or were delivered. I hope they were.

### AMERICAN TANK

*It was while we were talking to the chief and friends at Bomboe village on Arundel that I asked if there was anything to see a mile of two east of the village where the fighting had taken place. I more or less figured that it would only be jungle. However I was told there was a tank there. Tank? I exclaimed. I knew all about tanks on Arundel. Wilber had described watching a tank attack against the Japanese positions with six U.S. Marine tanks. The Japanese battalion commander (Kinoshita) I had met in Japan also described American tank attacks as did the official U.S. infantry action reports. So I said: "A Japanese or a U.S. tank?" and the answer was, "an American tank", confirming that it could well be related to these events. So, I asked, of course, if we could go see it.*

Scenic inner channel en route to location of disabled American tank, near Sagekarasa Island, Arundel Island. [PHOTO: IAN WARNE]

*We left the village in Alfred's canoe with a local guide (Peter Evan). He directed us east a bit in the channel on the north side of Bomboe peninsula and then out into Blackett Strait and eastward toward Sagekarasa Island, a long, narrow offshore island that was fiercely defended by the Japanese. At the far east end of Sagekaraasa, he guided us back into the lagoon inside the offshore islands by going between Sagekarasa and Stima peninsula – a little channel only 20 feet wide. We paddled through (without motor). There were people and houses on Stima peninsula and Alfred and Peter talked to them as we paddled slowly the 50 yards or so. We then paddled across the lagoon to the "mainland" (Arundel) to exactly where the Japanese had the strongest concentrations.*

*Peter led us into the jungle to the west (more or less following the lagoon but inland a few dozen yards) for 100 to 200 yards, hacking bushes and vines and plants with his machete as he went. It was very thick and impossible to traverse without a machete. He went this way and that, looking for the tank, and finally found it. It was in fine shape; the jungle had not succeeded in rusting away any of its thick armor plate, its basic armor. All of its hatches still opened and shut, and the rubber treads on its tracks were still largely there, and not rotted.*

*To get some idea of what it was like inside, I climbed down inside it. The top hatch was a tight fit for me. [I was then about 185 pounds at 6' 1.5".] I sort of sat on the upper small metal frame seat of the gunner (one of the 3-man crew) and then crawled down to the driver's seat down low in the front. It was so cramped I could hardly do it and had to shift the gear lever to another gear to get my rump past*

*U.S. Marine tank in North Arundel jungle. It was disabled in an attack on September 18, 1943.* [PHOTO: IAN WARNE]

*it. I then crawled out the forward hatch; it seemed like I might not have been able to wriggle my way back up out the top hatch. I don't see how the crew could have managed to exist in that cramped space.*

*I thought that this must be one of the tanks that had been destroyed by the Japanese antitank gun as described by Col. Kinoshita. We looked all over it, unsuccessfully, for the damage inflicted by an antitank shell. It just looked like a perfect tank. Alfred said that maybe the tank had burned, but I said that I knew that antitank shells had "destroyed" it; Kinoshita had told me. The tank looked like we could just put a new battery in it and start it up. Then Alfred saw two or three neat little (about one inch diameter) holes in the front armor plate down low which had penetrated the ~1.5 inches of steel plate! Now I know what antitank shells are. They don't blast the tank to smithereens; they are small shells, probably with a shaped explosive charge that creates a hypersonic jet of metal that can penetrate armor plate.*

*This, then, was clearly a tank Kinoshita saw destroyed. "I myself was standing beside the gun" he had said. The shells penetrated just in front of the driver and it is doubtful he survived. [In fact, the crews of the two damaged tanks were reported to have exited safely; Estes, p. 52.] Wilber's account describes the tank attack of the previous day, which went OK. He does not mention the destroyed tanks in the subsequent attack. However the operations reports do tell of them [Ops. of 27th Inf., p. 62].*

Again, I was walking in Wilber's footsteps. He had watched this and other tank attacks very close to this position, and had walked around the smoking battlefield with General Griswold.

*We then went back to the canoe and paddled and motored westward back to Bomboe Village, dropped off Peter, and then turned back eastward again to continue our circumnavigation of Arundel Island.*

### Ondonga

*Going eastward we (Alfred and I) again passed by Sagekarasa (the 3rd time!). I could visualize the terribly hard fighting on the west end and could see the adjacent "Island #1" where one of Wilber's "whispering chorus of observers" quietly observed the Japanese and whispered his reports into the telephone back to Wilber at Bomboe Village. On the other side of the Strait reaching up into the clouds was the mile-high extinct volcano of Kolombangara. The Japanese held Kolombangara during this action, and it dominated not only the military strategy but also the view.*

*Then we proceeded down the east side of Arundel, passing Piru Plantation where the "Eastern Force" of artillery was located during the Arundel battle and where the 169th FA Bn. subsequently was on defensive duty for four months. We then went* down to Diamond Narrows where the channel narrows to about 100 yards and flows very swiftly. The U.S. airfield on Ondonga Peninsula was there.

Now, there is a large Japanese fishing station (docks, houses, and processing plant) on Piru about where the Eastern Force was. So who won the war? I learned later that 95% of the lumber cut by the Lever Co. on Kolombangara is sold to the Japanese! The economic needs of Japan had a lot to do with the instigation of WWII. It looks to me like their economic needs are being satisfied in defeat and peaceably.

Before getting to Piru Plantation (no longer a plantation), I saw the group of islands to the west which form the outer boundary of Stima Lagoon. One of these was "Devine's Island" – across from "Carrigan's Beach" where Wilber started his unforgettable "Walk into Arundel."

Our canoe then took us down the west side of Baanga. We passed by the location of the naval guns but we couldn't see them, and arrived at Munda at about 5 p.m. for a much needed beer, swim and supper.

Alfred was pleased to see the tank. He had never seen it and had not known the story.

### Munda Rest House

*I am writing about this trip in my very plain but clean room [at Munda] with overhead fluorescent light. The windows are louvered and screened and there are no mosquitos in here. I have a shower and a working toilet. The food is good and very plain. Actually, tonight, we had cold "Crayfish" (crab meat) for the main course, quite exotic. Mayonnaise was provided for dressing, not so exotic.*

*The French fellow here with his 4-year-old (Claude and Julien) told me some of the pre-World War II history of this place. It seems that, until 1902, the natives had a headhunting practice. A bunch of them would take a very big "War Canoe" – elegant and decorated – to the Eastern Solomons, e.g. Guadalcanal, and collect some 100 heads (human) in surprise raids and return home. Only the arrival of missionaries (with guns) in 1902 stopped this practice. On the hill of a nearby island, there is a statue of a dog's head, which was supposed to warn the local natives of the approach of enemies. Two of the big canoes are near here. I may get to see them.*

*I am told that the Munda Trail is now an entirely passable road. I hope to go along there tomorrow to see the famous hills that were contested in the battle and also the former location of the Munda cemetery. The Trail was the road built to follow (and to provide supplies) to the American troops as they advanced from Zanana Beach westward toward Munda. It had been overgrown, but the government recently opened it up. I invite Claude and Julien to join us; I have good stories to tell about the fighting and he has a couple of cameras!*

So ended my second day at Munda.

I recounted the final days of my stay in the Solomons as I was returning to Port Moresby. I was at the Kieta airport in Bougainville on May 27 as I wrote this.

### Munda Trail, Wednesday, May 25

*Having done a lot of motorized canoeing my first two days at Munda, and having dunked my camera, I was ready for a more relaxed time on my last full day there. Our plans changed around a bit, but the upshot was that I hung around the Rest House for a couple of hours, went to Alfred's trial, and then went in a carryall (vehicle) down the Munda Trail.*

*Alfred had to go before the magistrate because he had socked a person who came onto his property several times and maybe into his house; I forget. He was fined $40.00. The cash he got from me must have come in handy. He showed up in neat trousers (blue) and shirt (yellow) and sat, respectfully, in the very simple one-room courthouse with about 20 chairs for spectators. The magistrate was English and normally stationed at nearby Gizo Island. His salary is partially (mostly?) paid by the English, a form of temporary subsidy to the Solomon Islands since their independence in 1978. The public defender was a 25-year-old (approximately) woman from Australia who likes scuba diving.*

*After the trial, we drove down the Munda Trail, first down the beach, then inland toward Zanana, passing Horseshoe Hill on the left and then Bartley/Reincke Ridge (Map 8). The Munda military cemetery had been on Reincke Ridge according to Alfred. Continuing toward Zanana, the road remained dry, solid, dirt and gravel. In addition to Alfred Basili, Claude, and his son, we were with the carryall owner, Ron Parkinson, an Australian who lived at Munda. Alfred says he helped tell the Americans where to build the road so it would be on dry ground.*

*The road crossed the Barike River (a stream a couple of yards wide). One branch of it was supposed to be the line of departure (Map 7); the troops of the two regiments were to line up there at attack time. It was also most probably the stream that Wilber mentioned jumping into, which encouraged the following soldiers to do likewise. We then came to the place of the July 5–8 Japanese "roadblock". Here a small company of Japanese blocked the trail and hence the advance of the entire 169th Infantry toward the Line of Departure. There is a wrecked weapons carrier (3/4 ton truck) just off the road here, which Alfred says was damaged at that roadblock.*

*We then reached Zanana, the point of the original Munda landings. It is definitely an unimpressive small little beach. It is hard to imagine two full regiments disembarking there. I always thought that Zanana must have been a poor place to land because it meant five miles of slugging through jungle to reach Munda. However, Alfred assured me it was a good place because the Liana-Munda area was heavily fortified. At Zanana, the landings were completely unopposed. Alfred told me that he joined the lead barges at Sasavele as a scout to help guide them into the beach.*

Alfred's testimony of the events near Munda was interesting, but of course was sometimes incomplete or even wrong. I later was told by Naylor, 1st battalion commander, 172nd Infantry, of the confusion and failure the first night they tried to get in through the narrow channels. He said the natives were supposed to mark the channel with lights in their canoes. However, that didn't work, and many of the American boats got lost or went aground. No one got onto the beach that first night.

*On the way back up the Munda Trail to the airfield, we stopped at the roadblock, took photos of the old weapons carrier, and then went on to the Barike River. We got out and hiked about 200 to 300 yards upstream to a delightful waterfall about seven yards high. At the bottom was a pool, circular about ten yards across. So we stripped to our shorts and swam in the clear clean cool (but not cold) water under the tall jungle trees with dappled sunshine coming down between the leaves, beautiful, a jungle paradise. If the tall trees had had vines on them it would have been a perfect place to swing out over the pool and jump in. This recreational pleasure was a far cry from the 1943 scene.*

*After the swim, we continued toward Munda and stopped at Horseshoe Hill. Alfred knew that name and it is so labeled on Map 8. We hiked past a garden and up a ridge on the Munda side to the top; it was only a ten-minute stroll. At the top, one saw a series of low rolling hills; the "horseshoe" shape of the one we were on was difficult to discern.*

*These Japanese-held ridges were in front of portions of five regiments of the U.S. Army when they attacked from a new Line of Departure on July 25. It was during this attack that Christian ("Cris") and French, both long-time friends of Wilber's from Washington State, and also his own Lt. Malone, were killed. Horseshoe Hill is the hill that Wilber plastered with artillery and for which (in part) Wilber received the Legion of Merit. The critical nature of Horseshoe Hill is apparent on Miller's map, in that it took until August 1 for the front to reach the other side of these ridges. The Japanese defense was fierce and tenacious.*

*From the top of Horseshoe Hill, one could see straight across flat land (largely planted with palm trees to Munda airfield. On the left was the water and on the right was the series of hills leading to Bibilo Hill, just north of the airfield. The 161st and 145th Regiments had to fight through these. We could also look across to where the cemetery had been; it was now overgrown mostly with low bushes. The bodies had since been moved to the National Cemetery in Manila or returned to the U.S.*

## COMBAT AND NEW LIFE  PART 11: INTERLUDE 1983

The hill just northwest of Horseshoe Hill was Christian Hill, named for Wilber's former sergeant of the 161st Infantry who was killed there. [Karolevitz, map p. 48]

*On the way down Horseshoe Hill, we saw a "scarecrow" in a garden. It was a pair of crossed sticks with burlap for a cloak, and an old rusty G.I. American helmet on top for a head that seemed to be looking toward Munda. It was a potent symbol of what had occurred there.*
*We then came back to Munda for a welcome beer.*

### SASAVELE, AGAIN, THURSDAY, MAY 26

The next morning, my last at Munda, we took Alfred's canoe eastward toward Zanana Beach and stopped on Nusa Banga where we saw a newly made war canoe of the type used by the head hunters of the western Solomons in their head-hunting raids in the eastern Solomons. We then visited Sasavele again, where we found the likely location of the fire direction center pit as recounted above.

That afternoon, Thursday, I departed Munda on Solaire for the ten-minute flight to Ringi Cove (Vila airfield) on Kolombangara. It was the beginning of my trip back to modern civilization. However, my adventures in the Solomons were not yet over.

*Scarecrow constructed of a cross of sticks, burlap, and a rusted American GI helmet, in a garden on Horseshoe Hill, New Georgia, May 1983.* [PHOTO: CLAUDE COLOMER]

# 10

## *Kolombangara: the way out*

### May 1983

The travel arrangements in the Solomons had a charming informality and uncertainty about them. Each step of my journey out of the Solomons was a minor triumph. My long absence from my host institute in Japan was close to violating the terms of my fellowship there. I was still at Munda Thursday morning, and it was my goal was to reach Port Moresby in time for my long-scheduled 3 p.m. Saturday flight to Japan.

I continued my account, still at Kieta airport on May 27.

**TRAVEL CHALLENGES, THURSDAY, MAY 26, CONT.**

*I had learned that I could fly to Port Moresby by flying directly northwest up to Kieta on Bougainville Island via Solaire and taking a jet from there. The alternative was flying 210 miles southeast to Guadalcanal (the wrong way), and then reversing direction in a jet that would fly over Munda at 30,000 feet altitude en route to Kieta. The direct Solaire flight would be a lot less mileage in a small plane at low altitude, and I would thus see a lot more of the northwest Solomons. So, I needed my ticket rewritten. That had to be done in Honiara (Guadalcanal), so my plane coupon (for Solaire) had been sent there, carried by a Solaire flight, and it came back OK.*

Political lesson: Kieta is on Bougainville (Map 2), the largest and most northwest of the Solomon Islands, but Bougainville is part of the sovereign state of Papua New Guinea (PNG), the capital of which is Port Moresby, my destination. I was currently in the sovereign state of Solomon Islands. In short, Kieta was across a national border. However, it was a border I had successfully crossed en route to Guadalcanal a week earlier.

*On the day before my departure from Munda, I was told (surprise!) by the local Munda representative of Solaire that I needed a visa to enter PNG and that to get it, my passport would have to go to Honiara. On the day before leaving! I was given a long form to fill out. I protested mightily that when I went through PNG a week earlier no advance visa was required. I was assured that it was necessary and that if I didn't get it, I would be put right back on the plane at Kieta (PNG) and sent back to the Solomons! So, in view of Solaire's demonstrated efficiency with my traveler's checks and tickets, I gave up my passport and held my breath.*

### RINGI COVE, KOLOMBANGARA

*The flight from Munda to Vila airfield at Ringi Cove on Kolombangara (the volcanic island across Blackett Strait from Arundel) took only a few minutes, and provided beautiful low-altitude views of Baanga and Arundel. It was there that I would pick up the flight to Kieta on the following day (Friday the 27th) and, hopefully, my returned passport would arrive there on that flight, which originated in Honiara. At Ringi Cove, there is no town or rest house, only a timber company, so I was put up by a hospitable young English couple, Ian and Liz Warne, who were with the timber company. They had two boys, and their home was modern and comfortable.*

*After arriving at the famed Vila airfield, I went off with my hosts to a lovely clear stream for a swim in a little pool about one or two yards deep (at most) and five yards across. Upon our return I spent some time with the radio operator talking to Honiara about my visa, but that accomplished little. My hosts thought it very unlikely my passport would arrive the next morning and urged me to relax and enjoy Kolombangara and their hospitality during the likely multi-day wait for later airline connections.*

> In short, they advised this anxious professor to calm down and smell the roses. It was sometimes hard for me to do that.

*That evening, I saw a movie at the timber company "Club" with a subdued but friendly group of about 15 people (mostly or all English). It was a warm tropical evening. The movie projector didn't focus too well because of a hard-to-cure fungus growth on the lens I was told. The movie was John Wayne in "Alamo"! It was all macho, manhood, stand up and die, etc. etc. I could feel so much of that in the islands and jungles around me. I could see where such attitudes got people like Tomonari, the soldiers of the 27th Regiment, and eventually my father. The movie amplified my sense of the place despite its [the movie's] blatant artificiality.*

*After the movie, one of my hosts took me down to the docks in order to show me Blackett Strait in the light of the full moon. The little offshore islands of Arundel seemed very close even though they were almost a mile away. To that peaceful*

CHAPTER 10    *Kolombangara: the way out*

*Liz and Ian Warne and their two sons, Peter (one year) and Alastair (four years), my hosts on Kolombangara Island, May 1983.* [PHOTO: IAN WARNE]

*scene, I superimposed Japanese barges, lights, frantic reinforcement activity, and artillery shell explosions. I could sense the excitement and fears of the Japanese as they looked out onto the same scene, though to my host, standing beside me, it was just a story.*

The moon was exactly full that night, May 26, 1983. In September 1943, it was full on the 14th, the day before Wilber arrived at Bomboe Village. As the week wore on, the early evenings would have been dark with the moon rising an hour later each evening. It rose at about midnight when the Japanese were completing their evacuation on the 21st. Moonlight facilitated accurate artillery fire.

*This imagined time travel would have been even more vivid if I had been around a few weeks earlier to hear the old buried artillery shell or bomb explode unexpectedly near the Kolombangara Camp in the middle of the night. In the Solomons, it is OK to burn vegetation off your fields, but you stand well back to avoid unpleasant surprises.*

### Gizo and Ballale, Friday, May 27

*I rose early the next morning and packed my bag on the off chance that the passport/visa problem would work out. Indeed it did. The pilot had my passport, and told me that a PNG visa was not needed if I was only in transit – just as I had said! Fortunately, I had my bag with me and was ready to hop on the plane. My hosts were quite surprised that it all came together and that I was actually leaving.*

*On taking off, I saw Devil's Island (now Lighthouse Island) and Stepping Stone Island. Both are prominent in Wilber's story. Plum Island was passed shortly; this is where Jack Kennedy swam with his men after PT-109 was sunk. We then landed on a tiny island, of diameter only the length of the dirt runway. The non-runway part was grass covered. This was the airport that services the bigger adjacent island of Gizo. The attendants pumped fuel into the aircraft here while a steady stream of gas poured from the leaky pump onto the ground. The pilot commented that he had suggested they fix this some time ago. They had all of us out of the plane for this operation. I was a bit concerned about my luggage: notes, exposed film, etc. Fortunately, the gas didn't ignite.*

*We left Gizo with me in the co-pilot's seat and headed for the Shortland Islands and specifically the airport on the small island of Ballale. This is small but bigger than the Gizo airport islet. It has jungle surrounding the airstrip. This was a big Japanese bomber base in WWII. "All the good runways in the Solomons were built by the Japanese," said my pilot. The Shortlands are the most northwest islands of the sovereign state of Solomon Islands, and are just off Bougainville. Flying around these small islands in small planes is fascinating, fun, and beautiful. What a wonderful way to see the Solomons. Our pilot walked me up and across the Ballale runway and into the trees where there was a wrecked Japanese Betty Bomber, probably disabled by American bombing. I regretted not having a camera.*

*I went through PNG customs at Ballale, though I was still in Solomon Islands. The air terminal was like a bus stop shelter; it had enough sun cover for a couple of tables and a few chairs.*

The plane continued on to Kieta in Papua New Guinea where I was to get a jet plane to Port Moresby. Kieta was on the east coast of Bougainville. High jungle-covered mountains rose up inland from the coast. Our flight path was westward over these huge mountains. I had a long wait and so had time to write up much of the above.

CHAPTER 10    *Kolombangara: the way out*

### Kieta Airport, May 27

*I'm in Kieta, PNG (on Bougainville) in an open terminal waiting room with overhead fans providing a warm(!) breeze. The terminal is small but large compared to those at Ballale and Gizo which were more like bus stops. It is very poor but cosmopolitan and Caribbean-like: blacks, whites, babies, etc. It is a very different world than Boston or Tokyo.*

*My plane to Port Moresby is here finally; it is 1:45 p.m. (Kieta time). Somebody gave me sandwiches so I did not starve. The flight to Rabaul, is here too, despite an earlier announcement that it had been cancelled to the disgust of waiting passengers who have since left the airport. It would have been fun to go to Rabaul to see the many war relics there. The goal of all the fighting in the Solomons was to neutralize the great Japanese naval base there.*

Our plane took off and headed straight for the mountains in a steep straight climb. I gathered that the plan was to clear the mountains on this flight path. We climbed and climbed as the terrain underneath us rose and rose, up to almost a mile high. The peaks still far ahead looked rather ominous. There were numerous military airplanes in World War II that had crashed into the often rain-shrouded New Guinea mountaintops. Some of those wrecks were not found for decades. Thanks to my careful attention(!), our plane did indeed clear the peaks of Bougainville without deviating one bit from its straight-line rising flight path.

*Port Moresby; I made it!!!*

### Port Moresby, Saturday, May 28

*The next day finds me in Port Moresby beside the hotel pool soaking up the sun. My plane leaves for Hong Kong at 3 p.m. This is the flight I had originally scheduled long ago, and here I am, much to my amazement, actually ready to board it.*

Thus ended my week tracing Wilber's footsteps in the Solomon Islands. It was an adventure into another world and time. Legends from the war came alive for me. Soldiers of two nations were there again as were their struggles, sufferings, deaths, and pride of accomplishment. Looking back on my visit now, in 2014, that week in the Solomons and indeed my entire month-long Pacific adventure seem like a dream.

In the next pages, Wilber's story continues, as the 43rd Division settled into a defensive posture on Ondonga Island in the Solomons with time for recreation, training, and reflection.

# PART III

# ONDONGA PALM GROVE

NEW GEORGIA (SOLOMON ISLANDS)
OCTOBER 1943–JANUARY 1944

★ ☆

# 11

# *"Swan doesn't polish those insignia very much"*

## Ondonga, New Georgia
## October 1943

With the end of the Arundel combat, the different components of the 43rd Division moved to defensive positions on the New Georgia and Russell Island groups. Two batteries (B and C) of Wilber's outfit, the 169th Field Artillery Battalion, remained at Piru Plantatation, Ondonga (New Georgia), but moved to new positions there. Wilber returned to his unit at Ondonga September 26, and Battery A returned from Bustling Point on September 29. For a few days, Japanese artillery (dubbed "Pistol Pete") on Kolombangara Island occasionally fired into the 169th area, but with little effect. The Americans had invaded Vella Lavella, the island beyond Kolombangara, on August 15, thus bypassing and isolating Kolombangara, which the Japanese evacuated on October 3. The 27th Infantry Regiment landed on Kolombangara a few days later on October 6, and Wilber visited it on October 8.

The Japanese offered no ground resistance to the American forces on Vella Lavella, but resisted American efforts to resupply its troops there with heavy but largely ineffective air attacks. The Japanese successfully evacuated 600 troops from the island despite American efforts to prevent it. In that encounter, the naval Battle of Vella Lavella (October 6 and 7), one Japanese and one American destroyer were sunk and two other American destroyers were damaged. After this, no organized Japanese troops remained in the New Georgia area.

## COMBAT AND NEW LIFE   PART III: ONDONGA PALM GROVE

But the possibility of a Japanese counterthrust remained, so the mission of the 43rd Division was initially defensive as well as rest and rehabilitation of the soldiers and equipment. With time, as the threat of attack receded, the focus of attention became the training for the next combat.

As Wilber's unit began this recuperation period, Norma was beginning the last month of her pregnancy in Washington, D.C. Wilber's letters during the four-month period on Ondonga revealed a relaxation of the tensions of combat, reflections on that combat, and the gradual rising of spirits and health; but this was tempered by Wilber's growing concern about Norma's life and activities.

x · o · ø · o · x

By October 3, when this next letter was written, the 169th Field Artillery was fully assembled on Piru Plantation with Wilber present and in command. Other elements of the division were elsewhere in the New Georgia group on defensive duty; division headquarters was at Munda, nine miles south of Ondonga. As Wilber put it, the battalion "is my baby now." The Japanese had just evacuated Kolombangara, so they could no longer fire on the 169th area, but enemy bombers posed an occasional threat. Wilber settled down to comment on his forthcoming promotion party and to catch up on letters he had received from Norma. He also provided us with more insight into the recent combat.

### OCT. 3, 1943

Dearest Nana — I'll just stick a note in with a letter I want you to have and get it ready to mail now. Gagner is going to Div. Hq. and can mail it. It's Sunday + I am giving, with our Doctor [Charles D'Avanzo] who is also just promoted, a little party to my officers and Downen. It is the so-called "wetting of the leaves" and is often quite an alcoholic matter. ["Leaves" referred to the oak leaf insignia worn by majors and lieutenant colonels.] Now the chief feature will be lobster stew, a Tom Collins (improvised), and a chicken dinner (from the Doc) plus misc. items sent from the States such as sardines, jam, and clam chowder. Just what will result after it all goes thru the cooks' hands is questionable but combat is over for the time being and it's our first chance to sit down together. Time 3:00 P.M. this afternoon. I wish you could be the hostess.

More mail up to Sept. 13 came and packages galore. I've received the razor, film, blades, mirror, talcum, Vit. "C," and probably some other things which came while I was a bit rushed.

CHAPTER 11    *Swan doesn't polish those insignia very much*

*Officers of the 169th Field Artillery Battalion at the promotion party hosted by Wilber (at head of table) and Charles D'Avanzo, the battalion medical doctor, at Ondonga on October 3, 1943. The large canvas tent in the background was probably where Wilber and Captain Rainey lived. If so, the canvas covered two smaller tents [letter 10/30/43]. These were the officers who carried the 169th through three months of Solomon Islands combat.*
[PHOTO: CHARLES D'AVANZO]

… Now I'm back in a cocoanut grove where things are more quiet and where I hope to rest and rehabilitate my men. Don [Downen of the 161st Infantry] is about 300 yards away so I hope to see him often. Barker just received the Legion of Merit medal, which is the 4th highest given by our country, and I think he earned it. — I love you Sweetheart Mine. Wilber XXXOOO

During this period, Wilber occasionally sent home photos taken by the battalion medical officer, Charles D'Avanzo. In 1985, I asked Howard Brown,

*Captain Charles D'Avanzo (left) and Wilber relaxing outside (Wilber's?) tent, Ondonga, September 1943. D'Avanzo was the battalion medical doctor and an avid photographer.*
[PHOTO: CHARLES D'AVANZO]

a veteran of the 169th Field Artillery what had become of Dr. D'Avanzo. D'Avanzo had died, but he referred me to his widow in Longmeadow, Massachusetts. I called on her and had a wonderful visit. It turned out that the doctor had been an avid photographer and had ever so neatly organized and labeled his large collection of photographic negatives. She graciously gave me those from the few months he was with the 169th. I reciprocated by giving her a booklet of prints of them. D'Avanzo was injured during the Luzon landings but survived to practice medicine for many years in Springfield, Massachusetts.

D'Avanzo's photographs of Wilber's "party" captured the officers of the 169th Field Artillery Battalion in a special relaxed moment. These were the citizen soldiers who led the battalion so capably through the Munda, Baanga, and Arundel actions.

x·o·ø·o·x

### [PIRU PLANTATION] OCT. 3, 1943

Dearest Lover of Mine — I've just finished a "quickie" letter to you so it could start today. I'll try to make this one a little more satisfactory and complete. Business first. – On Sept 29, I sent you two checks: #15823 for $108.30 and #16015 for $221.50. They represent three months pay of that portion I have been getting. [The other portions went directly to Norma and his parents.] I asked for checks for greater safety during combat. Now I'm broke but will get cash next time and can then pay Swan [his orderly and driver] for the five months I owe him and other items such as postage, barber bills, etc.

The [silver lieutenant colonel] leaves came within two days of the time I was notified of my promotion. I also have two others: one presented by the Exec of the 27th Inf. and the other by the G-3 of our division. They happened to match so that is a third pair. Confidentially I like yours [the ones you sent] best. They are smooth surfaced and will look best when shined. Of course the others are better for combat. I wear my insignia in combat so the infantry enlisted man will know the artillery is really right with them. It's heart warming to see the look of appreciation on the face of a tired, dirty and maybe discouraged private who is on the way forward to possible blackout [death]. However I must admit Swan doesn't polish those insignia very much, and I haven't complained at all....

> Snipers tried to identify officers as the more valuable targets.

Last night and the night before were so peaceful. No bombs and no shelling by Pistol Pete. Maybe Col. Hill [C.O. 192nd Field Artillery Battalion] finally located Pete and dropped a few on him. [Hill's 155-mm guns had a greater range than Wilber's 105-mm.] Anyway our sleep was uninterrupted. Regarding the massacre on the Munda Trail of our wounded, don't get too upset about it. Some of my friends were killed then, so we all work at fighting that much harder now. The only answer I know is to drive the Japs back to their island and keep them there....

COMBAT AND NEW LIFE   PART III: ONDONGA PALM GROVE

Wilber was clearly suppressing feelings about losing friends in that "massacre."

I know you will never leave me. You haven't a chance if you tried. You keep reassuring me, and I "ain't" even worried. You're hooked, Lady, for the duration. You are my most solid rock and I'm counting terribly much on you to be there when I come back. It is the most wonderful thing I ever knew to have you with me thru this war. The war seems so trivial beside your love for me. It gets noisy now + then, but the music of my Nana sounds clear + pure thru the noise + confusion to me. Sometimes it is fearfully tiring but Nana's love comes by with a little extra help and everything is well. When danger seems close, your spirit is closer and keeps my mind clear and my eyes + ears sharp. All in all you seem to be a pretty necessary part of this soldier's equipment. When I get home I'll chain you to my belt so you'll always be near. I do so love you.

Was Norma reassuring Wilber that she would never leave him, or was she reassuring herself? His response in this letter was written while she was a full eight months pregnant. Her reassurance was likely genuine; perhaps she had already decided that she would cast her lot with Wilber, not with Monte. Her plan for her baby would be revealed by her later actions.

… I agree very heartily on the plans for the children. Did I tell you I had made an allotment of $5.00 per month to each for extra needs. I required no limit on how it was to be spent but did ask for a monthly account by items of how it was spent. The first check should reach them Nov. 1. Remember too many phone calls and letters will be considered as a "hanging on" and a nuisance eventually. Don't over do it + don't become their errand girl.

… Anyway I'm up to Aug 29 in your letters + must stop. Today I go to Bairoko harbor to bring Goff back. It's my baby now [the 169th Field Artillery]. I love you and hold you close. — Wilber

x·o·ø·o·x

Wilber wrote to his father with a number of insights into jungle warfare.

**OCT. 4, 1943**
Dear Father — I've practically no idea what I have told you of my recent actions. At least you know the Munda job is old now. Did I tell you my battalion was in the Baanga Island action? Probably so since that was in August. For September, the

169th went into business again on Arundel I. There we practically eliminated the Jap l3th Inf., which was rated as one of Japan's best two regiments.…

I wish I could have a few of the things you can grow and have on the farm. Today I ate my first fried eggs for a year, and it was a storage egg. In some ways you had an advantage in France [in World War I]. However, I wanted to fight the Japs and I'm satisfied. They may get me pretty soon, but I have already credited myself with a Jap regimental [Col. Satoshi Tomonari] and two Jap battalion commanders of the 13th Inf. and also the complete destruction of the C.P. of the Jap 229th Inf. [probably on Baanga Island]. Consequently even if they do catch up with me, I'll feel the score is still in my favor.…

> This attitude was not unique to Wilber; General Griswold considered Colonel Tomonari a personal adversary [this work, p. 105]. War was a very high-stakes personal game in the eyes of some senior officers. Your life was on the table, and you could win even if killed! Unfortunately the pawns were living human beings.

Answering yours of Aug. 4th. The matters of escaping death by a "narrow margin" as you say have had no bad effects. The wounds were both trivial and only one bothers me at all. The bone over my eye is probably fractured. The surgeon thinks a bone splinter will work out eventually so I'm waiting. In the meantime it only bothers me – Oct. 7 – when I bump it. As you know narrow escapes are pretty common in war, and in the jungle one always is aware of numerous possibilities. Some can be guarded against, but often the only way to know if an area is clear is to walk thru it. Fortunately the Jap sniper is a very poor shot at moving targets. I have repeatedly walked thru sniper fire without any unusual feeling of hazard, but have seen several men killed there at the same time because they stopped a minute.

> His repeated mention of the sniper fire put the lie to "without any unusual feeling of hazard." The psychological effects of these repeated threats to his life went unmentioned or were vastly downplayed. Was his father impressed by his son's "sangfroid" [imperturbability, or literally, cold blood] or could he see through it?

The Jap with a machine gun is another story. One does well to see them first, which is not always possible. They have an annoying habit too of letting 2/3 of a group pass before opening fire. The tendency is to call them masters of camouflage. However all anyone needs to do to be camouflaged in this country is not to wear a red uniform and to sit or lie still. The Marines built the Jap up to a superman with fanatical death-desiring courage and great shrewdness of combat. Most of that is baloney. In the jungle, anyone on the move is at a disadvantage. We are on the offensive, which gives the Jap that advantage. The Marines were on the defensive [on Guadalcanal] so have no excuse.

In many ways the Jap is quite dumb. For example: I was able to completely knock out five efforts to reinforce Arundel just because all their barges stopped at Devil's Island. One would have thought they paid toll there. As many as thirty times I fired on boats that stopped there. D.I. was too small to have more than a few men on it, (not more than 75 yards long), but all boats stopped.

They are not brave in a personal way. I have repeatedly seen them throw away their guns and run wildly away from my artillery fire. They scream like children or pigs when I get fire right on them. To date, altho I've seen a lot of our wounded receive those wounds, I've never heard an American soldier give way to pain or fear to the extent of screaming. We (the 169th) have several times literally chased them by artillery fire into the open so disorganized that our infantry could shoot them at will.

Their organized areas are usually quite filthy according to our standards, with feces likely to be anywhere and food fragments on the ground. However most areas are strongly and well organized and difficult to take.

> I am torn here by these criticisms of the marines and also of the Japanese. Norma's half-brother, Stoney Sparlin, served as a medical corpsman with the Fourth Marine Raider Battalion, which fought on New Georgia Island and elsewhere. He was a wonderful fellow, but was deeply critical of the army's slow deliberate ways and presumed incompetence. The antipathy, fueled by inter-service rivalry, went both ways, it seems. There was some truth in both sides' criticisms; neither branch was ideal. The marines' initial failure to capture Bairoko Harbor in northern New Georgia mirrored the army's performance at Munda.
>
> After earning my PhD in 1961, I worked closely with Japanese colleagues in cosmic rays and x-ray astronomy and during my 1983 sabbatical leave in Japan. Two Japanese academics became valuable mentors to me. In my experience, the Japanese culture is typified by cleanliness and reserve, which runs counter to these stories of screaming and filth. (Perhaps we should ask why it was that the American soldiers didn't "scream" when injured or fired upon, or perhaps they sometimes did.)
>
> The filth that Wilber encountered in Japanese quarters may have arisen from Japanese commanders in the Solomons being less concerned about disease than the American. As for "dumb" actions such as boats stopping at Devil's Island, every army and navy has its share of "dumb," stubborn officers. Another possibility was that the American artillery fire disrupted Japanese communications, and Japanese coxswains were following earlier orders that could not be changed.

CHAPTER 11  *Swan doesn't polish those insignia very much*

The fact that so few prisoners are taken is not an indication of the Japs bravery. I think it is normal to the jungle. One doesn't take the risk of ordering surrender; one shoots or is shot by the time the first two seconds of an encounter have passed. The enemy is usually only a few feet away when you see him or he sees you and from then on it's a case of who moves first. If one is wounded, the cover gives him a chance to crawl or be carried away. The final factor is the basic distrust between the two races. Every American is pretty well agreed they would fight to the finish rather than be a prisoner.

> The Japanese army was notoriously cruel to its own soldiers. Some of these soldiers in turn were savagely cruel to those under them, such as American soldiers who had been captured, because surrender was disgraceful in their eyes.

When they attack, as you have read, the Japs always yell before they charge the American lines. I have heard it several times and have yet to recognize the "banzai" they are credited with. Some officers though say they have heard it. When I have been with attacked groups it has just been a plain yell like "yea" prolonged. I don't know if this interests you or not, but I'm sure a lot of hokum gets in the papers from some of our returned "heroes." My predecessor [Lieutenant Colonel "Knight," a pseudonym] is one. He, it now seems, is home because of a severe wound received in Guadalcanal. Actually he was wounded by the rumor that we were going into Munda. Anyway he has since been released from the Army and is making many speeches on "Slow Starvation in the S. Pac" "The Horrors of Life in the Jungle" "Jap Jungle Tactics" etc. All get into the paper and come back here [for us to see]....

> This was a pretty devastating comment to make about his former commanding officer. In an earlier letter [of 5/29/43], Wilber had acknowledged that his predecessor really did appear to have health issues when he was relieved.

Last week I took a physical exam and was pleased to find myself still in good shape. I am very tired, but that isn't too surprising since I have been in nearly continuous combat for three months. It has just happened that my Bn. got all the big jobs. Anyway except for the first few nights out, I sleep like a log and that helps. Twice, tho, I've renewed my little-sleep habits. Once on the Munda job I went without for six days and nights. More recently on Arundel, I slept for five days and nights only between 3:00 A.M. and 6:00 A.M., thereby confusing a lot of Japs and amazing the infantry I was supporting. So I feel fine but tired now.

... This letter has rambled a lot but I thought you would like a few sidelights on some of the situations I have seen. — I love you, Wilber

# COMBAT AND NEW LIFE    PART III: ONDONGA PALM GROVE

x · o · ø · o · x

Wilber was presented with a surprising opportunity.

**OCT 8, 1943**

Dearest Wife of Mine — This will be a "quickie" letter for it will be dark soon.…

This is a problem facing me now. My answer has been "No!" but of course in the Army if a Lt. Col. says "No" and the general says "YES!" the decision is made. I find myself in the highly flattering position of being asked(?) to become the Regimental Executive and Second in Command of the 169th Inf. by both the regimental commander (Col. Holland) and the division commander (Gen. Wing). It is one of the most unusual situations I ever saw for an artillery officer to be requested to become an infantry officer in a higher position. Barker tells me that it is because I have a reputation and that the opportunity is really that they want me to take command of the regiment after about six months. That would mean, if I make good, promotion to Colonel in about a year. As I said above, I am trying to decline on the basis that my training is not what I would want for that position, if I were choosing a regimental executive.

> Colonel Holland had again assumed command of the 169th Infantry on September 16. A direct path to command as a full colonel was non-existent for an artillery officer in the triangular organization of the 43rd Division because there was no regiment of artillery. (A regiment is normally commanded by a full colonel.) There were only infantry regiments. The typical promotion for an artillery lieutenant colonel would have been to executive officer of division artillery, a colonel's position, but that was not a command position.

To me (and that is selfish and will not be considered), the situation is that I already am pretty well a marked artilleryman throughout the XIV Corps, and I could become a poor regimental commander if things weren't going good with an equally [widespread] but less desirable reputation. Anyway there it is. Papa is on the spot. DeBlois says "Here is your chance to be a general." I offered it to him, but of course he isn't up for consideration. It will be settled soon and I'll let you know if I make the change. Meanwhile, I'm still your artilleryman. Don't let this get any publicity.

Today I went to Kolombangara and to Vila Field [on Kolombangara]. It's fun to fire on [Japanese] territory then a little later walk over ground and know it's U.S. Territory. You feel you have paid back a little of the debt to Washington and Jefferson and Lincoln and those who created our country. It was interesting, and the volcano (extinct) is majestic. I'd like to climb it but one can't for a long time for there will be stray Japs in the jungle. So I've been on another of the Solomon Isl. [Islands]. It's dark.

CHAPTER 11   *Swan doesn't polish those insignia very much*

I do love you above all else. Don't worry about my last problem. Whichever way it goes I'll make it turn out all right. — XXX Wilber

On October 10, the army took an official portrait of Wilber. In it, he had a disquieting appearance that reflected, it seems to me, the previous three exhausting months of jungle combat.

*Official army portrait of a tired-looking Wilber, taken on October 10, 1943, shortly after the end of the Solomons combat. His right eyebrow showed no sign of the shrapnel lodged in the bone there. He wore his newly acquired lieutenant-colonel insignia, the silver oak leaf, on his right collar. On the other, he wore the crossed cannons of the field artillery.*
[PHOTO: U.S. ARMY]

COMBAT AND NEW LIFE    PART III: ONDONGA PALM GROVE

x·o·ø·o·x

On October 14, René DeBlois, Wilber's executive officer, moved with about half of Wilber's staff to Bustling Point to command the reconstituted (so-called) Provisional Battalion there. The next day, Battery A followed them there [169th History and Journal; letter 1/25/44]. This was a repositioning of forces for defensive purposes. Wilber, as C.O., then had to take on the responsibilities of the executive officer for the rest of his battalion remaining on Ondonga. This was a substantial administrative burden.

### OCT. 16, 1943
*[Note to me by Norma:] Hale: Please return.*
Dearest Norma — I've been writing to Dean Cloke [at U. of Maine]. It has taken a week so you can see what my schedule is like now. In the first place it has mostly been busy work and every so often someone up top would change his (and our) plans. For the time being, my battalion seems doomed (?) to a quiet period.…

Oct. 17.… I'm still an artilleryman and expect to stay so. The C.O. 169th Inf. growled at me about it, but I said I'd be up front with him anyway [as his artillery commander], to which he agreed. I finally decided I was too tired to tackle a new field this late in the war. It was interesting tho that Don's regimental commander [161st Infantry] strongly advised me to take it saying he would jump at the chance to have a good artillery officer on his staff. He further said he had discovered an unusual loyalty to me in his regiment, that numerous of his officers had spoken most highly of me. Because of what he had seen of my methods and my reputation in his own regiment, he had every confidence in my success in the infantry. So I didn't take it. If I can come home Lt. Col. of F.A. in good standing, I'm going to be content and won't even wonder if I could have been Col. of Inf.

> Why did Wilber decline the infantry position with the prospects of a regimental command and a promotion? He probably was reluctant to expose himself to failure in a more visible position, for which he did not have the usual qualifications. Earlier, General Barker had made such a move when he was appointed commander of the 43rd Infantry Division, and it did not work out well for him. This surely was one consideration for Wilber.
>
> Later, in 1945, prior to the planned invasion of Japan, Wilber did make exactly this transition, from artillery to executive officer of an infantry regiment. He was not given a choice and by then probably had a higher level of confidence that he could handle the job.

CHAPTER 11   *Swan doesn't polish those insignia very much*

There are some compensations to being in the 169th FA Bn. One officer in the 43d Div. Arty and the General are to have two weeks leave in New Zealand as a rest. It is a reward and recognition too of outstanding service in combat. Barker offered it to me. I declined and asked for the chance to name one of my officers....

It was good to read the letters to you from our [Pullman, Washington] friends, but I know they probably upset you. However it is nice to be upset by kindness and thoughtfulness. I have felt bad about Cris and French too. Both died within two hundred yards of me [during the July 25 attack toward Munda airfield]. The old group is diminished. Those two are dead, Langley transferred, Hudleson evacuated with rheumatism, Faler with malaria, Lamont with machine gun wounds, but Don and McCalder are still OK. I told Don I'd like him in my Bn. He said he'd like me to take his, so we parted in good spirits.

> McCalder was killed in combat in Luzon in 1945; Downen survived the war. Wilber's connection to his friends in Company E of the 161st Infantry was warm and intense. He deeply felt the departure or loss of its members.

Wasn't Lake Louise [British Columbia, Canada] wonderful [on our honeymoon]? DeBlois + I are going to take our wives + family there some day. We've discussed it thoroughly and seriously both knowing the wives will make the final decision. Anyway, even there, the most beautiful breathtaking thing was my lovely bride. That was one of so many perfect days with you. No. We stayed at L. Louise two days and one night. Papa was counting his finances and stayed two nights and one day at Sicamous [BC] for half the price....

> Norma was apparently recalling details of their honeymoon in 1927. Her state of mind at that point is painful to contemplate today. Was she trying desperately to re-connect with Wilber or was she cynically digging up their history just to keep his morale up? Honeymoon memories were an unlikely choice for the latter. This and her subsequent actions suggested she was determined to "do the right thing" by Wilber. (Of course, this could well be the wishful imagining of a surviving son.)

I'm just tickled to death about Hale's school. It sounds like a wonderful place and I'm sure Hale will learn a lot and enjoy it too. We may yet land on a farm after this war. I hope he does learn a trade such as printing or typing too. It's dark. I love your letters. Don't worry too hard. — [No closing]

x·o·ø·o·x

# COMBAT AND NEW LIFE    PART III: ONDONGA PALM GROVE

It was on October 20–22 that Wilber had sat down to write the four long letters recounting the Arundel combat that appeared in Chapter 6. The beginnings and ends of those letters, heretofore omitted, provide some of the minutiae of his life at Ondonga and give us context for his writing the Arundel story.

### OCTOBER 20, 1943 [EARLY]

Dearest Wife — … the Pac[ific]-Asiatic ribbon came, also the blades, also the soap. Thanks for all three. The ribbon was the first one we had seen, and the men and officers were most interested.

[Here he recounts the Arundel Story, Part 1.]

[Marginal note:] I am taking your suggestion of using Paul's home [Wilber's brother in Washington D.C.] as my home address. Will make changes on [dog] tags. — Love, WEB

x·o·ø·o·x

### OCT. 20, 1943 [EVENING]

Yes Dearest I'm back again — And I love you and wish I could see you and hold you in my arms tonight. It is after seven P.M. and I've just finished with a battery commanders' meeting. Supper was at four thirty. It is dark now but Rainey who lives with me has a gasoline lantern and we can read and write in luxury. Now we are so far back of the front lines that lights are permitted if they do not shine up. Of course they go out in a hurry in the event of a raid.

[Here he presents the Arundel story, Part 2.]

How about starting three washcloths my way? I'm about out. — Goodnight Lover. WEB.

x·o·ø·o·x

### OCTOBER 21, 1943

Dear Darling of My Dreams — It's seven again after supper, and I'm thru for the day. Tomorrow Barker will be here for an inspection of our men and area. So today has been a good housecleaning day. Rainey and I had to move our tent, so Swan and R's [Rainey's] orderly and R. & I worked all A.M. on personal and unofficial labor. Very satisfying too, for I now live on a floor. We stole it when another unit moved out before the next found it.

[Arundel Story, Part 3] — XXXOOO Wilber

## OCTOBER 22, 1943

It's evening again Darling — I'm just thru with a dish of ice cream. The CBs [Construction Battalions] have an ice cream machine, and they have twice helped us give our men some for dessert. Believe me, that's a real treat here. We will probably all join the Naval Construction Battalions in the next war. The doctor has cultivated a few of their doctors and came over tonight with a dish of some he had gotten for his men and himself. I was holding a staff and battery commanders' meeting, so that dish was shared pretty thin, but the morale went way up.

Barker is off to New Zealand for his leave. He inspected us the last thing before he left by plane.... Our inspection went well, and because of that I declared the rest of the day to be a holiday. It was little [enough] to do [for the men].

[Arundel Story, Part 4]

I never wrote up the battle of Baanga for you. It was a depressing and unfortunate affair in several ways. We did our part well but it was expensive to us. Heidelberger is missing in action there, and three of his men were wounded [and one died]. He was one of my best officers, and I sent him in to a bad spot. It's good to be able to sleep nights, as I can now, and not to have to send officers and men [to dangerous] places.

... Answering your Aug. 21. I'm afraid my wounds are a bit too trivial to be justification for all those letters. Most people visualize a leg or arm shot off – movie stuff. It's queer how impressions are so rigid. It is true tho that the first wounded soldier I saw had exactly that kind of wound – a leg off at the hip joint, so I had a rather rough initiation, but not so rough as his. We do laugh at the home front generals. "It's about all the fun me and DeBlois gits."

> That first person was a sailor wounded, probably fatally, by the bomb that wounded Wilber on July 4th at Rendova. The sailor was on the ship (LCI-24) adjacent to Wilber's. "Home-front generals," civilians who would second-guess military decisions, claimed to understand the realities of war.

... I'm now in process of claiming pay as Lt. Col. because I commanded the Bn. in combat as a major who was not the senior major. Someday I'll win that too, but now it's gone to Wash. D.C. for a ruling.... I love you. — XXXOOO Wilber

An airfield at Ondonga peninsula on the southern end of Ondonga Island (and Piru plantation) was completed on October 23. Its defense was

COMBAT AND NEW LIFE   PART III: ONDONGA PALM GROVE

*Road ("Camp Street") through the Ondonga campsite amid the coconut trees.* [PHOTO: CHARLES D'AVANZO]

*Signpost in the bivouac area of the 169th Field Artillery, a Rhode Island outfit, with directions to various places and facilities, some quite wishful. From the top: East Providence (RI), Pawtucket (RI), Cranston (RI), Battalion Hqtrs., Laundry, Mess Hall, 1st Echelon, Tailor, Latrine. This predated a similar sign often seen on the humorous TV show, MASH, set in the Korean War. They must have been a common sight throughout the Pacific Theater during World War II.* [PHOTO: CHARLES D'AVANZO]

the mission of the 161st Infantry (Wilber's former outfit), which was supported by Wilber's artillery battalion. The army was not forgetting Pearl Harbor. The next day, planes of the Royal New Zealand Air Force flew in and then onward to support landings at Torokina, Bougainville.

**OCT. 24, 1943**
Hello There Wife! — It's a quiet Sunday here and all is well with me.… The war is getting a bit out of my reach now, and I've a definite feeling this will be true for some considerable time. So stop worrying. I'm just doing the same things now I was doing in [Camp] Shelby: inspections, saluting, training etc.…

Your explanation about the [Hotel] Altamont was very good. I'd have stood around the desk, too, waiting for you to get your mail. Where will you be for X-mas? Your presents will come to Box 923 [Baltimore, MD] and I'm afraid you won't get it [sic] for Christmas.

> I do wish I had Norma's "explanation." Wilber had been writing to Baltimore, believing she lived at the Altamont where some man was "waiting around the desk" for her to come by to pick up her mail. In any case, it must have been fiction. She was surely by then living in Washington with Monte and his mother. Her baby's due date had already come and gone.

… I'd like to have a good weekend in a hotel with you again. Another reason I didn't go to N.Z. was the fact you weren't going to be there.… You see, all thru the active combat, I'd see one of my soldiers looking a bit sorry for himself and ask him how he felt. If he said he wanted a rest or to be sent to the rear, and I thought he didn't need it, I'd say, "Well I can count on you staying up here as long as I do, can't I?" He would usually grin + say he guessed he could stick as long as I did and that was that. Actually I never let an officer (except Mushik + Heidelberger) stay up front as long as I stayed, and I relieved enlisted men even more frequently. Now I still don't want my men in the next combat to say "He had a leave in New Zealand so we are supposed to be all set for combat." …

I'm glad the children are doing so well and that their schools are so good. Hale's choice of printing is showing good sense. He is going to be able to get thru college OK.…

It's time to stop and tell you how much we all (H + V + I) love you. You are my sweet little wife and I'm missing you all the time. Your letter saying I'm getting such a wonderful watch for X-mas just came and I'm going to be awfully proud of it. It will be doubly precious too because you selected it. I can hardly wait for it to come. Good Night Lover. I love you. Take care of you for me. — XXXOOØ Wilber

At St. Bernard's School, there was a required work period during the day. I volunteered to work in the print shop, which was a good way to avoid cleaning and other prosaic jobs. Once assigned, a student tended to stay in the shop for long periods because it took a while to become adept at skills such as setting type and running the presses. The shop did small commercial jobs that provided income for the school. I made stationery for my father with his military address neatly printed on each sheet and envelope. I set the type and printed them myself.

x·o·ø·o·x

## OCT. 26, 1943

Dear Father — Another month has slipped by since my last letter. It has been a quiet month except for the first few days when I found myself in the embarrassing situation where the Japs could place artillery fire on me and I couldn't reach them. I had wanted to move up to be within range but was overruled so had to rely on some one else to silence the Jap guns.

It was done in time, but it was the unanimous opinion of my men that we could have done it much more rapidly and efficiently. However, the main thing is that my men have been out of combat now ever since the Arundel action was completed. It's good to see the men in clean uniforms with shaves and haircuts. Also it's good to have a chance to heal up the various sores and ulcers and skin infections that we get in the jungle. They heal slowly tho and it will take quite a bit of time to be completely rid of them....

My battalion has received three letters of commendation (from infantry regimental commanders) for the work it did during the past months. That has given the men some pride in their outfit. They now classify infantry as either the type who commend us and who are the "really good outfits," or as the type who take us for granted. The latter of course, my men think, lack something.

We have been supplementing our rations by some hunting of beef in the jungle and fishing in the sea. It gives a change. I saw a turtle in the sea the other day. It was about three feet from the front to the rear of his shell. He was about six feet below the surface of the water and swimming. We had no tackle in our boat and no one volunteered to dive in after him, so we simply passed. It would be good tho to get one and try the meat. A 200-pound turtle ought to make a lot of soup. All my travel is either on foot in the jungle or by boat. It is quite amazing to be so bound up on boat traffic. For example, Thursday I go to a Div. meeting of commanders [at Munda] and will travel nine miles each way by boat. — I hope you are OK. Love, Wilber

CHAPTER 11    *Swan doesn't polish those insignia very much*

*Howitzer (155-mm) of 192nd Field Artillery Battalion, Battery C, 43rd Division on Bibilo Hill, New Georgia, adjacent and above Munda airfield (not visible) on December 24, 1943. It stood in a pit that allowed firing in any direction and protected the howitzer and personnel in the event of an air raid. The sea, nearby islets, and Rendova Island are seen in the background.* [PHOTO: U.S. ARMY SIGNAL CORPS, SC 233453]

The defensive nature of the 43rd Division's mission was well illustrated by a photo of a 155-mm howitzer of the 192nd Field Artillery Battalion at Munda. It was located on Bibilo Hill immediately north of the airfield in an emplacement that permitted firing in any direction.

At home, the birth of Norma's baby was imminent. It was already well overdue according to Norma's testimony in later years.

# 12

## *"Norma Day"*

### Ondonga
### NOVEMBER 1943

At the end of October, Wilber's battalion had reverted to clean uniforms and close haircuts under the palm trees of Piru Plantation (Ondonga), and in the United States, Norma had reached the end of her pregnancy. Wilber presciently, but unknowingly, nails the delivery day exactly with an enthusiastic pertinent greeting.

**OCT. 29, 1943**
Today Lover is Norma Day on this Island. — I wake up thinking how much I loved you, spent the day interrupting my work to recall your sweetness, and after supper read your four letters dated the twelfth, and now am ending the day to you. So today was Norma Day. I'll have others too on other islands.

It truly was Norma Day, in more ways than Wilber imagined! On this date Norma gave birth to Gale Alice Bradt in the Georgetown University Hospital in Washington, D.C. The birth certificate gave Norma and Wilber as the parents. She was a "legitimate" baby.

… We are still revelling [sic] in peace and freedom from Jap shells. It's wonderful. We even have lights at night and can read. Of course the bombers come over once in a while but we don't expect them to be very accurate and so far they aren't and the boys bet on them and enjoy it.

I'm thrilled about the watch and can hardly wait until it comes. Of course I'll like the metal strap just because you bought it. I'll try to take care of this watch and just use it myself. The one I sent back for repair needs a general overhaul and

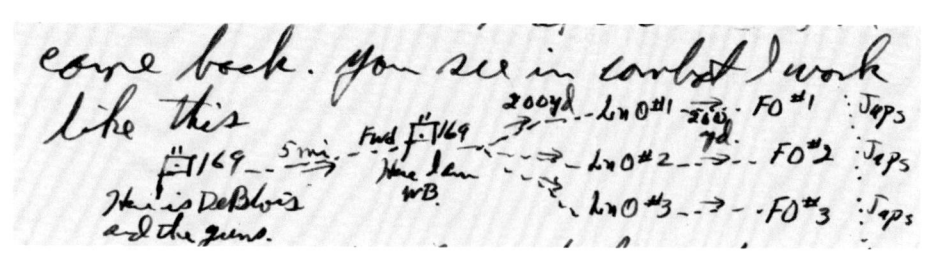

*Sketch from Wilber's letter of October 29, 1943, showing the team that delivered the artillery support to the infantry: the guns and fire direction center five miles to the rear on Sasavele island (left, "Here is DeBlois and the guns"), the forward command post near the front lines ("Here I am, WB"), the three liaison officers 200 yards farther ahead, one with each of the three infantry battalions of the regiment the 169th was supporting, and finally the three forward observers 200 yards farther along with the infantry facing the Japanese.*

brighter numerals for night. It has seen a lot of things. One of my officers wore it for a few days + returned it to me just before being killed. Another was wearing it when wounded and wore it to the hospital and until he came back.

You see, in combat I work like this [sketch]. Everything travells [sic] along the line of the arrows [forward]. My forward observers use it + lose it. The liaison officers replace it and ask me for more. They take my coat, my compass, field glasses, radios, telephones, maps, watch and canteens. Everything moves to the front except calls for more artillery fire and those go back. So you see how my watch saw so much. Sometimes I'm closer to the front than 400 yds because sometimes that supply line runs alongside the Japs and I am as close as the F.O. [forward observer] in which case all of us are acting as observers. Nearly any outfit can shoot, but to keep the stuff at the front makes the shooting more continuous.

… The Lt. Col. stuff is a bit "confusin" to me yet too. It's a shock to be given so much courtesy and to be listened to as if I might expect it. Oh well I'll probably get used to it. I hope I do a good job and don't take myself too seriously.

… I'm enclosing a really good picture of myself, Maj. Bill Bailey and a Capt. Ryan who used to go to the Ch[emistry] Dept, U. of Me, summers while I was there. The picture was taken on Arundel at the end of that job. Bailey was a very new major + I was wearing my new leaves for the first time. I believe you could have it re-photographed and enlarged and send one to Hale + Valerie. I'd like a copy to go to father too + Paul. Paul could send it if you prefer not [to do so].

We had a bombing the other night, some "near misses" but no damage. It was funny because before breakfast the next morning, practically every one of my men was doing a little improvement on their dugouts. It's very reassuring to see how they react to Jap bombs – no excitement – just in their holes or flat on the ground until it's over then a big argument about how close they landed.... Love Love Love from me to you. — Wilber

So ended a day that still resonates warmly in our family, the day little Gale was born. The next day, Wilber wrote the only daughter he knew.

x·o·ø·o·x

### OCT. 30, 1943

Dear Daughter [Valerie] — It has been quite a while since I wrote you but I do think of you each day. Things are going very well here now for me. No fighting for the time being and a lot of rest and sleep....

I live with Capt Rainey in a pair of small wall tents that leak. We put a large tarpaulin over them to shed the rain and built a board floor so we are very comfortable too. The double canvas makes it cool. Rainey says it looks like a Mongolian yerk [sic]. Since I don't know what a "yerk" is nor how to spell it, you will have to tell me. [It is "yurt."]

*Wilber on the phone in his "office" at Ondonga. To his right was his "command car."*
[PHOTO: CHARLES D'AVANZO]

I love you Sweet Heart. Let me know how you are and tell me the news about Nana & Hale. I wish I could see you. — Wilber

Captain Rainey was the battalion's highest-ranking staff officer under Wilber as S-3 (operations) in the absence of DeBlois.

x·o·ø·o·x

Here, Wilber reflected on what Norma was likely telling him about her putative piano playing for remuneration.

### OCT 31, 1943
Dear Norma — You seem awfully busy. I do hope you aren't getting yourself well run down for the winter. It's too bad there are so many business details for you to do. I know how depressing bills are too. Don't let them get you down. I wish you could be comfortably settled down doing the things you enjoy. I know you enjoy playing but to play a concert for $10.00 seems too bad. Why don't you give the concert free if you want to play there? Let me pay for the ten dollar and fifty dollar jobs. Keep yourself out of the cheap class Darling. You are not the only one in this firm, you know. Keep yourself out of the position where a ten-dollar bill will buy what is worth either far more or is a wonderful gift.... — Wilber

[Note on side:] I sent my Purple Heart to you in another letter today. WB

Norma had apparently revealed her discouragement to Wilber, disguised as financial worries. It was doubtful she was playing commercially at all in those last weeks of her pregnancy.

x·o·ø·o·x

The following wonderful letter of praise from Wilber was to June Goff, wife of Dixwell Goff, one of Wilber's officers. It is one of several he wrote to the wives of his officers. I interviewed Dix Goff several times in Rhode Island in the 1980s. He bound two copies of my book of Wilber's letters beautifully in leather and presented them to Valerie and me only a few months before he died in 1988.

### OCTOBER 31, 1943
Dear June — Relax. Everything here is all right. I know a letter from me could be bad news but this one is not. It's very quiet here now.

*CHAPTER 12    Norma Day*

Dixwell and I were together thru some of the most difficult days in the Munda action. I want you to know he was just as efficient and willing as any man could be. I watched him go into dangerous places to do a job. I saw him save scores of lives for our infantry by placing artillery fire exactly where the Japs were sure we couldn't put it. I watched him in a critical time adjust our artillery fire so close in to our troops that shell fragments fell all around those of us fifty yards farther back than Dixwell. That time he came back with that big grin and his eyes sparkling because he knew he had done a real Goff job. I watched him bounce on and off logs to help the infantrymen locate themselves while most of them were saying for him to keep down. Dixwell is an infantryman's hero. Several Infantry officers told me he did more for the morale of their men than any one else....

 You may be sure too that I will do everything possible to get him back safe to see that baby. This letter is partly to her.... — To the Goffs, from Wilber Bradt

x · o · ø · o · x

At my New Jersey boarding school, I was getting acclimated to eighth grade, having been advanced from seventh grade.

**St. Bernard's School, Nov. 7, 1943**
*Dear Mother — This is my second week in the 8th grade and I have been getting fair marks as far as I know, and I am not working too hard. I do my Latin with Mr. Hubbell (our teacher and dorm. master). The rest of the work I do in study hall.*

*I have the school magazine on paper and will send it home when I have read it. We have been working a long time setting it up in the print shop. I will mark some of the parts I set. Mr. Nicholls [the headmaster] got your letter. I sit at his table now [at meals]. Mrs. Nicholls plays the organ in church (St. Luke's in Gladstone), so she knows what you mean about violin.*

Norma wanted me to practice my violin. My recollection is that I never played it that year.

*It only costs a nickel to call Valerie. Today she told me she was in the infirmary because of a rash between the fingers but it was nothing. She has some boys' skates from you, are they mine? She thinks so. She also has the bikes. I am going to write a letter to the faculty and ask for a day off to go see Valerie [at her school, six miles distant]. She said she does not have time to write you. I asked her too [sic] as you are worried. She weighs 108.*

*I was in the infirmary for two nights (50¢/day) for a bad sneezing spell (running [sic] nose). Will try to avoid them because of money. I sang a duet with another boy in chapel this afternoon. Here are the words....*

*Since you are writing again your finger must be better. I am glad of that. I lost weight in the infirmary but will try to gain more. I wrote Monte. — I love you a lot. Hale*
*PLEASE! ALMOST OUT – SEND VITAMINS*

Norma somehow got our bikes out to Valerie's school for storage or use; we had no car. We did not use the bikes that year, nor had we the previous year in New York City. She apparently explained the gap in her letters as due to a finger injury when in fact it was the birth of Gale.

Note that I considered Monte close enough to write to occasionally. I probably had to be reminded by Norma to thank him for some helpful act.

x · o · ø · o · x

### NOV. 10, 1943

Dearest Nana — Your letters of Oct 23 + 25 just came with assorted letters from Evie, Gerry J., + Irene Bray. Yours are the nicest, of course. We had pork + beans for supper – good too.

The Armistice Day will be a religious service for our dead who are in this island. It will be a sad Armistice for us for Lts. Payne and Malone and Heidelberger will be there in the cemetery [at Munda] from the 169th [Field Artillery]. However each was doing a grand job when his time came. I think I feel the worst about Payne because he had a boy a little younger than Hale. It doesn't help much to know that each was where I had sent him but of course that is one of the aspects of the commander's responsibility....

We are still comfortably seated in our cocoanut grove letting the war go off and leave us. It is just as well for the boys are gaining weight + getting rid of these so called "jungle rot" infections that vary from varieties of athlete's foot to ringworm. Just now I'm taking the malaria cure to try to knock out a few bugs. It, the malaria doesn't bother me at all, probably due to the atabrine [an antimalarial drug used during the war], but I am trying to get rid of it anyway. A hospital with all kinds of equipment moved into our backyard so we are really getting well cared for....

Yes Files is at Div. Arty. Hq. He is the Div. Arty. Exec. next in rank to Barker. His letter was nice, wasn't it? He is prejudiced toward this Bn. because he used to command it. His present work is non-tactical and desk work. He is lonesome for the artillery type of action, I think. One day he came up to my island [Piru Plantation at Ondonga] to furnish his boat for me to make a reconnaissance. It was a particularly disagreeable day and pouring rain. We had to wade thru swampy island shores several times. I remember I fell once in the water and that once we went thru a thick growth of thorned bushes. Files was as happy as he could be and on the way back said to me "Do you realize this is the first reconnaissance I have been on for over a year? I wish I could get out this way often." I felt sorry for him except that [being older] he probably hasn't the physique to do much of it. I must stop soon for tomorrow we are up at 4:30 A.M. Too Early!

… Good night Lover. I'll have a grape juice before bed. Another 30 [cents] down the hatch! — Wilber XXXØØ

> In 1981, I went to a luncheon in Providence, Rhode Island, in honor of General Files's 90th (!) birthday given by his national guard comrades. He was in better shape than Wilber thought.

x·o·ø·o·x

### NOV. 16 [15?], 1943
Dear Valerie — … We attended a religious and military memorial service on Armistice Day in honor of our dead comrades. We stood at salute while the firing squad fired a volley for each battalion or regiment that had one or more men killed. For us the speaker said "For 1st Lt —, the first to fall in the 169th F.A. Bn. and his brave comrades that followed." Then the volley was fired. It was a beautiful spot that had been made into a cemetery and the service was lovely but so, so sad. I hope too many more don't "follow" in the next year.…

I am going to bed now Darling. Give Nana a big kiss for me and write me about your school. I love you. — Wilber (Daddy) Bradt XXXXX

x·o·ø·o·x

> The pace of training was again picking up.

### NOV. 17 [16?], 1943
Greetings to my Moscow Mt. Girl [Norma] — … Today I have been working on our miniature [model firing] range and have set it up for officer + N.C.O. training. We built roads, trenches, pill boxes, an air field and other things on it and observe it thru field glasses. The officers are showing a lot of interest and are studying hard. We also are doing a jungle exercise on defensive measures against Jap infiltration or assault attack. I don't think the Japs would like the measures. — XXXOOØ Wilber

*Munda Cemetery, New Georgia, July 8, 1944, a year after the battle began. These graves were moved either to the Manila American Cemetery in the Philippines or to the U.S. after the war.* [PHOTO: U.S. ARMY SIGNAL CORPS, SC 526385]

x · o · ø · o · x

### NOV. 18 [CORRECTED TO] 17, 1943

Rose of my Life — I'm in love with you. It's soon going to be birthday time [on Nov. 30] for you, Little Wife, and I want you to remember I'm in love with you....

Rainey, Davis + I went into the jungle today on reconnaissance. Tomorrow we take in all officers + "non-coms" in a series of three groups. I am doing some original training on security of artillery battalions while in position and firing. For years the artillery has been saying, "The infantry is supposed to protect us." Maybe so, but when they are the busiest is the time we are most likely to be attacked by the Japs. So – I decided to do some training so the 169th FA could defend itself. It starts tomorrow along my ideas. These are quite different from those usually recommended. Col. Files is quite interested and is coming up to see what we do. I can promise any Japs that want to try us that we will put on a show that isn't in the books. I think that now the men will realize the importance of such training and take it seriously....

Good Night Sweet. I'm thinking of those lovely arms. — XXØØØ Wilber
How much longer will that Box 923 [Baltimore] address be OK?

> Wilber's infantry training in the 161st Infantry gave him insight into how to handle potential Japanese raids on his artillery positions. This would become important in the Philippines.

CHAPTER 12    *Norma Day*

Norma was still using the Baltimore address while living in Washington. It was not clear how Norma and Monte managed this. I doubt they drove because that would have expended valuable rationed gasoline. The train would have been practical but time consuming; mailing a letter could have taken a half-day or more.

x · o · ø · o · x

Life on Ondonga Island had interesting variety for the men of the battalion.

### NOV 21, 1943 [SUNDAY]

Lovable Norma — You could never guess what I've been doing. Eating my Christmas olives. I hadn't thought of olives for months. And did I enjoy them! I lapped up the juice and thought how you used to save it for me. Thank you, Wifey, that was a real treat. This is a request for more when it is convenient. Are olives rationed? We had a rather flat lunch today so I treated myself to a dessert of olives. They were surely big ones.

The olives were probably Alfonso olives (large dark reddish Mediterranean style and cured in red wine) from Chile. We learned to savor them in New York where we were enjoying Lebanese cuisine prepared by Monte's mother and by Norma. Norma probably sent Wilber's Christmas package shortly before she gave birth.

The handkerchiefs came too and are put away with my two new towels. The lobster + pineapple are being saved but not for long. The Vit C. is cached until I am next doing strenuous exercise. Lover you spoil me....
[We have] several new officers, all Second Lts. Their names are Bivenour, Gowl, VanCamp, Merck, Grounds, Brichta, Waterman, Miller and Johnson and Gong. That brings our officer strength up to the [censored] level. You can see we went to a pretty low ebb for a time....

The censor would delete a word or words by literally cutting them out with a sharp knife. This would also remove any words written at that location on the reverse side of the stationery, as was the case with the first words of the preceding paragraph. Wilber's letters rarely had such excisions because he knew what he could and could not write.

It's very hot here today. I'm sitting in my tent shirtless + sans shoes + sox. (Off duty time). I've encouraged the men to play games in the afternoons and we now have six teams, and four play a game each day so a large group of the men participate. It has cheered them up a lot. Further I've just gotten from Wing orders to send my battalion [softball] team to the [censored] just for the morale effect. The orders are published + the boys are pretty pleased. They know that in combat I'll expect unreasonable things of them, so I want them to know too that, in rest times, I balance the books a bit.

That is why we have arranged for ice cream for them occasionally thru the C.B.s [Construction Battalion] and a movie every evening too. Mornings we train and afternoons have athletics and improve our living areas. Once or twice a week we have all day problems or fire. For officers, the schedule is heavier.

> It is imperative that a large group of men be kept active, lest a general and contagious discontent take hold.

Good bye, Lover. I'm thankful for so many things this year and you are the number one item. I love you, My Adored. It's so good to rest + to have time to think of you. — XXXØØ Wilber

Later – I saw Abbott + Costello in "Pardon My Sarong" the other night. Do you remember when we saw it? Another night I saw a movie about "High Explosives." There were several big blowups. At the end of the show, some G.I. yells, "It's OK to come out of your hole now, Frank." Goodnight Lover. [My] arm is around you tonight. I love you. Wilber

> "G.I." referred to the ordinary enlisted serviceman (soldier, sailor, marine, or airman). It was adapted from "general issue" or "government issue" meaning any standard item of equipment issued by the government.

x·o·ø·o·x

## NOV. 24, 1943

Norma Dear — It's tonight again and you are my darling. I'd like to have Thanksgiving with you tomorrow but since that is out, I'll just be your special boy tomorrow. It is so wonderful to know such a wonderful wife is waiting for me back home. I do want to come back to you, you know. That is terribly important to me; so important that there is only one thing more important.

I want my children to know that even if I don't come back, I will still be glad to have served my country and the things it stands for. I will be thankful that I have done part of my share already. It's something that I can't ever have taken away from me. Sometimes I try to think what the country means to me and I decide it's you, and Hale and Valerie, and your friends, and their friends and their friends' friends.

CHAPTER 12   Norma Day

> To me, this was very touching. Wilber was really in this for the principle of it, not just because he had to be or because he sought adventure, and he wanted us to know it.
>
> Now we are still sitting beside the trail to Tokyo watching others move ahead. It's their turn to be the "spearhead." That was our part of the New Georgia job....
>
> Another item, less pleasant, had to do with Lt. Heidelberger whom we lost in Baanga. It has just been ruled that he was killed in action. He was seriously wounded and we carried him as missing. A body was found and partially identified as his. I still hope he will show up as a prisoner of war but the chances are poor....
>
> In your letter of Oct 28, you assumed I was on the move again. Poor Nana, all full of worry. You should relax....

Norma was still conscientiously writing on October 28, the day before she gave birth. I can picture her, uncomfortably pregnant by now, at a typewriter beside a south-facing upper window of the Q Street row house, with the sun streaming in, working away on a letter to Wilber, never mentioning where she was and what loomed so large in her life.

> Not too long ago I took Downing, Zebrowski, Rainey, Davis and Mushik in a boat. We went up Kula Gulf, past Kolombangara to Enogai [Map 9, inlet just east of Bairoko Harbor] where the Japs had had some large guns. They are still there and were of the same general type as the two Davis and I had knocked out on Baanga. The Gulf was quite choppy and we bounced all over the water. As Davis said, "over one and under the next." We were soaked but it was real fun. I told the cox [coxswain] that it wasn't an emergency trip and not to continue if he thought he might lose his boat. I didn't mention the possibility of losing me but I had that in mind. He said "If you want to go, I'll take her thru." I did + he did.
>
> Our trip took us along the side of the island [Kolombangara] [where] a valley cuts the rim of the crater [of the extinct volcano]. We could look thru this gash into the crater proper + see the opposite walls. It was certainly an intriguing sight. All the mountain is jungle covered. No rock shows anywhere, but the erosion ravines and the faults still show. You would have loved the beauty and challenge of the doorway into the heart of that mile high island.... — Wilber XXXOOO
>
> [Note on side:] Happy Birthday to Nana [Nov. 30, her 38th]. Wilber

x · o · ø · o · x

It was Thanksgiving, and Wilber was thankful for (almost) no short rounds and for turkey provided by Uncle Sam.

189

*Captain Russell Davis, Ondonga, fall of 1943. Wilber was in the background.*
[PHOTO: CAPT. LAWRENCE S. PALMER, DDS, DC, COURTESY OF HIS SON, DAVID PALMER.]

### NOV. 25, 1943 [THANKSGIVING DAY]

Darling Wife — Today I think of you as with the children. I hope it is a happy day for you and I know it will be a real treat for them. I wish I could have met your train. That look of pleased surprise that I catch now + then on your face by unexpectedly meeting a bus or a train is worth more than two months' salary to me.

Norma had apparently intended to visit Valerie and me on Thanksgiving but we did not see her until Christmas when we all met in New York City.

CHAPTER 12    *Norma Day*

I did like your quotation from "The Fountain" [a 1932 novel by Charles L. Morgan]. It was good and beautiful but wrong. God never let go of his hand. It's pretty comforting too in times of stress. Do you recall the statements that there were no atheists in the foxholes on Guadalcanal. That was probably pretty accurate. God held my hand a good many times when I brought our fires so close in that, as a scientist, I knew some "shorts" [artillery shells which land short of the target] would fall on our men. The fact that, out of 29,000 rounds, none did is directly opposed to the statistically accurate fact that over 300 shells should have fallen short. Every day I knew, as a scientist, I would see some of those shorts come in our lines and everyday I was thankful God held my hands.

It didn't happen until we were near the 50,000th round, and I couldn't even feel then that I had any complaint. The expected percentage is 1.3. It's no fun to go to the Aid Station and see the casualties you caused. Another time some of our troops walked into my fires and that was pretty tough. There is nothing to do except to say it is my responsibility, which I did, and I thought it was pretty fine for the infantry major to come up + say he had gone outside his zone into the area I was supposed to be firing on and that it was his fault....

> I, as son and physicist, must jump in to point out a problem with Wilber's assessment. For only one to fall short when 300 are expected is statistically unrealistic. The dispersion assumed in the artillery calculations must have been greater than the actual dispersion. This would exaggerate the likelihood of shorts and thus lead to more conservative firing with fewer injuries to friendly troops.
>
> Nevertheless, prayer was still called for as the explosive-laden shells hurtled toward the front lines. Any small error would invalidate the statistics, and Wilber was acutely aware of that. Fifty thousand prayers would expend a lot of mental energy and subconsciously he probably did expend it.

... Uncle Sam did very well by his boys for Thanksgiving Dinner. He furnished turkey generously and the "makins" for dressing, cake and fruit. The boys were just as happy as kids. Afterward they lay on their bunks trying to out-groan the others. We made ice cream and got the CBs to freeze it for us. Fifteen gallons for 150 men. There were no complaints. So far as I know, the 169th was the only outfit of the 43rd [Division] that had ice cream. Pretty soft!

I'd love to get my cheek against your breasts tonight and just dream and feel at home and all right again. — I'll be dreaming you. WB

x·o·ø·o·x

## COMBAT AND NEW LIFE　　PART III: ONDONGA PALM GROVE

**NOV. 27, 1943**
Lively Lady of Mine — … A letter just came from Capt. Wild. He was still in New Zealand and had just received the Distinguished Service Cross. That is the first decoration received by the 169th Field [Artillery]. I'm very proud of that. He did some great artillery adjustments and twice personally shot up a Jap machine gun with a pistol. On the first occasion it was a borrowed pistol. On the second there were three other officers (one mine) who also assisted. I hope when he gets back to the States you can talk to him. He is quite conceited but could tell you more of what we did in Munda than anyone else either there or here. He was at the front about three weeks in Munda, missed Baanga, and was back on the job in Arundel.
… Goodnight Wife with the lovely hands. — I love you, Wilber.

> The Distinguished Service Cross was and is a very prestigious medal awarded for personal heroism in combat. It is second only in rank to the Congressional Medal of Honor. It was likely that Wilber recommended Wild for the medal. He may have had some ambivalence about it because Wild had disobeyed Wilber's orders not to take risks by engaging in personal combat [letter 8/24/43].

x·o·ø·o·x

**NOV. 28, 1943**
Little Snow Maid [Norma] — How is the weather for you Sweet Heart? I'm sorry you had a cold. You have been holding out on me, no word of a cold except that it's about over. I knew it tho because of the gap in my mail so I worried anyway. It's wonderful to have such a nice girl to worry about, and dream about and think about and to love. Do you still have the little crease marks on your arms?

> Actually, the "cold" was the delivery of baby Gale in Georgetown University Hospital. Wilber was just then getting letters written by Norma after Gale was born—Norma had picked up her letter-writing duties quite promptly.

Today I wrote to Mrs. Norbert J. Heidelberger of 1111 Whitesboro St, Utica, N.Y. about her son Bert who was a 1st Lt. in the Bn. He was missing in action and had been so reported until we had all the available facts collected; then he was reported killed in action. It was a hard letter to write because I could say so little that would be a comfort to her. He was a fine boy who had done a wonderful job everywhere he worked. When the Japs got him they really hurt the battalion. I couldn't even tell her he had gone easily because he had traveled a long way thru

Jap territory after being wounded but all of it the wrong way. It was a pity that such a dogged determination to live was defeated by loss of direction. Anyway I told her how much we liked Bert and that I was with him at noon of his last day and some of the things he did that saved the lives of many American soldiers.

Your letter of Nov. 15 came on Nov. 27. You must not worry so much about me Dear. Adm. H. [Halsey] has other troops beside the 169th and even uses them now + then. I'm still sitting under the same palm tree rehabilitating. — Wilber

> I talked to Heidelberger's brother by phone in 1981 and shared this letter with him. He could not believe that Norbert would have lost his way because he loved fishing and hunting and was at home in the wilderness.

---

In Russia, the onset of winter and rapidly strengthening Russian forces, aided by supplies from the U.S. through "Lend Lease," led to solid Russian advances on all fronts. Hitler, fearing an Allied invasion of France, halted the shipment of troops from France to the Russian front. Kiev on the Dnieper River was captured by the Russians on November 3, 1943.

On November 20, 1943, army and marine troops landed in the Gilbert Islands, on Makin atoll and Tarawa atoll respectively. The former was captured quickly, but in the several days of intense fighting on Tarawa, the U.S. Marines encountered fierce Japanese resistance that resulted in about three thousand marine casualties. This was the beginning of an island-hopping campaign in the Central Pacific by Admiral Chester Nimitz (Map 3). The next landings further westward would be in the Marshall Islands, on Kwajalein (February 1) and on Eniwetok (February 21). The advance toward the Philippines and Japan would thus be two-pronged, with MacArthur directing the drive up the New Guinea coast toward the Philippines. The 43rd Division would participate in the New Guinea drive and thus would revert to army command.

## 13

## *"Poor Nana"*

### Ondonga
### December 1943

After two months, Ondonga Island was becoming like home for the 169th Field Artillery. As the front became ever more distant, preparations for future combat began to take precedence over defense. Meanwhile, Norma was adapting to her new baby and telling no one of it. Wilber was increasingly aware that Norma was withholding the details of her life, and his frustration was growing.

**DEC. 2. [1943]**
Dear Mother of Hale + Valerie — Do you realize that I'm the boy that you had asking you to be the mother of his babies some wonderful years ago? You did say "yes" and you did give me such wonderful children. I'm so happy about your loving me Dear.…

I'm wondering if you still are working on the morale circuit. You may not realize it but your letters have certainly lost all geographic significance. Don't you ever eat? Or go to shows? Or sleep anywhere? Or see anyone you know? Mysterious Norma. If you have joined the FBI, I should at least get a receipt for one very nice wife, slightly used, value priceless.…

> Norma's letters, mailed from Baltimore, lacked the little day-to-day items she would usually recite and were often delayed. Wilber attributed this to secret work she was doing, possibly on the "morale circuit" playing piano for the troops at remote locations with the USO or possibly using her secretarial and organizational skills with the FBI. He was growing very concerned.

*Weapons carriers lined up for inspection by the division, "all in spotless condition," on December 4, 1943 [letter 12/5/43].* [PHOTO: CHARLES D'AVANZO]

We are still concentrating on the inspection which is due day after tomorrow. It rained two days + put us behind schedule but I think everything will be ready in time. I hope it goes well but don't intend to worry if it doesn't. The men have done a lot of work and the equipment is as well prepared as possible to date. Later it will be better. I've arranged a couple of surprises, a manner of reporting + alerting the men that hasn't been done in the 43d yet. It will be interesting to see how the inspector reacts. I think Harold [Barker] will be a bit shocked when the battery commanders say "Prepare for Inspection! Pass it on!" and a quarter-mile line of drivers in turn shout the command to the next. It sounds like they are daring the inspector to come down that line.

It is business but I mailed you four MOs [postal money orders] #68200, 68201, 68202, 68203 each for a hundred dollars. In case they don't show up in a reasonable time consult your husband. I love you Nana Mine. — Happy Hale Day, Wilber

The closing referred to my forthcoming 13th birthday on December 7.

x·o·ø·o·x

Inspections became a real driving force in the life of the battalion, and firing exercises were an excuse for humor.

## DEC. 5, 1943

Yes Lover — I'm thinking of you again. It's a day so like many we've shared; cool and rainy. I have been reading and once found I was under the impression I was in the study hearing the rain patter outside on our Maine porch. It was such a comfortable and wonderful thought that it interrupted my detective story and I saw: cocoanuts! What a slump!? Anyway it's nice to have remembered.

Nana Mine, the inspection turned out to be a major celebration. Gen. Ross who is now assistant division commander and who formerly commanded the 172d [Infantry] was the inspector. The men were as clean + well shaved as if they were starting home. They sirred him and saluted him and did reporting to perfection. The vehicles were all on the line, all freshly painted and all in spotless condition. Over three fourths had been given a thorough technical overhaul since combat. Records were OK, kitchens spotless, not even one fly showed up, tents were spick + span and areas were tops. Barker was along and he grinned like "Chessie" [Cheshire Cat] most of the time.

Ross found himself complimenting men and officers most of the time. He criticized some vehicles because they showed too much oil in the motor. We rolled one on to level ground and showed that they were exactly right. He checked spare gasoline cans, and I said they were empty by my order. He said "OK I'll find some with gas in them." After he had examined over a hundred he said "I still think I'll find just one." He didn't. He repeatedly said, "Bradt, I knew you had a good shooting battalion but I didn't know it was this good." When he left he congratulated me and said "No infantry battalion that I have inspected has reached the standards you have set today." For lunch we gave him Vienna sausages so it wasn't bribes.…

We have another man who received a decoration. Corp. [Samuel B.] Morgan of Bty. C. has just received the Silver Star for gallantry in action in Munda. The boys are pretty proud of him but the pleasure is not as high as if he were here to receive it. He was wounded in the Baanga Action and hasn't returned yet. [Morgan was in the Heidelberger party on Baanga.]

… Tomorrow we fire again. We plan to + usually do fire once a week for refresher training. The other day a high staff officer turned in a complaint that we fired too close to his boat. He said we fired as near as 800 yards from him. Our observer said [he] measured it with his instruments [and] that it was nearer 2000 yards. [Lt. Col. Edward W.] Berry ["S-3" on Barker's staff] stepped into the matter with the remark that we were a veteran artillery outfit + that the infantry was used to our firing within one or two hundred yards of them and liked it. However he said that probably this officer wasn't used to that and he would advise me to stay over a thousand yards away from boats. It was really funny and now when I fire Barker says, "Now, don't scare [any] high ranking officers today." …

It's late Lover. Day after tomorrow is Hale's birthday. It doesn't seem thirteen years ago does it? I love you Corinne [Norma's middle name] Dear. — Wilber XXXOOØ

## COMBAT AND NEW LIFE   PART III: ONDONGA PALM GROVE

x · o · ø · o · x

**DEC. 9, 1943**
Hello Sweet and Precious — At last some letters came thru from you. It has been so long to go without mail. A letter is so much nicer than a package. It seems the P.O. Dept. has been specializing on packages recently for very little first class mail has been delivered during the past three weeks. You see I'm not accusing you of neglect. Two letters came, one dated Nov. 4 and one Nov. 8. Both were mailed Nov. 16. You must have been sick for some time to hold them so long. I worry about you much more this year than last and that makes letters seem farther apart too.

> Norma had been busy with the baby and getting the letters to Baltimore was not easy. Nevertheless, she did write a letter to Wilber only five days after the October 29 birth. And the one she wrote four days later was, as Wilber noted, a "masterpiece of encouragement" but also depressing in its lack of information about herself. I can imagine her mulling over what to write in a rocking chair as the baby nursed; there was so much she could not say. Her creativity had failed to produce a credible alternative life for Wilber's consumption.

I wish you weren't so isolated. You never mention meeting any friends, nor what you do on off days (I assume you cannot discuss your work.), nor [do you] even seem to have a place to spend Christmas. Poor Nana, this is being a lot harder on you than on me. I wish I could do something about it. You speak of not enough money for carfare to go see the children. Please Lover, don't be silly about trying to save too much. I don't know what conditions are like there, and I write about paying off debts, but I want you to have enough money for keeping the family together by visits. I know the children are OK but I don't feel that you are at all. I'm not going to say any more about paying off the debt on the house or buying bonds.

All I can do for my family now is furnish them money. That always seemed to me the least important of the things I should be giving them and now it still is the poorest of the things I want to do for you. Since that is all I can do, please use it to take care of yourself and the children. What good would a paid-for house be to me if everything wasn't all right in the family. There is on the way to you now quite a bit of money. Surely you can go see the children when you want. Just so you can check, there were M.O. #67442, 68200, 68201, 68202 + 68203. mailed on Nov. 26 and Dec. 2. They are yours Nana. Please use them. I do hope you are OK....

CHAPTER 13    *Poor Nana*

His anguish was clear, nearly palpable. He could only provide money, when he wanted to do much more. He knew it had been his own choice to join the active army, which took him away from his family, and he was suffering the consequences of that choice. But it is likely his suffering would have been no less had he been back home while his former comrades were fighting in the Pacific.

You are most flattering Lover. I'm just working here and trying to kill all the Japs I can. It's a wonderful thing to have a country of people like ours to fight for and to know they make good guns, good clothes, good food and ships so we can win this war. Your Nov. 8 letter is a masterpiece of encouragement and inspiration for me. Please don't worry about me. This war business is not too bad.… Must stop Lover. Take care of yourself and Merry Christmas to you + Hale + Valerie. I love all of you. — Wilber

x · o · ø · o · x

The next day, his frustration was still evident, but he moved right on to a less charged topic.

### DEC. 10, 1943

Dearest Wife — … Sweet Heart another day went by without mail from you. I do hope you are all right. I thought maybe mail delivery was delayed but I've gotten mail from other sources such as Evelyn, Cloke, M. Hirsch, New Eng. T. [Teacher's] Assoc., Ruth and relatives of my officers in different parts of the States. Probably you are just busy and maybe you're forgetting to mail it. One letter you wrote the 4th was posted the 16th I believe. Imagine my absent minded professor wife. That watch is the nicest thing I've ever had given to me and I think it came from the sweetest wife in the world too.…

Today I spent most of the day writing three recommendations for decoration. Unfortunately the award of a decoration is closely related to the write up of the recommendation. Two of these were for the Silver Star and one for the Legion of Merit. They will run a gauntlet of about five higher headquarters each of which may disapprove, approve or request a rewrite or change it from one to another decoration. In one case I recommended for a Silver Star, was told to rewrite for Legion of Merit, then to rewrite for Silver Star, again to rewrite for Legion of Merit all of which took three months after which the Silver Star was awarded. I thought after it was over that maybe I should have gotten the decoration for effort. One of those I wrote today was for Dixwell [Goff].

COMBAT AND NEW LIFE   PART III: ONDONGA PALM GROVE

We still sit in our cocoanut grove and I still love it. The sun came out for a short time and dried my shorts that Swan had on the line. I love you little Bed Mate. Please take care of yourself. I'm still trying to take care of you but you must help. What do you eat? — Kiss me Wilber XXXOOØ

x · o · ø · o · x

Off-duty times for the officers on an isolated island were not without simple pleasures, but yearnings for home could take a firm hold without the diversion of combat.

### DEC. 11, 1943

Nana Mine — I've just heard the Brahms' First Symphony over at the neighboring naval unit. They have a grand phonograph. Last week their Doctor (Cushman) started an hour of symphonic music each Saturday evening. This is the first I have heard and also the first good music except radio I have heard for a year. It was as wonderful as Brahms can be, which you know I feel always just fails to reach the perfection he leads one to expect. Next week, if I can go, I'll hear The "Emperor" Concerto, Beethoven 5th....

The officers just came in with some ice cream. Very juicy, but cold. No flavor, but good. We sat around + guzzled and told stories about Syracuse U., Wisc., Cornell, McKenzie River, Chinooks and Rhode Island Clambakes. In the mean time a whole flock of night fighters [airplanes] took off from the local field and started "orbiting," then later took off with all the appearance of wanting to do a little business. One never knows where, why, or what here. It's just like seeing five minutes of a movie and trying to guess the rest....

I'll stop now until tomorrow, Lover. I miss you so much when things aren't so strenuous.... Good Night Dear. I love you. — XXXOOØ Wilber

The battalion was quite close to Ondonga airfield

x · o · ø · o · x

### DEC. 12, 1943

Sweet Wife of Mine — It's Sunday afternoon and Rainey, Davis + I went to the Episcopal services this morning. There Rainey + I had communion and Davis who fancies himself a sort of No-Church Christian waited. It was a small group of Marines, Sailors + Soldiers. One carried a tire gauge on his belt, several others knives, another a lot of keys, another was a lumberjack from Maine – a rather interesting group.

It's later, after supper + after a show. The show was "Moon + Sixpence" and the sound didn't work, so it wasn't so good. The moon is full now and it shines thru the palms as bright as molten silver. Our planes that go overhead carry red + green lights.... — Wilber, I love you.

As Wilber's atheist son, I puzzle over my scientific father humbly taking communion at a church service. Was he really a believer, down deep? I suspect he really was; there seemed to be no social pressure for him to attend or take communion in this instance.

x·o·ø·o·x

Wilber heard back from Mrs. Heidelberger. Her generosity of spirit was admirable, although her heartbreak was evident.

**1111 Whitesboro St. Utica NY, December 13, 1943**
*Dear Lieutenant Colonel Bradt — I cannot begin to tell you or thank you enough for your lovely letter to me today. Whereas in our respect it was the saddest day in our lives because of what it confirmed; it was a great comfort to us to know just what really happened to Norbert. We feel very badly about his death, but we are very, very proud of him. He was a fine boy. The Army did much for him, but he was fine even before that....*

*Please do not blame yourself for anything that happened to Norbert. I am sure he is proud of you because he did his job so well....*

*May the war end very soon and may God be with you at all times so that you will soon be back safely and well. — Sincerely, Mrs. Cara K. Heidelberger*

Wilber apparently had shared with Mrs. Heidelberger his own feeling of responsibility for sending her son into a bad place. Unfortunately, the Heidelberger family no longer has Wilber's letters.

x·o·ø·o·x

It would take a couple of weeks for Mrs. Heidelberger's letter to arrive. In the meantime, perhaps sensing that he could well be losing Norma, Wilber's letters were becoming more solicitous and tender. He reenters the courting mode, which "he could do so well," as Norma told me many years later. Nevertheless, he started this next letter with a bit of reproach lightly masked in black humor.

# COMBAT AND NEW LIFE   PART III: ONDONGA PALM GROVE

**DEC. 15, 1943**
Hello There Sweet and Lovable — How's your handwriting today? I haven't seen any samples recently so still wonder if you really are finally ready to discard your old man....

The other day I decided that when I come back to you, I will court you all over again. That would be so you could be sure I really loved you. Besides I never had any more fun in my life then when I was making you love me. Do you remember, Dear. The moon has never been so bright as it was those days. The air was always so soft and you were so charming and sweet that I could hardly believe I was really awake. I'm so glad you decided to love me. It is the most wonderful thing I have ever had happen to me. How I would like to look down into those lovely eyes now, and to tousle that silken hair, and lay my cheek against yours and hold you so tightly. Oh My Little Norma I do so love you. It's late Dear + I must stop now. I'll try to add more tomorrow. G'nite.

Dec. 16 — Darling, Darling, Please be all right. I want to be with you again as soon as possible and never to have to be separated from you. Good night red lips, white arms and golden hair. I love you. I adore you and I'm hungry for a look at you. Besides, I am Your Husband. — XXXOOØ Wilber

x · o · Ø · o · x

**DEC. 17, 1943**
Dear Wife, Today is another day that I love you... — Hallelujah! Letters from Nana just came. I'm so relieved. So relieved. Now I know you have just been too busy to write and I can stop worrying. They were dated Nov. 18 and 20, were mailed Nov. 27 and arrived Dec. 17. Not so good as it might be "but good." "I'm eatin' it, ain't I?" At least you don't say you have been sick. I notice tho, you don't say you weren't sick either, so maybe it isn't so good. You sure have a knack for not saying a word about yourself. Don't you ever buy a new dress, or eat a special dinner, or see a show or a dog fight. Don't the men ever try to date you and do they? What are you playing now? Is the little crease mark still on your arms? Is your fur coat all shot by now? Do you wear snuggies [women's knitted undergarments]? How much sleep did you get each of the three nights before you get this letter?

> Wilber may have been relieved but he still worried. Not being under the pressure of combat gave him time to fret. Norma probably had no idea he would be comparing postmark dates with her letter dates or that the

CHAPTER 13   *Poor Nana*

absence of personal details would be so revealing. The covert life was not her strong suit.

Answering your 18th of Nov. I'm so glad to have a letter to answer. You sure had me worried. I had written to Hale asking him to check up + let me know if you were OK and when. I do love you so much.…

I'm happy most of the time Darling. This war isn't going to get the best of my spirit even if it does mess me up physically. Don't get too worried about how I look in pictures. It's just that dopey look of mine. The "terrible and soul-searing" business is more movie and commentator education. The terrible and soul-searing things are what we are trying to stop by a nice clean war. Killing and wounding men is nothing to what went on in Europe before we started to fight. No, Wife of Mine, I'm not going to come back with a lot of the conventional mental scars. I'll just be tired and lazy and cantankerous and in love with my family.… It's Saturday A.M. Dec. 18. I'm still feeling wonderful about your letters.… Please take care of yourself. — Wilber XXXOOO

If the mental scars were indeed "conventional," they would not have been easy to avoid.

On this date, December 17, at St. Bernard's School, I sang a solo (soprano) as one of the "Three Wise Men." It was part of the last-night festivities before Christmas vacation, which began the next day and ended on January 3. It was to be a real treat for Valerie and me because Norma came to New York City to be with us. It was our first time together since June.

Valerie, Norma, and I spent at least some of the time with the Linfords, in Leonia, New Jersey, just across the Hudson River from New York City. Henry Linford had been a PhD student of Wilber's in Pullman, Washington, and was then (1943) a professor at Columbia University. They were close family friends. One decade later, Henry would serve as father of the bride at Valerie's wedding in the Columbia University chapel.

x·o·ø·o·x

In the midst of his concern about Norma, Wilber did not forget his two children at their New Jersey schools.

**DEC. 22, 1943**
[To Valerie] Today Darling is Valerie Day for me. — A very sweet letter came from you today and I enjoyed it a lot. In it you offered to make a bargain with me about

a letter once a week.... Norma sent me your Nov. 13th grades. It looks like about a "B" average, which is pretty good. You probably will be planning to get rid of all those "C's." A "C" means just ordinary or "about half tried" so I know you are able to do better.... I was very pleased and proud of your grades in Order and Conduct. In my opinion they are the most important of all the grades. You have done very well Little Lover....

Good night, Little Sweet. It's late and I must stop. I just came back from a plane ride. It was wonderful to sail along over the ocean and to see ships and islands and reefs about a mile below. That would be "five angels." Do you know the pilots say "angel" for a thousand feet of altitude.

Did your allotment come OK? Please do write me a short letter soon. I'd love to answer it. I love you Valerie. THIS IS POP SIGNING OFF. — XXXXXXOOOOOO Your Daddy, Wilber

> Wilber was pushing his daughter to improve her grades; the teacher in him came to the fore. The plane ride was probably his first in this theater and possibly the first of his entire life. Many of us know the beauty of tropic islands, water, and coral from the air. (And many years later, in 1983, I was flying in those same skies over those same islands.)

x·o·ø·o·x

## DEC. 22, 1943

*[Note in corner by Norma:] Hale Please return. [and I did!]*

Dearest Wife — I just returned from a trip by SCAT [South Pacific Combat Air Transport] to see Whitney [i.e., the 152nd FA Bn. in the Russell Islands]. He is about an hour's flight away on another group of islands. It was most interesting. We were out of sight of land for a short time but much of the time were over islands and reefs and ships. Once I saw a plane on the bottom of the sea. It looked as if the pilot had very carefully landed it there. Maybe he did. Once we flew over the top of an extinct volcano. I had a day with Whitney [his battalion] then came back....

> The 152nd Field Artillery Battalion was Wilber's former unit from Bangor, Maine. He knew many of its men and wrote Norma news of them, which I omit here. He continued this letter the next day.

Dec. 23, 1943 — ... One of your letters dated Oct. 19 came. It must have loitered a little on the way. Pop had a minor operation today for piles (thrombosis type). It only took a few minutes and was done at the Marine hospital near me. Right

CHAPTER 13   *Poor Nana*

now sitting down is done by a very cautious ritual, but the doctor says I'll be more comfortable tomorrow. It is another item corrected in getting myself in the best possible shape before the next combat. The doctor says I should have a hemorrhoid operation also in a couple of weeks. It too will be a minor matter, probably four or five days in the hospital. There are two very fine ones near here.

Probably I shouldn't mention these matters to you because you may worry.... Don't get hysterical, Maw.... It's late Dear and I must to bed. I love you so much Darling. My arm is about your waist, My Love, My Own Wife. — XXXOOØ Wilber

*Next page spread: Instructions for flying with the South Pacific Combat Air Transport Command (SCAT). Wilber was flown from New Georgia to the Russell Islands on December 20, 1943, and back on the 22nd. In the Russells, he visited the 152nd Field Artillery Battalion, his old unit from Bangor, Maine.* [SCAT, IN WILBER'S PAPERS]

COMBAT AND NEW LIFE    PART III: ONDONGA PALM GROVE

*Dec. 20 + 22, 1943*

**SOUTH PACIFIC**   **COMBAT**
~~COMFORT~~
YOU ARE GOING TO TRAVEL
WE DON'T PROMISE MUCH, EXCEPT TO GET YO...

IF YOU MUST BE UP NORTH TOMORROW
WE'LL PULL SOME IMPORTANT CARGO
AND GET YOU ON THE VERY NEXT PLA...

WE GIVE YOU THE
PRIVILEGE OF CARRYING
YOUR OWN BAGGAGE.

WE CARRY COMBAT SUPPLIES —
SORRY THAT YOU HAVE TO
SIT ON THEM.

AND WHEN WE GET THERE
WATCH YOUR OWN GEAR —
SCAT VALETS WILL BE
NOTICEABLY ABSENT

SCAT HAS A JOB
YOUR COOPERATION WILL AID IN...

CHAPTER 13   *Poor Nana*

AIR TRANSPORT COMMAND

...L ON A SCAT "FLYING BOXCAR."
...OU TO YOUR DESTINATION SAFELY

...LANE.

IT MAY SEEM SILLY TO GET YOU UP AT 2 AM TO TAKE OFF, BUT THIS IS WAR AND SCHEDULES COME BEFORE PERSONAL COMFORT.

For Hale

STAY PUT WHEN WE TAKE YOU TO YOUR PLANE, WANDERERS GET LOST IN THE JUNGLES AND RED CROSS CANTEENS WHILE PLANES TAKE OFF WITHOUT THEM.

MEN TO KEEP PLANES CLEAN ARE SCARCE - STUFF THAT HALF-EATEN SANDWICH IN YOUR POCKET.

WE DO NOT RUN HOTELS, IF YOU HAPPEN TO FIND ANY BED BUGS THEY DO NOT BELONG TO US.

...OB TO DO,
...ITS SUCCESSFUL COMPLETION

## 14

## *"He'll have a little trouble with me"*

### Ondonga
#### December 1943–January 1944

Wilber spent his second Christmas in the Pacific. The first was beside the Ouenghi River in New Caledonia and this one was in a palm grove on Ondonga Island. They were winding up the third month of their four on Ondonga. He captured the scene on Christmas Eve and morning in this letter to Norma.

**DEC. 24, 1943**
Darling Nana — It's Christmas Eve now and I'm just back from a K. Hepburn show called "Holiday." I spent most of the time at the show remembering you and how much fun it was to make love to you and how wonderful it was to find you wanted to do the things I wanted and to go the places I would find. She (K.H.) was much like you in her mannerisms. You are much prettier, so it was much easier to believe you and I were together again.

Dearest Wife, I do love you more than I can explain. Someday again I'll be able to hurry away from work to steal an extra hour with you. I knew that it was wonderful. I knew it at W.S.C. [Washington State College] when we walked on the campus and sat on the stone bench. Do you remember you asked me if I had ever had any relations with any girl? I am proud to say now my answer would have to be different. Thank you for all those precious moments and hours spent in your arms. You are a most seductive young lady, and it nearly caused your downfall more than one night.

> Here Wilber revealed that his first "relations" were with Norma, further suggesting that their premarital courting had been chaste. Wilber definitely had not been a "ladies' man" in those days; he was busy with his chemistry.

… It is a quiet night here now. I am sitting in one of my new chairs that Swan made for me. Capt. Davis, Mr. Gagner + Major (since 5:00 P.M. today) [Richard] Rainey are sitting beside me around Dick's gasoline lantern. Davis + [Chief Warrant Officer H. A.] Gagner are reading my Sat. E.P. [Evening Post magazine] and Dick is writing. Outside a motor is thrumping to charge a battery. My radio is singing "In the Gleaming" and I have within reach a bottle of beer and some peanuts. In the distance the Protestant service is in progress. They are singing something by Gounod, the Messiah, and some other lovely selections. Dick + Davis and Hugh Blain + I all planned to go together, but Dick had work and I'm not quite recovered enough to walk that far in the dark. We plan to go to Communion together Sunday. Blain + Dick are Episcopalian and Davis has leanings from going to an Episcopal school.

I wonder if you + the children will be at Grace Church tonight. Wherever you are I pray God to watch over you and to keep you safe (all of you) in 1944. By the way, did you "Watch the 43d [Division] in '43!"? That is what the boys have said for three years and I guess they were right.…

> The year 1943 was indeed a special year for the 43rd Division, given those three months of combat.
> Norma had probably written that she would see Valerie and me in New York. I only barely recollect that Christmas. We may well have attended the Christmas Eve service at Grace Church with its wonderful music reminiscent of my two years in the choir. Wilber later heard from Norma that we visited Valerie's former school in Greenwich Village [letter 1/12/44].

Dec. 25th, Christmas Morning. I have eaten hot cakes, pork sausage, peaches + coffee for breakfast. The food you are saving in the States is getting here all right. In fact the last issue was of good variety too.

Next I shaved and had my first bowel movement since my operation (What a relief!) and took off my shoes + shirt (not permitted except on non-training times) and called the battery commanders and wished them a Merry X-mas. So now I can sit down to my favorite recreation of the war – communing with My Wife.…

Do you know Darling I haven't been bombed since early in October. It's getting so peaceful here that I've almost forgotten the way a Jap Bomber sounds up in the air. I haven't forgotten tho how the bombs sound on the way down. It is certainly wonderful to have quiet nights and of course we owe them to the outfits up forward. I've quite a few friends up there now and know they don't find it quiet.

Since we won't have a car maybe we should all take a hike down the Appalachian Trail and sleep in the shelters along the way. Or maybe we would prefer to stay

CHAPTER 14   *He'll have a little trouble with me*

home and go to a beach close to a grocery store. Right now a good hotel sounds pretty attractive; we might go to Quebec and if we really wanted to waste our time the most efficient way, I suggest Lake Louise.... — I love you, Wilber.

[Note on side:] Happy New Year from the Cocoanut Grove.

x·o·ø·o·x

### DEC. 27, 1943

Dear Hale — Today General Barker came up to my island [Ondonga] to give Lt. Mushik a Distinguished Service Cross. It was quite a program....

Afterward the band played a concert, the photographer took a lot of pictures and congratulated Mushik. The men looked fine as they marched by the reviewing stand. We are all proud of Mushik.... He is just the plain ordinary American that is as good and as brave as anybody's king or duke or lord. The more I see of just plain people, the gladder I am to be one of them.

... I've just received letters from Norma so I know she is OK. I love you. — XXXOOO Wilber

*Wilber saluted as he led his battalion in review past General Barker (sunlit officer at attention) and Lt. Donald Mushik (to Barker's left) following the presentation of the Distinguished Service Cross (DSC) to Mushik, December 27, 1943.* [PHOTO: CHARLES D'AVANZO]

COMBAT AND NEW LIFE   PART III: ONDONGA PALM GROVE

*Band (at left) concert, Ondonga. Bradt and Rainey (?) were watching from inside their tent. Note the short military haircuts and neat uniforms and the air raid dugout right center. This was probably the band concert of December 27 [letter 12/27/43], after the presentation of the Distinguished Service Cross to Lieutenant Mushik. Captain Rainey likened their tent to a Mongolian yurt.* [LETTER 10/30/43; PHOTO: CHARLES D'AVANZO]

CHAPTER 14   *He'll have a little trouble with me*

*Wilber Bradt (left) and Donald Mushik on the day Mushik received the Distinguished Service Cross, which he wore here, December 27, 1943.* [PHOTO: CHARLES D'AVANZO]

*Below left: Officers of the 169th Field Artillery Battalion after the Mushik Distinguished Service Cross ceremony in front of the battalion chapel, Ondonga, New Georgia. Valerie as a little girl circled her daddy's (Wilber's) face with crayon. Mushik, wearing medal, is third from left, front row, and the executive officer, René DeBlois is between Mushik and Wilber. Seated, left to right: Butler, Keegan, Mushik, DeBlois, Bradt, Rainey, Goff, Bremer, Davis. Standing, left to right: Patenge, Zebrowski, Mayne, Blair, McAuliffe, Farrell, Goul, Maffei, Van Camp, Downing, Newman, Waterman, Gagner. Many of these men were featured in Wilber's letters.* [LETTER 10/30/43; PHOTO: CHARLES D'AVANZO]

## COMBAT AND NEW LIFE     PART III: ONDONGA PALM GROVE

Wilber sent home photos of the ceremony taken by D'Avanzo. They show soldiers marching in review amidst palm trees, a band concert, and the officers of the 169th Artillery in front of the battalion chapel.

x · o · ø · o · x

An opportunity for leave in New Zealand would have been tempting for many, but Wilber had his own take on it.

### DEC. 29, 1943

Dearest Norma — It's a Norma night here tonight, warm, bright stars, night noises making a Silly Symphony that isn't at all silly. I'm wondering if you got your presents all right. Did you like the Stradivari perfume? Was the jacket cute? Did Jo [Probably Josephine, Paul Bradt's wife] like the Scarf? Do you love your husband? You must, for another box came yesterday. Lobster too! And Candy! And radio tubes! You are all so sweet to me. I was particularly glad for the candy, since I've been eating a lot from the officers' gifts and am glad to return the gift. The radio is working fine now and I get the news regularly....

Gen. Barker just called and said he could send two officers to New Zealand for a leave and would I go if he named me. No I would not go unless he ordered it. Further, I expected to need a leave someday and then I would ask for it. OK Says he "So you don't want to go! All Right! All Right! That is fine! I just wanted to give you the chance." OK Gen. Thanks a lot. I'll buy a bond with that money and sleep on my own cot on my own island instead of being lonesome in someone else's city. Let me know the next time you will be in New Zealand and I'll ask for a leave.

I love you Dearest, Please hold me close in your thoughts and arms tonight. I'll be dreaming you. — XXXOOØ Wilber

This was the second time Wilber had been offered and had declined leave in New Zealand [letter 10/16/43].

x · o · ø · o · x

### JAN. 3, 1944

Dearest Wife — It's another day that I love my Darling. I wonder if there is any new way to tell you that I love you. It must seem monotonous to always know just what I'm going to say about it. However maybe the simplest words are the best. "I love you." …

… We have this island so clean that a fly carries his own rations if he comes here. A general was nearly assaulted the other day by one of my mess sergeants. The general asked, "Where are your [flies]?" The sergeant said very quickly and definitely, "I don't have any flies, (long pause) Sir." He didn't either. It's a pleasure to see the men looking so well and feeling so confident of themselves.

My new officers are developing very well. Which reminds me, I need to prepare a two-hour lecture on artillery for an infantry officers' school. You know, "Field Artillery taught in two easy lessons".… Your husband. (I love to think of that husband business). Have you ever slept with a Lt. Col.? — Wilber XXXØØØØØ

x · o · ø · o · x

Wilber took time to write Washington State friends and to recall yet again the loss of Christian and French in the Munda action.

### JAN. 4, 1944

… I was about 400 yards away when Cris was killed and was less than 200 yards when French died. Of course I didn't know they had gone until later but then I found I had been watching the latter take his men into combat.

x · o · ø · o · x

The military life had its moments of mutual adjustment.

### JAN. 6, 1944

Dearest Nana — Here is that man again broadcasting from the same cocoanut tree.… we have now built another walk. Did I ever tell you our system? First, I say I want a gravel walk from here to there. Second, some Sergeant supervises the gravelling of a meandering path from "here to there." Third, I say I want it straightened. Fourth, I notice it is now a series of general trends in the direction of "there." So Fifth, I say "What about getting that walk straightened?" and the battery commander says "I'm afraid the sergeant is going to have a little trouble with that." Then sixth I opine, "He'll have a little trouble with me if that walk isn't straight tomorrow." Seventh, it's straight.

It's raining again. It rains easy here now. In fact I think this one started because I spit outside just now. The coxswain of my boat is the son of a Reg. Army Colonel of the Air Corps. He is quite a character; very small, talkative, has been wounded, and either seen a lot of service or lies well. His crew is named "Junior" and Junior

*Path at Ondonga, possibly the one Wilber ordered straightened [letter 1/6/44]. The medical aid station far down the path was marked by a banner.* [PHOTO: CHARLES D'AVANZO]

is not letting this war bother him at all. For example, yesterday I told the coxswain, "I want to go to\_\_\_\_ next," \_\_\_\_ being about three miles away, I then went to the stern and sat down + started to read a book. Pretty soon I noticed our wake was very crooked.

The cox was also on the stern, so I said nothing knowing that the Navy always does its best work voluntarily. Finally the cox looked up from a chapter of "They also serve" and said, "Jeeminy Crickets, Where is Junior going now?" and dashed up to the cockpit for a conference. Junior's calm explanation was that he hadn't understood where we were to go so he just decided to circle until someone explained it all to him.

Next the bilge pump stopped working and the boat began to fill. We went slower + slower then headed for a convenient (there is always one) island. So I inquired what was up now. The coxswain explained + said he couldn't make it back and would have to beach the boat + repair the pump. So Junior climbs up in the bow and we ease into the shore. The cox says, "How's it look, Junior?" Junior just looks + keeps quiet. The cox says, "Well is it OK to go in, Junior?" Junior doesn't commit himself. So we go on farther in when Wham, Scrape, slide, scrunch and with a jolt we stop on a rock. The cox says "Junior, you should ought to tell me about those." We back off the rock with a lot of unpleasant scratching noises and the cox remarks to me, "These old boats are getting worse every day."

Farther on I ask the coxswain what about beaching the boat + he allows as how maybe he can make it home. Since the last three mile stretch didn't have any convenient islands I picked a beach + told him to pull in to it. So Junior takes the bow + away we go. On the way in the cox pleads with Junior for signals + words to guide him in. Finally Junior relents + says, "I kain't see nothin so just give'r the gun + we'll know if we hit something." So we did and didn't.

Good night Darling. When you go to bed tonight think of me. I'll be dreaming of you. — Wilber. XXXOOØ

x · o · ø · o · x

One aspect that distinguishes an excellent artillery unit is explained in this next letter.

**JAN. 10, 1944**
Dearest Wife — Dick [Rainey] + I have been talking it over + we have definitely decided that we have the nicest two wives in the world. However don't get too conceited because we also think you have a pair of very extra special husbands....

Our service practice has been very interesting. I've been emphasizing the need for speed in getting the shells on the targets and the officers have done very well. In fact so well that I am told we are way ahead of the other battalions in that particular item. To make it all the nicer, we just received word from [Fort] Sill that Speed of Adjustment is the latest thing, so Barker is all for speed. Ain't we got fun? The boys are getting pretty good too, some of them are cracking down on the target on the first volley and most of them are getting effect on the third.

… My cold is nearly gone and I'm feeling much better. I love you. — XXXOOØ Wilber

x·o·ø·o·x

### JAN. 12, 1944
Dear Daughter Valerie — How is my Tumblebug today: Fine, I surely hope. Norma wrote that you three were all together [in New York City] for Christmas and that you took some candy to PS #41 [which Valerie attended the previous year]. I'm glad you remembered them. It makes people happy to be remembered.…

Happy New Year, Little Lady of Mine, Your Daddy loves you. — Wilber XXXOOOOO XXX

x·o·ø·o·x

Norma had occasion to write to Wilber's father.

### JAN 13, 1944
*Dear Father — Hale showed me your letter and your expressed wish to have some pictures of the school.*

*It happens I have some pictures Hale took, and so here they are. Hale is in one of the pictures.*

*We are fine. I am trying to locate in Washington to be near Paul and Jo. I have some prospects for work there. The children wish to be near Paul in the summertime, so as soon as I locate some work and an apartment there, I will move.*

*Hale was so very pleased that you wrote him. — Love, Norma*

Norma apparently wanted to stay in Washington where she had Monte's and Terkman's support in taking care of Gale. Valerie and I would finish out the school year at our New Jersey schools. Norma was already in Washington, but for public consumption was now discussing a "move" there from Baltimore.

x·o·ø·o·x

Wilber reported to his father, as usual, on the activities of his battalion. He also gave him the fresh news that orders had been received awarding him the Legion of Merit medal. He would receive the medal itself later in an awards ceremony. He took some pains to examine his feelings about the award and was appropriately modest, but was clearly proud nonetheless. There were still flashbacks to the combat. Wilber replayed them for his father but probably also for himself.

JAN. 15, 1944
Dear Father — It's a particularly nice day here today with some haze in the sky so the sun isn't too hot, and what is less common and even nicer, there is a good breeze. I'm under the same cocoanut tree and have just had a very good dinner.…

I'm enclosing a small picture of myself taken recently and a copy of the order awarding me the Legion of Merit medal. I thought you would like the order and I have another copy for my files. Personally I think the statement made in the order is actually a statement of the high accomplishment of my battalion.…

There is one aspect of this medal that I prize much more than the award itself, and this must not be repeated where it might be given publicity. It was told me by a general [probably Barker]. He stated that two other of his officers had been recommended for this award and that the So. Pac. board that passes on these had sent them back as a commendation in lieu of a decoration. My general [Barker], when this happened, went to one of the present fronts and saw the Corps commander about my decoration. He said he told the Corps commander [Griswold] he acquiesced in the case of the other two being commended, but that if the board so ruled on me, he wanted assistance in pushing a reconsideration of my case. The Corps Commander said he certainly would take it up personally because he had watched me at the front several times and was aware that I could always be found on the job there. He said other nice things I don't recall accurately and stated again that he would personally see that I was given this decoration. As it turned out the award was made in the routine manner without any adjustments. I told my general that the fact he felt that way about me and that the Corps Commander would say those things about me meant more to me than the award. So you see I feel pretty good about it.

We have had entertainments, boxing, ball games, movies, and other activities and recreations. I work them [the men] hard every morning – then give priority to athletics over fatigue [physical work]. It isn't too hard for men to develop an interest in some form of a physical game if by doing so he avoids an afternoon of heaving ammunition or road building. We, also being on an island [Ondonga on New Georgia], push swimming. This is particularly important because of our always being in amphibious operations where the most critical times are ship to shore periods. After these boys had gone over the side of a transport a few times they didn't need to be urged to learn how to swim. While we were in New Caledonia, we camped along the Ouenghi River, and that gave them a lot of chances to swim.

The waters of the Solomons were now considered safe for swimming. That had not always been the case. While on the Russell Islands (March 28, 1943), Wilber had written, "Brightly colored fish are common and an occasional octopus will squirt black ink around himself. Sharks, barracuda, rays, dolphins and tuna-like fish have all been seen. The enthusiasm for swimming is a little low."

We have been working hard on getting our equipment in first class condition since combat. The fact that there are no roads at all at the front, the salt water, rain and shortage of repairs makes a truck go down fast. The G.M.C. 6 by 6 is a wonderful truck. I've seen them move ammunition over coral ledges where it seemed impossible. In combat once or twice our ammunition got critically low, and then the trucks really took on loads. If I admitted what I've hauled on a 6 x 6, I'd either be branded as a liar or made to pay for the truck. So now we have been getting all of them overhauled and completely repaired....

Don't take the decoration [Legion of Merit] too seriously. Remember, in the artillery there is only a hundred yards between a hero and a heel or between a decoration and a court martial.... I love you. — Your Son, Wilber

x · o · ø · o · x

### JAN. 15, 1944

Dear Son Hale — I'm sending you my copy of an order awarding me the Legion of Merit medal. Please take care of it because it is my only copy. After you are thru with it, please send it on to Norma. You will be the first one of the family [other than my father] to know so you can write Norma and Valerie about it please. This doesn't mean I'm a hero. It means more that my battalion is a fine outfit, and I'm very proud of them....

> He shared his only other copy of the award with me and trusted me to tell the family of this momentous news, so as not to appear too conceited about it; it was his Indiana modesty. Recall that I was away from home, so some action was required on my part. Unfortunately, I apparently did not get the significance of the award and failed to pass on the news [letter 2/20/44].

Norma tells me you made the highest grades in your class. Was that the highest in every subject or was your average the highest? I am wondering because the last card I saw had a weak spot in it where some grade must have slipped a little. It's probably back in place now. How do you like that school? It must be pretty cool

CHAPTER 14    *He'll have a little trouble with me*

work on the farm now. I know it always seemed a bit chilly around the edges when I used to do the chores in winter....

Do you have a silo on your farm? I always loved the smell and warmth in the silo. It always seemed so clean, and I could imagine the cows and horses liked it a lot. We have three horses here now, one with a white star in his forehead. They graze around our tents, and the men climb on and off them and ride around without saddle or bridle. The horses were left here by someone who left before the Japs came, and they took good care of themselves.

Good bye now Hale. I love you and hope 1944 will be the last whole year we'll be apart, but if it isn't I know you are working just as hard at your job as I am at mine. — Your Daddy, Wilber

You can show the order [awarding the medal] to your friends if you wish. — WB

Wilber enjoyed memories of his boyhood on the farm. Meanwhile, his relationship with Norma was about to undergo a significant change.

# 15

## *"Civilization is catching up with me"*

### Ondonga
### January 1944

Wilber's time on Ondonga was drawing to a close; there would soon to be some very good news for the division.

**JAN. 15, 1944**

Dearest Wife — It's Saturday afternoon and for a while the sun was hot and a nice breeze was blowing. Then during a very short time the wind came up and the rain came down in sheets. Now it's back to the drip stage and everything smells sweet + clean. Such is life now in the Sopac [South Pacific] – all April weather....

I've been reading your letters of Dec. 21 and 24 again. They were the nicest I've had for a long time. You seemed to have really sat down and told me of yourself and the children. You have no idea how much I'm interested in your room, how the children look, how you feel, and what you are doing. It was so nice to feel I knew your room, to hear about the Curie [French scientists] movie and the Handel movie and to have word the M.O.s had come. All in all the letters were tops....

> Norma was with Valerie and me in New York and thus could write the details of our time together, whereas she could not write of caring for two-month old Gale in Washington, D.C. Her separation from little Gale during this two- or three-week period must have been difficult. Her instincts, though, took her to New York so she could give some attention to her two older children.

Barker was over to watch us fire and seemed very well satisfied. He critiqued several officers severely then called me off in a corner + said not to be too concerned because we were well ahead of the other battalions "but not good enough yet.…"

My tent floor is a great luxury and now my life is complete for I have a broom. Two were issued the other day and there are only two floors in the Hq battery so I sent word that I would like one kept at my tent. The supply Sgt. sent me word that he had issued one and was using the other himself but that he would try to get another for me. Corp. Swan told him to send one down to my tent and then to try to get another one for himself. Apparently Swan was convincing for I now have a broom and Swan no longer sweeps with a clothes brush.

We are marooned today by high seas. But I didn't want to go anywhere anyway, and besides they are nothing like what we [saw] in Maine that spring so long ago. I gave my bed roll a coat of paint the other day so it is now water proof again. My tent is dry and my roll is dry and this is the rainy season. I'm glad I'm not trying to take New Georgia in January. It would be a wet job. However it [combat] must be much worse in Italy in January.…

Mrs. Keegan wrote to Ed [Keegan] today as follows "I made you an applesauce cake and seasoned it with brandy so it would keep." Keegan said the next sentence was, "The cake looked so good we ate it for supper." That little event practically kept the officers in stitches for two days. They all wonder how he enjoyed the cake his wife baked for him.

I love you Sweet Heart. Every night I wish we were together again. Each day I spend some time remembering your loveliness, your charm and your sweetness. I don't want you to feel you must have an apartment because of me.…

I wonder if you are worrying too much [about me]. I know now you don't tell me when you are sick and have relapses and have to go back to bed, so I wonder all the time if no mail means you are sick. Please don't hold out on me. The one thing I asked for when we were married was to carry part of your load. Now you are believing the propagandists instead of me, and I hear afterward you have been sick. Would you prefer for me not to tell you of my illnesses + wounds? Please? … — XXXOOØ I love you. Wilber

> Norma continued supporting Wilber with letters and shipments while caring for her newborn. She strove to keep a positive face on things so as to keep her army husband content and thus safe from worry that could endanger his life. Wilber, for his part, desperately wanted to "carry part of [her] load" as his part of the marriage contract, but she could not bring herself to share her secret burden. One wonders whether Norma's enabling of his idyllic view of women and marriage might have been more damaging to their relationship in the long run than being forthright, but of course honesty was inconceivable in this case. They were both trapped by their human nature, the war, and the norms of the day.

CHAPTER 15    *Civilization is catching up with me*

x · o · ø · o · x

**JAN. 18, 1944**
Sweet Norma — It didn't rain quite so much today.... Civilization is catching up with me; tailors, exchanges, refrigerators are all beginning to appear....

I wrote to Don yesterday and to Col. Eason whom I haven't seen since he was relieved [from Command of the 169th Infantry] on the Munda Trail. He + I had spent a pretty nasty week together and I had come to like him very much. He is in the States now.

> The "pretty nasty week" was Wilber's only acknowledgment of how badly things had gone for the 169th Infantry in the early days of the drive on Munda.

McAuliffe has furnished us our most recent laugh. A cousin of his in the Army has developed War Neurosis. He is stationed in Texas. Things must be worse in the States than I knew. It doesn't run in the family tho, for I've sent Mac into more than one place [from which] I doubted if he would return. He always went + so far has always returned and in good standing.

Good Night Lover, I'll be dreaming of you tonight. How I do miss you! — XXXOOØ Wilber

x · o · ø · o · x

**JAN. 21, 1944**
Dear Father — Here is my Legion of Merit [medal]. I am sending it to you because I have tried to do as well as I know you would have done. I know you tried to be part of the Spanish-American War, am proud of your service in World War I and think I know how much you regret not being in the armed forces this time. So it is yours with the reservation that I would like Hale to have it some day. I shall continue to try to do this job according to the standards which you have always shown. — I am your loving son, Wilber

> Wilber honored his father while also calling attention to his own deeds for which he sought his father's approval. I believe Valerie now has the medal, while I have the Silver Star that Wilber earned in the Philippines.

x · o · ø · o · x

COMBAT AND NEW LIFE   PART III: ONDONGA PALM GROVE

*Captain Francis A. McAuliffe (left) and Lieutenant Mushik, Ondonga, fall of 1943. Both were officers of the 169th Field Artillery, Wilber's outfit.* [PHOTO: CAPT. LAWRENCE S. PALMER, DDS, DC, COURTESY OF HIS SON, DAVID PALMER.]

CHAPTER 15   *Civilization is catching up with me*

On January 22, the battalion was alerted to a move that would begin January 26. This likely necessitated a great deal of preparation as well as joy because the ultimate destination was New Zealand, western civilization. This was Wilber's last letter from Ondonga. In it, in apparent anguish, he pleads for his wife's understanding and with great emotion acquiesces to a shift in their relationship.

**JAN. 23, 1944**
Dearest Nana — A fine long letter came from you today. Apparently I'm a little off balance about something, for you are suggesting I get me a Providence wife. [Many of the 169th Field Artillery officers were from Providence, Rhode Island.] I deny everything, and if any of my letters are incriminating, I'll plead temporary insanity. I'm satisfied with my present connubial arrangements, that is, if you haven't made any alterations …. I'm still sitting under the same cocoanut tree. It's practically home to me now.

Jan. 25, 1944 — How time flies. Things have been going around and around since I started this letter. The Army can certainly make much of little. DeBlois is returning to me. He has been commanding a Provisional Battalion [on Bustling Point, Arundel] ever since combat ended. I have been very short handed because he had almost half of my staff. Also I've been my own Executive, which gave me a double load of work. I'll sure be glad to see him when he pulls in today.

I received a very long letter that you wrote Dec. 30. The one you regretted having written the 27th has not arrived. I think I told you I wouldn't read it. Dearest you should know that I don't mean to criticize you or your letters.…

Please try to realize my situation, Darling. I like letters. I don't care for them except as they help me keep in touch with my family. All my life I have wanted to be the kind of husband and father that did know what went on in his family. The war, I knew, would make this difficult but I was determined to overcome that difficulty. However, I guess it is too long and the war wins. Of course the children write very seldom and I don't expect them to, but I didn't feel any confidence in their telling me if you were sick, and they didn't tell me. I have often wondered why you keep your residence from me. It's been five months almost and I have written repeatedly asking about you personally, what you do, where you go and how you spend your own time. I don't expect to know what you are doing, for you have said it required some secrecy. Of course I can understand that. However I cannot understand why you have apparently lost all interest in your music and writing, or perhaps you think I'm not interested.

Dearest Wife, don't mistake my words for my thoughts and intentions. That one important thing is my love for you. All the things I say poorly or fail to say are still an effort at the expression of my love for you. You are having a hard time there and I realize it is harder for you than for me. I was at home too during much of the last war, so I know about it. You don't want to worry me, I know, and I appreciate that. From now on I won't say anything about these things. You can write as often or seldom as your situation requires and I will understand that it is OK. If there is a reason why I should be told so little about you, that too is all right, and I will be sure you are doing what your judgment requires.

I do hope you can be doing the things you want to do and that it [sic] won't keep you away from your music too long. When I hear the piano on the radio, I try to pretend it's my Darling and can't. Don't feel that I'm wanting you to have an apartment. That is of no concern to me since I can use Paul's address for filling out routine reports. In other words, Lover, I'm all thru meddling in things I should leave entirely to you. I'll still be standing by tho Dear. You can consider me as a consultant rather than as a co-administrator from now on. Don't forget tho that I'm still your very-much-in-love, altho difficult, husband. That is one thing I won't stop doing even to win a war....

In one of the published orders by higher headquarters was the following: "It has been observed that flies are prevalent around latrines and kitchens. The latrine flies often go to the kitchen and the kitchen flies to the latrines and vice versa. Corrective action will be taken immediately." This isn't an exact quotation but it's no worse than the exact one. Since then one of the local news letters came out protesting the injustice of such an order and pointing out that some kitchen flies go [to] the latrine for pleasure but that some "have to go" and further that the latrine flies certainly were reasonable in [making] their trips to the kitchen at meal time. Morale is up ten points....

It must have been wonderful to be with the children [at] Christmas. I hope they didn't wear you out chasing over the city.... I must stop now. Please keep them turned up at the corners Lover. I love you and I won't worry you any more. — Your Husband (AWOL) XXXOOØ Wilber [AWOL = Absent Without Leave; a punishable offense in the military]

> Wilber's anguish was real. I think Norma desperately wanted to make the relationship with Wilber work, but knew she could not share with him her most emotional experience (having a beautiful new baby) and the painful limits she had placed on herself in an attempt to protect both Wilber and herself.
>
> Typically, Wilber softened a serious topic with an abrupt switch to a benign, humorous one about flies.

x·o·ø·o·x

CHAPTER 15   *Civilization is catching up with me*

The defensive mission of the 43rd Division on Ondonga thus came to an end. It was ordered back to New Zealand for further recuperation and training of replacements. The division was critically short of infantry troops. On January 26, 1944, the first detachment of the 169th Field Artillery Battalion, with Wilber, departed on an LST for the overnight trip to Guadalcanal. Four weeks later, they would board large ships for Auckland, New Zealand.

Wilber's wife and children had settled into their independent post-Christmas routines. Valerie and I were by now quite at home in our New Jersey boarding schools, though I was a bit blue and even teary as I rode the train on a gray rainy day back to school after Christmas. But once there, I settled into the routine of classes, working in the print shop, and passing scouting tests. Valerie soldiered on with her nun-teachers and classmates. Norma had returned to her life in Washington with baby Gale. She was probably working at her writings and possibly piano practicing if a piano was available.

---

While Wilber was at Ondonga, the advance up the Solomons toward the strong Japanese base at Rabaul on the northeastern tip of New Britain (Map 2, left panel) continued without the 43rd Division. Landings in the Solomons (Map 2, right panel) on Choiseul Island and the Treasury Islands on October 27 and on the large island of Bougainville on November 1 made possible the establishment of airfields, radar sites, and PT boat bases that would serve to support further advances. The western end of New Britain itself was invaded at Arawe on December 15 and at Cape Gloucester on December 26. Rabaul would eventually be neutralized (March 1944) by landings beyond it in the Admiralty Islands (350 miles northwest of New Britain) and further advances up the New Guinea coast. Air support for these operations was highly visible to Wilber; he was located alongside the Ondonga airfield and on the air route to the front from airfields in the Russells and Guadalcanal. In the Central Pacific, landings in the Marshall Islands were imminent.

In Italy, the Allies had been slogging their way up the Italian peninsula since the early September landings at Calabria and Salerno. In December, they were stalled by a defensive line at Cassino, well short of Rome. An Allied landing at Anzio behind the German lines on January 22 was contained by the Germans for several months. It would not be until May/June that the two Allied forces would break through the German defenses, join up, and liberate Rome. Allied resources were being husbanded for the planned invasion of France the following June. Thus, reinforcements and support that could have shortened the Italian campaign were not forthcoming.

The Russian Army had made advances across its entire front and had finally broken the German siege of Leningrad on January 19. The siege had gone on for a full thousand days causing great hardship for its Russian inhabitants.

# PART IV

# WESTERN CIVILIZATION AT LAST!

GUADALCANAL AND NEW ZEALAND
FEBRUARY—JULY, 1944

★ ★

# 16

## *"Before their souls could be hurt"*
### Guadalcanal
### February 1944

Early in 1944, the 43rd Division moved to Guadalcanal and after one month was shipped to New Zealand. The division had not seen Guadalcanal in nearly a year, and the island had become a busy supply hub of the Pacific War. The division was without its equipment, so training was not an option. Its month there was a very wet one; heavy rains flooded tents and surrounding areas.

New Zealand was a country stripped of its own young men who were off fighting with the British in faraway places. The 10,000 American men of the 43rd Division who had been in the Pacific islands for 15 months would soon arrive there. The division was low on manpower, especially infantry, due to casualties and illness, and here it would be restored to fighting status.

Wilber's letters gave snapshots of how he and the New Zealanders (called Kiwis) dealt with the sudden merging of two quite different cultures: Kiwi civilians and battle-weary American soldiers.

The Bradt family at home maintained its status quo for the balance of the academic year. Norma was with baby Gale—now three months old—in Washington, D.C., pretending to be in Baltimore, while Valerie and I continued in our New Jersey boarding schools. Our much-needed reunion in New York City at Christmas brightened the winter. Wilber remained concerned by the absence of information in Norma's letters about her activities and living arrangements. Delayed postmark dates on her letters continued to trouble him.

COMBAT AND NEW LIFE   PART IV: WESTERN CIVILIZATION AT LAST!

x · o · ø · o · x

When Wilber wrote this letter to Norma, he was on a Landing Ship Tank (LST) taking the first contingent of the 169th Field Artillery Battalion from Ondonga to Guadalcanal, an overnight trip.

**[AT SEA ON AN LST] JAN. 27, 1944**
Hello Darling — It's a lovely sunshiny day and I am thinking how nice it would be if you were with me. This morning the old cocoanut tree wasn't there when I woke up. I had slept in a bed with a spring mattress and it sure felt good. For breakfast we had coffee, figs, beans, toast and butter and PAPER NAPKINS. How times change! I'd forgotten there was ever any napkin except in my hip pocket.

This sea is as smooth as a Maine lake and is so restful and blue. It's nice to get away from my usual island hopping. We are not moving into combat. I told you Ray [DeBlois] is back with me again. Last night we sat by the rail and talked for an hour or so. He is already taking over most of the details [of running the battalion], and I'm on the verge of having some more time for the general planning and actions. The flying fish are again the main items of interest and even they don't interrupt my relaxation very often. I am sitting in my canvas chair on deck, just lazily absorbing rest. It's wonderful not to be hemmed in by jungle or palms.

This letter of course cannot be mailed until this movement is complete, and I can't tell you where I have been for the last five months for quite a while yet. After current events have definitely become history, the censorship rules permit their being mentioned. Anyway the last area was pretty good after the shooting stopped and there is some satisfaction after a battle to holding the battlefield and watching the enemy leave. I feel sad about leaving Malone + Payne + Heidelberger here. It still seems impossible that they are gone. Sometimes I think they are still part of the battalion and are by their examples still leading us in combat.

It was very interesting that you should get a report on us from a returned soldier. I think he gave you a rather ambiguous answer. Didn't he? You know our infantry [the 169th *Infantry*] also made quite a [poor] reputation and the contrast was all in our [169th *Field Artillery*] favor. Consequently stories are often confused. After the Inf. Rgt. C.O. [Colonel Eason] was relieved, they got a good grip on things. There never was anything wrong with the men. That colonel was a close friend of mine so I felt badly about him, but of course war is tough on men.

> Recall that it was the 169th Infantry that had had discipline problems and many psychological casualties in the early days of the Munda action. This was the second time Wilber commented on his friendship for Colonel Eason despite the colonel's apparent shortcomings as a leader. I was told by

a former officer of the 169th Field Artillery, Howard Brown I believe, that the 169th Infantry was a good outfit except for "poor leadership," a view Wilber apparently shared.

Dearest I won't be getting mail now for a while because of this move but it won't worry me because I will know you are writing and will have no reason to think you may be sick....

If I were to tell you how it rained all the time we were loading yesterday and how muddy it was and [how] wet I was, it would just remind me of a trip into Yellowstone and how well you cared for me when I had a cold there. That was so nice that I'll never forget it. I was so all in and fagged and discouraged that I didn't want to do anything. You made the decisions, did the work, and I never felt so wonderful about anything in my life. Since then I've learned to lean on your sweetness. I am in love with you and want you in my arms. — Wilber XXXOOØ

> This was a rare admission by Wilber of the depression that occasionally afflicted him. His housemate in Washington State, when both were bachelors, told Norma that it was important to get Wilber going in the morning [NB letter 2/3/41, Book 1]. His responsibilities and activities as commander may have kept this tendency at bay. How he would respond to a forthcoming leave in New Zealand was an open question. He had previously declined a leave there because he had not wanted to be "lonesome in someone else's city" [letter 12/29/43].

x · o · ø · o · x

The next day Wilber wrote from Guadalcanal.

**[GUADALCANAL] JAN. 28, 1944**
Hello Nana! — How are you feeling today Darling. I mean the day you receive this letter. So far as today is concerned, My Love, I hope you have a grand day. Your old man is back on land again [Guadalcanal]. Yesterday we arrived here about noon. The Navy had given us a fine dinner in which roast beef was the high spot. I left Ray [DeBlois] in charge of the unloading and went down to find our bivouac area several miles away. We actually traveled on roads and that was something new for us. This was the first time I had driven 25 miles per hour since last January. Also I remembered that I had seen very little of dust [on the roads] for the same time.

Just as I arrived at the new area, I met Barker + we went together + looked it over. It is pretty fair altho we kept our record intact for moving in the rain. Ditch digging seems to be indicated. Near my tent is a patch of banana plants but the fruit

*Rainwater flooding tent of two 43rd Division soldiers, Guadalcanal, February 6, 1944.*
[PHOTO: U.S. ARMY SIGNAL CORPS, SC 188316]

is green. One kitchen is in the middle of a patch of wild sweet potatoes. A few large trees furnish shade for the officers and for some of the men. The rest of the area is a meadow of tall grass. Mosquitos are thick and huge but I've seen no anopheles [malaria-carrying mosquitoes] and my mosquito lotion is doing well by me now.

This is a clear day with a light breeze and a hot sun. The men are busy setting up kitchens, tents, caring for equipment, ditching, cutting away brush + grass and generally getting settled. They are a little out of practice, having been in the [previous] place five months. They are tending to become more a lumber-jack type than ever before. An axe seems a pretty normal accessory to a soldier down here and a machete is more useful than a razor.

Dearest, I didn't mean to do it, but I cheated. When your letter of the 27 of Dec. came the postmark looked like the 26th, so I opened it and started reading it. I really had checked the postmark but it looked safe to me. Then in spite of your apologies, I found it was a very nice letter. There was nothing in it to worry about. I know you have been worrying about me + trying to keep my morale up. I don't intend in any way to try to run your life and if you have really decided you want a home life instead of a career, I'll be very happy about that. Just when the "fight" comes in, I don't quite see. It was one of the nicest letters I've received. Besides I know you are my own sweet wife and that means everything to me. Apparently I've missed some mail for I still don't know where you live but you don't know where I am so I guess we are about even. Furthermore as I said before, I don't expect to worry about it anymore.

> Norma was apparently wrestling with her feelings and uncertain future. She defended her independence, but had a desire for a "home life." Would that mean a life with Wilber? The "fight" referred to her resistance to his probing of her secrecy. Meanwhile, Wilber "knew" she was his, but in reality may not have been quite so sure.

Barker + Files + Berry + Bailey just dropped in for a half hour. They were purely social minded and seemed satisfied with our progress. I had just returned from an inspection around the area. We are near our infantry [169th Inf.]....

You are my Darling, the Flower of my Life and the most precious Jewel. I told you once I would go to Hell for you and this war business is only a sample of what I would like to do for My Nana. The night you get this I will be walking with you My Princess. Try + see if you can sense my presence. I'll be very gentle and considerate. — XXXOOØ Wilber

x·o·ø·o·x

### JAN. 30, 1944

Dearest — You do try so hard to spoil me that I'm embarrassed. Today I received seven letters. It was fun too but you don't need to do it you know. As long as I hear from you often enough to know you are OK, I'm not worried. Of course I'd like to hear from you every two hours. Am I wrong to keep sending my mail to Wash. D.C.? I've been afraid to send it to Baltimore for fear you would have in the meantime gone back to N.Y.C. As soon as you give me definite instructions, I'll send it where you say....

I'm pretty well rid of my assorted fungus infections now. The ringworm is gone from my feet and crotch + the inside of my thighs. I still have a spot on the head of my penis which seems slow to heal; and also on one of my big toes is another type of infection. Now that we seem headed away from the jungle fronts, I hope to clean up both places. The first would be embarrassing if we were where some of the men were picking up some of the more social types of infections. Don't be concerned for it is not serious, just irritating and annoying. Did I tell you we don't need fox holes here. This is the first time since Feb. that has been true. It's good for the morale too.…

It's nice of Monte to still keep in contact with the children. He has the knack of doing the things for them I would like to do. I liked him very much and wish we could have had more time together. He is certainly interested in you and I feel sorry for him in a way. It is his feeling for you that enables him to do for you + the children the same things I would want to do. I hope he hasn't too many talents that I don't possess. It is a peculiar situation but in a way I'm glad he is standing by in case I'm liquidated. However I am going to try to keep the lead I now hold. I do love you so dearly that it's very clear to me why others feel the same way about you.…

> This has a sad and painful poignancy. Wilber was directly addressing the ambiguous role Monte was playing in their relationship, a role Wilber considered helpful. Wilber was wise enough to know and admit that he could well be liquidated and that Monte would be a safety net for the family. Norma surely realized this too. It was the wild card in Wilber's and in every soldier's hand in wartime.

Good bye for now Darling … I love you. I kiss your hair, I hold your hands in mine and someday I'll carry you across the threshold of our home. — Your Husband Wilber. XXXOOØ

x · o · ø · o · x

> The next day, Wilber turned his attention to me.

**JAN. 31, 1944**
Dear Hale — I just found out why you hadn't mentioned the present I bought for your Christmas present. It just came here today. Apparently the company was so used to fathers sending presents to sons in the army they thought it should have been mailed here.…

I'm sure if you dropped Latin it was for a good reason. Your judgment is good enough for me. The main thing is not what you study but how you do it. I hope you don't let the boys get you in the habit of criticizing your school. It undoubtedly has both good and weak points; all schools do. They are certainly spending a lot more these days than we pay to send you there. I can't forget either how much better it is than what the children in Europe can have now. A school is, next to a church, one of our most precious blessings. I've always been happy about the way you have taken part in each of them. I went to a Catholic Mass yesterday. I love you Son. Happy 1944! — Your Dad, Wilber

CHAPTER 16    *Before their souls could be hurt*

x · o · ø · o · x

### FEB. 7, 1944

Darling of Mine — Yesterday I started a letter to you saying it was a clear cool Sunday but I was interrupted by a trip to the other side of this area. It took until two thirty and we arrived dirty and wind burned and tired. I bathed, ate a couple of sandwiches, and assumed what Joe Dinsmore [?] called "The Position of a Soldier" on my bunk. After supper I read "c/o postmaster" by St. George. It is much better than "Pvt. Hargrove" and is very much more accurate as to detail.… Interruption – I love you. — XXXOOØ Wilber

I see by a letter [from you] to D'Avanzo's wife forwarded [here] to D'A that you now have a Washington, D.C., address. That is once I found out in spite of the distance. WB.

> It looked here like Norma's cover had been blown. Actually, it was not. She had informed Wilber of it in a letter he received a few days later (see below). She likely acquired the apartment at 1754 Q Street NW, a mile from Monte's home, upon returning from Christmas in New York, so as to have a respectable address. She could have moved there with baby Gale, but more likely she used it only as a pied-a-terre for her daily mail and for her children's expected spring vacation visits.
>
> Monte's rented home was a multi-story row house with lots of room for Norma and the baby. His mother Terkman, and possibly his sister Alice (an army nurse), would have been a great help in managing the baby. Monte was not very adept at practical things and being from an older generation, he most likely contributed only minimally to Gale's care. He would turn 50 that February 28. On the other hand, a new baby in his home would likely have provoked awkward questions. Any course would have had its difficulties. Norma surely took Gale for strolls in her carriage on nice days, hopefully without neighbors raising eyebrows.

x · o · ø · o · x

### FEB. 8, 1944

Hello SweetHeart — … Another letter I'll enclose in this one is a letter from Ensign [Marshall] Dann. He was in charge of a pool of small boats in our last combat and, so far as we were concerned, did almost the impossible to keep the 169th in the fighting. You can realize how difficult things can become when my observers and liaison groups were on one island, my advanced C.P. [command post] on another, my howitzers on a third and the division C.P. on a fourth. That has happened to me twice [on Baanga and Arundel] and when times were critical I sometimes was moving in a lot of different directions all at once. Dann and a bull-dozer driver were my pals. More than once I rode a boat a general had expected to use. The "dozer" driver was another story. Anyway whenever I told Dann it was urgent, he got me boats. It didn't matter either how close to the front, tho sometimes I felt pretty nervous about enemy shells.

He was reassigned a short time ago and I wrote a letter of commendation for him without mentioning it to him. His letter [below] is a result of what developed. He is a nice young college graduate from Detroit and someday we may stop + see him there.... — XXXOOØ Wilber

> Regretfully, Wilber never wrote the story of the bulldozer driver, or it was lost.

x · o · ø · o · x

### 31 January 1944
*Dear Colonel Bradt — Today I received a most pleasant surprise when the commanding officer "read me off" with a citation from Admiral Halsey. It mentioned boat work with an unnamed field artillery unit at Baanga and Arundel from Oct. 1 to Dec. 16. I knew this to be your work, and wish to thank you for such consideration. You might be interested to know that the routing for endorsements took it over much of the South Pacific with great accumulation of gold striped [high-ranking officers'] names.*

*... Please extend my warmest personal regards to Maj. Rainey and the other officers and men of your organization. — Very sincerely yours, Marshall Dann, Lt (j.g.) USNR*

> Wilber's mention of Detroit enabled me to locate Dann's family, although the route to it was not perfectly straight! I found that there had been a Marshall Dann who became a sportswriter for the *Detroit Free Press*, but several queries to the paper went unanswered. There was also a Marshall Dann who had been executive director of the Western Golf Association (WGA) for many years and who had died in 2000. Finally, in 2011, I was motivated to call the WGA and was immediately put in touch with his family who confirmed that the boat officer, the sportswriter, and the golf official were indeed all the same person.

I sent his daughter the original handwritten letter from Dann to Wilber. It arrived on Christmas Eve of 2011. She wrote, "My brother, sisters, and I miss our father every day. Reading my father's words in his oh-so-familiar handwriting was the best Christmas gift I could have received." Almost a year later, I discovered another testament to Lieutenant Dann's services in General Barker's book [Barker, pp. 98–100], and forwarded that information to the family as well. I got more than a little pleasure from connections like this as I pursued this story.

x·o·ø·o·x

Wilber, after recounting a humorous scene, gently tells Norma that her descriptions of her life are somewhat wanting in consistency.

**FEB. 10, 1944**
Lover Mine — His nibs your husband is speaking to you. Pay close attention, draw close, put your ear to my lips – here is a kiss. I'll send this letter to 923 [Box 923, Baltimore] and all others [until instructed otherwise]....

Yesterday I fell flat in a mud hole of black mud + water about a foot deep and the watch came thru fine. Incidentally I was on the way to a meeting of the commanders of the division. One item taken up was that there was no excuse for wearing dirty uniforms. The Chief of Staff looked a bit dazed at me but went thru with his exhortations. It was quite funny because I further mystified him by neither explaining nor apologizing, just acted as if it was my usual afternoon dress....

These last letters are wonderful. They take me right with you and show me yourself and I think you're lovely.... You still seem to feel that I am critical of you and I feel badly about that. I've tried so hard to let you see I was worried by the dual factor of having no address except a P.O. Box and by the fact that your last letters said you had been ill. You also say, "Maybe I had talked too much about the places we played, etc., plants [factories] in and near Baltimore." To me that is startling news for the only thing I have received was a statement that you could not tell me those things. You told me in one letter that I received that you were traveling with a group + playing [piano]. It's too bad I worried you + made you feel I was "upset" or had "had a fight" with you. I didn't mean to. There have been several times when I have had no mail for weeks at a time and I didn't mention it because I was getting no mail from anyone and could tell that it was boat + plane trouble....

Thank you for the birthday date. I love you. I love you. Yes you. My own Precious Wife. — XXXOOO Wilber

Wilber turned to his daughter Valerie. He knew she needed attention from him as well as from Norma. He opened, as he so often did, with a vivid natural scene and then joined Valerie in her doll world.

### FEB. 11, 1944
Dear Valerie — This is a very still quiet evening. It has been raining and the trees are still dripping. The Katydids are singing in the brush. I am sitting in my tent door looking at the sky where the sun set an hour ago. There are tents on each side of a path we call a street. At the end of the street are four great ragged trees. They stand dark in front of the sky. I am writing in the dark so cannot see the words. They may be hard to read....

For dolls' names, I like Bernadette better than Tumblebug because Tumblebug is something special to me. [It was his pet name for Valerie.] They call the Australian soldiers "Diggers" so that might be a good name for a Panda that came from Australia. How do you like "Digger?" I'm afraid if you used Colonel or Artillery, the girls might think you were bragging. Please tell me what names you select.

… Goodbye now. Little Daughter. I love you. Try to be a good soldier by helping the other girls to be cheerful. Someday we'll be home again. — XXXXXOOOO, Wilber

### FEB. 11 FOR FEB. 12, 1944
Dearest Golden Daffodil [Norma] — It's just a lovely evening after a hot day....

Answering your Jan. 21 – So you are settled! Now I'm wondering if "Que" St. is "Q" St. Not that it matters except the general opinion here is that you live on "Q" St. However I admit you should know so Que it is. I'm glad for now I can go to you if I have to. Wouldn't you be surprised if I showed up at your door some day? …

I hope you do like Washington. It should be fun and you can see a lot we would have liked. You will learn a lot and be so educated I won't dare express an opinion. It is a new chapter in your life. What does the "free lance for CBS" mean? Have I missed some more letters? …

Good bye now. My Love. Be cheery. I'll be thinking of you the night you see this letter. — XXXOOO Wilber

Norma had made her "move" to Washington public. She confirmed the 1754 Q Street NW address that Wilber first learned from D'Avanzo. Washingtonians often wrote "Eye" for I Street and "Que" for Q Street to avoid confusion with 1st, L, and O Streets.

x · o · ø · o · x

**FEB 14, 1944**
Happy Valentine's Day Darling — You can't be mine this year for I asked Valerie. Of course my heart takes a big flipflop every time I think of you.… Yours of Jan 24, 31 and Feb. 3 came today and I loved each.

… I sent Mrs. Heidelberger the First Lts. bar [insignia] Bert [Heidelberger] wore in his last combat. He didn't hide his insignia. She must be a very nice mother. Unfortunately two of the three officers I lost by death were the ones I would have picked as the very nicest and cleanest of all. It almost looked as if they were too good for this business and the Lord took them away before their souls could be hurt.…

> It had been 18 months since Heidelberger had died (killed in action), and Wilber had not forgotten him or the others. Note the value he placed on an officer not hiding his insignia in combat. The risk of being identified as an officer by an enemy was outweighed by the encouragement your presence gave to your men.

Don't worry about Mother + me. That was bound to happen no matter who married me. I knew it, but really couldn't believe she would cherish resentment so faithfully. It is just as well and my only regret is for Father. He would so much [like to?] have Hale with him, I know. However I'm so glad the children know Paul + Jo.…

> This left little question that Wilber's mother faithfully cherished resentment. It had been three years since the bitter dispute (recounted in Book 1) about money owed, and she still would not write to Wilber.

Tonight I've written to you, Hale, and Valerie, so that is my "Round and Round" to all of you Oh! How I love each one of you! Good Night Dearest. — Wilber ØØØØØØ

> In a "round and round," the four of us would hold hands in a circle when, say, we were sitting around a table.

x · o · ø · o · x

### FEB. 14, 1944 [SECOND LETTER THIS DATE]

Darling Wife — Answering your Jan. 26 – I'm glad you liked the picture of the officers in front of the chapel.…

I've just read O River Remember [by Martha Otenso, Dodd Mead & Company, 1943] and it is Norma Shaleen [one of the characters in the novel] whom I loved almost as much as my Norma Sparlin. She was (and her aunt too) so like you that I nearly cried several times. Bn. commanders aren't supposed to do that and I just wanted to. The mother in the boys' family was so much like my own I wouldn't dare send the book home and the father was much like my father so you see why the book moved me so. It just reminded me again how much I loved you and how precious you are to me. Everything between us was and is just right. Your letters are so sweet, your love so dear and faithful. I don't wonder if you will approve of me. I know you are so loyal and generous that you would stay beside me even if I was mean and selfish toward you.…

I love you Darling. My lips kiss your breasts. — Wilber

x · o · ∅ · o · x

### FEB. 17, 1944

Darlink — Beside my tent are some banana plants. I suppose the leaves on some are five feet long and one and a half feet wide. Some have bananas on them, but none are ripe right now. The path to the officers' latrine goes past the banana plants (there is a regular thicket of them) and winds thru great green banks of morning-glory vines. This morning enormous purple trumpet shaped blossoms brighten the green background until it reminds me of a scene in "Blossom Time." Overhead are these enormous trees with the vines hanging in them.…

I never told you of a job we did on Kolombangara some months ago. There were Jap graves there, some well marked and fenced. I had examined them and we had a few pictures, which turned out poorly. Anyway some over-zealous soldiers, or possibly but not probably, natives trampled down the fences + flowers and knocked over the marker posts. At that time we were on a nearby island and were given the job of restoration. I sent Maffie over with about twenty men. They cut poles, built fences, set out shrubbery and re-set the marker posts. The rules of Land Warfare and the requirements of International Law were met. You can just imagine the comments our men made about that job. They liked the job mainly because of the opportunity for griping and making cracks. That is probably nothing to what the inmates of the graves thought about being dressed up by U.S. soldiers. The Jap

CHAPTER 16    *Before their souls could be hurt*

marker is a wooden post about five feet tall and four or five inches across each face. On it is carved or burned his name and the other identifying information.

… We are doing no training at present and the days are dull. It is usually too wet to walk and our equipment is not available now for training. So we give the men an hour of exercise in the morning and take them swimming in the afternoon.…

Did I tell you there would be a break in my letters soon but that it would not mean any additional hazard to me? I do love you. — Wilber XXXOOO

> A "break in letters" meant a voyage somewhere, often toward more danger. Norma may not have believed Wilber's assurance.

x · o · ∅ · o · x

### FEB. 20, 1944

Hello Golden Girl — Yesterday I wrote to Hale, inspected the battalion, went for a walk after supper, read a cheesy murder mystery, and went to bed. On my walk I went down to the beach and watched the waves for a while and saw three ships going by. I wondered and wished I were on one of them headed for the girl I love. I've sent many a ship-load of love to you by smuggling it on ships headed for Frisco.

A Jan 15 letter of yours answering my Jan. 1 letter just came with a letter from Hale, which I will forward soon. When I came to his mention of my decoration, I laughed + laughed and laughed. I guess he didn't know it [the Legion of Merit] is the fourth highest honor the country ever gives an individual and rates higher than a Silver Star… Probably I should have explained it to Hale but I was pretty sure he would be showing the letter to some of his friends and didn't want him to find I was too conceited. Anyway I won't be now, for he shifted immediately to the subject of cows.…

> I probably should have shown more enthusiasm about the medal; Wilber's care in not appearing "too conceited" actually revealed his pride in it.

We are having a big police [clean up] today, and the men are burning a lot of surplus junk. It is necessary to do this every so often in order to have room to live. I must stop now but will write again in about a week. In the meantime you will be constantly in my thoughts. My next letters will not be dated.

I love you Dear One. Don't ever forget that you are my precious wife and that I want you all to myself after this war is over. No choirs, no organs, no [National] Guard, nothing but things we can do together. Hand in Hand Nana. Please. — Wilber XXX∅∅∅∅∅∅∅∅∅

This plea, "things we can do together ... hand in hand," displays Wilber's idealistic view of romantic love. He seemed to be losing sight of the role of love in the context of everyday commitments and activities. When men live in isolation from women, fantasies tend to substitute for reality.

The cleanup presaged their departure from Guadalcanal two days later. This apparently was Wilber's last letter from Guadalcanal.

x·o·ø·o·x

Norma wrote to her father-in-law, revealing an awareness of her own contribution to the long-standing financial misunderstanding. She wrote from her new Washington address.

**1754 Q Street N.W., Washington, D.C., Feb. 20, 1944**
*Dear Father — Enclosed is a picture of Wilber, which he wanted [me] to send to you. It was originally with two other officers, and I did not have the negative, so it took longer to get them.*

*I hope that all is well with you. If you think it would do any good to write a letter of apology to Mother, I would be glad to do so, as I really and truly now feel that I should apologize for my disrespect. I do not ever expect her to receive the children and/or myself in her heart, but do hope and pray that soon she may feel differently toward Wilber and write to him. He is in such mortal danger all the time, and I know that his heart aches for word from her.*

*Hale and Valerie are well, although Valerie has been exposed to scarlet fever, which is epidemic here, in light form, on the east coast. It is treated with sulfadiazine. Valerie's term grades are wonderful. Hale's do not look so good to me, but he is 1st in his class, 2nd in the Grammar School, and 3rd in the entire preparatory school. They seem to grade very low.*

*I wrote a letter of objection immediately, when I heard he was promoted [skipped ahead from 7th to 8th grade], but the Headmaster felt that Hale needed the stimulation of harder class work. — Love, Norma*

Norma was deeply empathetic toward Wilber's pain over his mother not writing to him. This letter confirmed yet again that her mother-in-law Elizabeth was still harboring the hurt from the 1941 financial dispute, which was why she was not writing to Wilber. She surely also remembered the quick private marriage of Wilber and Norma in Washington State, about which the Indiana Bradts were informed only after the fact.

CHAPTER 16  *Before their souls could be hurt*

x·o·ø·o·x

On the morning of February 22, 1944, Wilber's battalion, the 169th Field Artillery Battalion, boarded the USAT Willard Holbrook. This was another older ship; it had served as the President Taft during the prewar years. It departed Guadalcanal at noon that day en route to Auckland, New Zealand. (Map 1) The departure must have been a great moment for these troops. They were about to return to western culture after a 15-month absence.

*Troops of the 43rd Division (169th and 192nd Field Artillery Battalions) board the USAT Willard Holbrook at Guadalcanal on February 22, 1944. Wilber sailed with them to New Zealand. Note the manmade pier built off the open beach; Guadalcanal had no harbor.*
[PHOTO: U.S. ARMY SIGNAL CORPS, SC 221865]

## 17

## *"Our plan is to get away from soldiers"*

### Tour of New Zealand
### MARCH 1944

The 43rd Division arrived in Auckland, New Zealand, at 5 p.m. on February 27. At 11 p.m., the 169th Field Artillery Battalion arrived at its base in Papakura (Opaheke) about 20 miles south of Auckland (Map 14). Artillery headquarters was located nearby in the Manurewa area. The other artillery units were located elsewhere in the environs of Auckland. There are no existing letters from Wilber during the voyage to New Zealand. Those undated letters he mentioned may never have been written or mailed.

Liberal leaves were granted during March, and many men, including Wilber, availed themselves of the opportunity to see New Zealand, and this led to a little romance for Wilber. In April, serious training would begin with emphasis on infantry-artillery cooperation. Replacement soldiers were integrated into the units and educated in the skills needed for combat.

**[OPAHEKE NEW ZEALAND] FEB. 28, 1944**
Dearest Wife — … How I would like to have heard your concert. There is no doubt in my mind about it being the best they had ever heard. I can also imagine how lovely you would look too. It must have been a wonderful day for you.

… I'm living with the staff in a real house. We are planning to buy a few chairs and rugs to make it nice. And tonight I'm writing in front of a cozy fire in a fireplace. Will wonders never cease! …

Good night Dearest. I was up late last night [getting settled here] but I still love you. — Wilber

### COMBAT AND NEW LIFE   PART 1V: WESTERN CIVILIZATION AT LAST!

Norma was responding to Wilber's frequent pleas that she share the details of her life with him. She was creating a fictitious life; I doubt there ever was any such concert.

x · o · ø · o · x

Wilber finally was facing up to the actuality of a vacation.

**MAR. 1, 1944**
*[Note on top by Norma to me or Valerie:] Please return.*
Dearest Nana — Just now several of your letters dated Feb. came. One was so typically Sparlin that I laughed out loud – where you re-iterated all about your missing letters. What a Girl! I suppose you will worry about whether I worry for fear you are worrying about whether I'm worried or not, and if I'm not worrying about you, you'll worry about why I'm not worrying....

My vacation is practically in effect now. Last night I saw [the movie] Fantasia in a theatre, sat on plush seats in a balcony with real white families – all for one [shilling] and six pence [about 20 U.S. cents in 1943]. During intermission Davis bought me an ice-cream cone. Isn't that something? Half of my boys are on vacation now, and Ray [DeBlois] + I hope to get away next week some time. He is going with Downing and I go with Davis. Our plan is to get away from soldiers. Ray + Downing plan to fish and will probably sit in the canoe back to back so they will not need to see any soldiers.

Rus. [Capt. Russell Davis] + I are planning to drift thru the small towns and take walks in the pine forests and climb mountains and sit beside rivers and stop at little hotels and read and rest and eat different than army foods. If it isn't too expensive I plan to forget the Bn. for two weeks. Today I went to the American Red Cross Office here for information as to where to go. The lady who talked with me wanted us to stop and see her mother who lives in the area we planned to tour. She said rather apologetically that her mother was "quite old" but would be so proud if we would stop a day or two with her. I mention it to show you how hospitable people here are. The lady said her husband was an engineer officer and that he had been in service "over seas" for five and one half years. It sounded like a long time to me. Don't worry. I'm not interested in her nor she in me. Davis once did a bicycle tour of England so he should be good company on a walking and bus tour.

Oh Yes, I'm living in a real house too. The Staff + I have a six room house with a big tree in the front yard, a back porch with a wonderful view of meadows, hills and hedges and two fireplaces. We hung drapes on the windows that we made of burlap and it looks quite homey. When we arrived it was at night and we detrained and marched down a gravel road. The odor of evergreen was heavy in the air and it was cool, and the rotten odor of the jungle was all forgotten in the joy of clean perfumes of trees and flowers and the odor of fresh cut hay and of cows + horses. One house behind a neat hedge was lighted and the freshly mowed lawn and the lighted windows were to me the most beautiful sight I had seen in many months.

How I wish you were here to share my vacation. You must need one as much as I, and there are so many things here you would love. The country looks here like Vermont except that all the roads are bordered by hedges, all the yards are marked by hedges, and many of the fields [are] too. Houses are painted white + usually have red roofs. I told one man I might move here after the war and he said I wouldn't like it. When I asked why, he said "You Yanks do things. You don't have red tape. Don't you know?" He was sure they were too slow + easy going for us because he was in Canada once and knew about us.…

I'm glad you + Paul were pleased about my L. of M. [Legion of Merit medal]. I might as well tell you now that, altho it did not develop, Col. Holland recommended me for the Silver Star. I would have been very proud if it had been given me but am not surprised that it fell thru because I didn't do anything that I would have recommended one of my officers for a Star for. I am proud tho that Holland felt that way about me and you should know but do not speak of it to anyone else. Too many cheap imitators are being quoted as expecting decorations.

I do love you so much that all I can say is that you are my whole life. — Wilber XXXØØ

> The Silver Star was, and is, given for personal heroism, whereas the Legion of Merit was for "exceptionally meritorious conduct." Wilber would later be awarded the Silver Star three times for actions in the Philippines.

X·O·Ø·O·X

## MAR. 2, 1944

Sweet Wife — I'm sitting by my fireplace watching the coals glow and dim into ashes. The men are having a dance at the Red Cross Hut in our camp and I have just gone down (10:00 P.M.) to see if everything is going as it should. There were seventy girls (?) and about a hundred of our men all apparently as happy as they could be. Everyone was behaving very well too. I met the lady who was in charge of the girls and her daughter. They were both very busy carrying cakes + coffee to the couples. Mrs. B—? is a farmer's wife who lives just three houses down the road. She is much like Mrs. Brann [the wife of a University of Maine colleague].

In my last letter I spoke of how beautiful the lighted windows of a house had looked to me. It was her house and she said her husband had had the curtains up when we marched by "because it looks so much more homelike, don't you know?" It did to me....

Barker + Files were here today just for social purposes. I had released half my officers the day before and was glad I had because Files said I could let ten percent go. So they were safely away for a week's rest. He considered requiring me to recall forty percent of them but decided against it. I got B. [Barker was Files's boss.] steamed up on the theme that the officers had earned all the rest I could arrange and that I wanted it for them. It looks now as if he is going to back up my ideas on that.

Yesterday René [DeBlois] and I went to the city [probably Auckland] to check on vacation tours and fishing points. I'm not sure but that the best vacation for me would be the loan of a Chem. Lab., but I don't dare do it or my men would know I was nuts. I guess I'm normal mentally for the thought of a vacation appalls me. I'm in a real depression trying to figure out something I'd like to do. Probably if I fish for a week or so, I'll welcome combat again.

*The prospect of two weeks of vacation seemed to dismay Wilber.*

Mar. 3 ... This is a beautiful countryside. Everything is green and fresh as in Maine. The firs + cedar and spruce are used for wind-breaks and hedges, and some are so tall that the houses are completely hidden from the road. In one case I saw a cedar hedge so high that the front gate was a door cut thru the hedge, which was about six feet thru and twelve high. I like these hedges and would like one around our back yard. They trim them straight up + down on the outside and I suppose on the inside too so they make a dense green wall. You would like it too.... Good night Darling. My arms are around you. — XXXOOØ Wilber

x · o · ø · o · x

*Wilber turned again to his son with a play on an idiom and other "manly" topics.*

**MARCH 3, 1944**
Dear Son Hale — Thank you for the birthday letter. It was one of the very nicest I have ever received. March came in like a lamb down here and has been a lamb since. It probably never is a lion here [in the southern hemisphere]. I can imagine it was pretty lionish with you.

CHAPTER 17    *Our plan is to get away from soldiers*

I'm very glad to hear your grades are doing well.... You surprise me by being [promoted to] a Second Class Scout [so soon]. I'm glad you are a Scout. It is a famous organization that has done many fine things.

> Second Class is the third rank one can attain in scouting, after Scout and Tenderfoot.

The bullet bent when it hit something before it hit me. It evidently ricocheted and hit me … The Legion of Merit is a medal given to some soldiers by order of the President. It is the same thru all our Army. Yes Horseshoe Hill is the one I told you about where we blasted the Japs off it, so our infantry could capture it….

I love you Son. You are doing all right and I'm proud of you. — Your Father. Wilber

> I found scouting, with its focus on individual achievements for the earning of merit badges, as opposed to team sports, very much to my liking. St. Bernard's School had a scout log cabin on the property to which I repaired on many an afternoon to work on scouting skills: knot tying, lighting a fire without matches, cooking over a fire, identifying trees in winter, and so on. One of our teachers, the elderly, shy Mr. Hobbe, was our scoutmaster, and he was often available to help us. I was a First Class scout by the end of the year.

x · o · ø · o · x

### MAR. 5, 1944

Dear Norma — Do you still have those cute little creases on your forearm? If so consider them kissed … Your letter mailed Dec. 16 came today as fresh and clean as if mailed last week. It was a sweet letter about our last Christmas in Bangor with love in every word. I felt so happy after reading it. You said you had had the flu but were up again. It was just one other reason that I love you so much. Little Mother! …

> Wilber made no mention of the much-delayed arrival of this letter. In this case, the delay may have been the military's problem because it was apparently postmarked on December 16.

I'm sleeping long hours and can't seem to get too much of it. In fact, I slept long hours in the tropics except during actual combat. Even then I slept easily when I could. It is one of my real assets and so is the old trick of turning the mind blank and not thinking of anything. Do you remember how you used to worry about that Darling? It's a good way to rest between bouts. Maybe I should go to a town where there is a good library, movies, and hotel and read + sleep for a week.

This is one place you would like. It renews my intention for us to repeat our honeymoon trip only more leisurely. How about on our twentieth anniversary? [in 1947] … I love you Darling. Don't forget me. — Wilber XXXOOØ

This is the last extant letter from Wilber to Norma until the end of April, except for one on April 6, and there were only a few in May. Letters from Wilber could have been misplaced, and Wilber admitted to some gaps in his letter writing due to his vacation travels. There are, in contrast, letters from him to me, Valerie, his father, and his brother during this period.

Life became complicated for Norma in March and April. She would be caring for a six-month old, hosting spring vacation visits by Valerie and me, and suffering an injury in a traffic accident.

x · o · ø · o · x

Wilber's first monthly letter from New Zealand to his father started with a scenic description followed by an overview of his and his men's activities.

### MARCH 5, 1944

Dear Father — I'm sitting on the back porch of a house and looking across clean meadows where cattle and sheep are grazing. In the distance are green hills and pine covered slopes. Altogether it is a beautiful spot. It is the fall of the year, and the orchard has in it ripe peaches and lemons. The yard is full of flowers native to your own area – Crysanthemums, Dahlias, late lilies, etc. Nearly all the fields are bounded by hedges of flowering shrubs, red haw, black haw, cedar, fir, pine, gorse, and others I don't recognize … All in all we are better quartered than any time since 1941. The men and battery officers are in hutments, which [are] the best they have seen for a year and a half.

I've moved several times since you last heard by the radio where we were. On one move, a box of my luggage went into the ocean, which didn't help the contents any. It was salvaged, and I spend a lot of time re-gluing things, oiling and cleaning compasses, staplers, drying out my books and throwing away items I have carefully carried around for over 15,000 miles.…

Now we are in a real rest area and our men are getting passes and trying to get drunk on the local beer and making the usual advances to the local girls. In some ways, as the C.O., I think I prefer the active combat when the men who make mistakes are evacuated or buried and don't get dumped on my doorstep. However I've very little to complain about for the boys are better than many other units, and my officers are all gentlemen both by act of Congress and by their own conduct. I don't believe we have as much trouble in this theatre from drinking as in the last war. The supply is too limited....

You write about the strikes and lack of support of the war. However I'm reminded that the very fact that people can squabble and criticize and strike is really our strength. Some such as you and I are jealous of our country while others we think lax will pitch in when the last fight comes and will make us ashamed that we have done so little.

> It pleases this liberal son that Wilber could see the true underpinnings of a working democracy despite his conservative political leanings. It had been almost a decade since he had been on strike duty with the national guard (Book 1), where his job had been to keep order in the streets. At that time, he had focused on keeping order, which had the effect of furthering the aims of the employers.

Here come the O.D.s [Officers of the Day to report to Wilber]. Goodbye, I Love You. — Wilber

x · o · ø · o · x

> Wilber was now off on an 18-day vacation on North Island and South Island, New Zealand (Map 14). He was with Capt. Earl Russell Davis for the whole trip, but they had started out with a Lieutenant Gong. They traveled mostly by bus [letter 3/1/44], but perhaps sometimes by automobile ["car," letter 3/14/44], and were required by army regulation to be in uniform in public. This made them quite conspicuous and the center of much attention. The beginning of fall was a wonderful time for such a tour; the trees were colorful and there was minimal snow on high-altitude trails. Wilber wrote to me with fatherly advice in the moral sphere.

**[ON LEAVE, TOURING NEW ZEALAND] MARCH 10, 1944**
Dear Hale — I am having two weeks vacation and this is my third day. Yesterday we drove very leisurely thru mountain country and sheep meadows. There are certainly a lot of sheep here and they are very pretty against the green hills. Capt. Davis and Lt. [J. H.] Gong (My Chinese officer) are with me. We decided to get away from all uniforms and telephones that would call us. It, so far, has been a wonderful rest. I had been a bit jumpy and very tired but now am feeling much better already.

For breakfast this morning, I had ham and mushrooms and tea. Before I was up, the hotel maid brought a hot cup of tea to my room. It is a good way to wake and very helpful since the dining room only opened at 8:00. Last evening for supper, I ate in a seafood restaurant and asked for oysters. They had none but did have a crayfish with a big tail like our lobster. All the claws were small, and the shell was covered by sharp spikes. They serve it cold with tomatoes, and it is very good. In fact I could not tell if it was at all different in taste from our lobster.

I'm glad you are getting a chance to live with other boys and to have men teachers this year. It is important for each of us to decide what type of things we will and will not do. Of course it is easy to know that we won't steal or burn houses or anything like that. It isn't so easy to know just what to do about being a good fellow without doing some things that might cheapen you. Neither is it easy to know when to give in courteously and when to stand up for what you think is right. Every man must set his own standards and must be true to them.

I believe it is a good guide to do those things you won't be ashamed of later; to do those things that don't take some one's rights and happiness away from them. It means letting people have fun at your expense often enough to show them you are able to play a losing part but to hold [out against] certain demeaning things, which no one and nothing can make you do. I'm sure a school such as yours is giving you

*Postcard photo of Mt. Egmont (aka Mt. Taranaki) seen from the Stratford side. Wilber wrote on another photograph of this mountain that "Davis and I climbed this," but in fact they did not reach the summit because of snow [letter 4/9/44]. The peak, at 8,261 feet, is considered a moderate climb when free of snow. It is situated in Egmont National Park.*
[PHOTO: JAMES MCALLISTER (1869–1952), FROM WILBER'S PAPERS]

CHAPTER 17   *Our plan is to get away from soldiers*

*Souvenir picture card of "Mt. Ngauruhoe in Eruption. N. Z." in Wilber's papers. He wrote on the back, "I was here after the eruption. WB" This volcano erupted 45 times in the 20th century. It is situated in Tongariro National Park in the Central Plateau of North Island, New Zealand.* [PHOTO: NATIONAL PUBLICITY STUDIOS, N. Z., NO. 4858]

good chances to learn these things for yourself, and [I] want you to know I am sure you will choose a good way to live. I love you son. Nothing could make me happier than to have you here today. — Good bye Now. Wilber.

This fatherly advice was admirable in that it avoided defining specific do's and don'ts. He left the boundaries up to me, a smart strategy when dealing with a 13-year-old.

On this date, I too had begun a vacation, the spring break (March 10 to 20) from St. Bernard's School. I went by train to Washington, D.C., where I stayed with Wilber's brother Paul and his wife Josephine. I saw little or nothing of Norma; she was hospitalized after being hit by a car in Dupont Circle. I went hiking with Paul and Jo and was aggressively toured all around Washington, D.C., on buses, trolleys, and on foot by Aunt Jo's father, Mr. Irey. He had been a Capitol page [messenger boy] and taught me a great deal about the Capitol and many other famous Washington sites. He died that August at age 62; I was glad to have known him.

COMBAT AND NEW LIFE  PART 1V: WESTERN CIVILIZATION AT LAST!

*The famous "Drop Scene" on the Whanganui River, named for its stage-like perfection, on a souvenir picture card. It is situated in Whanganui National Park, North Island, New Zealand. Wilber wrote on this image: "We saw this too."* [PHOTO: NATIONAL PUBLICITY STUDIOS, N. Z., NO. 4289]

CHAPTER 17   *Our plan is to get away from soldiers*

The paucity of Wilber's letters and his silence on place names, possibly because of censorship rules, made my reconstruction of his New Zealand vacation itinerary somewhat difficult. He and Davis headed south from Auckland by bus or car and took the ferry to Christchurch on South Island [letter 7/7/44]—this much was known. When censorship allowed, Wilber sent home a few souvenir picture cards that he had annotated, and I found other such cards in his papers. These showed that while still on North Island, he and Davis had visited the Egmont, Whanganui, and Tongariro National Parks, all about 200 miles south of Auckland on North Island. To quote his annotations, they "climbed" the 8,260-foot Mt. Taranaki, "saw" Mt. Ngauruhoe "not in eruption," and "saw" the famous Drop Scene on the Whanganui River. The latter is a picturesque scene so perfect it could be the backdrop for a stage play. Visiting national parks had been Wilber's habit in the United States, and he continued it in New Zealand.

x · o · ø · o · x

Four days later, Wilber and Davis were in a hotel "in a large city," which probably was Christchurch on South Island. He wrote Valerie about the earlier week on North Island.

**MAR. 14, 1944**
Dear Little Tumblebug — Yesterday and the day before I was traveling in a car among pretty green fields over high steep hills and thru wooded ravines. The plants are different than ours and one often sees giant ferns which are taller than I. The names of some of the trees are native, for example the Wheki tree is like this [sketch] with each leaf like a great fern. On the other hand the Lekouri [?] tree has bunches of flag-like leaves just at the end of each branch like this [sketch]. The Norfolk Island Pine is a beautiful symmetrical evergreen that I wish you could see. Notice how all the limbs come out at the same level, then the tree grows up another step and sends out another ring of branches like this [sketch].... Someday maybe we can see them together.

I could not find any reference to a "Lekouri" tree. In 2012, I asked an Australian friend about it, sending him Wilber's sketch. He shared it with a national botany expert in New Zealand who instantly identified it. The sketched tree was surely the "ti-kouka" (known in New Zealand as the cabbage tree). Wilber probably got "Lekouri" from another similar sounding New Zealand tree, the Kauri, which grows to 50 yards, like the American Sequoia.

Sunday [March 12] I visited in a little town and a man took me out to the bowling green for the afternoon. There was a tournament being played and it was very interesting. I had never seen outdoor bowling before. They roll the balls across the lawn and try for the closest position to a small ball. There are no ten pins or alleys in it. The balls are made heavy on one side.... In the middle of the afternoon, we were given tea & tomato sandwiches. They wanted Capt. Davis & me to go hunting wild pig the next day but we declined.

That evening we went to Evensong at St. Andrews, Church of England. The service was almost the same as ours and it was the first time I had heard a pipe organ since we were together. They chanted more of the service but in other respects were quite low church.

Today [Tuesday], I'm in a large city [Christchurch], sitting in a hotel room listening to my little radio as I write. All this is a real rest from being in the jungle. I love you Darling and am very, very glad you are my girl. Please write to me once in awhile. — Daddy XXXXXOOOOO

It is likely that the church Wilber visited was St. Andrews, in Plimmerton, a seaside resort about ten miles outside Wellington. St. Andrew's offered Sunday Evensong services in

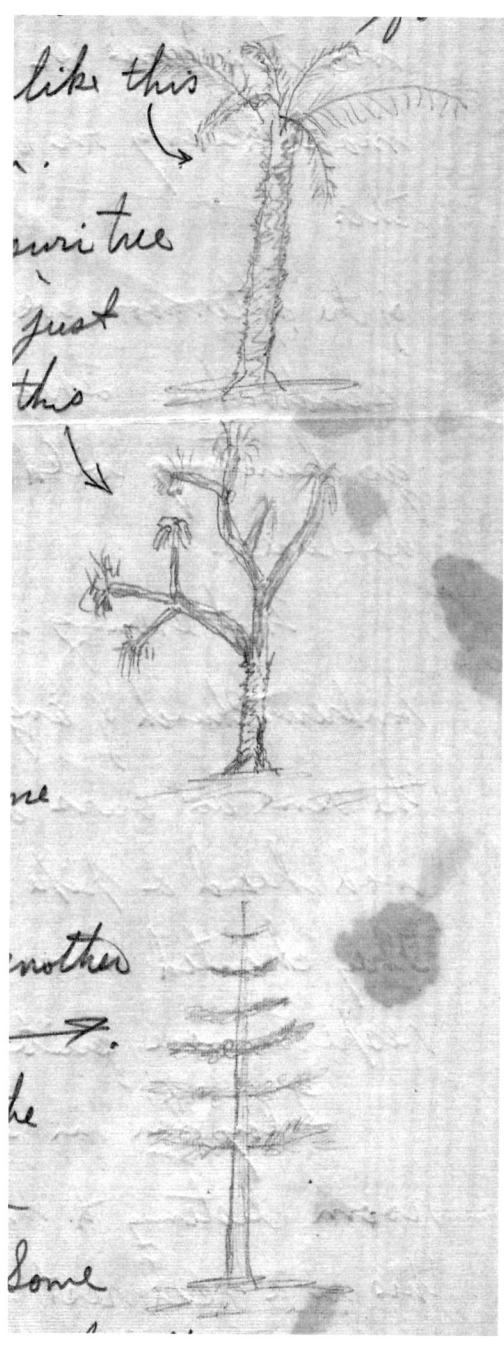

*Sketches of New Zealand trees in a letter to Valerie. From the top: Wheki, Ti-kouka ("cabbage tree"), and Norfolk Island Pine. The Ti-kouka was misnamed by Wilber.* [LETTER 3/14/44]

CHAPTER 17   *Our plan is to get away from soldiers*

*United Service Hotel, Christchurch, New Zealand, (in background upper right) in 1928. Wilber and Davis stayed here during their tour in March 1944. It was an expensive hotel, according to Olive Madsen. It was built about 1885 and demolished in 1990.*
[CHRISTCHURCH CITY LIBRARIES, CCL PHOTO CD10, IMG0008]

those days, and the town featured the Plimmerton Bowling Club, claimed even now as one of the best in the Wellington region. Wilber and Davis probably saved money by avoiding downtown Wellington hotels, but would enjoy that luxury on the return trip. The ferry to Christchurch (actually nearby Lyttelton) on South Island departed from Wellington, the capital city of New Zealand. During March 1944, it seemed that the departures were relatively infrequent and irregular if "Shipping Departures" listed in old *Wellington Evening Post* issues, now available online, were complete. The Pupeko departed for Lyttelton at 9:50 p.m. on March 13, and they may have been on it. In Christchurch, they stayed, I learned later, at the rather expensive and historic United Service Hotel. It was built about 1885 and was finally torn down in 1990. A number of souvenir picture cards of Christchurch sights in Wilber's collection—none of them annotated—suggested that they may have spent a day or two seeing the sights of the city.

# COMBAT AND NEW LIFE  PART IV: WESTERN CIVILIZATION AT LAST!

x · o · ø · o · x

Souvenir photos with his notations placed Wilber on the west coast of South Island at the Franz Josef Glacier, which flowed toward the Tasman Sea in the Westland Tai Poutini National Park. There was no direct road across the mountains from Christchurch to the park; one first traveled to the north or south (Map 14). The longer route to the south went through the spectacularly situated Queenstown, nestled in the mountains on New Zealand's longest lake. Today it is a must for most tourists and a natural bus destination 300 miles from Christchurch. I expect Wilber and Davis visited and stayed there. Wilber's collection of unmarked picture cards also contained an image of the famously dramatic Milford Sound on the southwest coast, which suggests that they did explore the southern route. They would likely have spent a few days in Queenstown hiking and boating and then bussed northward the 220 miles to the glacier areas of Westland and Cook National Parks. Mt. Cook is New Zealand's highest mountain at 12,316 feet.

By the time this next letter was written, Thursday March 23, Wilber was "on the way back to work." He and Davis were due back at Papakura early on Monday morning; their 18-day leave was coming to an end. From the known dates of their Wellington visit and ferry schedules, they must have already been at their departure port at the north end of South Island, probably at picturesque Picton, situated in one of the fractal-like multiple inlets of Marlborough Sound. Wilber felt relaxed and described conversations around the fire with an international group that he portrayed perceptively and with humor in this letter to Valerie, possibly written as he was waiting for the ferry to North Island.

### MARCH 23, 1944

Dear Daughter Valerie — How is my favorite daughter today? Probably wondering about spring. Is it warm in New Jersey yet? I suppose spring will really be there by your birthday [April 18]. Here it is fall and the goldenrod is blooming.

The other day I went climbing on a glacier [Franz Josef Glacier]. It was the first ice & snow I have touched since my last leave in New York in 1941. The guide cut steps in the ice and we climbed up the steep places wondering if our shoes would slip. In the crevasses were lovely blue colors where the light had reflected. One ice cave about as big as our living room was so lovely I'll never forget it. It felt good too to be cold again. All about us were great rocky snow capped mountains with little white clouds playing hide & seek among their peaks.

CHAPTER 17   *Our plan is to get away from soldiers*

*Image of the Franz Josef Glacier, New Zealand, on a souvenir picture card on which Wilber had written, "On my trip, I climbed this. WB." It is on the west coast of South Island in the Westland Tai Poutini National Park.* [PHOTO: NATIONAL PUBLICITY STUDIOS, N. Z., NO. 4261]

*The Franz Josef Glacier as seen from Waiho Chapel, New Zealand. Wilber wrote a note on the back of this souvenir picture card to Norma, "I was in this church too. You too someday. WB."* [PHOTO: NATIONAL PUBLICITY STUDIOS, N. Z., NO. 4266]

*Wilber on a hike with three companions, in New Zealand. These may be three of the people Wilber had mentioned sitting around the hotel fireplace after hiking [letter 3/23/44]. If so, this photo could have been taken in the hills near Picton on the northeast tip of South Island, from which Wilber and Davis probably took the ferry to Wellington.* [PHOTO: WILBER BRADT COLLECTION]

The people too are very nice. We found a small crowd here that all wanted to do the same thing. They were Jack and Shirley and Mac and Helen and Rita and Alec and Peggy and George and Aunty and Peter and Helman and Longfellow and Brownie and two or three others commonly called "Oh I say you there." Davis & I climbed with them, complained about our aches and sore muscles, and danced with them, and we sat by the fireplace together. It was all fun. I often wished I had my family with me. Jack & Shirley were on their honeymoon, Mac was a New Zealand aviator, Alec was a guide. George was fat. Aunty, I think owned part of the hotel because she was very bossy. Helen was engaged to the son of the hotel manager, Helman was a citizen [of New Zealand?]. Brownie was an American Red Cross worker who did all the talking. Longfellow was a full "chicken" colonel who went to college with me. Peter was the bar tender and Rita an American Second Lt. Nurse. Evenings I read in front of the fireplace and really enjoyed myself.

I love you Little Sweet. Someday I hope we can go places together again. I'm nearly thru my rest now & am on the way back to work. — Your Daddy XXXOOO Wilber

CHAPTER 17   *Our plan is to get away from soldiers*

Picton is adjacent to the Whenuanui Bay Scenic Reserve where they may have done the hiking Wilber described. The evenings "in front of the fireplace" could also have been in Picton.

x·o·ø·o·x

I learned a great deal about their next few days in Wellington from multiple sources: Wilber's departure (from New Zealand) letter of July 7, 1944, below, wherein he described his Wellington visit; my 1984 interview with a Ms. Olive Madsen of Carterton (see the following Interlude); a cricket match schedule; and train service availability. From all this, it is clear that Wilber and Captain Davis arrived in Wellington late Thursday or early Friday, stayed at the St. George Hotel, and returned to Auckland by train, a roughly 15-hour trip, two days later on Sunday, March 26. The Wellington visit wrapped up a marvelous grand tour of New Zealand, which was actually not as relaxing as Wilber had hoped.

Unmentioned in these letters so far was a bit of romance that Wilber found during this trip. As usual, significant events in his life emerged in his letters somewhat after the fact. We will hear of this one in that departure letter of July 7. The complete story would not be revealed until my own visit to New Zealand in 1984.

# 18

## *"I'm taking over another battalion"*

### Matakana, New Zealand
### April–May, 1944

As Wilber returned to his unit in the Auckland region, probably on Monday, March 27, Norma was struggling with what to do when Valerie and I finished the school year at our New Jersey boarding schools. Should she stay in Washington, D.C., with baby Gale and remain separated from us, or should she reunite the family, possibly in Bangor, Maine, where we owned a home and where Wilber's job as the university department head awaited him? Returning with the baby to Bangor, where all Wilber's academic and military associates' families lived, would certainly raise very awkward questions. Remaining with Gale in Washington where Wilber's brother Paul lived would raise similar questions. The social pressures of the day might well have driven Norma and Monte to consider giving up Gale for adoption, a thought that gives me the shivers, even today.

x·o·ø·o·x

Wilber's brother Paul was not a letter writer, unlike his wife Josephine. Thus Wilber wrote to her and got in a bit of boasting. This was his first day back on the job, and he had been greeted with news of a brand new assignment.

**MAR. 27, 1944**
Dear Jo, [wife of brother Paul] — … I'm taking over another battalion [152 FA Bn.] in a few days so have a big job ahead bringing it up to the level of the 169th. I asked the General [Barker] if the shift was due to any failure on my part. He punched me in the ribs + said, "I don't need to tell [you] but I will say it again. The Division

commander, the Assist. Div. Commander + I all consider you the best Arty. Bn. C.O. in the Div. That is why the shift." So I'm stuck and afraid he'll find out I'm a phony too. Goom-By. — Love from your brother Wilber

> The 152nd Field Artillery Battalion was Wilber's previous outfit in Bangor, Maine, before it was inducted into federal service. This move to the command of a different battalion of the 43rd Division was a lateral move; it did not merit a promotion. The 152nd was stationed about 40 miles north of Auckland at Matakana (Warkworth). Wilber replaced Norman Whitney who with another battalion commander, George Hill, had gone on leave in the States for subsequent reassignment to other units. Wilber's former executive officer, René DeBlois, took command of Wilber's former unit, the 169th Field Artillery Battalion.
>
> General Barker may have felt that the 152nd needed a strong commander, and Wilber may have been more qualified than other available officers. Also DeBlois, who had previously commanded the Provisional Battalion on Arundel, was available to take over the 169th. It was in General Barker's interest to have the best available officers command his four battalions of artillery.

x·o·ø·o·x

> In his monthly letter to his father, Wilber was unusually candid about his situation and condition. He also included more about Norma's accident.

**[U.S. ARMY HOSPITAL] 4/1/44**
Dear Father — I'm glad the L. of M. [medal] arrived safely and that you appreciated it. It apparently made very good time in the mail.…

Several things have happened. We moved back to civilization some time ago and I was given 18 days rest. It was nice but I was disappointed to find I still haven't rid myself of a tenseness and nervousness that developed in the "Islands." It isn't serious, but bothers me. I climbed some mountains, saw movies, went to church, ate hotel (rationed) dinners, and talked with a lot of the local people. It was all very pleasant and expensive but I don't vacation easily. The other event is the fact that I am taking command of the 152d FA Bn. today. I'm depressed about leaving the 169 [FA Bn.] but realize it's a war. The 152 is my home unit from Bangor, and I am glad to be back home. However I made this 169 famous all over the So. Pac. and really feel it was mine. Now I'm starting all over to try to do the same for the 152d. The former commander is returning to the states to join a new unit.

CHAPTER 18   *I'm taking over another battalion*

The final recent event designed to make me feel old at the age of 44 is the fact that I am in the hospital myself for a general check up and minor repairs. That shows how sympathetic Norma and I are for I just had a letter from her saying she was in Walter Reed Hospital, having been knocked down by a car on the street. She said X-rays didn't show any fractures but that they are holding her awhile and that she would have to be careful for some time. I'm afraid she is minimizing her injuries on my account, but am sure Paul will be keeping an eye on her.

Your letter about strikes and soldiers' notes was not censored.... It's true more men die because of strikes and democracy type bungling, but it's also true that to live isn't nearly so important as many people think. I think I told you I don't expect to live thru this affair, but the fact doesn't particularly dismay me. In fact it enables me to do things in combat that I would otherwise not be able to do. I realize it would be tough on the family but don't think it would bother me, now that I personally [have] piled up a score on the Japs they will never match.

> Wilber had succumbed to a discouraged and somewhat fatalistic view of his role in the war, clearly abetted by his being in the hospital and thus being inactive. He had yet to dig into the job of bringing the 152nd Field Artillery up to his standards.

Please give my greetings to Scott Henderson [owner of neighboring farm and boyhood friend] and tell him I'd like to drop in some day to see if he is as old as I feel. It's amazing how few people I know there, but of course one either goes forward or backward. I love you and hope this spring will be good to you. — Your Son, Wilber

x · o · ø · o · x

### APRIL 2, 1944

Darling Daughter of Mine [Valerie] — How is my sweet little flower today? ...Did you know you are "Comrade IV?" In Nana's (wedding) ring is engraved the word "Comrades" meaning we always stand and fight and work and live together. On the back of her watch are the words "Comrade III" and Hale's birth [date] just to show he was one of our Comrades. When you were born Nana gave me a Scabbard & Blade key and on its back is engraved "Comrade IV" and your birthday. You see we are a little more than just a family. We are a special family in which each one wants the others to be cared for and to learn to be good Christian neighbors....

I have heard of Norma's accident and hope she is OK now. Did you write to her while she was in the hospital? I think she is very lonesome for you....

Goodby Now, or as they say here, Cheerio! — I love you Valerie, Wilber

I still have the engraved watch. The National Society of Scabbard and Blade was, and is, a collegiate military service honor society that Wilber may have joined at Indiana University. He was at Washington State College when Valerie was born (1932) and might have been a faculty advisor to the society there.

x · o · ø · o · x

Next came a big letter from Wilber to me about sexuality, the counterpart to his father's 1918 letter to him (Book 1) about morality and in particular . . . . . smoking! I was 13 at this time and Wilber had been 18 when he received his father's letter. Perhaps he should have gotten the sex letter and I the smoking letter! As it was, I was never tempted to smoke, and to this date have never had so much as a puff. Wilber's letter was remarkable for its day in its progressive approach toward women. He wrote it from the hospital.

**APRIL 3, 1944**
Dear Hale — … I wish you could have been with me when I was climbing in the mountains and on the glacier. Climbing on the glacier was pretty jittery work for a while for me. I hadn't been on ice for so long that I was afraid to trust my feet. However on the way back I was able to slide down steep places and use my pike for a brake and really enjoyed it. The ice and snow were good to see again.

I've just been down to the mess for lunch. It was particularly good today – roast pork, sweet potatoes, milk and cauliflower and lettuce salad; I declined some cake and stopped at the Exchange and bought a candy bar. It's so comfortable here [in the hospital] that I'm afraid I'll get lazy if I stay long.

Norma tells me you are taking girls to dances now. You are certainly starting younger than I did. Just remember that girls are people too and should be treated accordingly. I'm sure you would always do that anyway. Do they give you much instruction on sex? If they don't, have Norma buy you some books. This sex business is pretty powerful stuff when you get a little older and can give you either a lot of fun or a lot of trouble. The thing to remember is that it is one of the most powerful instincts we inherit, just as that of self-preservation and therefore can't quite be treated as a bad habit.

Not all intercourse with a girl gets her pregnant because it depends on her own physical condition and health. Some people think it is wrong to take a girl except to have babies. I was taught that, but I know now that it is wrong to do anything that would harm either the body or spirit or reputation of another person. Doing anything, which a girl or you would look back on as being cheap or that would make either of you ashamed afterward, would be wrong. Since sex is based on a powerful instinct, you will see girls who will attract you that way. Only hypocrites say they aren't attracted. If you are old enough to marry one of these girls, it may grow to be a real love such as I hold for Nana; or, if she isn't the type you could love, [it] may be a dangerous thing to expose yourself to. One of the best reasons for never drinking enough to be even a little intoxicated is that alcohol causes one to lower his restraint and do things he would not do otherwise.

You must remember that girls have these same instincts, perhaps even stronger than men, and that it is therefore up to us men to see that our girls don't feel sorry for anything the next day or month. If an unmarried girl has a baby, people make life very hard for her and for her baby.

> Neither he nor I realized how close to the bone he was cutting here. I must have sent this letter on to Norma; it was in one of the collections I obtained from her.

One reason I am writing these things now is that I may never have a chance to talk to you, or you may be in the Army or Navy before I have that chance. I see here a lot of boys taking girls who will be sorry later. The girls are lonely for all their men have been away for years, and our boys have been away from women for a year and a half. When one is strong no trouble results, but when both are weak, serious trouble comes in babies and disease and disillusionment for nice girls back home.

It doesn't do to feel that these situations won't happen to you. I have never lain with any woman but Nana and never will, but there have been women who were attractive to me that way. I know tho that I'd feel cheap and dirty if I went back to Norma after doing any playing around with someone else. Only recently a woman asked me to "sleep" with her. I was quite surprised for she seemed very nice, but of course I thanked her and said I wasn't the type. I don't know if she was a professional whore or not, for these people here seem to feel that because we saved them from the Jap atrocities, they are greatly in debt to us.

I'm sure some people try to give the impression that possessing a woman's body is either awful or that [it] is something not to talk about. After one is married, it is legal and normal and there is nothing to be ashamed or embarrassed about it. It is really just another way to express your love for each other, is fun and rather wonderful to know you both enjoy it. If there are any questions you care to ask I'll be glad to answer them as well as I can. When you are older, I'll want to tell you as much as you like about how to make love to a woman this way.

Only one thing more – some boys as you probably know think a lot about sex and get into bad habits because of it. This may show up with a tendency to play with the penis, which is called masturbation, or to tell dirty stories or in getting too interested in girls. It would be just as bad to spend too much time on thinking about how you feel; your aches and pains; or whether you felt blue. In general try to be moderate in your habits. Avoid extremes of studious habits or of all physical habits. Mix up your actions of each day so that each day you exercise yourself physically, mentally and spiritually and you will have no real trouble with sex or anything else.

You can see now why I am so glad you are in a church school, working on a farm and getting ahead in the scouts. In the same way here, I hike and climb, go to church, study every day, and work on the battalion duties each day. That keeps me on a fairly well balanced keel and I don't get my mind too much on anything [any one thing].

Good bye now, Hale. I hope this long-winded letter doesn't bore you. I love you a lot. — Wilber

>Wilber was telegraphing here how he kept his own life in balance. The entirely voluntary statement "I have never lain with any woman but Nana" assures us yet again that Wilber's sexual experiences had been solely with Norma.

>I was impressed with his gender sensitivity: women had feelings too, he suggested, and could easily be hurt by men. He was also honest about temptations and desires on the part of both sexes and did not demonize masturbation (this was quite common in those days, as in statements like "it will weaken your mind.") I did read here, though, some tinges of male chauvinism typical of the era: it is the men's job to take care of the (helpless) girls. Finally, this remarkable father-son "talk" from the 1940s was preserved and memorialized in writing because father and son were separated by war, in an era when hand-written letters were still the norm.

>I do not remember getting this letter but I am sure it had an effect on me as I took my dad's letters pretty seriously. I myself didn't discover masturbation until the following year, so I certainly didn't understand his reference to it but may have thought I did. His advice probably influenced my later rather timid and fairly responsible approaches to the opposite sex.

x·o·ø·o·x

>A few days later, Wilber turned to a lighter subject as he received the stationery I had printed in the print shop for him. He made two suggestions for improvements in the next batch.

CHAPTER 18   *I'm taking over another battalion*

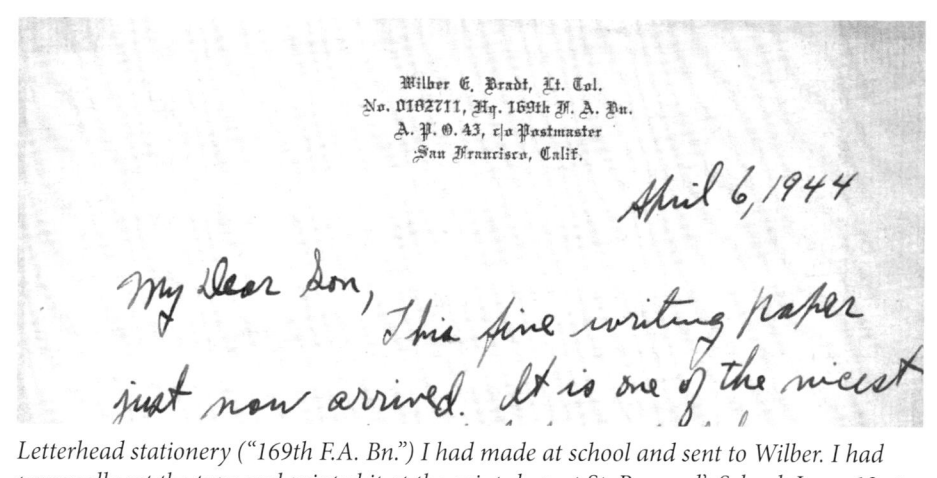

*Letterhead stationery ("169th F.A. Bn.") I had made at school and sent to Wilber. I had personally set the type and printed it at the print shop at St. Bernard's School; I was 13 at the time. It arrived just as Wilber took command of the 152nd Field Artillery Battalion, so it was immediately obsolete but of course still usable.*

### APRIL 6, 1944

My Dear Son — This fine writing paper just now arrived. It is one of the nicest and most thoughtful presents I have ever received. Thank you so much. Did you select the style of printing? I think it looks very neat. I'm wondering if you set the type. It surely is a good job. Of course I would change to the 152d just now [instead of the "169th F.A. Bn." on the letterhead]. However that won't make any difference in the way I like the present.

If you could have some more made for the 152d FA Bn. I would appreciate it. This will all be used up before that would arrive anyway. I like the address best on the back of the envelope too, but since I have to write it in the upper left corner perhaps it would be better to print it there next time.

I don't know when anything has made me as happy as this present Hale. You certainly picked a good one.

I'm sending Valerie and Nana some flowers for Valerie's birthday. I hope they arrive in time. Tomorrow is Good Friday and next is Easter Sunday. I hope to go to the Cathedral for services if I can get out of the hospital in time. If not I'll be thinking and praying that we may be thru with the war by another Easter.

I had a malted milk today with so much ice cream in it that I could hardly drink it. I'll bet you would have liked it. I wished I could have bought you one. It cost a shilling.

Major DeBlois now commands the 169th and I know he will do a good job with them. I'm going to try to make the 152d even better than the 169th. Good by Son. — I love you, Your father, Wilber

COMBAT AND NEW LIFE    PART 1V: WESTERN CIVILIZATION AT LAST!

x · o · ø · o · x

Wilber then turned to his brother Paul and wife Josephine, belittling his own hiking ability in order to celebrate theirs. There was a long-standing warm camaraderie between the two brothers.

[HOSPITAL] APRIL 9, 1944
Dear Jo + Paul — Your nice letters of Jan. 31 and Feb. 19 came while I was on the move again.…

Your accounts of your hike on Old Rag [a mountain in Shenandoah National Park] fill me with horror. Such [heavy back] packs, such expenditure of energy, such discomfort, so much food. Think how much nicer to sit in a warm theatre in a good comfortable seat and see a travelogue of a mountain trail. If you + Paul were to ever invite me on one of your trips, I'd slink off in shame at my own weakness. Do you realize that I usually don't even carry a pistol belt because it's too heavy. Normally I hang a canteen on my pants belt and a pistol in a shoulder holster with chocolate in my pocket. Here a blanket is surplus, thank goodness. I sure couldn't stand the pace you two would set. However it's wonderful to have relatives that can do those things.…

One of the mountains we climbed [in New Zealand] was a volcanic cone rising in a plain at sea level to over 8,000 feet. We went up one afternoon to over 5,500 feet for a practice climb then came back the next morning for a climb to the top but a storm stopped us at about the same height which was at the snow line then. A week later a friend found the snow at 2,500 feet so we were just in time. I practically freeze when the day is cool. — Best o' luck from your brother, Wilber

The mountain was surely Mt. Egmont, altitude 8,261 feet. Another letter written on this date to Wilber's other brother Rex said that he was still in the hospital. He was released soon thereafter.

x · o · ø · o · x

Wilber heard from me about my visit to Washington and about a dramatic encounter at St. Bernard's School.

[ST. BERNARD'S SCHOOL] APR. 23, 1944
*Dear Daddy — I got three letters from you dated Mar. 28, Apr. 3, 6. They were nice letters. I liked them a lot. I did not lose your bullet.*

*… If I did not tell you, I want to tell you what happened at Washington. I went on a train with another boy who got off at Baltimore. The first weekend I went*

274

CHAPTER 18   *I'm taking over another battalion*

*camping with [Uncle] Paul and Jo.... It rained all day but we had fun. That night Mother was hit by an automobile. I kept visiting her all the time [by telephone?]. I saw the House of Representatives in session. While I was there the clerk read the roll (435 names) and read the names of those who did not answer again. They were discussing how you should vote. "Soldier's Vote Bill." I didn't see [Senator] Brewster [from Maine] because the Senate had already adjourned.*

*Speaking of girls, there is going to be a dance May 6. I already have mine picked and I asked her. She said she would come.*

*There is a boy whose mother died last year and his father is a Lt. Col. in Italy. He was promoted about the same time you were. The boy is awfully slow [in doing his tasks]. The dorm-master has a habit of hitting him. Last night Helmer (the boy) was slow getting undressed, so Mr. Hubbell started hitting him with a strap. Helmer broke loose from him and started to run downstairs. Now Mr. Hub. is a very fat man. He started to run after Helmer, but his feet couldn't keep up with him so he made a 3, or 4, or 5 point landing on his stomach. He hit his arm against a doorway and broke it in two places. Helmer was awfully slow getting undressed and always is, but Mr. Hubbell had no right to hit him without having him lie down on a bed or something of the like. If you want to you can decide who is guilty, but I wouldn't bother if I were you.*

*I will have the stationery printed as you asked.... — Your loving son, Hale*

>  My recollection, possibly flawed, was that I did not see Norma at all that week in March, except possibly the evening I arrived. She was in Walter Reed Army Hospital and there were most likely restrictions on children's visits. This was the second spring vacation that Paul and Jo had taken me in. Valerie spent her spring vacation with Norma later, in mid-April. I surmise that Norma had made the 1754 Q Street NW apartment her headquarters for the visit and that baby Gale had been kept out of sight at Monte's house one mile to the west.
>
>  Mr. Hubbell never recovered and died within several months of his encounter with Helmer. Hubbell had befriended me and coached me in Latin outside of classes. His life there at the school had seemed to me quite lonely and sad.

x · o · ø · o · x

**[MATAKANA, N.Z.] APRIL 28, 1944**
My Dear Wife — I'm sitting at 10:00 P.M. in my hut beside my oil stove, thanking you for my warm pajamas with every shiver. I should feel very smart with my

paisley robe but instead I find myself very lonesome. Recently I've realized how hard things are for you these days. It is the weekend, and camp is nearly deserted. I'm staying in camp because I prefer it but I should be out with you. You are right when you say it is no fun to be out with people to whom you don't belong. I want to be sentimental and to make love to you. No one else will do, and I'll be glad when I can get back to the jungle and won't be seeing couples together and children playing in yards or lighted windows. Don't you hate single beds? …

I'm sorry, Dear, you aren't getting mail. It is not so good here for I'm off the direct mail routes. However the long delay was due to the fact that while I was on vacation, I couldn't send letters for we cannot use civilian channels. I sent four letters out when I was half thru my trip but it looks as if Swan never mailed them. While in the hospital I wrote almost daily and you probably have received those letters now. [These letters were apparently lost.] Since coming to the 152, I've missed writing for there are many things to straighten out here. I would never run a battalion like Whitney did this one. He had 2d Lts doing jobs for 1st Lts and vice versa, junior officers above their seniors and gave everyone the highest ratings officially even in cases where he said the officers were N.G. [no good].

> Nevertheless, on May 18, Wilber wrote in another context, "There is no question but that Lt. Col. Whitney had developed a fine outfit." Norman Whitney was the well-known owner of a fuel-oil distribution company in Bangor. Wilber justly trusted Norma not to pass his critical comments on to Bangor friends.

[Maj. Gen. Leonard] Wing [C.O. of the 43rd Division] came up to talk to the men and because I was here got mixed up and thought he was talking to the 169th. He really laid it on thick and the boys looked as if they didn't recognize themselves. He and Gen [David M. N.] Ross [assistant division commander] stayed for lunch and we really had a good visit. He [Wing] has always been cordial since Choate and I supported his brigade in maneuvers [in Louisiana or South Carolina] but he is really friendly now. I've always thought he was competent and he is proving it.…

> This was a fine tribute to General Wing, a Vermont National Guardsman. Col. John F. Choate was commanding officer of the 152nd Field Artillery Regiment in Camp Blanding before the 43rd Division was reorganized. He and Wilber had been close friends, but lost touch after the reorganization.

April 29, 1944 … This afternoon I spent all my free time studying the records of my officers. The information I gathered was quite encouraging. Several are college men and even the two Whitney said were N.G. may have been mis-handled. The

CHAPTER 18   *I'm taking over another battalion*

general attitude of the officers toward me is apparently very good. They seem to like what changes I am introducing and apparently my combat reputation didn't suffer any by the retelling in the 152. Maj. [Waldo H.] Fish [Jr.], my Exec[utive Officer], told Berry he was very happy now. So you see I'm really quite encouraged. I told Wing to watch this Bn. during the next combat and that I expected to make it the best in the division. He said that would be no surprise. That same day the Div. inspected our kitchens and said those of the 169th and 152d were the best yet inspected and that most of the division had been inspected.

Dearest, I'm so glad you have recovered from your accident. I practically have the horrors whenever I think of you alone and hurt. We really shouldn't be apart.... Take care of my Lover, my arms are still close about you and my spirit is with you each day. Don't forget, I love you. — XXXOOO Wilber

x·o·ø·o·x

### MAY 3, 1944

Hello Bright Eyes! — In your last letter you decided I was in combat again because you were receiving no mail. I'm wondering if you are in combat for I seem to be missing mail now....

It is cold here now; spit snow yesterday and I suffer quite a lot of discomfort. The first Maine winter is going to [be] hard on me. I'm still sitting waiting for some general to get up some morning and say "Where in the h— is the 43d [Division]?" In the mean time I'm getting fat again so have just introduced the new era of eating no more butter + gravy or potatoes. I may have to drop milk too but it is such a treat I'll keep drinking it for a while yet....

DeBlois has his silver leaves [lieutenant-colonel insignia] now and looks very cheerful over them. Goff is now Major and Steve Nichols a Lt. Col. The two last are in the 192 FA Bn. Did I tell you my Exec is Maj. Waldo Fish and my S-3 is Capt. Sam[uel F.] Pierson. Fish is an engineering graduate from Brown U. and Pierson an Arts graduate of Princeton. Both are good men. In that respect I am better off than the other Bn. COs.

Yesterday and also last week I gave talks in the Div. Officers' school to new officers. Tonight Fish + I go to the 3d Bn. 103d [Inf.] where Fish talks. I've a lot of getting acquainted to do in the 103d Inf. However the Reg[imental] C.O. and S-3 were with the 169 [Inf.] + 172 [Inf.] in New Ga. [New Georgia] so they are definitely pro-Bradt and I expect real cooperation there. Also it seems the 103d [Inf.] thinks Tommie DeWolfe is about tops, so with him + Mushik as Liaison officers I'll have a real pair there that I can rely on.

> Wilber knew well the officers formerly with the 169th and 172nd Infantry Regiments because his former unit, the 169th Field Artillery, supported those two infantry regiments in the Solomon actions. His new unit, the 152nd Field Artillery, normally supported the 103rd Infantry Regiment, (Chart 2) so "he had a lot of getting acquainted to do."

Next week we go into the mountains for a month of exercises. That means fewer letters, I'm afraid, so don't draw any heroic conclusions. It will likely be a lot colder there than here but it is a volcanic area and I may settle down in a nice warm geyser and refuse to come out to play with the General.

I've been interrupted repeatedly during this letter so it sounds pretty poor as I reread it. The main idea tho is that I love you more than I ever did before. You are my very special little mother and I'll be seeing you some day or year. — Your Husband (I'm proud to say), Wilber XXXØØ

> The divisional exercises were to be in the Rerewhakaaitu range outside Rotorua, some 120 miles south of Auckland (Map 14). Rotorua is famous for its hot springs. But southward higher elevations meant colder weather. The New Zealand winter was settling in.

x · o · ø · o · x

> Two weeks later, Wilber was in those mountains and wrote to me. Three days later, he wrote to Valerie.

## [ON FIRING RANGE] MAY 18, 1944

Dear Son — For the past two weeks I have been on the firing range with the Bn. It is a lovely area with a volcano on one side that erupted in 1880 and a lake in the impact area. We find gun positions in valleys behind high hills and shoot out into a large rough plain. All the battalions here have been doing the same thing and we shoot at the same targets, so it is interesting to watch and see who comes the closest to the targets and which Bn. is the fastest. In three exercises, the 152 [Wilber's unit] has not only been the most accurate but also the fastest. The 103d [FA] is taking second place. There is no question but that Lt. Col. Whitney had developed a fine outfit [the 152nd], and it is improving every day.

This area is supposed to be like Yellowstone Park but it is really a lot smaller and not so pretty. The nights are very cold and since we are not used to the cold, we really notice it.

May 22 — I've been interrupted again. We are really working pretty hard – up at 0530 and on the way to the range at 0630, with conferences, plans and orders each evening. It is good tho to be busy especially when things are working OK.

Yesterday we fired over the heads of our infantry, with them up close where the shells were falling. Before we started, one high-ranking officer wanted me to place fire closer than I planned. I objected and fired it my way. When one "short" landed only 200 yards in front of him, and fragments were flying all around he turned to me and said, "I guess that target is close enough all right." The new men were very impressed, but the veterans had seen it closer before in combat.… — Love, Wilber

x·o·ø·o·x

### MAY 21, 1944

Dear Valerie — This is a nice brisk morning and I am just thawing out from a very cold night. Frost was thick everywhere when I got up. We have a volcano for a neighbor here and this morning had quite a heavy earthquake. I looked out to see if the volcano was starting to smoke, but it wasn't. Too bad, for some nice warm lava would have melted the ice.

The 152 has been doing a lot of firing lately and doing a fine job. I'm very proud of them and hope in our next battle that we will do a good job.…

You must have had quite an adventure on your way back to school. There is a cute comic record about the Del. Lac. R.R. [Delaware & Lackawanna Railroad] It starts, "Where do you worka John? On the Delaware Lacawan. How do you worka John? I push. I push. I push." It goes on in a very silly way, and I can't remember anything except that I liked it. Some day you will get on the wrong train and end up in Colorado if you aren't careful.

I can buy Ginger Ale here so there is a bottle on the floor by me now. You can imagine what a treat it is for me. It is stronger than the kind we used to buy at home. Did you get the Jap cards? Good luck darling. I love you. Please write me what you are doing this summer. — Love and Hugs and Kisses from Your Daddy Wilber

Ginger ale was always a big favorite of Wilber's.

x·o·ø·o·x

Valerie still remembers that train adventure. She was returning from her visit with our mother in Washington, D.C., on Sunday April 23. The trip did not go well, as she wrote in a 2009 essay.

### Train Ride from Hell

*By Val Hymes (2009)*

*It was 1944. I had just turned 12 [on April 18]. I was supposed to return from Easter vacation to boarding school in New Jersey by train from Washington, D.C., accompanied by an upperclassman. My mother took me to the train to make sure I got on the right one and waited for this person to show up. When she did not, Mother gave me detailed instructions how to change stations and trains at Newark and I was sent off by myself for the first time.*

*All went well until I arrived in Newark, got off the train and found a cab to the other station that would put me on the Delaware Lackawanna line to Morristown, near the school. A station wagon would be waiting to drive me to Mendham as long as I got there within a certain time. I got out of the cab and left my purse behind, with my ticket, money and instructions.*

*I had enough cash in a pocket to purchase a child's ticket, but I was too old. The station master gave me a child's ticket anyway and directed me to the train. I got on, the train left, and the conductor came. I froze, waiting to be exposed as a criminal. He asked me for my ticket. I gave it to him. He looked at it and said, "You're going the wrong way." I burst into tears. The conductor and passengers consoled me and told me to get off and wait for the next train back to Morristown.*

*I finally got on the right train, but I feared I would arrive too late for the station wagon ride to the school. Another whole wave of anxiety washed over me. But when I arrived, finally, there it was, the welcoming station wagon to take me to the school that I would come to call home. I felt guilty for years about losing my mother's alligator purse.*

x · o · ø · o · x

For Wilber, Sunday provided a break in the intensive training and testing. In addition to the above letter to Valerie, he sent one off to Norma.

### MAY 21, 1944

Sweet Heart of Mine — It's so nice to have a talk with you again. The past week has been very strenuous for me but a triumph for the 152. Our firing has been far superior to our friendly competitors. The old outfit [169th FA] had a hard time holding on to 4th [actually third] place (4 competitors). DeBlois is learning of the problems of Bn. C.O.s. It isn't sufficient to know all about gunnery because the C.O. isn't able to be at FDC [fire direction center] to see it done right anyway. He will learn tho and get them back in shape in time. Our firing was as good as any I have ever seen and was right on the button. Most of it was beautiful. We fired a lot of air bursts so it was necessary to have distance, direction and height of burst all correct. That takes training and skill on the part of many men.

Yesterday and today I wrote each of the children. Don't ever think it is a burden to write them. I do as often as I can, and I'm just as proud of them as you are. Please don't worry about your difficulty with Valerie. She is sound and is just her mother's daughter who at her age probably didn't want to be babied either. These Sparlins are an independent lot, you know, and how I love them. In my opinion you are right not to force yourself and Valerie to go back to Bangor. If we can afford their schools I think they have worked out satisfactorily this year. At the risk of monotony tho, I insist we must save money now for I expect hard days afterward and things at the U. of Me. are such now that [Dean] Cloke has twice offered to take temporary work elsewhere to ease their [financial] problems. I may not have employment for a time.…

Here is an arm around you. — Wilber XXXOOO

[Note in margin:] Probably no more letters for about ten days so don't worry. Next Sun. I'll be firing day + night. BBrrrr!

> Norma was no doubt expressing to Wilber her dilemma about what to do come June, though of course without revealing Gale's existence. He in turn recognized that he had to step back in the face of those "independent" Sparlins. At the same time, he was planning ahead to postwar times with some concern that there might not be a job for him at the University of Maine.
>
> The final days of the 43rd Division's month in the mountains would terminate with intensive graded artillery tests.

x · o · ø · o · x

> On the next Sunday, Wilber wrote again to Norma even though the firing continued. He also found time to relax and establish rapport with some of the officers of his new unit.

**MAY 28, '44 [SUNDAY]**
Darling Wife — How is my Sweet Little Cripple today? I hope the lame knee isn't making too much trouble. In fact I rather feel that it isn't going to be too bad. In the latter days of New Ga., I had so much trouble with rheumatism that I could hardly get up after sitting awhile. I loaded myself up with salt and water and was rid of it before Baanga started so it wasn't rheumatism at all. Maybe we will find a good solution for you too. If not, I'll like having my wife hanging a little closer to my arm.…

I'm sitting in my hut and have an oil stove on one side and a glass of beer on the other. A very nice situation further improved by the fact that it is Sunday and I'm wearing my slippers and a clean wool uniform. Last evening, six of us (Maj. Fish, Capts. Mushik, Ackerson, Green, + Lt. Landers) went to a hotel for dinner and to a [movie] show later. I didn't realize it at the time but it developed later that the previous Bn. C.O. had never done such a thing. I'm afraid I don't realize the aloofness and austerity that the rank of Lt. Col signifies. However I think in combat other things such as personal relationships will mean more.

Dear One, … I must stop now for we go in the field in an hour. We are still shooting bull's eyes. Love, I love my beautiful wife. My lips are in your hair. — Wilber

x · o · ø · o · x

### MAY 31, 1944

Dear Father — I've just finished a rather strenuous month in the mountains of [Rerewhakaaitu]. We are not in combat but have been training our replacements, working with our infantry, and doing the tests required of all artillery units in the States before they sail. It has been a very gratifying month. On our tests, the scores for the four Bn.s involved were:

| [Bn.] | Test 1 | Test 2 | Test 3 | Av. |
| --- | --- | --- | --- | --- |
| Bradt's Bn. [152] | Sat | 95.5% | 100% | 97.5 |
| McCormick's [103] | Sat | 70% | 94.5% | 86.7% |
| DeBlois' Bn. [169] | Sat | 57% | 72.5% | 64.7% |
| Nichols' Bn. [192] | Sat | 52% | 54.7% | 53.4% |

You will note the mathematics of the scoring board is a little weak, so it may all be a mistake. The values, of course are only relative and do not compare with units taking the test in the States because fewer points were graded here. Anyway the 152 was away out front and I hope it means they get the hot point in the next push. I've asked for it, but of course it is a matter affected by the mission of my Infantry, the 103d [Inf. Rgt.]....

As you see by the news, Adm. Halsey has moved to a new assignment because the So. Pac. [phase] is completed. I regret our no longer being under him and will always be proud to have served under him....

> The 43rd Division was now, or soon would be, under General MacArthur's *Southwest* Pacific Area command (as distinct from Halsey's former South Pacific Area command). Wilber was not shy about getting his unit

CHAPTER 18   *I'm taking over another battalion*

into the hottest combat, and I doubt there was a rush for the "hot point" by the other battalion commanders.

A few minutes ago my orderly brought in a half a pheasant he has wrangled from some local family. You can imagine how quickly I interrupted this letter. Such things don't happen very often.... It's 11:30 P.M. so good night. — I love you. Wilber

In 1945, Wilber told us that General Barker had assembled the divisional artillery officers and angrily criticized them for their poor performance on the tests described in this letter. It went on for two full hours, the first being all about "what the h— have you been doing during your training?" and the second about "the expected dismal performance of your battalions in the next combat." When it was all over and everyone was leaving exhausted, one of the 152nd officers said to an officer from one of the lower-ranked units, "That sure was a lot of hell to take for only 2 1/2 percent!"

The 43rd Division was entering its last days in New Zealand. Final preparations for combat, and the enjoyment of western life and the New Zealand people, were the order of the day.

---

On April 22, MacArthur's forces had advanced westward 580 miles by sea to the central New Guinea north coast in landings at Aitape (Map 1) and, 120 miles farther west, at Hollandia, thus bypassing the Japanese 18th Army. The goal was to capture and improve Japanese airfields for Allied use. The landings were a total surprise to the Japanese, so opposition was minimal. However, since the landings isolated the 18th Army from its sources of supply, its survival depended on the elimination of the new Allied positions. The 18th Army began a westward land-based movement toward Aitape; a major battle was anticipated.

On May 18, MacArthur's troops moved 100 miles farther west in New Guinea to the Wadke Islands. By this time mopping-up actions at Hollandia and Aitape were well in hand and airfields at each site were operational. The Japanese 18th Army to the east of Aitape remained a threat. Landings at Biak Island, another 200 miles westward, took place on May 27. Biak is at the base of the Vogelkop Peninsula (the head of the New Guinea "bird"; Map 1). MacArthur had promised the Filipinos that he would return, and he was now poised to do so.

# 19

## *"I've asked for the point of honor"*
### New Zealand
### June–July, 1944

The battalion was back "home" in Matakana, north of Auckland. It was mid-winter, and the men were given some days off to compensate for their extra work in the recent exercises. This gave Wilber time to write Valerie and Norma.

**JUNE 1, '44**
Dear Daughter — I've just been looking at your picture and have decided I have a very pretty girl. Thank you for having it taken and for sending it to me. I've been keeping it in my Prayer Book; so last night when I was reading the prayer for "the absent," there you were all ready to peep out at me the minute I opened the book.

We are back from our training in the mountains and are giving the men three days rest because of the weekends they worked. One night I slept out on the ground, [and] an inch of ice froze in my canteen, and my roll was coated with ice where my breath had congealed. It was pretty country with lakes, mountains, evergreen forests, and in some areas hot springs and geysers. One volcano erupted in 1880 and has a big hole in the top. It really wasn't so cold as it would be in Maine in the fall but I notice it more. Today it is blowing a lot and has practically stopped raining....

The other day a few of my officers and I went to a small hotel for dinner. Our dinner was chicken soup, fish, curried sausage & rice with chutney, roast beef (rare), leeks, roast potatoes, turnips, passion fruit, banana trifle and tea & cheese. Then we went into the lounge by the fireplace and had coffee. It was nice to have silverware and napkins. They cover their sugar bowls and cream pitchers with little crocheted pieces with heavy beads around the edge. I believe they are called "cozeys." [cozies].

I poured the tea and there is a right and wrong way to do that. The milk must be poured in the cups first, then some tea and afterward the hot water. I don't believe it matters when the sugar is added. With the tea one eats small sandwiches, biscuits & butter or cookies. It's a very nice idea. Maybe I should start the habit of getting home for tea at four with my family. I hope I can.

Goodbye now. I love you Sweet Heart. Keep my home happy this summer, I'll be along some of these months. — Your Father, Wilber

x · o · ø · o · x

### JUNE 1, '44

Hello Wife of Mine — What are those pretty legs of yours doing right now? It is going to be really a thrill when I see them again. Kisses to you.... We have just returned from our field exercises and tests.... However, my luck was with me for the Bn. really went to town.... We are trying to act modest but it is hard.

Barker called me in and complimented the Bn. very highly, excusing himself by saying "He had to go by the figures." I assured him we weren't 97% perfect but that I would rate the Bn. at about 85%. That cheered him immensely and he admitted I probably knew weak spots they did not know of. I reassured him that such was the case, but that I proposed to take care of matters. Before we changed the subject, he felt better, having been convinced I wasn't going to retire from active training.

> Wilber's immediate superior, General Barker, had a difficult time passing out a compliment. For him, the level of training, no matter how high, was never adequate. Wilber admired him but generally stayed out of his way. Wilber could not better characterize Barker than he did with, "I assured him we weren't 97% perfect."

I told him I did not desire rotation but that I would probably want a leave in lieu thereof. He said that was his decision for himself too. We agreed we preferred to fight it out in this theatre. He said he would like me to stay there with him if things worked out that way. All in all it cleared the air pretty well and he knows where I stand regarding the rotation, and I have increased my chances for a leave home sometime after October. In the meantime maybe the 152 can get in a few more rounds with the Japs. I've asked for the point of honor in the next action so we may get a chance. This Bn. did a lot of sitting around in N. Ga. while the 169 had business.

> Presumably, by the "point of honor," Wilber meant the position most critical to the success of the battle. After taking leave in the States, one could either return to one's former position with the 43rd Division or could report to a unit in training in the States followed by overseas duty with it

("rotation"). Rotation could result in a higher position and promotion for an officer with combat experience, but it did not interest Wilber.

June 2 — This is Fr. [Friday] P.M. and nearly everyone has left for town. Only the "duty officers" for each battery and one for the Bn. will be staying – except for me. Maj. Pierson and Maj. Fish still worry about my not going social each weekend. They have observed that I have a good time with people so have decided I just need encouragement. For example, that naval officer whom I met in New Caledonia who is a friend of Hauck's [president of University of Maine] is here now. Pierson met him and is very anxious that I resume the beautiful (?) friendship by spending a weekend at his [naval officer's] headquarters. I decline and Pierson says he is sure I would have a good time. I agree and he gets encouraged until I comment that I'm not going. I consistently agree that all their proposals for moving into the private home of "lovely people," or having a date with a "wonderful girl," or spending a weekend at the races, or with the navy would be lots of fun; then [I] point out that I would prefer a quiet week-end minding my own business. It is a shame to worry them for they mean well. You know the type of people who always rush around and never have a quiet evening at home.

Wilber's homebody inclinations contrasted markedly to those of most soldiers with free time in a strange country. He went on to paint a cozy picture of his surroundings.

… I'm sitting in my slippers, pajamas, robe by my oil heater writing, and my little radio is giving me a piano recital of some piece you play, I don't know what it is but it sounds like Beethoven … Will you have your piano this summer? I'm afraid the War is taking too many things away from you. Be careful to hold close to the most precious ones.… Good night Lovely Wife. — Wilber XXXØØ

x · o · ø · o · x

This day, Allied forces landed en masse on the Normandy coast of France. They had finally taken the war into the heartland of Europe. The forces were led by the Supreme Commander, the four-star American General Dwight D. (Ike) Eisenhower.

**JUNE 6, 1944 (INVASION DAY!)**
Hello Babe — How are those corners [of your mouth] today? Turned up I hope. So the invasion [of France] is on! In a few weeks we will know what is ahead – an early victory or a long war. I've every confidence in "Ike." Did I ever tell you that Choate + I decided back in the days after the La. [Louisiana] Maneuvers [in

August/September 1941] that to "go places" one should be on Eisenhower's staff. I considered trying for it but decided I wouldn't have enough background to do the job he deserved from his staff. Think of the load he is carrying now and the people who awaited his coming so long and so horribly. Because of that I would like to be with one of his battalions. However this [Pacific theater] is still my choice. So far Jap killing hasn't injured any bystanders and I'm thankful for that simplifying aspect.

Invasion Day! I've hoped so long for it. Darling it's another step toward the end. Thank God for an Administration that gave our men training and equipment before asking them to cross the [English] Channel. Many will die but at least they had a chance and that is worth much.

> Wilber was definitely in accord with the early interventionist policies of President Roosevelt, but he never voted for him.

Just now I've joined the British Empire in its moment of silent prayer while Big Ben [the great bell in the tower of Westminster Palace in London] rings thru my radio. I do pray things go well in Europe.…

Speaking of the Pontoon Bridge in the "Canal" [Guadalcanal], did I tell you of the Negro driver of the [large] Diamond T Truck? When he came to this narrow track laid across those not too steady boats [the pontoon bridge], he stopped his truck and: [M.P. is Military Policeman directing traffic]

M.P.: – "Come On! What are you waiting for?" Sam – "Boss, I kain't drive acrost that there." M.P. – "The Hell with that stuff! Lets go." Sam – "No Suh, I kain't do it. I just kain't." M.P. – "Say, what's the matter with you anyway?" Sam – "I just kain't drive this here big truck acrost that little bridge." M.P. (Light Dawning?) – "Aren't you a Diamond T driver?" Sam – "Yessuh I'se a Diamond T driver all right but…" M.P. – "Well 'but' what? Get going before I take you out of that cab and take you apart." Sam (with faint hope) – "But Boss, I just been a Diamond T driver since brekfus." M.P. – "The Hell you say! Get over, You'd probably wreck the bridge anyway." Sam – "Yessuh! (Happily) YESSUH!"

I was so disgusted by the traffic jam that it wasn't funny until after I had been at sea a day or so; then I really laughed. On the same day Keegan was riding with a negro driver and reported later this:

Silence driving along dusty road for several miles. George, "Cap'n Suh, has you all been over heah very long?" Keegan, "About a year and a half." Silence for two miles. Geo., "Pears lak a mighty long time to be from home." Keegan, "Sure does." Very heavy silence, dust for three miles. Geo. (Cautiously), "We'uns has been here six days." Keegan (trying to appear interested), "Is that so?" Extremely thoughtful silence, heat, dust and inward turmoil for about five miles then Geo., "Cap'n, that pears lak a mighty long time to me." Keegan (Callously) "You'll get used to it, Soldier." Geo. (Sadly), "Yessuh." Silence resumed to end of trip. — XXXØØ I love you Sweet, Wilber.

> In Wilber's telling, one can well imagine the traffic jam, the dusty road, and the emotions of the participants. These stories, with their black dialect and implied slow-wittedness, displayed the racist stereotyping of blacks that was so prevalent in those days. Wilber, of another generation, was completely oblivious to this, and so was I when I first read the stories in his letters in 1944.

x·o·ø·o·x

**JUNE 9, 1944**
Dear Little Wife of Mine — It's another rainy night (6:30 P.M.) and I'm sitting in my hut with a cozy oil stove beside me. On the stove is heating my bath water. On the walls are my maps that you sent me showing the dates of our advances in the different theatres. In one corner is my table, a phone, and along one side my cot + bedroll. Opposite the door is a cupboard that I use for a wardrobe [and] a box of equipment. In another corner are six bottles of beer, one of "GA" [ginger ale] (the other eleven are empty) and a bottle of sherry. Across from my bunk is my trunk and two chairs. In the last corner is my helmet + pistol and that is about the story of my environment.

Monday I drove down to see Col. Files and talked over current business with him. I had worked out a new technique on "sound sensing" of artillery in the jungle that was independent of the volume of sound of the bursting shell. When the strength of the sound is used, it often misleads the observer. For example if the shell falls in a ravine or behind a hill it sounds farther away than if it falls on a slope facing the observer. In Munda it happened once that Mushik thought it was 800 yards in front of him and decreased the range 200 yards, which caused the next shell to land almost in his face. To say he was surprised is too mild. He was discombooberated. Lt. Col. ____ whom I know did the same thing except the shell landed 100 yards behind him.…

> Wilber did not care to divulge the name of the officer who made such a grievous mistake.
>
> Wilber's "new technique" may have been a refinement of the method described in his letter of July 31, 1943: one measured the time interval from the shell passing overhead to the sound of the explosion.

Last night I was invited over to Mr. + Mrs. [Olive] Croker's house for tea. Three other officers went with me. It is the third time I've been there. They have some of our men over nearly every night and officers about once a week. The Crokers are dairy farmers and are very nice, hospitable people. If we ever come here together I will want you to meet them; Mrs. C. serves a mean table. It is a meal such as one seldom sees. I never eat breakfast after I've been there and should fast for a whole day afterward. You can tell your flyer's wife that I've been most royally treated by her countrymen. I hope the Americans are as nice to their ally's soldiers + sailors....

> I visited Matakana in 1984. Mrs. Croker had died several years before and Mr. Croker long before, but I did visit with others who remembered the Americans and those days.

Don't worry about my being fit for combat. I've no intention of hazarding my men by going in if I'm not up to it. I feel fine, am on a program now of eating less than I want. I've two field jackets, size 40 and 46 and the size 40 is getting snug. I wore a 46 in Shelby and am trying to stay near the 40 size....

I'm glad you are getting our [Bangor] house in shape again. It probably needs it badly. Your idea of being with the children pleases me too. I wish I could be with you too. The only thing that worries me is infantile paralysis [the name given to polio in the 1940s] from swimming in the pools in a hot part of the country. I know you will watch that tho.

> It appeared that Norma had decided to return to Bangor with Valerie and me; baby Gale would remain in Washington with Monte and his mother. Being separated from her baby would certainly become a severe test of her ability to conform to the straight and narrow life demanded by the times.

This is Friday eve. and I'm thinking of going to town tomorrow to a show. We have been authorized three days leave, which I haven't taken but perhaps I do need to get out of this hut. Hotel rooms here are not heated so our usual method doesn't appeal. Besides this is the month I didn't get paid [because of an overpayment in 1943] and my cash on hand is low. However I may stay overnight + go to church.

Good night Beloved. I'm so happy about my family that will soon be together. Be sure you have a room where you can entertain gentlemen next winter. I might be along. — Love + my arms about you Wilber.

x·o·ø·o·x

CHAPTER 19   *I've asked for the point of honor*

**JUNE 12, 1944**
Sweet Wife — It's another gray day and I'm in love with you. Yesterday was bright and I was in love with you then too. It must be a chronic case or at least weather proof. I have gone into town [probably Warkworth] for the weekend and taken a room at the local hotel. By tomorrow I'll be ready for the trip back to camp and Army food. Besides they are out of toilet paper at the hotel. "Nize Plase!" [Nice Place!]

However they have a nice fireplace in the lounge, which I do enjoy. I've read my copy of the "Rubyaat" [Rubaiyat] and am now reading "The Road Back to Paris." This A.M. I expect to take a walk and do a little window shopping wishing you were along. Saturday I went to a movie and saw "Mokie" and shed tears copiously. Mokie was a little boy with a little boy's troubles.… — XXXØØ Wilber

x · o · ø · o · x

The closing exercises of the year at St. Bernard's School were held on June 14 at 8 p.m. I graduated from eighth grade after a spring term interlaced with print shop work and scouting. Norma surely was at the graduation. Most probably, we went directly from there to our home in Bangor, Maine, by train as we had no car.

x · o · ø · o · x

The 152nd Field Artillery Battalion at Matakana was well north of Auckland Harbour, and division artillery headquarters was well south of it. (The Auckland Harbour Bridge would not be built until 1959.) It was a long (60 miles) interesting drive interrupted by a ferry ride.

**JUNE 15, 1944**
Dear Wife — Today Pierson, Fish + I went to Div. Arty to a meeting. It is an all day job since the trip takes three hours each way and the general usually takes up another two. It was good to see DeBlois + Goff + Rainey and all the others again. This was one of those harangues such as the Sales Mgr feels called on to produce every so often. Very interesting but most of the language won't help me much in civilian life. I told Barker afterward that I had notes on his talk in my files; that I took them down after the La. [Louisiana] Maneuvers [in 1941]. Same stuff! Same objective! He laughed + said he should have remembered and used them and saved himself some work.

Our route to Div. Arty. is very pretty. The hills incline toward mountains, and the road winds about between them occasionally courageously climbing well up on one then losing heart and slipping back into the valley. At other places it will creep along cliffs over the sea then run down to a beach just before attempting another mountain. Occasionally it will stumble across some pretty little British town or be monopolized by a herd of sheep or cattle or scores of cycling school children, finally ending at the ticket office of an ocean ferry all out of breath. You would love it and I would too if you were along.

Nana I hope your bruises are all gone and that you have a nice place to live. Please have a "Round + Round" for me so I'll know where to send my spirit when it's lonely. I think of you so much these days.... Do you realize that it was almost exactly 17 years ago that I met you. They have been wonderful years for me Lover; each one of them even the last two. This should be our locust anniversary. Would you be interested in signing a contract for another 17 years at twice the loving? That is an offer. — I love you. XXXØØØ Wilber

> The next day, June 16, 1944, the army took official photographs of groups of officers, prior to the division's move on to combat. Wilber was in

*Staff of the 152nd Field Artillery Battalion on June 16, 1944, three weeks before departing New Zealand for the next phase of combat. From left, seated: Capt. Frank Burns, ME; Maj. Waldo Fish, RI; Lt. Col. Wilber Bradt, ME; Maj. Sam Pierson, CT; Capt. Thomas DeWolfe, ME. From left, standing: Capt. Donald Mushik, ND; Lt. Rhiner Deglon, WA; Capt. Benjamin Green, MI; Capt. Tilden Mason, RI.* [PHOTO: U.S. ARMY, PROVIDED BY WALDO FISH]

one of them with the eight officers of his staff. These were the men about whom Wilber would be writing for the next year. The photo may have been taken the day of the big inspection mentioned in the next letter.

x·o·ø·o·x

**JUNE 17, [1944]**
Hello Little Wife — Today was a red-letter day with three letters from my Girl. It is so wonderful to get letters from you. They always bring me back home again. I'm more in love with you now than ever before.

This weekend I'm staying in camp doing some studying and planning. Our inspection was quite a complete affair with division officers from Arty, ordnance, survey, signal, motor vehicle and supply branches – 12 in all. Altho I haven't received the written reports yet, they all left amid a barrage of favorable comments. The General (B.) [Barker] was up [here] and spoke very favorably of what he saw and heard. His attitude toward me has changed a great deal in the post Munda period. Yesterday he talked over matters with me that I am sure he had never mentioned to anyone else. I think it, in part, is because of my declared intention of staying with this Div. until the war is over and part, of course, is the fact that the 152 [FA Bn.] is "hot."

This is the year for the 152. It was OK to say "Watch the 43d [Div.] in 43." When I came here I told Wing to watch the 152. They all are now, and I predict they will be busy watching the 152 thru 1944. The 169 had suffered with "Knight" [the former C.O.], and DeBlois + I put it back on its feet and it did a real job. This Bn. is good and I expect it to [be] the top Arty Bn. of the S.W. Pac by the end of the year. I hope I can keep up with them. You will be interested to know that Hussey's [Battery B's] kitchen was rated "Superior" last week by the Div. and that was the first one rated that high in the entire division for six months.…

> Captain Robert S. Hussey was commander of Battery B in Wilber's unit and also a prewar Bangor friend.

You asked about my salary for 1944 and its sub-divisions … my taxable monthly income is $463.00. If you use that figure, you will be very close to the accurate annual figure, which is furnished me by the finance office.…

> Wilber's taxable income amounted to $5,556 per year. He also received a nontaxable annual rental allowance of $1,260. Together these amounted to about $90,000 in today's dollars.

I've just given my Surgeon a little instruction on good table manners and common courtesy such as offering a lady the comfortable chair rather than grabbing it himself. The local women who serve tea to the men stay for the movie + have reserved seats except when the "Doc" gets there first. Bn. C.O.s have some very unusual things to do. He commented that his manners always suited him at home which I thought was a very revealing remark, but I confined my admonitions to the present situation – little matters such as eating the choice foods before the Majors get any or eating all the dessert when some officers have had none. What a life!

[Later:] Lamb Chops for lunch + the Doc very careful of his table manners! …

June 19 … Weren't you thrilled that we have landed troops in Saipan. I told you we were on the last half. It begins to look now as if it were the last third. About one more step and Japan [the homeland] will be in the war too. Then there was the news of our B-29s bombing her, which must have shaken Tojo a little and given him a nice fresh nightmare. It's also a fine feeling to know that we now have a lot of company in this theatre. It will move things faster. We felt a little lonesome when we first arrived and discovered there were only three other Army divisions here too.

The landings on Saipan in the Mariana Islands and the first B-29 raid on Japan (Kyushu) from China both occurred on June 15.

…I'm not using codes or hints but will keep you informed as soon as it is legal. Radio news is so up to date that letters can often tell of action and events as soon as one gets around to writing. I'm not taking any chances with the censor. They busted a Maj. Gen. in England for that.

Early in his overseas duty, Wilber had dropped hints regarding his locations, as did many. His attitude on this point had clearly changed with time.

… I can't tell you yet which Army we go to [will be assigned to] but it may be possible later after we get our name in the papers. I'm so glad you aren't having hay fever. Please take good care of my family. They are just about the best in the world. I need you, Mate o' Mine. Must Good night now. Here is my arm about you. — Love, XXXOOØ Wilber

x·o·ø·o·x

Wilber was back in the hospital and wrote to his father.

CHAPTER 19    *I've asked for the point of honor*

**JUNE 24, 1944**
Dear Father — This letter is a little early but I'm writing it now for two reasons – first the doctor has his clutches on me again and second my schedule looks a bit heavy for the next week or so. I'll tell you about it later. I'm in bed with a cold and persistent cough. A year and a half in the tropics apparently didn't prepare me very well for winter climates. I'll be glad to get back to the jungle for more than one reason. This cold isn't anything for you to be concerned about. I expect to be up again in a day or so. In fact it was almost cured once; then I ran into a strenuous week of almost no sleep and a lot of exposure, so the normal happened.…

I must stop now and do some sleeping for the Doc. I hope things go well with you and that you are well. — Love, Wilber

x·o·ø·o·x

Wilber now knew that we had returned to Bangor and wrote to Valerie about getting along with schoolmates. He related his own experiences coming home to the Indiana farm from college.

**JUNE 29, 1944**
Dear Valerie — Notice how dirty this page is. The other night I left my tent [actually a hut; see letters 4/28/44 and 5/28/44] for awhile and the oil stove smoked. When I came back there was soot all over everything. My blankets were black and some of my clothes, papers and other stuff. It took Victor Miller almost all day to clean things up and me some time to clean myself up. You should have seen my black face the next morning.…

Thank you too for the Father's Day cards. It was nice to be remembered then too.

I suppose you are glad to be back in Bangor. You must be careful not to seem to brag when you talk to your friends who have not been away. They might feel badly and wish you had stayed away. They may be a little hard to get acquainted with right away because they are used to getting along without you.

When I was a boy and away at college, it was always hard to make my friends near the farm accept me when I came back. They always watched to see if I had "gotten stuck-up." If I was very careful not to talk much about myself and to listen to them and talk about the things they were interested in, then they soon forgot that I had been away. After that we always had fun. Most people prefer to talk about themselves and anyone who listens well is usually considered pretty fine.

… It's still cold nasty weather here. I've had a cold for a few days but am up and around and feeling OK now. I love my favorite daughter and wish I were with her now. Someday before too long I'll drop in on you. In the meantime take good care of my family. Goodbye now Darling. — Your Father, Wilber XXXOOOO

Valerie and I got along easily with our Bangor friends. We had been absent more than three years and we had all grown a lot. Come September, I would be in ninth grade, one grade ahead of my former classmates due to my skipping seventh grade at St. Bernard's, and Valerie would be in seventh. I recall no resentment or awkwardness in these reconnections. In fact, my close friends that year were generally not old friends, but new acquaintances. At age 13, and after three years of boys-only schools, I was also taking note of my female schoolmates.

x·o·ø·o·x

The 43rd Division was about to be shipped to New Guinea. The move to the ship in Auckland was imminent, but Wilber did not mention it. Lacking any confidential information, the letter could be mailed immediately.

## [JULY] 3, 1944

Dear Wife and children — I'll have to make this letter short because I've quite a few things cooking just now.…

I'm enclosing two more citations, one for the 169 file and one for the 152 [FA Bn.]. Since I've come here, I've obtained 18 Bronze Stars for the 152 men for acts performed in New Ga. They didn't see as much action nor as hot action in the 152 as the 169 boys did.

There was less opportunity for them to win medals, but even so, many were deserving of these belatedly recommended bronze stars.

I see the boys on Saipan ran into something of the same type as we saw in New Georgia. Some of these islands have been taken so fast that it looked as if we [the 43rd Division] just didn't know how. The casualty list is comparable too. Maybe what we have already seen is as tough as what we will see. Anyway we'll see what we see, and I'll come back + tell you about it.

The Russians are surely going strong. "Bye 'n bye, no more Germans." That, with the success of the Normandy operation, speaks for a "Christmas in Berlin." Tell Valerie not to worry about the Japs "invading" us. Japan is worrying about us invading her. There are a lot of us here now… I'm glad you're home and together again. I love all of you + each of you. — XXXØØ Wilber

x·o·ø·o·x

Later that same day, Wilber began a vivid description of the hurried move of his battalion of 500 men to Auckland for the boarding of the transport ship, USAT Sea Devil. The battalion was 40 miles north of Auckland, the ship arrival and loading schedule was quite uncertain, and the supply of trucks was limited. Wilber vividly portrayed the stresses, strains, and hard work of such a move. These letters would not be mailed until the move was history. This would be Wilber's eighth voyage since leaving San Francisco. (Map 1)

## JULY 3, 1944 [MATAKANA, N.Z.]

[note on top:] To be mailed Aug. 17, 1944

Dear wife + children — This is the first of a series of letters that will not be mailed until our censor says we can say we have moved. Today I am in our camp at Matakana, N.Z. We have just received word we are to move and in a hurry. I've sent Maj. Fish and four staff officers to Auckland to take care of things at the port and on ship, also Burns to Div. Arty. as a liaison officer. We have loaded all our trucks with impedimenta and sent them down to the area assigned to us until the wharf is free. The batteries are cleaning up their so-called luxury furniture and extra junk ("Little things they have collected").

About 1100 [hours] Fish called and said everything was quiet, no ship had come in and that we could relax. At noon he called again and said Hussey's battery [Battery B] should get down (70 miles) as soon as possible and that he would have quarters for them. They were to be a loading detail to load the ship. They have gone just now amid much perspiration. No one behind a desk ever quite realizes what work is involved in a movement. All is quiet for the rest of the day. We clean up Hussey's area, collect his unused rations and wait. I think of you in my spare time + decide I love you, — Wilber.

> The 70-mile distance given by Wilber suggests the heavily loaded trucks took the long route westward through Helensville to avoid the ferries; neither the Harbour Bridge nor the Upper Harbor Bridge had been built.

x · o · ø · o · x

## JULY 4, 1944

Dearest ones — This is a fair morning with hope of sunshine. We set up fifty pyramidal tents that came in wet, hoping they will dry. If they go in a [ship's] hold wet they will rot. We also collect our surplus oil and gasoline (for ranges) and load them to be hauled back to the division supply. One howitzer is found [to be] out of order since yesterday. We rush it off to ordnance for a check-up and repair. One doesn't go toward the combat zone with howitzers in questionable condition.

At 1000 [hours] Fish and Burns call with the report that no loading has started, with a lot of details to be checked, and say Div. Arty. is sending us more trucks from Nichols's and McCormick's Bns. We send out all our trucks again loaded on the general idea that what is gone won't have to be moved later.

At 1130 Fish calls again and says to rush McIntire's battery [Battery C] down. Loading is under way and division is in a mood to rush. He needs more men. Our borrowed trucks arrive just in time to be loaded + started back with orders to check with Fish before returning. We relax a little for we've no trucks so can't do anything even if we do receive orders.

> The letter continued on July 5, with the remaining events of July 4 [152nd FA Journal].

July 5 — At 1300 Fish calls again + says everything is under control, our trucks are started back and it looks like we might be here a week yet. I tell him to release half the borrowed trucks (McCormick's) and to send the others up to me to stand by overnight.

At 1500 he calls back and says the ship has suddenly decided to load vehicles that night, that he needs more stuff. I decided to move the rest of the Bn. down starting at 2000 [8 P.M.] and tell him to send me every truck he can spare from the loading. He sounds a bit worried but says he will go to work on a place for the men to stay until they go on ship. I call Maj. Pierson and the remaining three battery commanders and say "get ready for charge Ten" [meaning unknown], then tell them to be ready to clear out in five hours or less if possible. This time they can't leave anything to someone else because everyone is going except Maj. Pierson and six men who will get an official clearance from the N.Z. Army for the area and camp equipment [being in good condition]. That can't be done until the next morning. I leave with Mushik, DeWolfe, and Meier at 1700 and join the "Fish" C.P. [Command Post] in Auckland. As I pull out, trucks are arriving. The drivers are tired already too. They always take a beating on these moves. Between 1500 and 1700 there have been three changes of decision as to where the Bn. will go.

It's cold on the way down and I notice it more than usual because we had ice cream for supper. Since it was my last ice cream for I didn't know how long, I ate a lot, and so nearly froze. However Ruhlin had kept reserved for me for the past week a room [in] an officer's rest camp and I find good accommodations.

Fish has all hands working and word comes from Pierson that the Bn. is on the road [at 2000 on the 4th; 152nd FA Bn. Journal]. I go to bed. And dream of my dear ones, of trucks, of our house, ships, changes in orders, [and] combat, and spend a rather active night so far as dreams go. I love you, My Wife and my son and my daughter. I hope you don't worry too much about this break in my mail. — XXXOOØ Wilber

x · o · ø · o · x

The balance of the battalion arrived in Auckland at 1:15 a.m. on July 5, according to the battalion journal. The battalion apparently rested easy on July 5, a Wednesday, after the strenuous move of the day before, as there are no further journal entries for July 5. Perhaps liberty was granted to some, but perhaps not, in order to ensure that everyone would be available to board the ship.

**JULY 6, 1944**
Dear Ones — Here is that man again. I get up late (0830) [July 6] and purposely sleep thru breakfast so I'll get plenty of rest. I think of how you would approve and thank my stars for two such field officers as Fish and Pierson. By 0900, I'm at the wharf and discover I'm the commander of all the troops on board. That is a very unpleasant little surprise but Fish has been on the job. I find he has tentatively appointed a ship's executive (Rainey) and a ship's adjutant (an infantry officer) and has arranged for a meeting at 1100.

I go on the ship [USAT Sea Devil] + contact the ATS officer on board. He is a captain and seems to have a personal feud with the skipper, which doesn't simplify my problems at all. At 1100 we assign the ship's details (totaling about 500 men) to the various units, make plans for embarking the men and getting them fed as soon as possible. The infantry to go aboard are those I fought with down the Munda Trail [the 169th Inf.] so I get plenty of cooperation. The other artillery is DeBlois's outfit [169th FA Bn.], which is also to the good.

The ship's "details" were groups of soldiers who had specific duties during the voyage, such as in the kitchens and mess halls as well as for guard and cleaning duties. Keeping order among several thousand men aboard a ship was not a trivial matter.

At 1150 [General] Barker shows up and takes me to lunch. I eat oysters on the half shell, fried oysters and steak. Barker underestimated me so I had to help him pay for the dinner. He was much embarrassed.

Oysters on the half-shell were a favorite of Wilber's. He evidently did not hold back on how many he ate; see the following letter.

By 1300 I was back at the ship to watch personnel go aboard. My Bn. is first. They go on quietly and rapidly. The billeting officer (Bremer) later told me they were the least trouble. About 1400 [General] Wing [C.O. of 43rd Division] came down to say good-bye. At 1500 we are still loading personnel and impedimenta. The mess officer at 1600 tells me he has just now received his rations for supper and that the galley detail from my Bn. was the hardest working crew he ever saw. At 1730 he started feeding the men on board but we are still loading personnel. That is finished at 1800. I place a guard around the ship.

Two come over the side of the ship in an effort to go AWOL. The guard catches one and picks the other up before he leaves the wharf. Four field officers [senior officers] from Div. Hq. want a pass to leave the ship for the evening. I ascertain that it won't sail until the next morning and give them passes, also one to Fish who has some loose ends to clear up.

> It turned out [letter 7/7/44] that Fish had a special friend to meet one last time.

Then Wing sends orders "No passes except for me and absolutely essential missions." One of the above staff officers hadn't yet left and is he sad! The next development is that Wing overlooked the fact that three other ships are moored to the same wharf. I find myself issuing passes to scores of people who come in [to the wharf] to load them and can't get out except on my signature. By 2300 my ship is thru loading and men are below decks. I post an officer guard and tell the M.P.s that Wing didn't mean it and to use their judgment from then on.

At 2330, I go to my stateroom. There is only one on this ship and I share it with the Div. chaplain Fr Connelly (Rom. C.). There I find no one [had] made up his bunk. My orderly has fixed mine. So down I go to the Troop Hq and get that arranged. By midnight I'm really in bed. It's a good bed and I really sleep and don't dream except about someone's flat feet – mine! However, I still love you and pray you are all well and happy. I decide I'll sleep late again and let Rainey work at Troop Hqs. without me until after a late breakfast. — Love, Wilber XXX OOØ

> The ship was finally loaded with its 2400 soldiers and ready to sail; Wilber could relax.

x · o · ø · o · x

> Wilber described the ship's departure and then attended to his social duties upon leaving hospitable New Zealand. He also tried to clear the air about his vacation "romance."

CHAPTER 19   *I've asked for the point of honor*

### [USAT SEA DEVIL] JULY 7, [1944]

Hello My Fine Feathered Friends — Ye olde man slept thru breakfast this morning on the theory that the six-dozen oysters he ate yesterday would sustain him for a little longer. It was a grand feeling too because I was quite tired. I didn't care if we had sailed or not and if the whole twenty four hundred [men on the ship] had deserted, I didn't intend to go after them anyway. It later developed that, on the contrary, we had gained a few recruits during the night; men who were AWOL but had no intention of missing the ship. Probably they just had wanted to miss the work of loading.

> Was six-dozen oysters an exaggeration? I think not; Wilber was a great fan of raw oysters. (One alleged "world record" was 46 dozen in ten minutes.) Even so, it should have been Wilber who was embarrassed, not his host, General Barker!

It is a cool cloudy morning and the ship is nosed away from the wharf about 1000 and out into the stream. We sat there a little while, then move out with a British ship, which we very promptly leave. The pilot is dropped at 1100 and I enter in my record book "Lv. Auckland on [USS Sea Devil] 1100 July 7, 1944 WB," so it's official. We are really off and on our way back to the combat area. The harbor is beautiful as we pull out. A. is really a lovely city. I'll show you some day.

> Norma never made it there, but I did.

Before we leave the N.Z. subject there are some people here to whom I wish you would write if you have time. First Mr. + Mrs. Sidney (or Sydney?) Smith, Matakana, N.Z. He is the local butcher. Matakana is just a cross roads town of a dozen homes. The people here are nearly all country people and I have never known people anywhere try as hard for so long (five months) to make us feel at home. The Smiths found I liked oysters and they repeatedly spent many cold wet hours gathering some for me. He frequently sent me steaks that would cost two dollars apiece in a U.S. Hotel and never took a penny for them. While I was sick, they were always trying to do something about it such as fresh eggs (very scarce) for my breakfast. I owe them more than I can ever pay. I gave Mrs. Smith a pin of novelty jewelry, a black boy dancer that Jo sent me for X-mas, and the olives you sent. They cannot get them here. If you see something nice please send it to them.

Another is Mrs. (and Mr.) S(?) A(?)Croker. The name is in the cookbook that you will receive. The emphasis on the Mrs. is because Mr. never says a word. He just sits and smiles and answers all questions by one word. Mrs. C. has more or less organized all the entertainment (local) for my men. For example, she specialized in fine and fancy cooking. A normal week for her, I found was to run the dance for our enlisted men each Monday. This included getting girls of good character

*Minnie Smith (far left), Minnie's mother (center front) and Sidney (right), about 1942. (The woman in back and her child are the Smiths' friends.) Sidney was the local butcher in Matakana. Wilber wrote of them: "I owe them more than I can ever pay."* [PHOTO: SIDNEY SMITH]

to come, chaperoning the dance and getting them home. On three or four other nights ea. week, she had as guests in her home – from four to eight of our men; on another night a group of our officers. These evenings consisted of tea (our supper) which is a good substantial meal of soup, salad, vegetables, meat and dessert and, about three hours later, supper (!!!) which is your departure snack. It consists of tea, about eight kinds of cakes, cookies, sandwiches, patties, scones, puddings and "trifle." One eats some of each and is assisted to the car. Usually one such event is all the human system can stand in a week.

The thing that impressed me was the work involved in preparing such a meal and I knew she milks 15 cows daily. I don't know how many Sam milks because he

*Sam and Olive Croker about 1950. Sam "never says a word," wrote Wilber, and Olive "more or less organized all the entertainment (local) for my men." They both had died before my 1984 visit.* [PHOTO: DAWN JONES PENNEY]

doesn't say. I don't know what type of present she would appreciate, but I was present when she received some perfume from a boy from the States. She was pleased. Both ladies are in the graying stage but both dress neatly. If you write to Mrs. C. and I hope you do, please also mention the Jones girls. They are numerous and are practically her Lieutenants. I've met them repeatedly but never got their first names straight. Personally I suspect they may have had marital hopes but none of the boys seemed to make good.

Mrs. C's address is also Matakana, N.Z. I have noticed repeatedly that a letter from one's family in the States means more to these New Zealanders than anything else. They feel that we just came in time in 1942 and want to show that they really appreciate it. Also N.Z. boys in the States write home of the fine way Americans treat them and they (here) try to repay that courtesy. It has resulted in a wonderful feeling in many cases. Numerous marriages have occurred and of course there

*The Jones Girls, Matakana, New Zealand, ca. 1944. From left, Dawn, a friend, Gwen, Meryl, Yvonne, and Ida in front. They energetically helped with dinners and dances for the soldiers of the 152nd Field Artillery Battalion.* [PHOTO: DAWN JONES PENNEY]

are always cases where Americans have imposed on this feeling and unfortunate incidents have happened.

> Wilber was full of gratitude for the kindnesses of these people and wanted Norma to help him return his thanks. He was also creating a record of names and addresses that would survive him should the worst occur. I looked up some of these people when I was in New Zealand in 1984.

There is only one other letter and it isn't so important. That would be to Miss Olive Madsen, Wairasa [Wairarapa], N.Z. That isn't the complete address but I think it is OK. If I find the rest after we reach my trunk I'll correct this. She + her mother I've mentioned before as part of my vacation contacts. [That letter is missing from the collection.] I met them on the boat going to Christchurch, N.Z. from Wellington and liked them. I found she was taking her mother on a vacation, the main purpose of which seemed to be to meet some N.Z. aviator. On one of his duty nights, I took her to a movie and then on my return to Wellington ten days later, we (Davis + I) were invited out to their farm. We couldn't go, so the daughter came into town and spent the day with us. In fact she nearly walked me to death. That was that and OK, but I never saw the farm. One reason was that both she +

her mother have horses and just love to ride. You can imagine how I reacted to that. You're right.

> Wilber never rode horses to my knowledge, but he may have as a boy. The few stories I know placed him behind the horse in a wagon or plow. This letter suggested he was quite averse to riding possibly because he had had more than enough of it as a boy.
>
> The embarrassed prelude to the above, "it isn't so important," might have sent a loud signal to Norma. Apparently she had heard of Miss Madsen in a previous letter, but here Wilber revealed more of their encounters. Wilber would have done well to drop the subject there, but in fact he went on with more (incriminating?) details!

As I said above, this letter isn't urgent. I think I paid for dinners etc. to settle that aspect of things. In fact I sent her a corsage [!] and learned later she ran a florist shop. It should be a lesson to me. She wrote a few times and I finally wrote that I would only have time to write you and suggested she end the correspondence. She wrote one more letter, which I haven't and won't answer in which she said "of course she would never want to do anything which would hurt my family." Since she rather accurately read my mind, I was a bit ashamed and felt a bit embarrassed. If you write and say you appreciate her kindness and her mother's kindness to me, they will know I hadn't felt she had any designs on me. I could write that, but I don't want to get involved again in a morale building correspondence. I really don't have time to answer even tho I do appreciate the intent (e.g. the M. Hirsh case).

> A corsage. How romantic! Was this a complete account of his meetings with Olive and his feelings about the meetings and correspondence, or was there more to it? The boyish awkwardness of this "confession" revealed the feelings he had for her. Their connection was surely brief; she lived 400 miles south of his home base. Whatever the circumstances of their meetings, it is evident that Wilber was attempting to clear the air and his conscience before re-entering combat. I did meet Miss Madsen on my 1984 visit to New Zealand, and she completed the story for me as recounted in the following Interlude.

I guess that completes the account of my international entanglements. Some time if we can get to N.Z. together, I'll want you to meet all these people. They have each helped me personally and/or my boys as much as they could in the nicest way they knew. There is another address, Mrs. Joy Simmonds, Takapuna, N.Z. She is very much in love with one of my officers [Fish] and he with her. It may result in a wedding some day. I made it possible [for] them to have several extra hours

*Olive Madsen wearing the corsage given her by Wilber in Christchurch, New Zealand, March 1944. She is pictured here at the modest Ambassador Hotel where she and her mother stayed. She gave me this photo on my 1984 visit.* [PHOTO: OLIVE MADSEN]

together during our last mad rush of embarkation and she sent me a present as appreciation....

To finish my July 7th record, the rest of the day was spent in issuing plans + orders for the troops, feeding, recreation, sanitation, discipline, security for a trip thru the [censored; Coral Sea]. I wonder if we'll pass over the Lexington [U.S. carrier sunk in the battle of the Coral Sea in 1942]. We had our first boat drill and sub drill. We had conferences and decisions. The Skipper is reported not to like

CHAPTER 19   *I've asked for the point of honor*

soldiers. He and the Army Transport Officer are feuding; the ATS officer hopes I'll "make this voyage a lesson to the Skipper." I opine that a ten-day voyage isn't long enough for me to solve his problems, and besides all I want from the Skipper is a landfall in the right place. I may meet problems, but I'll not hunt for them.

I love you all three. These letters are for all of you and are just the story of how I left the South Pacific. — Goodnight XXXOOØ, Wilber

x · o · ø · o · x

The 43rd Division was off on a new mission: landings at Aitape, New Guinea, on the north central coast, to the west of the Japanese 18th Army, to reinforce American units already there. The shipment of the 43rd Division to Aitape was hurried because of indications that the bypassed (and trapped) Japanese 18th Army was preparing attacks westward in an attempt to dislodge the Americans and capture American supplies and the American held airstrips.

---

While the 43rd Division was in New Zealand (February through June 1944), MacArthur moved altogether 900 miles westward in New Guinea to Biak Island and was now poised for an attack on the Philippines. But first, he would have to deal with the trapped Japanese 18th Army.

In the Central Pacific, the Allied advance on June 15 to the Mariana Islands, the next closest group to Japan, was made secure with the end of Japanese resistance on Saipan July 9 and the capture of Tinian and Guam Islands on August 1 and 11 respectively. The Japanese fiercely resisted the Saipan landings, but as their supplies ran out, large numbers of Japanese combatants died in hopeless banzai attacks or by suicide rather than facing capture. These advances bypassed the strong Japanese naval base at Truk in the Caroline Islands, provided a base from which B-29 bombers could reach Japan, and were a large step toward the northern Philippine Islands. Airfields at Biak could have supported the Mariana landings, but unfortunately they were not yet operational. Operations in the two theaters (New Guinea and Central Pacific) were coordinated because available air and naval support had to be shared.

The naval Battle of the Philippine Sea (June 19–20, 1944) took place while portions of the fleet were still supporting the Saipan landings. It featured Admiral Mitscher's naval Task Force 58 and intrepid feats by American submarines. Three Japanese carriers were sunk and three others damaged, as were a cruiser and a battleship. [Morison, Vol. VIII, pp. 288–301]. Other major elements of the Japanese fleet survived due to the conservative use of the stronger American fleet, which had to protect the Saipan landings. The battle effectively destroyed the Japanese naval air arm of 430 carrier planes; only 35 survived the two days of battle. On June 19 alone, 243 Japanese planes were shot down in the "Great Marianas Turkey Shoot" [ibid., p. 319]. The Japanese naval air arm would never recover. American air losses were minor in comparison and no American ships were lost.

On the India-Burma front, the Allies repelled a major Japanese offensive. After months of bitter fighting from March to June, the Japanese, without supplies and decimated by disease, retreated back to the Burmese plains. Fighting continued farther north and in China.

Throughout the spring, the Russians had been advancing westward in Europe. A renewed attack began on June 22. On July 3, in the north of the Russian front, Minsk fell, and on July 8, the nearby surrounded German Fourth Army surrendered. Sixty thousand German captives were marched through Moscow a week later. The Russians were outside Warsaw, Poland, by August 1, 1944.

In Italy, the Allies had broken through the Cassino defenses in May and entered Rome on June 4. The Germans retreated over the next two months, June and July, to the "Gothic Line" near Florence, which they would hold through most of August. In the meantime, of course, the Normandy landings in France had occurred on June 6. The battle to break out of Normandy continued until early August. On August 15, the Allies established another front with landings on the southern coast of France.

All in all, the Allies were on the move, but as the Axis forces were pushed closer to their homelands, their supply lines became shorter and fighting intensified. Exacting the greatest possible cost from the Allies with the greatest possible delay was the goal of both Germany and Japan. If the Allies became sufficiently dispirited, perhaps an armistice could be obtained that was more favorable than the outcome demanded by the Allies, which was unconditional surrender.

# PART V

# INTERLUDE 1984

NEW ZEALAND
OCTOBER 1984

★ ★

# 20

# *Waldo and Wilber*

## Rhode Island and New Zealand
## SEPTEMBER–OCTOBER, 1984

In October 1984, I was scheduled to join again my young colleague, Ronald Remillard, to conduct astronomical observations at the Siding Springs Observatory in Australia. I took that opportunity to visit New Zealand for the week prior to our work, as I had done in May 1983 with my visits to the Philippines and the Solomons. I had learned then how wonderfully rewarding such a visit could be, so I felt compelled to sample the life Wilber had found in New Zealand: the scenery, the towns, and the people.

Wilber's scientific habit of recording names, addresses, and dates in his letters allowed me to meet people he knew or members of their families. I could walk in his footsteps in the villages and towns where he had been, and I could satisfy my visceral yearning to get closer to my father through those connections. My queries and observations would also serve to fill in and enrich his story. And I wanted to learn more about his and his executive officer's romances! As I left for New Zealand, it was this latter topic that intrigued me the most, I confess.

### WALDO AND HIS FAMILY

Recall earlier in this account that Wilber allowed Waldo Fish, the executive officer of Wilber's unit, the 152nd Field Artillery Battalion, to leave the ship in Auckland the night before it sailed; Waldo had had "some loose ends to clear up." Wilber's subsequent letters [e.g., letter 11/19/44, Book 3] made clear that Waldo and a "Margaret Simpson" (not her real name), had developed a very close relationship in New Zealand. (In gratitude, Margaret later sent Wilber a beautiful set of napkin rings, each carved from a different New Zealand wood, a set we had in our home for many years.) Wilber admired Margaret and wrote Norma that Waldo was considering a divorce from his Rhode Island wife so he could marry Margaret. Wilber and Waldo worked together throughout subsequent combat in the New Guinea and Philippine campaigns, and Wilber came to have a very high regard for his executive officer. Waldo's competence had already been demonstrated by his organization of the unit's embarkation in Auckland.

I had met Waldo in 1981 during my early conversations with Wilber's Rhode Island associates and had established a rapport with him. Of course, I had not asked him about Margaret. But before leaving for New Zealand in 1984, I wanted to get his thoughts about Margaret—at the very least, to find the answer to the question Wilber had left hanging. Did Waldo finally marry Margaret? Since my 1981 meeting with him, Waldo had lost his (second) wife and had had one or more strokes. I had met his second wife but knew nothing about her background. On that September 1984 visit, I found him taking the sun in his driveway. His caretaker provided me with a chair, and it was there that we talked. He was 76; I was 53.

I shared with him some of the photos and documents I had found during my Wilber research. Then, with some trepidation, I told him that Wilber's letters had made it clear that he (Waldo) had been very much in love with a New Zealand woman and that marriage had been discussed. Without saying a word, he pulled an address book from an inner pocket and slowly opened it up to a page that had "Margaret Simpson" written in large script, with an address that dated back to 1944. I asked if he had married her. He replied that no, he had not. When I asked him why, he answered slowly that she had been in an automobile accident that had disfigured her for life.

Somewhat later, Waldo's ex-daughter-in-law arrived with her young boys, his grandsons, for a visit. She told me that Waldo had indeed written home from the Pacific that he wanted to marry a New Zealand woman, and that this led to his divorce from his first wife, a wonderful woman; this had sadly distanced him from his then-six-year-old son. That son later became the (then ex-) husband of my informant. I was able to tell her boys about some of their grandfather's exploits in the war and show them some photographs from that time. They were quite fascinated.

I began to imagine re-connecting two lonely elders if I could find Margaret in New Zealand. The daughter-in-law told me that Waldo had earlier suggested that she take him to visit New Zealand without indicating why. Later during my trip, I learned that Waldo had written friends (the Smiths)

CHAPTER 20   *Waldo and Wilber*

*Waldo Fish, the executive officer of the 152nd Field Artillery Battalion during the New Guinea and Luzon campaigns, at his Rhode Island home during my visit there in September 1984. He was a highly competent officer whom Wilber much admired. Waldo died in 1990. His son, Waldo III, died in 2008.* [PHOTO: HALE BRADT]

in New Zealand saying that he wanted to locate Margaret. I wondered if I could possibly do this for him.

My main objective from the start had been to learn more about Wilber's time in New Zealand by finding the people who had befriended him, and the Waldo story was only a sidelight. But it nearly overwhelmed the Wilber story! I had one short week in New Zealand and a lot to do. I made a couple of telephone calls before I left in an attempt to jumpstart some of my searches, but without much success. My plan was to drive to Matakana, just north of Auckland, where Wilber's unit had been stationed in 1944, and go from there. I flew from Boston to Auckland with a long nighttime stopover in Honolulu. My journal, with excisions and edits, continued my story.

### The Jones girls and Smiths, October 6–7, 1984
*Immediately upon arrival in Auckland (Map 14) about 11 a.m. on Oct. 6, after 32 hours of air travel, I drove to the Auckland suburb that had been the 1944 home of "Margaret Simpson" and asked around for an old timer who might know of her.*

*Dawn Jones Penney in Matakana, New Zealand, October 1984 with a granddaughter (left) and friend. She was one of the Jones girls who helped Mrs. Croker entertain the troops of the 152nd Field Artillery.* [PHOTO: HALE BRADT]

*I got no more than a false lead to a Simpson who was no relation to her. I then telephoned some other Simpsons in the area with no luck.*

*I then drove on up to Matakana (1.5 hours) where the 152nd FA Bn. was quartered for five months in 1944. Matakana had a main (essentially the only) street with about 20 houses and a butcher shop. Since my dad's letter mentioned Sidney Smith, the butcher who gave him free steaks and other foods, I immediately went to the house across the road from the butcher shop where the butcher's truck was parked (it was Saturday). It turned out to be a different butcher, but his wife, Dawn Jones Penney, was one of the Jones girls (there were six of them) mentioned in my Dad's letter as helping with all the dinners put on by Mrs. Croker for his men and officers.*

*I had a lovely chat with Dawn (she is 59 now – in 1984), was given 1940s photos of the Crokers (deceased), the Smiths, and the Jones girls. She took me to the farm (Whistler's farm on Port Wells Rd.) a few miles away where the camp had been, and I met the farmer, saw the cows being milked, and walked among the remains of the camp – a few concrete tent bases, etc. She also showed me the former Croker home where the sumptuous meals took place. My visit went on for one afternoon and the next morning. The intervening evening I stayed about five km away in Warkworth, which has three motels and a hotel. There I learned the advantage of early reserva-*

*Minnie and Sidney Smith at their home, 1984.* [PHOTO: HALE BRADT]

*tions and the cleanliness, low prices, and good food (breakfast) offered by the small motels ("Lodges") in New Zealand. (In America, "small" often means cheap in price and quality.) She told me where the Smiths live (Devonport). I called them and arranged to visit them that next afternoon.*

A battalion of 500 men suddenly arriving in the midst of this tiny town must have made quite an impression. I learned that this camp had been used by other troops at other times. Dawn told me about the dances and dinners, and her memories were in accord with the descriptions that Wilber had given. She did not remember my father specifically. The entire visit gave me a strong sense of Wilber's experiences and, in general, a sense of how small towns all over New Zealand had handled the influx of American soldiers. There must have been many of those overwhelming tea suppers and, in return, many shared American goods.

*The next afternoon (Oct. 7), I drove down (about 1.5 hours) to see Sidney and Minnie Smith and found both of them nimble and alert despite the fact that I had heard Sidney was very ill. They remembered my father well, the first people in the Pacific to remember him in all my travels in the Philippines, Solomons, and heretofore in New Zealand. They had an autograph book with his inscription:*

"To a good neighbor with a real wish for a reunion some day at 204 Broadway, Bangor, Maine. Wilber E. Bradt"

Reading this now (2014) brings tears to my eyes.

*Minnie still had the little "black-boy" pin Wilber had given her [letter 7/7/44]. They told me about entertaining the men in their home. Wilber may have eaten in their home about 12 times and they ate at the Camp about six times. "Wilber loved to come and sit in front of the big open fire. Some of the men smoked cigars and played blackjack." More than once, he arranged for the Smiths and others to get some scarce groceries or delicacies, e.g. sugar and sockeye salmon, to compensate for their expenses in feeding the men in their homes.*

On a subsequent visit to New Zealand with my wife a couple years later, we looked up Mrs. Smith and had a nice visit. Mr. Smith had died in the meantime.

### Margaret, October 8–9

*This day, I did a lot of digging in local town records trying to trace Margaret. I visited several town halls to search voting records and a library in Auckland attempting to learn Margaret's current name and address with no success. I learned of a former husband (deceased) and attempted to contact his second wife, but she was on vacation with her new husband according to her sister whom I did meet. The sister, understandably, did not know the whereabouts or current name of her former brother-in-law's former wife! She did share some of the Margaret's former husband's family history, which was quite dramatic; it involved serious legal difficulties and an aviator's death in the Battle of Britain. A search of school records also failed to help. I was learning a lot of intriguing personal history, but was not getting closer to locating Margaret. I was becoming obsessed and frustrated.*

### World's fastest tour of the South Island, October 9–10

*Disgusted with my growing obsession and already four out of the seven days in NZ expended, I drove to the airport, booked and boarded a flight with a ticket for Christchurch (to stay overnight) and Queenstown (2 nights) on South Island, and then to Auckland from whence my flight would leave for Australia. I could follow Wilber's footsteps on his leave and possibly see glaciers he may have seen. Everyone extols the beauty of the South Island, and I was loathe to miss it entirely.*

*On the flight down, the plane stopped briefly at Wellington, the capital city of New Zealand (on North Island). This was the next obvious place to search for Margaret (at the National Births/Deaths/Marriage Registry). However, I went on to South Island as planned, spent the night in beautiful Christchurch, the principal city of South Island. There I met a nice family with a handicapped boy in a restaurant, and then refreshed, decided to renew the search for Margaret by making my Queen-*

*stown visit the next day only about eight hours, (including a flight to Milford Sound) and to go back to Wellington that very day! Another motive was the fact that Olive Madsen, the woman my Dad took to the movies, might still live in the Wairarapa, close to Wellington. I had no idea if she was still alive. An attempt to phone her from Auckland had failed.*

*So, after one night in Christchurch, I went on to Queenstown, which entailed a hair-raising landing and takeoff at Mt. Cook and then the beauty of Queenstown. It is a small resort town in the mountains on New Zealand's longest lake. I found it to be very touristy, like Aspen, Colorado, and hence not very appealing to me. It was raining in Milford Sound so we could not fly in there. I rode a jet boat in a river, took a gondola up a nearby mountain (hill), and hiked around before catching my plane back to Christchurch and on to Wellington that same evening. This was probably the world's shortest visit to the South Island and a poor excuse for a meaningful visit. However, the payoff was huge; I was able to find and meet both Olive and Margaret.*

Looking back now (2014) at my tour of New Zealand, I realize how little I saw of the natural wonders of New Zealand that Wilber and Davis experienced. At the time, I had not reconstructed their likely itinerary as described earlier and unknowingly bypassed the national parks of the North Island and caught only glimpses of them on the South Island.

## 21

## *Olive and Margaret*

### Wellington and Auckland
### OCTOBER 1984

WAIRARAPA AND OLIVE, OCTOBER 11

*T*oday, my luck changed. Actually it stayed good; I was having a great time meeting people and seeing interesting places. After supper in my Wellington hotel, I asked telephone information for the phone number of an Olive Madsen in the Wairarapa district. Immediately, I had her number and her on the phone. She was delighted to hear from me, remembered Wilber and invited me to her home. We arranged to meet the next afternoon after I visited the Registry in Wellington.

The next morning, I was off to the Births/Marriages registry. With some sympathetic help from the clerks, I soon (in two hours) located two of Margaret's marriage certificates (one before the war and one after), and her present address which was in the Auckland area near her 1944 address! Sympathetic help was necessary because bureaucratic impediments are in place to keep genealogy addicts from overwhelming the Registry. The clerks looked up Margaret on their [new] computer system for me. [Remember, this was 1984.]

I am scheduled to leave NZ (Auckland) the morning after tomorrow! Time is short! Perhaps I can look her up when I return to Auckland tomorrow.

At about noon, I was off to Carterton, Wairarapa, about two hours to the north, to see Olive. I drove in my Avis rental over a beautiful yellow-flowered mountain: lots of hairpin turns (nobody told me to expect that) and then into flat warm sheep country. I loved it – what a tour!

The visit with Olive Madsen was an absolute delight. I was warmly welcomed and spent several hours chatting with her in her sitting room before returning to Wellington. She is 69 (b. Jan 10, 1915) and very perky. She had cancer of the cervix 18 years ago and a stroke 18 mos. ago of which I could see no evidence. She never

*Olive Madsen, 1944. She gave me this photo on my visit in October 1984.* [PHOTO: OLIVE MADSEN]

CHAPTER 21  *Olive and Margaret*

*Olive Madsen and me at her home in Carterton, New Zealand, October 1984. She died in 1989.* [PHOTO: HALE BRADT]

married, lived with her mother for years, and operated a flower shop for 16 years and then a Ladies Wear shop for 16 years, both in Martinborough (in the Wairarapa). She moved to her present home in 1972. She rents the front part of it. Her story of her meetings with my father vividly filled out his versions. More or less, it went as follows:

"I met your father (Wilber) and Davis (the officer he was traveling with) on the Ferry from Wellington to Christchurch on South Island. I was on holiday with my mother. In Christchurch, Mother and I went to our modest Bed and Breakfast hotel (the Ambassador), and Davis and Wilber went to the expensive United Services Hotel. The next day, while I was out, flowers arrived from Wilber with an invitation to go to the movies. The flowers were orange to match my frock – it was nice he remembered. I was in quite a tizz, being a country girl (age 29) with a Lt. Col. (age 44) paying attention to me. (My mother was unusually attractive, and it was she who usually drew the attention.)

I think Olive herself was also quite attractive, according to a photo from that time.

"We went to the movies and it turned out that he had previously bought tickets and inspected the reserved seats to make sure they were OK. When he took me

*Wilber (left) and Russ Davis on leave in Wellington, New Zealand, March 1944 in a photograph taken by Olive Madsen. Wearing uniforms while off duty was a requirement of the military.* [PHOTO: OLIVE MADSEN]

back he kissed me goodnight, but other than that never made a move for me, unlike most of the many other G.I.'s I had met. Wilber had told me he was married, but never discussed his family or job. That was that for Christchurch. Davis and Wilber continued their tour and we our vacation.

"Some time later [about ten days later on Friday, March 24], I received a call from Wilber from Wellington; he and Davis were returning north. They had very little time and so Wilber asked me to come down to Wellington for the evening and following day. He would pay for my hotel room in their hotel (St. George). Ordinarily, I would never accept such an invitation, but since he was so perfect a gentleman, I accepted and took the bus to Wellington.

"That evening, Davis, he, and I had supper together. Your father and Davis were like brothers. We then spent the rest of the evening in the hotel lounge with a charming group of New Zealand and American people. Later Wilber spent 1/2 hour with me in my room, but nothing serious occurred. We sat on the side of the bed and chatted. At one point I leaned across his lap to reach for something and he kissed me lightly on the neck. He remembered that later in a letter he wrote.

"The next day, we ate breakfast together [with Davis probably] and walked around Wellington with Davis. Wilber made no attempt to exclude Davis. Wilber took me into a bookstore and bought a book of poems that I still have here [and which she showed me]. He sort of romped into the bookshop in a little boyish way. We then went over to see a cricket game at Basin Reserve at Courtney Place by tram [trolley]. I tried to explain cricket to them, probably not successfully. We stayed only about 1/4 hour. [Two New Zealand teams were playing that Saturday afternoon.] We then walked to Oriental Bay to see the boats, expensive houses, etc. I took a photo of Wilber and Davis there. Then, back to St. George's Hotel, and then I got the bus for home.

"Wilber wrote to me at most two times and I wrote two or three times. He had asked me to 'please write'. I no longer have his letters; I had them in a folder with those from a number of G.I.'s and Marines I had met and threw it out when I moved here. One of my letters must have been forwarded to Washington, D.C., because your mother wrote me that Wilber had died of head wounds. I then wrote her with, more or less, the story I told you because I felt she would want to know about some of the pleasant times he had while overseas. I never heard from her thereafter.

"The whole episode must have meant a great deal to me if I can remember so many details of it now."

I asked her if she had hoped that maybe he would come back, i.e., was he her "lost love" for whom she stayed forever single? No such luck:

# COMBAT AND NEW LIFE  PART V: INTERLUDE 1984

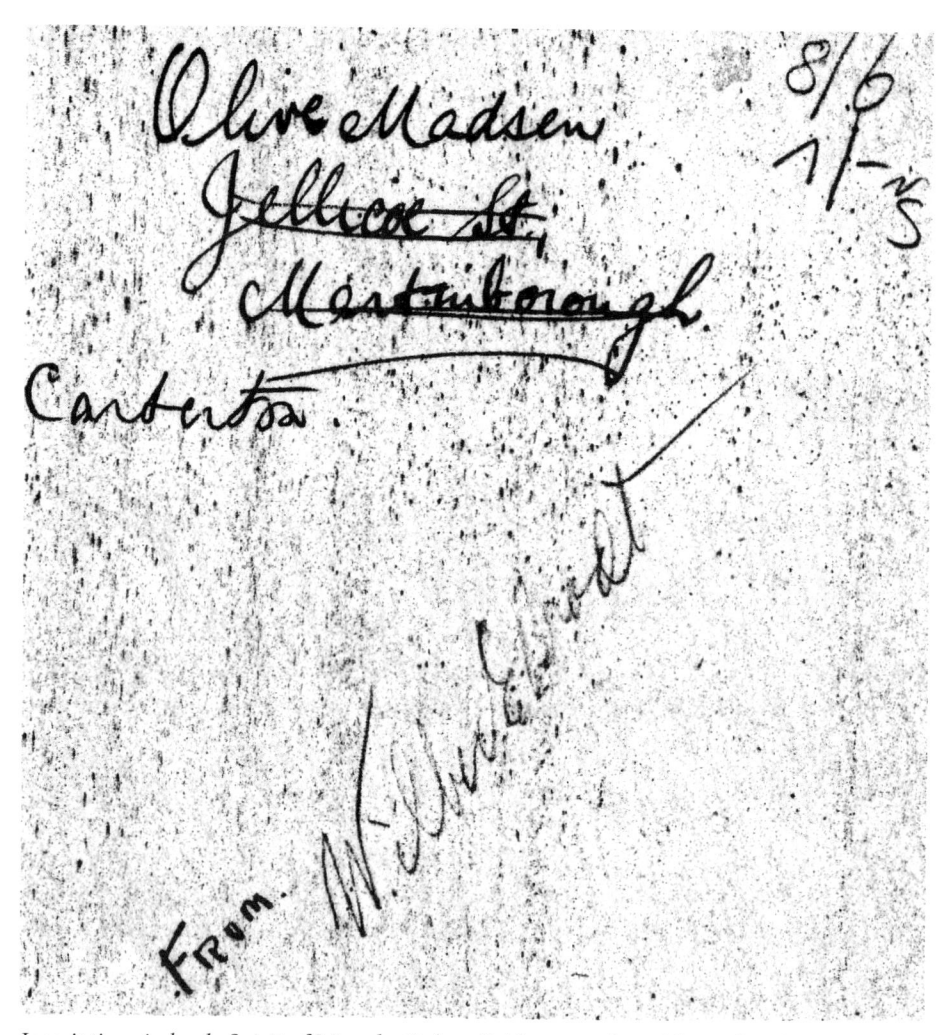

*Inscriptions in book,* Spirit of Man, *by Robert Bridges, purchased by Wilber for Olive Madsen. He signed it and she added her name, addresses, and the "From." The prices are in the upper right. It was 8 shillings 6 pence, reduced to 7 shillings 0 pence.* [FACSIMILE: COURTESY OF OLIVE MADSEN]

*"I knew he was married, and goodbye was goodbye. I had a number of other American correspondents. I was very leery of marriage – possibly because my parents were quite unhappy – and my close association with my mother probably didn't help" – a slight tone of regret here.*

*She showed me photos (1940's and 1980's) of her American correspondents, and told me that some of the marines who had been stationed near her town were later killed in Tarawa. She came up with some remarkable mementos of Wilber: the book*

324

CHAPTER 21   *Olive and Margaret*

*of poems, the negative of the photo she took at Oriental Bay, and a Lt. Col.'s silver oak-leaf insignia Wilber had given her.*

*I had long known of the photo of Wilber and Davis and have copies. However, I had never known where, when, and why it was taken. Both officers are in winter khaki uniforms. My father was quite heavy at the time (he oscillated between 190 and 210 pounds at 6'0" height and looks very severe (serious) in the photo. Davis is younger, slim, and quite handsome. I asked her if she were at all interested in Davis. She said, "no, he showed no interest in me."*

*As for the book of poems: Wilber had written "Wilber E. Bradt" in the front cover – and, as Olive carefully explained, she had prefixed this with "From" so no one would think she had kept someone else's book.*

> The book was *The Spirit of Man* by Robert Bridges, an anthology of poems and philosophical writings, which Norma had sent to Wilber before he went overseas [letter 9/12/42] and which he mentioned reading for much of the following year. He knew just what book to ask for when entering the bookstore.

*The Lt. Col's insignia was not an inconsequential gift. Olive offered it to me, and I suggested that it would mean more to her than to me. She agreed and kept it.*

*After leaving Olive and Carterton, I returned to Wellington and visited the St. George hotel where Olive, Wilber, and Davis had stayed. I already had reservations in a small motel so did not immerse (drown?) myself in nostalgia by staying there. The small staircases up to the rooms probably dated from the 1940s or earlier as did the rather narrow halls and solid wooden banisters. I ate in the "hotel" restaurant on the ground floor, and felt very nostalgic until I asked how long the restaurant had been like this. I was told that it was only about two years old and had been rebuilt from a former bar!*

*I left the hotel and went to a movie and then to my Wellington motel for my second night there. As I zipped around in my Avis rental car – my fourth in New Zealand; I was by now quite a hotshot left-lane driver – I got pretty badly lost a couple of times. The Avis city maps were awful. Once, when I wanted to know where I was, I finally saw a pole at a corner with two street signs on it. I stopped, backed up, and discovered that I was at the corner of "Grant Street" and "Ladies Toilet"! Anyway, Wellington is not all that big, and one pretty quickly comes to the Cricket Stadium no matter which way one goes.*

> My visit with Olive was the high point of my week in New Zealand. It was very touching and moving to see this other facet of my sometimes-too-serious father. His romantic streak—testified to by my mother and very

evident in his letters—was still there in 1944, and it was briefly directed toward Olive. Consider his gifts to her: the flowers, insignia, and the book of poems and philosophy.

I can imagine the bedroom scene in the hotel as if it had been me rather than Wilber: the mixed feelings of romance, chivalry, and physical desire combined with timidity and nervousness about whether and how to proceed. Inexperience with adultery combined with Christian morality given his married state would have been a big inhibitor. The desire must have been great but the fear of rejection and the loss of self-respect even greater. Olive may not have sensed Wilber's mixed feelings in that hotel room. She probably suffered from the common misperception that all men had the confidence to go after sex if they wanted it and that they were either "aggressive" or "gentlemen." Confused, mixed feelings in men were, and are, surely common. Olive surely had similar feelings.

Olive's candor in recounting these details gave me confidence that her story was correct in its essentials, including that the relationship progressed no further. This was reinforced for me by the embarrassed, guilty-boy, confessional tone of Wilber's letters to Norma and the fact that his story was totally consistent with Olive's. If he had been hiding a sexual encounter, he would surely have omitted the details that might have been (and actually were) misconstrued by Norma. Then, too, there were his voluntary candid statements in later letters to Norma and me [letters 4/3/44 and, in Book 3, 10/5/45] that he had never slept with another woman. The brevity of the two encounters with Olive during his leave and the large distance (400 miles) from his unit's station and her home—along with Wilber's own fidelity to Norma—stood in the way of a deeper relationship. Olive and Wilber were two ships passing in the night of war.

At times, I find myself wishing he had had the experience of a full romantic relationship during those long three years overseas, but if he had, I doubt he could have risen above the shame and guilt he would have felt, given his romantic idealism. For her part, Norma took all of this as a clear indication that Wilber had had a sexual affair with Olive, or so she told others. Her belief may indeed have served as justification for her own actions—and as a bolster for her own sanity.

Beyond the romantic drama, Olive's story was rich in the details of ordinary facets of Wilber's and Davis's tour of New Zealand. They stayed in the better hotels, they had no vehicle and so mostly traveled by bus, their tour of Wellington that day was on foot and tram, and they routinely wore full uniforms.

CHAPTER 21   *Olive and Margaret*

I had a warm correspondence of a few letters with Olive for several years thereafter. She sent me pictures, loaned me the book Wilber had given her, commented on other details of those days, and speculated on what she might have written to Wilber that caused him to cease writing. We have already heard Wilber's take on that in his confessional letter of July 7 wherein he was "a bit ashamed" about the whole affair.

**MARGARET, OCTOBER 12**
*The next morning I flew up to Auckland, and again drove to the suburb where Margaret lived. It took a lot of nerve to drop in on her to ask about an old romance. The electoral rolls showed her still married to the man she had married shortly after the war.*

*Well, I did see her, for ten minutes only. She is a very active, attractive, and well-groomed woman in perfect health, and still active professionally in business with her husband. She lives in a beautiful suburban home, with carefully maintained gardens. She was quite formally dressed with a perfectly maintained hairdo. She had a somewhat formal, distant demeanor. Her husband was not there, thankfully.*

*She graciously invited me in. She remembered my father and was interested in hearing about Waldo; I showed her a picture of him. She said that there were many happy times in those days, that she worked in an administrative position for the U.S. in Auckland, that she remembers visiting the unit when they were training in the Rotorua area, that she thinks of Waldo occasionally, that there isn't much point in exchanging addresses with him ("It was so long ago"), but that yes it was OK to tell Waldo she was in good health. Had she ever been in an automobile accident? "No, I have never had a day of ill health; when I think of it, I have had a rather fortunate life." Had she considered marrying Waldo? "No, I would never have left New Zealand." I then thanked her and backed out of there feeling horribly intrusive and not daring to ask if I could take her picture.*

The scars of war do heal over time, but the memories and effects carry on. The lives of Wilber, Waldo, Olive, and Margaret were surely altered in ways visible and invisible through those encounters. I do wonder if my visits to Waldo, Olive, and Margaret might have given rise to an upwelling of old emotions or had they become muted after so many years? Sadly now, their emotions survive only in the speculative retelling; all four are now long deceased.

Upon my return to the States, I did not contact Waldo. I felt it better that, during his last days, he should live with the memories and fantasies he had carefully nurtured for so long. It was likely, I think, that Margaret had written falsely about her disfigurement to cool his ardor. I had also learned at the registry that her first marriage had not been officially terminated until shortly before her second marriage; she had not been free to marry in 1944 or 1945. Waldo had been under the impression that her husband had died in the war [letter 11/19/44, Book 3], a fiction based on the wartime death of a relative of her first husband. Waldo, in his last years, did not need to hear the sad truths; he lived on for quite a few years, until 1990.

After this rich exploration of many corners of New Zealand, my week was up; the next morning, October 13, I departed Auckland. It was quite a shock to re-enter 1984 as I flew to Australia and met Remillard for our astronomical observations. I told him about the pleasure of finding Olive and of my digging into Margaret's complex personal life. He commented with a chuckle that "it's a good thing you were not doing that in Sicily as you would probably be dead now."

My emotional response to leaving "wartime" New Zealand was surely dwarfed by the feelings of the soldiers of the 43rd Division who sailed out of Auckland Harbour that July day of 1944.

x·o·ø·o·x

This completes the second of three volumes of the story of my family in World War II.

Wilber and the 43rd Division had been through an intense three-month period of combat in the Solomons and had recovered, insofar as possible, with a period of defensive duty in the Solomons followed by rehabilitation and training in New Zealand. The division was now en route to Aitape, New Guinea, for its second phase of combat in the war.

The family at home had moved back to our Bangor, Maine, prewar home without baby Gale as Norma attempted to re-enter the proper life of a dutiful mother and faculty-military wife. Meanwhile, in the summer of 1944, the war was progressing in the Allies' favor on all fronts, but not without setbacks and serious losses; the Axis resistance was fierce and vicious. The war was far from over.

The final volume (*Victory and Homecoming*) of this trilogy follows Norma's attempt to rectify her life and takes Wilber through the New Guinea combat, the massive invasion of Luzon in the Philippines, the subsequent extended combat there, the occupation of Japan, his return home, and finally his unexpected death and its aftermath.

# *Acknowledgments*

I have been pursuing the story of my father Wilber and mother Norma for nearly 34 years and have been aided by so many individuals and organizations that it is not possible to properly acknowledge them all, but I will do my best.

First and foremost, my sisters Abigail and Valerie deserve my utmost gratitude for letting me tell our family's story and for moral support throughout. Abigail's husband Tom has been an enthusiastic supporter, and Donald, Valerie's husband, has provided sage editorial advice.

This work could not exist but for those who husbanded my father's letters for the 35 years it took me to wake up to their existence and intrinsic value, namely my mother, my Bradt grandmother, and my cousin Alan, all of whom are now deceased. My aunt, Wilber's sister Mary Higgins, chose to give me a collection of letters between Wilber's mother and father written in the 1910s and 1920s, and between Mary and her mother in later decades. These shed important light on the familial relationships that were so influential in my father's life.

In the early 1980s, I hired students and secretaries—Trish Dobson, Pam Gibbs, Brenda Parsons, and Nancy Ferreira—to type Wilber's letters into a primitive stand-alone word processor. They were persevering, patient souls who took a serious personal interest in the story. I used those files to create the volume *World War Two Letters of Wilber E. Bradt* (by Hale Bradt, 1986), a complete compilation of Wilber's letters of which I created only 40 copies, mostly for relatives. The current work is, as described in the Prologue, a distillation of the complete letters with much more supportive material.

General Harold R. Barker, Wilber's immediate superior in the 43rd Division, wrote his *History of the 43rd Division Artillery*, which is rich in technical detail—operation orders, maps, and rosters of officers, medal winners, wounded, and killed. It pertains directly to the units Wilber commanded. This, along with other published histories and documentation in Wilber's papers, provides context for the events Wilber describes. At my request in 1981 when she was 75 and still quite alert, my mother typed an eight-page summary of her life that was a valuable view of her life as she then, perhaps somewhat wishfully, remembered it.

Conversations and correspondence with Wilber's military and civilian associates and his siblings in the 1980s materially enriched this story. Especially helpful were Howard Brown, Waldo Fish, and others of the Rhode Island National Guard; Donald Downen of the Washington State National Guard; Irwin Douglass of the University of Maine; and Robert Patenge, formerly of the 169th Field Artillery Battalion. My 1983 conversation with Japanese Colonel Seishu Kinoshita, who fought opposite Wilber on Arundel, was an emotional highlight for both of us. Howard Brown died this year (2014); the others long before. My aunt Mary Bradt Higgins was especially helpful with her wonderful memory and facility with the typewriter. Her sister Ruth and brother Rex were also generous with their recollections and so were my mother's relatives, especially her sister Evelyn and Evelyn's daughters, Jane and Julie. My Bourjaily stepbrother, Paul Webb, and the former wife of his brother Vance, Tina Bourjaily, were helpfully responsive to my queries.

My visits in 1983 and 1984 to the Pacific sites of Wilber's odyssey (Solomon Islands, Philippine Islands, New Zealand, and Japan), and my meetings with the people he encountered added important dimensions and perspective. In New Zealand, Olive Madsen, Minnie and Sidney Smith, and Dawn Jones Penney were most helpful. In the Solomons, my guide Alfred Basili got me around efficiently in his motorized canoe, Liz and Ian Warne provided hospitality on Kolombangara, and Claude Colomer took photos for me after I had immersed my camera in seawater, and so did the Warnes. In the Philippines, Mrs. José Dacquel whom Wilber had known, Emma Peralto, Boysie Florendo, and the deLeon family made my visit most fruitful. Boysie spent a day driving me to sites on the Laguna de Bay, and young Edgar José drove us to Lingayen Gulf in his 1969 Ford Mustang with the music playing loudly as we cruised down roads reminiscent of the U.S. in the 1930s. These Pacific visits were facilitated by my residence in Japan while on sabbatical leave in 1983 at the Japanese Institute of Space and Astronautical Science. I remain grateful for its generous support of my scientific endeavors.

I was fortunate to have started this project when many of my informants were still living. In recent years, I have been in contact with families of soldiers and in one case a sailor who served with Wilber, namely the families of Charles D'Avanzo, Robert Patenge, Donald Mushik, Lawrence Palmer, Saul Shocket, and Marshall Dann. Their recollections and generous sharing of memories and photographs further added to the story.

## Acknowledgments

Faculty, archivists, and librarians at the universities Wilber and Norma attended or taught at (Washington State University, Indiana University, University of Cincinnati, University of Maine) helped flesh out those aspects of their lives. Staff at the National Archives in Suitland, Maryland; Washington, D.C., and College Park, Maryland, on my half dozen visits over the years were expert at finding needed documents. Also helpful were librarians and archivists in New Zealand (Auckland, Christchurch, and Wellington), and at the City of Nouméa, New Caledonia; Bancroft Library of the University of California, Berkeley; Columbia University; Tacoma Public Library, Washington; Seattle Museum of History and Industry; U.S. Army Center for Military History; Japanese Center for Military History of the National Institute of Defense Studies (IDS); and elsewhere. It was Dr. Hishashi Takahashi of IDS who put me in touch with Col. Kinoshita.

I am most grateful to Robin Bourjaily, Maura Henry, and Richard Feyl for readings and editorial comments on near-final drafts. Frances King did heroic service as editor and manager of the final phases of this work, and Lisa Carta's attention to detail and superb design sense created a most attractive set of books. Suzanne Fox, Richard Margulis, Kate Hannisian, and Michael Sperling contributed much appreciated marketing advice.

The many Bradts, Sparlins, and Bourjailys I have queried and visited over the years have helped create this story. In many respects, it is their story too. Many friends and colleagues have suffered my recounting parts of the story to them over these past decades. My daughters, Elizabeth and Dorothy, and my wife, Dorothy, have borne the burden more than most, and they did so with grace.

I, of course, take sole responsibility for errors and misrepresentations herein.

# *Bibliography*

The following references have been particularly helpful to me in creating the Wilber's War Trilogy.. They do not by any means comprise a comprehensive list of World War II Pacific Theater sources. Many of these volumes and documents are now available on the Internet.

**Official military journals, histories, and operations reports of the following units during World War II, U.S. National Archives and Records Administration (NARA):**

172nd, 103rd, and 169th Infantry Regiments of the 43rd Infantry Division.

152nd, 169th, 103rd, and 192nd Field Artillery Battalions of the 43rd Infantry Division.

27th, 145th, 148th, and 161st Infantry Regiments; see also Karolevitz reference below.

*43rd Infantry Division Historical Report, Luzon Campaign, 1945.*

*History of the 103rd Infantry Regiment, 43rd Division, January 1, 1945 – May 31, 1945.* [Detailed narrative history of the entire Luzon campaign for the regimental combat team that included Wilber's artillery battalion]

**Logs of naval units:**

LCI-65

LCI (L) Group 14

**Histories sponsored by the U.S. military:**

*United States Army in World War II, The War in the Pacific Series.* Sponsored by the U.S. Army Chief of Military History, U.S. Government Printing Office, 1949–1962:

Morton, Louis. *Strategy and Command: The First Two Years.*

Morton, Louis. *The Fall of the Philippines.* [1941–42]

Miller, John, Jr. *Guadalcanal, The First Offensive.* [Guadalcanal campaign, 1942–43]

Miller, John, Jr. *Cartwheel, the Reduction of Rabaul.* [New Georgia campaign, 1943]

Miller, Samuel. *Victory in Papua.* [Eastern New Guinea campaign, 1942]

Smith, Robert Ross. *Approach to the Philippines.* [Northern New Guinea campaign, 1944]

Cannon, M. Hamlin. *Leyte: The Return to the Philippines.* [Leyte campaign, 1944]

Smith, Robert Ross. *Triumph in the Philippines.* [Luzon campaign, 1945]

Williams, Mary. *Chronology 1941–1945.* [World War II events]

MacArthur, Gen. Douglas, *The Campaigns of MacArthur in the Pacific, Reports of General MacArthur, Volume 1,* U.S. Army Center for Military History, CMH Pub 13-3, 1994.

Morison, Samuel Eliot. *History of the U.S. Naval Operations in World War II.* New York: Atlantic, Little, Brown, 1948–60:

*Vol. III, The Rising Sun in the Pacific.*

*Vol. V, The Struggle for Guadalcanal.*

*Vol. VI, Breaking the Bismarck Barrier.*

*Vol. VIII, New Guinea and the Marianas.*

*Vol. XII, Leyte.*

*Vol. XIII, The Liberation of the Philippines.*

*Memoirs and histories by participants:*

Barker, Harold R. *History of the 43rd Division Artillery.* Providence RI: John F. Greene Printer, 1961.

Eichelberger, Robert L. *Our Jungle Road to Tokyo.* Rockville MD: Zenger Publishing Company, 1949.

Halsey, William F. and J. Bryan III. *Admiral Halsey's Story.* Rockville MD: Zenger, Publishing Company, 1947.

Krueger, Walter. *From Down Under to Nippon.* Rockville MD: Zenger Publishing Company, 1953.

Ockenden, Edward. *The Ghosts of Company G.* Infinity, 2011. [The TED Force in New Guinea]

Sledge, E. B. *With the Old Breed.* New York: Ballantine Books, 1981.

Zimmer, Joseph E. *History of the 43rd Infantry Division 1941–1945.* Baton Rouge, LA: The Army and Navy Publishing Company, undated, probably late 1940s.

*Other histories and memoirs:*

Bauer, K. Jack and Alan C. Coox. "Olympic vs. Ketsu-go," *Marine Corps Gazette,* August 1965, v. 49, No. 8.

Bourjaily, Vance. "My Father's Life," *Esquire Magazine,* March 1984, p. 98.

Donovan, Robert. *PT 10.* New York: McGraw-Hill, 1961.

Drea, Edward J. "Previews of Hell." *Quarterly Journal of Military History,* vol. 7, no. 3, p. 74. Aston, PA: Weider History, 1995. [Planned invasion of Kyushu]

Drea, Edward J. *Defending the Driniumor: Covering Force Operations in New Guinea, 1944,* Leavenworth Papers No. 9, Combat Studies Institute, 1984.

Estes, Kenneth W. *Marines Under Armor.* Annapolis MD: Naval Institute Press, 2000.

Goodwin, Doris Kearns. *No Ordinary Time.* New York: Touchstone, Simon & Schuster, 1994.

Hammel, Eric. *Munda Trail.* London: Orion Press, 1989.

Hasegawa, Tsuyoshi (Ed.) *The End of the Pacific War, Reappraisals.* Stanford, CA: Stanford University Press, 2007.

Keegan, John. *The Second World War.* New York: Viking Press, 1989.

Knox, Donald. *Death March.* New York: Harcourt, Brace, Jovanovich, 1981, pp. 181–184, 227. [The Lumban bridge story]

Karolevitz, R. F. (Ed.) *History of the 25th Infantry Division in World War II.* Nashville, TN: Battery Press, 1946, 1995. [Actions of the 27th and 161st Infantry Regiments]

Larrabee, Eric. *Commander in Chief.* New York: Simon & Schuster, 1987.

Paull, Raymond. *Retreat from Kokoda.* Australia: Wm. Heinemann Press, 1958.

Potter, E. B. *Nimitz.* Annapolis MD: Naval Institute Press, 1976.

Skates, John R. *The Invasion of Japan.* University of California Press, 1994.

*The Official History of the Washington National Guard*, Vol. 6, *Washington National Guard in World War II.* State of Washington: Office of the Adjutant General. [Also contains WW I and the 1935 strike duty]

*Unpublished or self-published documents:*

Antill, Peter, *Operation Downfall: The Planned Assault on Japan, Parts 1–4,* http://www.historyofwar.org/articles/wars_downfall1.html (1996).

Bourjaily, Monte F., "Re: Monte Ferris Bourjaily," 1936. [Résumé with references]

Bradt, Hale V. *Story of the Bradt Fund, the F. Hale Bradt Family, and their Versailles, Indiana Farm (1906–2001).* Self-published, 2004. [Early years of Wilber Bradt's life]

Bradt, Hale V. *The World War II Letters of Wilber E. Bradt.* Self-published 1986. [The nearly complete letters, transcribed and privately bound and distributed]

Bradt, Norma S. *Memoir, 1981.* [Eight page self-typed document]

Bradt, Wilber E. *Personal Journal (1941–45).* [Five handwritten notebook pages of dates, places, incidents]

Fushak, K. Graham. *The 43rd Infantry Division, Unit Cohesion and Neuropsychiatric Casualties.* Thesis, U.S. Command and General Staff College, 1999.

Higgins, John J. *A History of the First Connecticut Regiment, 169th Infantry 1672–1963.* Unpublished, 1963.

Patenge, Robert. *Memories of Wilber E. Bradt*, 1997. [Patenge was a survey officer in the 169th Field Artillery Battalion under Wilber Bradt in the Munda campaign, World War II, and later served with the 103rd Field Artillery Battalion.]

Saillant, Richard. *Journal of Richard L. Saillant.* Transcribed by Joseph Carey. [Saillant was an officer in the 118th Engineers of the 43rd Division until April 1944. The

Munda campaign is vividly described.]

Zimmer, Joseph E. *Letters from Col. Joseph E. Zimmer to his wife, Maude Files Zimmer 1942–1945.* Transcribed by Maude Zimmer. [Zimmer was an infantry officer in the 43rd Division who served in the 169th Infantry, 103rd Infantry, and other elements of the 43rd Division from 1941 until May 1945.]

*Newspaper archives, 1941–45:*

*Bangor* (Maine) *Daily News*
*New York Times*
*Wellington* (New Zealand) *Evening Post*
*Washington* (D.C.) *Post*
*Washington* (D.C.) *Star*

*Notable conversations with 43rd Division participants and one Japanese officer:*

Howard Brown (1981 through 2012)

Warren Covill (1981)

Seishu Kinoshita, Kyushu, Japan (1983)

Albert Merck (1984, 2009)

William Naylor (1984)

Robert Patenge (1997)

# INDEX  Book 2

**Bold** page numbers indicate a chapter or, if a page range is given, a part.
*Italic* page numbers indicate a photograph or map.
WB — Wilber Bradt; "Hale" is Wilber's son; "F. Hale" is Wilber's father

27th Infantry Regiment
    command post, Bomboe, *95*
    commendation for WB, 115
    visit by Halsey and Lodge, 108
    WB at command post, 80, *96*
37th Infantry Division
    reinforced 43rd Div., Munda, 25
43rd Infantry Division
    about to fold up, 22
    assault on New Georgia, *xxix*
    Brig. Gen. Leonard F. Wing commander, 63
    casualties in Solomons, 116
    command post attacked, 25
    en route Aitape, New Guinea, 307
    exercises in N.Z. mountains, 278
    Gen. Harold Barker commander, 56
    Gen. Hester relieved of command, 33
    Gen. John R. Hodge commander, 33
    Munda airfield captured, 43
    objective Munda airfield, **3**
    offensives in Solomons complete, 83
    on defense in Solomons, **159**
    ordered to New Zealand, 229
    organization of, *xx*
    under MacArthur command, 282
    voyages of, *xxiii*
103rd Field Artillery Battalion
    alongside, on Sasavele, 21
145th Infantry Regiment
    assisted 43rd Division, 25
    commendation for 169th FA Bn., 115
    sought 169th FA Bn. support, 43
    WB at command post of, 33
148th Infantry Regiment
    assisted 43rd Division, 25
    commendation for 169th FA Bn., 115
    sought 169th FA Bn. support, 43

152nd Field Artillery Battalion
    at Matakana, New Zealand, 291
    bronze-star medals for men of, 296
    move to Auckland for embarkation, 299
    officer assignments inappropriate, 276
    visited by air, 204
    Waldo Fish, executive officer, 277
    WB commanding officer, **267**
161st Infantry Regiment from Wash. State
    defense of Ondonga airfield, 175
    Lts. French and Christian killed, 51
    reinforced lines at Munda, 25
    supported by 169th FA Bn., 82
169th Field Artillery Battalion
    arrived at Barabuni Is., Rendova, **11**
    DeBlois new commander of, 268
    defended howitzer positions, 186
    fire direction center, 41
    firing exercises, scores in, 280
    firing not interrupted, Piru Plantation, 86
    former C.O. criticized, 293
    left Guadalcanal for New Zealand, 247
    left New Zealand, 299
    moved to vicinity Munda, 61
    officers at promotion party, *161*
    on Sasavele Island, 19
    positions on New Georgia, *xxxvii*
    regiments sought support of, 43
    rounds fired, Solomons, 28
    supported 169th Inf. Rgt., 20
169th Infantry Regiment
    attempted rescue on Baanga, 61
    began Munda drive, 20
    Co. L ambushed on Baanga, 59
    neuropsychiatric casualties, 22
    reputation at Munda, 234
    reunion with WB, 56

supported by 169th FA Bn., 19
WB offered executive position, 168
172nd Infantry Regiment
artillery for, Arundel, 86
brought into Baanga, 61
drive on Munda, 21
drive toward Laiana Beach, 22
landings on Arundel, *74*, 75

advice (sexual) for Hale by WB, 270
Alaikone, Jason, Guadalcanal, 131
at Japanese memorial, *130*
at U.S. Marine memorial, *130*
allotments ($5) to Hale and Valerie, 76
Armistice Day 1943, Munda, 185
artillery
assignments to infantry, xv
extinguished light, 100
fire support team, Munda, *180*
fired on boats and float planes, 100
organization of, Munda, 19
speed of adjustment, 217
statistics of short rounds, 191
test scores, New Zealand, 282
whish-whispering overhead, 38, 49
Arundel Island, **75**
first landings August 1943, *74*
lagoon, *144*
map and actions, *xxxv*
WB account, **85**

Baanga Island, **59**
beach where men stranded, *138*
map of actions, *xxxiv*
Bailey, Maj. William N.
commanded Provisional Battalion, 94
fire direction center, Bustling Pt., 99
newly promoted, 180
photo of with WB and Capt. Ryan, *82*
Ballale airport, The Solomons, 154
Baltimore, Maryland
fictional residence, 4
letters delayed, 198
Wilber writes to, 69
band concert, Ondonga, *212*
Barabuni Island
169th FA arrived at, 11
moved howitzers from, 13
Barike River
Hale swam in, 1983, 45
WB waded across, 45

Barker, Brig. Gen. Harold R.
acting commander, 43rd Div., 56
approved WB staying in Bomboe, 98
awarded DSC to Mushik, 211
commander 43rd Div. Artillery, xiv
commended Bn. C.O.s awkwardly, 57
complimented 169th FA, 30
gave div. arty. command to WB, 59
grinned at inspection, 197
harangue re bad scores, New Zealand, 283
leave in New Zealand, 173
lunch and WB's oyster consumption, 299
officer leaves, New Zealand, 252
ordered WB to rear, 37
pleased that 152nd FA not 97% perfect, 286
received Legion of Merit medal, 161
reverted to command of div. arty., 63
saw Griswold re WB decoration, 219
visited Sasavele, 14
WB best arty. battalion C.O. in div., 268
Basili, Alfred
at stern of his canoe, *140*
guide at Munda, 135
recoil spring, Baanga, *136*
Berry, Lt. Col. Edward W., S-3 Div. Arty., 197
bird calls imitated, 38
Blackett Strait
between Arundel and Kolumbangara, 96
controlled by artillery, 101
float plane on, 99
Kennedy PT boat sunk, 143
viewed at night by Hale, 152
Bloody Ridge aka Edson's ridge, 131
boat(s), small
coxswain "Junior" problems, 215
debarking from, onto Zanana Beach, *15*
en route Zanana Beach, *15*
in lagoon, WB en route Bomboe, 94
Japanese, destroyed, Arundel, 100
Kennedy PT-109 destroyed, 41
on lagoon near Bomboe, Col. Sugg, *103*
provided by Ensign Dann, 239
rusted landing craft, Guadalcanal, *133*
to Barabuni Island, 11
to Enogai, rough waters, 189
bombing
chart of, Rendova, July 4, *xxx*
of German cities, 118
of Hiroshima, 122
of Munda, 17
of Ondonga, 180

of Rendova, July 2, 5
   sketches of formation, *10*
   Wilber wounded by, Rendova, 9
Bomboe Village, Arundel, 95, **143**
Bourjaily, Gale aka Abigail
   birth of, 179, 184, 192
   Norma's choices re, 267
   separated from Norma, 290
   Terkman cared for, 218
Bourjaily, Monte F.
   home in Georgetown, 4
   met Hale and Valerie, 70
   Norma at his Wash. D.C. home, 218
   WB wrote of, 238
Bourjaily, Terkman (mother of Monte)
   cared for Gale, 218
   support for Norma, 4, 218
Bradt, Elizabeth P. (mother of WB)
   cherished resentment, 243
   Norma wrote of, 246
Bradt, F. Hale (father of WB)
   Legion of Merit order sent to, 219
   Norma wrote to, 218, 246
   set standards for WB, 225
Bradt, Hale V. (son of WB)
   Bangor, Maine, with family, 291
   Grace Boys Camp, 28
   Guadalcanal, 1983, 127
   lacked appreciation for WB award, 245
   letters from, *29, 35*
   met Colonel Kinoshita, 1983, 123
   New Georgia Island, visited by 1983, 135
   photograph of
      in Alfred Basili's canoe, *140*
      pedestal of coastal gun, Baanga, *137*
      with Waldo Fish 1984, *313*
   Solomon Islands, 1983, 45
   spring break in Wash. D.C., 257
   St. Bernard's (boarding) School, 70, 253
   Wash., D.C. with uncle, 1944, 274
   WB advice about friends, 295
   WB advice on sexuality, 270
Bradt, Norma Sparlin (wife of WB)
   gave birth to Gale, 179
   hit by automobile, 275
   idolized by WB, 40
   letters lacked details, 202
   location uncertain, 3
   met Hale and Valerie in NYC, 203
   moved family to Bangor, Maine, 291
   new address, Washington, D.C., 242
   recalled their honeymoon, 171

Valerie visited, 279
   WB worried about, 69, 227
   wrote father-in-law, 246
Bradt, Paul (brother of WB) & Josephine
   address used by WB, 172
   Baanga story told to, 62
   Hale visited, March 1944, 257
   Valerie visited, summer 1943, 5
Bradt, Valerie E. (daughter of WB)
   Bangor, Maine, with family, 291
   called Tumblebug by WB, 242
   Comrade IV, 269
   grades assessed by WB, 204
   relatives & summer camp 1943, 5
   St. John Baptist school, 71
   Train Ride from Hell, 279
Bradt, Wilber E.
   arrived New Zealand, 249
   artillery on Sasavele Island, 19
   Arundel story, 85
   awarded the Legion of Merit, 218
   Baanga action, 59
   Bomboe village, 78
   commanded divisional artillery, 61
   declined invitations to socialize, 287
   depression, 235
   destroyed Japanese guns, Baanga, 63
   fidelity to Norma, 209, 271
   firefight, Arundel, 92
   Guadalcanal en route New Zealand, 235
   hospital, New Zealand, 269
   imitated Japanese whistle signals, 38
   leave declined, 171, 214
   leave in New Zealand, 252, 255
   left Auckland with 152nd FA Bn., 301
   met Olive Madsen, 304
   Ondonga, 159
   ordered to rear, Munda, 38
   photograph of
      152nd FA staff, New Zealand, *292*
      at desk in tent office, Ondonga, *181*
      coastal gun, Japanese, Baanga, *65*
      officers of 169th FA, Ondonga, *212*
      official, with name board, *169*
      Ondonga, back turned, with Davis, *190*
      passing in review, DSC ceremony, *211*
      promotion party, *161*
      three hikers, New Zealand, *264*
      with Capt. Davis, Wellington, N.Z, *322*
      with Charles D'Avanzo, *162*
      with Maj. Bailey and Capt. Ryan, *82*
      with Mushik, DSC ceremony, *213*

promotion to lieutenant colonel, 83
refused move to infantry, 168
Rendova, 6
Russell Islands, 3
seeing last sun, 44
telegram re wounds, *25*
walk into Arundel, 88
with infantry, Munda drive, 20
wounded by bomb, 9
wounded by sniper bullet, 27
wrote recommendations, 115
Brown, Capt. Howard F.
169th Infantry a good outfit, 235
knew of D'Avanzo's widow, 161
story of WB on telephone, 44
Burns, Capt. Frank W.
liaison to div. arty., Auckland., *297*
photo of, with 152nd staff, N.Z., *292*
Bush, Lt. Col. George E.
executive of 27th Inf. Rgt., 98
in foxhole with three others, 99
Bustling Point
artillery at, 75
loading 155-mm shells into truck, *79*
Butler, Lt. Michael J.
adjusted fire, Arundel, 106
not sent into Arundel, 87
photo of, with 169th FA officers, *212*

Camp White for the Sheltering Arms, Valerie attended, 5
casualties, in landing craft, Rendova, *53*
cemetery
graves at Munda 1943, *52*
Munda 1944, *186*
Charlie One, firing mission, Munda, 47
children
crayon drawings by Japanese, 68
on Guadalcanal 1983, *129*, *131*
on Sasavele 1983, *138*, *139*
Warne family, Kolombangara, *153*
Christian, Lt. Louis K.
Distinguished Service Cross, 54
killed July 27, 1943, Munda, 51
photo of 1934, *54*
Christmas 1943, 203, 209
Cloke, Paul, Dean at U. Maine, 170, 281
Coast-Guard sailor
joined patrol into Arundel, 88
note to certify on patrol, 93
codes re locations, WB not using, 294

Colomere, Claude, tourist at Munda, 136
Combat, jungle, **1–118**
Congressional Medal of Honor, 98
Croker, Sam and Olive
dairy farmers, 290
photo of, ca. 1950, *303*
served sumptious "tea", 301
Cronin, Chaplain, service for natives, 77

D'Avanzo, Capt. Charles S., MD
avid photographer, 161
photo of, with WB, *162*
promotion party, 160
wife forwarded Norma's letter, 239
Dann, (navy) Lt. Marshall
commendation for by WB, 239
letter from, 240
Davis, Capt. E. Russell, Jr.
dancing in New Zealand, 264
Episcopal services, Ondonga, 200
forcing enemy into open with arty., 49
on leave with WB, New Zealand, 255
photograph of
chapel and 169th FA officers, *212*
in fire direction center, Sasavele, *42*
Ondonga, *190*
with WB, Wellington, N.Z., *322*, *323*
planned tour of New Zealand, 250
reconnaissance in jungle with WB, 186
rough boat ride to Enogai, 189
Davis, Maj. Charles W.
commander 3rd Bn., 27th Inf., on Sagekarasa & Medal of Honor recipient, 98
facing more machine guns, 100
open to suggestions on Sagekarasa, 106
DeBlois, Maj. René L.
at Rendova bombing, 9
called compliment "baloney", 42
commanded 169th FA Bn., 268
commanded Provisional Bn., 170
did work of two or three, 17
directed Eastern Force, Arundel, 78
managed fire direction center, Sasavele, 31, 38, 41, 47
photograph of
chapel and 169th FA officers, *212*
in fire direction center, *42*
promoted to lt. col., 277
Delaware Lacawan song, 279
Devil's Island, artillery target, *xxxvi*, 100

Devine, Lt. Col. James "Wally"
    at Devine's Island, Arundel, 87
    commander 3rd Bn. 172nd Inf. Rgt., 86
    relaxing with coffee, at Laiana, *26*
Distinguished Service Cross
    169th FA in review for Mushik, *211*
    Capt. Edward W. Wild, 192
    Lt. Donald L. Mushik, 47
    Lt. Kenneth P. French, 54
    Lt. Louis K. Christian, 54
Downen, Capt. Donald C.
    400 yards from WB, Munda, 30
    near Wilber, Ondonga, 161
    photograph of
        as major 1944, *55*
        with Japanese gun, *51*
        with wife 1985, *55*
    testimony re Lts. Christian and French, 54
dusty road & negro driver, 288

Eason, Col. John D.
    relieved of 169th Inf. command, 22
    WB liked very much, 225
Episcopal services, Ondonga, 200
Estes, Mrs., prayers for WB, 9
Evans, Col. B. F.
    C.O. 2nd Bn., 27th Inf. Rgt., 93
    rendezvous with Naylor's battalion, 93

family trees, xix
Farrell, Lt. Wm. A., Rendova bombing, 9
Files, Col. Chester
    90th birthday, 185
    commended 169th FA Bn., 114
    executive of division artillery, 114
    officers' leaves, New Zealand, 252
    on reconnaissance with WB, 185
fire direction center
    Bustling Point, 99
    Sasavele, 41, *42*, 48
firefight on Arundel, 92
Fish, Maj. Waldo H., Jr.
    dinner and movies with WB, 282
    executive officer of 152 FA Bn., 277
    loose ends to clear up, 300
    managed departure from Auckland, 297
    met by Hale, 312
    photograph of
        152nd staff, N.Z., *292*
        with Hale 1984, *313*

flies
    going to latrine and kitchen, 228
    must carrry rations, 215
French, Lt. Kenneth P.
    Distinguished Service Cross, 54
    killed July 28, 1943, Munda, 51
fungus infections, 237

generals
    laugh about home-front, 173
    told 169th FA the finest, 30
Gizo, Solomon Islands, 154
Goff, Capt. Dixwell
    adjusted fire, 31
    at front, Munda, 29
    kicked crab out of foxhole, 34
    managed forward command post, 111
    photo of, with 169th FA officers, *212*
    promoted to major, 277
    selected positions, Sasavele, 16
    WB letter to wife of, 183
Grace Boys Camp
    Hale attended, 5
    letters from, 23, *35*
Griswold, Maj. Gen. Oscar W.
    43rd Div. about to fold up, 22
    assumed command Occupation Force, 25
    Col. Tomonari his personal adversary, 165
    commander XIV Corps, xv
    in boat with Halsey and Lodge, *113*
    requested firing for Halsey & Lodge, 109
    visited front after attack, Arundel, 105
    WB adds technical ability, 27
    WB doing fine piece of work, 80
Guadalcanal
    flooded tent 1944, *236*
    Hale visited 1983, **127**
    photographs of children
        Alaikone grandsons, *131*
        Salia, *133*
        Stacey Wally, Guadalcanal, *129*
    WB arrived 1944, 235
gun(s)
    155-mm at Bustling Point, *79*
    coastal, Baanga
        destroyed, 63
        Hale visited 1983, 136
        mount and tube, *137*
        photo of, with WB 1943, *65*
    howitzer, Bibilo Hill, Munda, *177*
    Japanese, captured at Munda, *51*
    on Beach Red, Guadalcanal, *129*

341

Haffner, Capt., of 172nd Inf. Rgt., 88
Halsey, Adm. William F., Jr.
   citation to Lt. Dann, 240
   commander of South Pacific Area, 3
   in boat with Griswold and Lodge, *113*
   reassigned to Central Pacific, 282
   visited 27th Inf. command post, 108
Hamburg, Germany, firebombed, 118
harangue re firing scores, 291
Heidelberger, Lt. Norbert J.
   adjusted fire, 31, 47
   brother of, 1981, 193
   insignia sent to mother of, 243
   killed August 15, 1943, 61
   left battalion with Wilber, 60
   letter from mother of, 201
   letter to mother of, by WB, 192
   news photo of, *60*
   recalled by WB before Arundel walk, 87
   remembered on Armistice Day, 184
   ruled killed, 189
Helmer-Hubble story, 275
Henderson Field, Guadalcanal, 128
Hester, Maj. Gen. John H.
   commander 43rd Division 1941, xv
   did not sign promotion papers, 43
   relieved of division command, 33
   relieved of Occupation Force cmd., 25
Hill, Lt. Col. George M.
   C.O. 192nd FA Bn., 77
   his battalion silenced Pistol Pete, 163
   rotated to U.S., 268
Hodge, Maj. Gen. John R.
   commander 43rd Division, 33
   returned to Americal Division, 56
hokum by returned heroes, 167
Holland, Col. Temple G.
   169th finest artillery in world, 27
   C.O. 169th Inf. Rgt., 22, 168
   commander 145th Inf. Rgt., 30
   fought to get the 169th FA, 30
   recommended WB for Silver Star, 251
   requested WB as his executive, 168
Horseshoe Hill, Munda
   Hale visited 1983, 148
   infantry seized, 114, 253
   scarecrow, with U.S. Army helmet, *150*
Hussey, Capt. Robert S.
   C.O. Battery B, 152nd FA Bn., 293
   moved his battery to Auckland, 297

hut for officers, Matakana
   described, 281, 289
   soot from oil stove, 295
   with oil stove, 275

inspection
   prepared for, Ondonga, 197
   vehicles ready for, Ondonga, *196*
Interlude
   Japan & Solomons, **119–55**
   New Zealand, **309–28**
Italy surrendered to Allies, 73

Japanese
   13th Inf. Rgt., Flower of South Japan, 105
   antics at night in jungle, 65, 67
   antitank gunfire on Arundel, 104
   artillery on Kolombangara, 98
   children's drawings, 68
   coastal guns on Baanga, 64
   evacuation from Arundel, 83, 110
   gun captured at Munda, *51*
   pillbox, Munda, *30*
   reinforced Arundel, 78
Jones girls, Matakana, N.Z.
   Dawn Jones Penney 1984, *314*
   five sisters ca.1944, *304*
   helped entertain soldiers, 303
jungle
   barking lizards, 50
   noises at night, 38

Keegan, Capt. Edward J.
   cake, wife baked and ate, 224
   during bombing, Rendova, 9
   photo of, with 169th FA officers, *212*
   story of newly arrived driver, Guadalcanal, 288
Kennedy, Lt. John F.
   Hale met rescuers, Bomboe 1983, 143
   rescued by natives, 78
Kera, Angus, Munda Rest House, 135
Kieta, PNG, airport 1983, 154
Kinoshita, Col. Seishu
   assisted evacuation boats, 111
   battalion commander 13th Jp. Rgt., 144
   commander 13th Jp. Rgt., 125
   faced Americans, Arundel, 104
   Hale visited 1983, 123
   Naylor meeting with, 126, *126*
   photos of, 1942 and 1983, *123*
   proud not to have surrendered, 113

## Index

Kirker, Lt. Col. F.
  graveside service, Munda, 52
Knight, Lt. Col. (pseudonym)
  C.O. 169th FA Bn., criticized by WB, 293
  gave misleading speeches, 167
Kolombangara Island
  Hale visited 1983, **151**
  Japanese graves restored, 244
  Japanese stronghold, 75
  photo of, from Arundel, 96
  WB visited, 168
Kula Gulf
  boat ride to Arundel, 86
  naval battle of, 21
  rough boat ride to Enogai, 189
Kyushu, Japan 1983, **121**

Laiana beach, drive toward, 22
land crab in foxhole, 34
LCI-65. *See* ships
Legion of Merit
  awarded to Gen. Barker, 161
  awarded to WB, 114
  Holland recommended Silver Star, 251
  medal sent to father by WB, 225
  recommended DeBlois for, 17
Leningrad, Russia, seige broken, 230
letters
  from Norma delayed, 198
  Norma's lost, 45
line of departure
  fighting to reach, 21
  reached by 172nd Inf. and 169th Inf., 22
lineman puzzled by wire break, 39
lizard, barking, 50
Lodge, Senator Henry Cabot
  conversation with Hale, 112
  in boat with Halsey and Griswold, *113*
  visited 27th Inf. command post, 108

MacArthur, Gen. Douglas
  43rd Division under, 282
  commander SW Pacific Area, 3
  drive up New Guinea coast, 193
  landings at Aitape & Hollandia, 283
  promise to Filipinos, 283
  Wadke Islands taken, 283
Madsen, Olive A. C.
  book inscription by WB, *324*
  Hale telephoned and met, 319
  of Carterton, New Zealand, 265
  photograph of
    1944, *320*
    at Christchurch with corsage, *306*
    with Hale 1984, *321*
  WB wrote of meeting, 304
Malone, Lt. Arthur F.
  killed July 28, Munda, 32
  remembered on Armistice Day, 184
maps
  Arundel Island, with actions, *xxxv*
  Baanga Island actions, *xxxiv*
  Blackett Strait, *xxxvi*
  bombing pattern, Rendova, July 4, *xxx*
  Cartwheel area and Hale's travels, *xxiv*
  cleanup drives, New Georgia, *xxxiii*
  final drive to Munda, *xxxii*
  initial drive toward Munda, *xxxi*
  New Georgia Island group
    43rd Division assault, *xxix*
    artillery positions, *xxxvii*
  New Zealand, *xxxviii*
  Pacific Areas and voyages, *xxiii*
  Pacific command areas, dual thrusts, *xxvi*
  Solomon Islands with voyages, *xxviii*
Mayne, Lt. Joseph W.
  photo of, with 169th FA officers, *212*
  sent into jungle, Arundel, 86
McAuliffe, Capt. Francis A.
  cousin in Texas with war neurosis, 225
  photograph of
    on LCT en route Sasavele, *18*
    with 169th FA officers, *212*
    with Lt. Mushik, Ondonga, *226*
  sent into tough places, 225
McCalder, Lt. Robert W.
  close to Lt. Christian, 51
  killed Luzon, April 29, 1945, 51
McCormick, Lt. Col. William B.
  152nd FA borrowed trucks from, 298
  C.O. 103rd FA Bn., alongside, 21
McCracken, Kenneth, 127
McElroy, Corporal Norbert F.
  missing (killed) on Baanga, 61
memorials on Guadalcanal, *130*, 131
Merck, Lt. Albert W., 142
Mitscher, Adm. Marc, C.O. TF 58, 307
Morgan, Cpl. Samuel B., awarded Silver Star, 197
Moria, Capt. Kazen, 13th Japanese Rgt., 111
mud, WB fell into, 241
Munda, **19**
  air terminal 1983, *134*
  cemetery 1944, *186*
  final drive to, *xxxii*

Hale visited 1983, **135**
initial drive toward, *xxxi*
Munda Trail, 148
runway from approaching aircraft, *134*
Mushik, Lt. Donald L.
    awarded Distinguished Service Cross, 211
    called for volleys on Arundel, 109
    conducted fires, Munda, 46
    departed Auckland with 152nd FA, 298
    dinner and movies with WB, 282
    photograph of
        152nd FA staff, New Zealand, *292*
        169th FA officers, Ondonga, *212*
        relaxing, Ondonga, *47*
        reviewing battalion (DSC), *211*
        with Capt. McAuliffe, Ondonga, *226*
    transferred to 152nd FA Bn., 277

natives
    assisted Zanana landings, 149
    headhunters, 147
    religious service for, 77
    rescued Americans, 77
    scouts for 145th Infantry, 17
Naylor, Lt. Col. William H.
    battalion driving east on Arundel, 108
    battalion in firefight, 92
    commander, 1st Bn. 172nd Inf. Rgt., 86
    meeting with Col. Kinoshita, 125, *126*
    party sent to reach in jungle, 87
    patrol reached his battalion, 91
    photos of, 1943 and 1983, *90*
neuropsychiatric casualties
    43rd Division, Munda, 22
    a case in Texas, 225
    numbers in Solomons, 116
    problem of leadership, 234
New Georgia Island group, **1**
New Zealand, **231**
    43rd Division ordered to, 229
    civilization, **231–308**
    Interlude, **309–28**
    map of, *xxxviii*
    Rerewhakaaitu range, 278
    WB leave and tour
        Christchurch, 259, *261*
        Drop Scene, Whanganui River, *258*
        Franz Joseph glacier, 262, *263*
        Mount Egmont, aka Mt. Taranaki, *256*, 274
        Mount Ngauruhoe in eruption, *257*
        Picton, 262
        Plimmerton, 260
        sketches of trees, *260*
        Waiho Chapel and glacier, *263*
        WB with hikers, Picton(?), *264*
Nichols, Lt. Col. Stephen L.
    152nd FA borrowed trucks from, 298
    C.O. 192nd FA Bn., 277
Nimitz, Adm. Chester
    began Central Pacific advance, 193
    commander Pacific Fleet, 3
Normandy, invasion of, 287

Ondonga, **157–230**
    Hale canoed by 1983, 146
    office tent for WB, *181*
    road through camp, *174*
Otenso, Martha, *O River Remember*, 244

Patenge, Lt. Robert W.
    photo of, with 169th FA officers, *212*
    prepared artillery positions, Sasavele, 16
path, how to get straight, 215, *216*
Pavuvu, Russell Islands, 133
Payne, Lt. Earl M.
    had son younger than Hale, 184
    killed July 14, 1943, 23
    prepared communications, Sasavele, 16
    remembered on Armistice Day, 184
Penney, Dawn Jones, photo of 1984, *314*
Philippine Sea, naval battle of, 307
picnic in 1927, WB remembered, 8
Pierson, Maj. Samuel F.
    left New Zealand with 152nd FA Bn., 298
    New Zealand, 287
    photo of, with 152nd staff, *292*
    S-3 of 152nd FA Bn., 277
pillbox, Japanese, Munda, *30*
Piru Plantation
    batteries moved to, 75
    Eastern Force location, 78
    passed by in 1983 visit, 146
pontoon bridge & negro driver, 288
Port Moresby, Papua New Guinea
    entry into Solomons 1983, 128
    flight to, from Kieta, 154
    Hale transited 1983, 155
postcard, Hale to Norma 1943, *29*
promotion party, 160
Provisional Battalion at Bustling Pt., 75
PS 41 in NYC, attended by Valerie, 218
Purple Heart medal
    sent to Norma, 182
    WB awarded, with cluster, 114

Rainey, Capt. Richard N.
   C.O. Battery A, 169th FA, detached, 94
   children played instruments, 111
   cleared ridge with artillery, 31
   Episcopal services, Ondonga, 200
   lived with WB, Ondonga, 172
   photo of, with 169th FA officers, *212*
   reconnaissance in jungle with WB, 186
   rough boat ride to Enogai, 189
   S-3 of 169th FA Bn., 182
   ship's executive, Auckland, 299
recommendations by WB for medals, 199
rehabilitation 43rd Div., Ondonga, **157–230**
Rendova Island, **3**
   43rd Division occupied, 5
   arrived at, 6
   chart of bombing pattern, July 4, *xxx*
   harbor, aerial photo of, *7*
   viewed by Hale 1983, 134
   WB wounded at, 9
Ross, Col. David M. N.
   assistant division commander, 197
   commander 172nd Inf. Rgt., 87
   difficult to satisfy re artillery, 108
   endorsed note for coast guardsman, 93
   inspected 169th FA Bn., 197
   led 170 men into Arundel, 87
   promoted to general, 108
   returned to Carrigan's beach, 91
Ruhlin, Capt. James R.
   at Sasavele with Gen. Barker, 14
   reserved room for WB, Auckland, 298
Ryan, Capt. Hugh E., photo of, with WB, *82*

Sagekarasa Island
   cleared of Japanese, 83
   clearing of, by 27th Infantry, 105
   held by Major Davis, 98
   Japanese barges landing at, 100
   map of Blackett Strait, *xxxvi*
Saipan, Mariana Islands
   compared to Munda, 296
   landings June 15, 1944, 294
   secured July 9, 1944, 307
salient in American line, Munda, *xxxii*, 67
Sasavele Island, **37**
   Battery C en route to, *18*
   children on 1983, *139*
   empty shell cases, *49*
   fire direction center, 169th FA, 41
   first howitzer on, 14
   Hale visited 1983, 138

   relic vehicle, *141*
   WB ordered to, July 30, 37
   WB returned to, July 13, 23
SCAT (S. Pac. Combat Air Transport)
   cartoon instruction flyer, *206*
   WB flew on, to Russell Islands, 204
shell cases, empty on Sasavele, *49*
ships
   LCI-24
      bombed, two men killed, 9
      listing after being bombed, *11*
      sailor wounded on, 173
   LCI-65
      bombed, one man killed, 9
      carried WB to Rendova, 6
      Hale found log of, 12
      listing after being bombed, *11*
      skipper, Lt. Christopher Tompkins, 12
      WB embarked on, 6
   LCI-69, Rendova Harbor, *7*
   USAT Sea Devil, to Aitape, 297
   USAT Willard Holbrook, to N. Zealand, 247
   USS Lexington, sunk Coral Sea, 306
Shreve, Capt. of 172nd Inf. Rgt., 88
signpost with Rhode Island locations, *174*
Simpson, Margaret (pseudonym)
   friend of Waldo Fish, 311
   Hale searched for, 316
   interviewed by Hale, 327
   records found, Wellington, 319
Smith, Sidney and Minnie
   butcher, Matakana, N.Z., 301
   Hale visited 1983, 315
   photo 1984, *315*
   photo ca. 1942, *302*
soldiers
   Battery C moving to Sasavele, *18*
   casualties in landing craft, Rendova, *53*
   debarking at Zanana Beach, *15*
   landing at Arundel, *74*
   loading shells, Bustling Point, *79*
   singing by
      169th FA boating to Barabuni Is., 11
      172nd Inf. arriving at Baanga, 61
   wading to Stepping Stone Is., *97*
Solomons, Interlude, **119–55**
souvenirs, collecting Japanese, 56
Sparlin, Norma. *See* Bradt, Norma Sparlin
spikes for shoes
   life savers, 32
   WB thanked Norma for, 80

St. Bernard's School, 70
St. John Baptist School, 71
stationery printed by Hale, *273*
Stepping Stone Is., soldiers wading to, *97*
Sugg, Col. Douglas, C.O. 27th Inf.
   foxhole for, WB shared, Bomboe, 99
   hired WB on the spot, 80
   photograph of
      in boat, Arundel, *103*
      with Capt. Van Tusk, Arundel, *97*
   tank attack, Arundel, 104
   WB reported troop locations to, 96
swamp: slimy, stinking, sticky, 93
Swan, Corporal (T/5) James H.
   brought items to Bomboe, 98
   did not polish insignia well, 163
   made chairs, 210
   orderly and driver for WB, 6
   Rendova bombing, 9
swimming encouraged, 219

Takabayashi, Maj. Uichi
   C.O. 3rd Bn. Japanese 13th Rgt., 111
   killed by artillery fire, Arundel, 125
Takahashi, Hishashi, 123
tank
   American marine, near Munda, *52*
   American, relic on Arundel 1983, *145*
   attack, American, Arundel, 104
   Hale visited on Arundel, 1983, 145
   marine, with crew, Arundel, *101*
telegram, WB wounded, *25*
telephone wire
   laying from reel, *16*
   loop circuit and lineman, *39*
   reel ran out on Arundel walk, 91
tent
   broom for floor, 224
   Col. Sugg's, Bomboe, 98
   dugout on Sasavele, 50
   like yurt, Ondonga, 181
   near banana patch, Guadalcanal, 235
   wooden floor acquired, Ondonga, 172
Thanksgiving dinner 1943, 191
Tomonari, Col. Satoshi
   commander Japanese 13th Inf. Rgt., 105

   grave seen by WB, 111
   killed by artillery shell, 111
   name in WB notebook, 113
Tompkins, Lt. Christopher R.
   Hale's conversation with 1983, 12
   photos of, *12*
   skipper of LCI-65, 8

Van Camp, Lt. W. H., 99
Vila, Kolombangara
   Hale visited, 152
   Japanese airfield at, 75
   Japanese troops landed at Vila, 21
   map showing airdrome, *xxxvi*
   U.S. artillery bombarding, 100
   WB visited, 168
voyages of 43rd Division, *xxiii*

Wally, Stacey, photograph of, *129*
Warne, Ian and Liz
   Hale's hosts, Kolombangara, 152
   with their boys, *153*
weapons carriers ready for inspection, *196*
Whitney, Lt. Col. Norman E.
   C.O. 152nd FA Bn., 204
   developed fine outfit, 278
   inappropriate officer assignments, 276
   rotated to U.S., 268
Wild, Capt. Edward W.
   cleared ridge with artillery, 31
   Distinguished Service Cross, 192
   liaison to 2nd Bn., 27th Inf., 93
   moved often and fast, 57
   shot up machine gun crew, 67
Wing, Maj. Gen. Leonard F.
   bid farewell in Auckland, 300
   commander 43rd Div. 1943, 63
   confused 152nd FA with 169th FA, 276
   wanted WB as infantry executive, 168
   WB promotion long time earned, 81

Zanana Beach
   debarking onto, July 6, *15*
   division command post near, 25
   first landings July 2, 14
   Hale visited 1983, 140

PORTLAND PUBLIC LIBRARY SYSTEM
5 MONUMENT SQUARE
PORTLAND, ME 04101

**American Red Cross**

July 23, 1943

Dear Son,

I thought you might like to get a letter written on a battlefield during a battle. Just now things have quieted down right here. However there are some Jap snipers in the trees around me. The men shoot one out every so often. Some fall, some are tied up so they stay. I have a very satisfactory slit trench with poles and logs, dirt over it. I am in it now.

I told you I was wounded by a bomb on the Fourth of July but that it didn't amount to much. On the tenth I was scratched in the side by a Jap bullet. Again it was nothing and is all healed now. I have the bullet for a souvenir. It came in thru my jacket, hit me in the side and dropped in my pocket.

July 24. General Griswold was in the next foxhole to mine the other day. I was

*"To furnish volunteer aid to the sick and wounded of armies ......" and "To act in matters of voluntary relief and in accord with the military and naval authorities as a medium of communication between the people of the United States of America and their Army and Navy......" The Charter of The American National Red Cross. By Act of Congress, January 5, 1905.*

Form 539A